The Biology and Chemistry of the *CRUCIFERAE*

The Biology and Chemistry of the *CRUCIFERAE*

Edited by

J.G. VAUGHAN, A.J. MACLEOD

Queen Elizabeth College
University of London

and

B.M.G. JONES

Royal Holloway College
University of London

1976

ACADEMIC PRESS
London New York San Francisco

A Subsidiary of Harcourt Brace Jovanovich, Publishers

ACADEMIC PRESS INC. (LONDON) LTD.
24/28 Oval Road,
London NW1

United States Edition published by
ACADEMIC PRESS INC.
111 Fifth Avenue
New York, New York 10003

Library of Congress Catalog Card Number: 75-34565
ISBN: 0-12-715150-8

Printed photolitho in Great Britain by
J. W. Arrowsmith Ltd., Bristol

LIST OF CONTRIBUTORS

L. A. Appelqvist, Department of Food Hygiene, The Royal Vetinary College, Stockholm 50, Sweden.

U. C. Banerjee, Gray Herbarium, Harvard University, Cambridge, Massachusetts 02138, U. S. A.

R. Bjorkman, Biochemistry Institute, 751 21 Uppsala 1, Sweden.

P. C. Crisp, National Vegetable Research Station, Wellesbourne, Warwick, U. K.

K. E. Denford, Botany Department, University of Alberta, Edmonton, Canada.

A. Finlayson, Prairie Regional Laboratory, National Research Council, Saskatoon, Saskatchewan, Canada.

D. J. Harberd, Department of Agricultural Botany, University of Leeds, Leeds LS2 9JT.

I. C. Hedge, Royal Botanic Garden, Edinburgh EH3 5LR.

J. S. Hemingway, Food Division, Reckitt and Colman, Carrow, Norwich NOR 75A, U. K.

V. H. Heywood, Department of Botany, Plant Science Laboratories, The University, Whiteknights, Reading RG6 2AS.

A. Kjaer, Department of Organic Chemistry, Technical University of Denmark, 2800 Lyngby, Denmark.

M. J. Lawrence, Department of Genetics, University of Birmingham, Birmingham B15 2TT, U. K.

A. J. Macleod, Department of Chemistry, Queen Elizabeth College, Campden Hill Road, London W8 7AH.

Joan R. Phelan, Biology Department, St. Mary's College, Twickenham, England.

R. C. Rollins, Gray Herbarium, Harvard University, Cambridge, Massachusetts 02138, U. S. A.

J. G. Vaughan, Department of Biology, Queen Elizabeth College, Campden Hill Road, London W8 7AH.

PREFACE

The papers here published were read at a Conference on the Biology of the Cruciferae arranged jointly by the Linnean Society of London and the Phytochemical Society and held in London from the 7th to the 9th of January 1974. They show how diverse are the interests which botanists, agriculturalists and chemists have in this family.

Species of Cruciferae have been cultivated since prehistoric times, and many are grown as ornamentals. The type genus *Brassica* is particularly important for its cultivated species which provide vegetables, oil-seed and cattle food throughout the temperate and sub-tropical zones. Yet in many laboratories the Cruciferae's only claim to fame is the powerful peroxidase obtained from the horseradish *Armoracia rusticana,* which hardly does justice to the academic and economic importance of the other three thousand species and four hundred genera in the family. Even the name "Cruciferae" indicates its importance, for the International Code of Plant Nomenclature makes a rare exception in permitting the continued use of the well-known name for the family; Brassicaceae is the name which fully complies with the Code.

The Cruciferae are a classic example of a "natural" family, being recognised as such by Linnaeus (as the Tetradynamia). Its species are united by an impressive list of distinctive features including the almost constant and familiar floral formula K 2+2 C 4 A 2+4 $\underline{G}$ 2 with its curious 2 "whorls" each of sepals and stamens but not of petals, and the unique replum developing as two curtains of tissue which grow across the ovary from the opposite placentae, meeting and fusing in the centre. And, as is often the case with such natural families, the Cruciferae present to the taxonomist formidable problems at generic and tribal level.

The Cruciferae is most closely related to the Capparaceae (Capparidaceae): both have a centrifugal development of the androecium, several genera of Crucifers have a gynophore similar to that which characterises the Capparaceae, and species of both families synthesise glucosinolates (also present in the other Rhoeadalean families Resedaceae and Moringaceae). It seems likely that chemical studies of the Cruciferae will be a more powerful tool to unravel phylogenetic strands within the family than the existing sources of information on relationship. The Linnean Society's President, Professor Irene Manton, who opened the Conference, made a pioneer cytological study of the family in the 1930's which showed how unsatisfactory were some of the tribal groups of O. E. Schulz even though his taxa were based on such diverse features as nectary characteristics, the form of hairs and the occurrence of myrosin cells in addition to the more traditional taxonomic characters of pod shape and the folding of embryos. The cytogeneticist still finds much to challenge him in the family. Laibach's dream of *Arabidopsis thaliana* as the vegetable Kingdom's answer to *Drosophila melanogaster* has been realised: in keeping with the times, *A. thaliana* has become a laboratory plant grown on agar in glass tubes! Self-incompatibility and self-compatibility are both frequent in the family which thus provides an excellent group in which to study the evolutionary relationships of the two breeding systems.

The Conference did not exhaust the interests which scientists have in the Cruciferae. The family exhibits phenomena which deserve fuller investigation: heterophylly is prevalent; heterocarpy is not uncommon; geocarpy occurs in a few species, as does acauly: we know little about the control of the expression of these characters or their evolution. Woodiness is present in some species of *Brassica* and in the Canarian endemic genera *Parolinia* and *Sinapidendron* while *Zilla, Vella, Ptilotrichum, Euzomodendron* and *Anastatica,* which are variously distributed from Iberia to the Near East, have evolved a tough, spiny habit. What relation do these have to the prevailing herbaceous habit? The Kerguelen endemic *Pringlea antiscorbutica,* the N. American genera *Streptanthus, Thelypodium* and *Stanleya* are possible links with the Capparaceae and the Asiatic *Megacarpaea megalocarpa* with monoecious flowers, up to 16 stamens and huge seeds, deserves to be better understood. But this is for the future; for the present we are content to offer this *resumé* of our "talk of many things, of shoes and ships and sealing wax, and cabbages and kings" without doubting that the Cruciferae rate more highly than footwear, boats, Royalty and even sealing wax in scientific enquiry.

We record our thanks to those who contributed papers and to those who provided texts for reproduction in this volume.

B. M. G. Jones

Department of Botany,
Royal Holloway College,
Huntersdale, Callow Hill,
Virginia Water, Surrey.

ACKNOWLEDGEMENTS

The organizing and editing Committee thank:

the Secretariat of the Linnean Society who provided the publicity for this Conference;

J. & J. Colman Ltd. who provided the reception for participants;

the Council of the Linnean Society in whose rooms the Conference sessions were held;

the authors of invited papers which appear in this volume;

those scientists who submitted papers or exhibited at the Conference;

Professor Irene Manton, F.R.S., President of the Linnean Society, who opened the Conference;

Dr. J. B. Harborne, Chairman of the Phytochemical Society, Professor A. Kjaer, Professor C. Gómez-Campo and Professor R. C. Rollins who chaired sessions of the Conference;

Professor Vernon Heywood who opened the final discussion of the Conference

We are also indebted to Mrs. Abigail Gillett, who typed the final copy for publication and to Miss Emily Wilkinson of Academic Press, who helped us throughout its preparation.

J. G. Vaughan

B. M. G. Jones

A. J. MacLeod

CONTENTS

A SYSTEMATIC AND GEOGRAPHICAL SURVEY OF THE OLD WORLD CRUCIFERAE

I. C. HEDGE

CYTOTAXONOMIC STUDIES OF *BRASSICA* AND RELATED GENERA

D. J. HARBERD

TRENDS IN THE BREEDING AND CULTIVATION OF CRUCIFEROUS CROPS

P. CRISP

SEED STUDIES IN THE CRUCIFERAE

J. G. VAUGHAN, JOAN R. PHELAN and K. E. DENFORD

TRICHOMES IN STUDIES OF THE CRUCIFERAE

R. C. ROLLINS and U. C. BANERJEE

VARIATION IN NATURAL POPULATIONS OF *ARABIDOPSIS THALIANA* (L). HEYNH

M. J. LAWRENCE

PROPERTIES AND FUNCTION OF PLANT MYROSINASES

R. BJÖRKMAN

GLUCOSINOLATES IN THE CRUCIFERAE

A. KJAER

LIPIDS IN THE CRUCIFERAE

L-Å. APPELQVIST

THE SEED PROTEIN CONTENTS OF SOME CRUCIFERAE

A. J. FINLAYSON

VOLATILE FLAVOUR COMPOUNDS OF THE CRUCIFERAE

A. J. MACLEOD

THE BIOLOGY AND CHEMISTRY OF THE CRUCIFERAE - GENERAL CONCLUSIONS

V. H. HEYWOOD

A SYSTEMATIC AND GEOGRAPHICAL SURVEY OF THE OLD WORLD CRUCIFERAE

I. C. HEDGE

Royal Botanic Garden, Edinburgh, Scotland

INTRODUCTION

For the taxonomist, the Cruciferae is a large, unusually homogeneous family which, for a variety of reasons, poses major difficulties of classification. In floral structure, it is remarkably constant. There are few exceptions to the formula of 4 sepals, 4 equal cruciform petals, 6 stamens—4 long, 2 short—and an ovary with two parietal placentae. Some species lack petals; some have zygomorphic flowers; some have less than, rarely more than, 6 stamens; some have stamens of equal length. But these are rare deviations from what, in the phanerogams, is a very unusual formula. In the same way that the flowers are uniform, so too is the basic structure of the fruit: a capsule with a false septum (so-called because it does not represent the wall between carpels). In these characteristics of floral and fruit homogeneity, the Cruciferae much resembles the Umbelliferae. It also shares with that family the feature that, although the fruit is *basically* uniform, it exhibits a vast range of variation of fundamental importance to any classification at any level. The fruit may be narrow-linear, short-ovate, spherical, dehiscent or indehiscent, stipitate or not, clearly divided into two sections, strongly winged or not, be compressed dorsally or laterally, the false septum may be absent; the seeds may be in two rows or one, many or few; and so on. The variants are almost legion. But although the fruit is the linchpin of classification there are numerous other readily observable characters. The sepals may be erect or spreading, coherent or free, saccate or not at the base, hooded or not at the apex; the petals may be oblong or have a distinct blade and claw, be emarginate or entire, regularly cruciform or with larger spreading outer petals. Similar ranges of variation are found in the nectary glands at the base of the stamens; the size, shape and form of anthers, filaments and stigma; the shape and folding of the cotyledons and the position of the radicle relative to them; and in the indumentum which varies from simple to bifurcate, to dendroid, to stellate, to peltate.

In addition to this wide range of macro-characters there are also several micro-characters such as the form and positioning of the cells in the false septum, the distribution of myrosin cells and, if mucilage is produced by wetted seeds, the type of mucus. Characters of an anatomical, embryological or palynological nature are, without doubt, important but as yet are not available on a wide scale throughout the family.

The general picture is therefore, despite basic uniformity, of a very large number of available characters from which, by permutation and combination, the taxonomist can build up his classification. Indeed, there are probably few plant families in which there is a greater and more varied range of taxonomic characters than in the Cruciferae. At a conservative estimate there are about twenty easily-used characters each of which may have six or more "states", the majority of which are widely distributed throughout the family. Because of this high number of available characters, it is not at all surprising that different authors have stressed different characters. The result is that many very varied systems of classification have ensued.

TAXONOMY

Classifications of the Cruciferae

One of the earliest attempts at a natural classification of the family was given by Robert Morison, better known for his early monograph of the Umbelliferae, in his *Plantarum Historiae Universalis Oxoniensis* of 1680. Morison laid particular stress on characters provided by the fruit and his two main divisions were the long-fruited "Siliquosae" and the short-fruited "Siliculosae". Although there were several strangers in these groups such as *Papaver* and *Glaucium*

(Papaveraceae), *Fumaria* (Fumariaceae), *Leontice* (Berberidaceae), *Epilobium* (Onagraceae) and *Veronica* (Scrophulariaceae), many of the plants that he considered within his subdivisions are, in fact, considered as related by the standards of three centuries later. Linnaeus in the *Species Plantarum* (1753) also used the same main two divisions, based on fruit length, as had Morison. Although subsequently there were gradual improvements in classifying the family, particularly by A. De Candolle (*Prodromus*, 1824), who seems to have been the first person to draw attention to the value and use of cotyledon/radicle characters, more recent classifications of Cruciferae stem from that in Bentham and Hooker's *Genera Plantarum*. In this, Hooker (1862) recognized 10 tribes based mainly on fruit length and cotyledon/radicle characters. This world-wide treatment was followed in 1890 by Prantl's account in the *Pflanzenfamilien* (with emphasis on indumentum characters; 4 tribes), and Hayek's revision of 1911 (stress on nectary glands and myrosin cells; 10 tribes). These three accounts varied greatly from each other both with regard to the number and definition of the tribes and the genera included within them. Although these earlier attempts at providing a working classification all had points in their favour—if only to draw attention to the value of a particular character—the foundation of the modern classification of the family, at least at generic level, was laid by O. E. Schulz.

Otto Eugen Schulz (1874 - 1936), a Berlin schoolmaster by profession and a botanist only in his spare time (Loesener, 1936), contributed enormously to our knowledge of the Cruciferae on a world basis. Over a period of 40 years he wrote numerous papers on the family, three major accounts in the *Pflanzenreich* and, the culmination of his life's work, the revision of the family for the second edition of the *Pflanzenfamilien*. This was published, shortly after his death, in 1936. Because I have used Schulz's classification as the basis for what follows—the tribes I use are those of Schulz—it is appropriate to discuss some aspects of it. He recognized 360 genera throughout the world, 120 more than Hayek had in his classification of 25 years before. These genera were divided amongst 19 tribes. The tribes differed markedly from those of previous authors both with regard to definition and generic content. He did not overemphasise one or a few characters, as had Prantl or Hayek, but used a very large number of features in circumscribing the tribes; characters of calyx, petals, ovary, glands, stigma, septum, cotyledons, radicle, fruit-length, indumentum, anthers and filaments. It is an excellent system for identification purposes being provided with numerous keys and detailed illustrations. Speculations of a phylogenetic nature do not play an important rôle in his work.

However, despite the importance of the *Pflanzenfamilien* account, it is certainly not the ideal one and it is easy to criticise many aspects of it. Janchen (1942) published a rather severe review of Schulz's system, not because of his generic concepts but mainly from the viewpoint of his tribes and the sequence of them. In Janchen's own proposed tribal classification (see Table 1), the total number of tribes was reduced from 19 to 15.

Table 1

Synopsis of the Classifications of Cruciferae by O. E. Schulz (1936) and E. Janchen (1942)

Schulz (1936)		Janchen (1942)	
I	PRINGLEEAE	I	STANLEYEAE
II	STANLEYEAE	II	PRINGLEEAE
III	ROMANSCHULZIEAE	III	ROMANSCHULZIEAE
IV	STREPTANTHEAE	IV	STREPTANTHEAE
	Euklisiinae		Euklisiinae
	Caulanthinae		Caulanthinae
V	CREMOLOBEAE	V	SISYMBRIEAE
	Cremolobinae		Thelypodiinae
	Menonvilleinae		Sisymbriinae
VI	CHAMIREAE		Descurainiinae
			Alliariinae
			Arabidopsidinae
VII	BRASSICEAE		Pachycladinae
	Brassicinae		Brayinae
	Raphaninae		Chrysochamelinae
	Cakilinae		Parlatoriinae
	Zillinae		Isatidinae

Schulz (1936)		Janchen (1942)	
	Vellinae		Buniadinae
	Savignyinae		
	Moricandiinae		
VIII	HELIOPHILEAE	VI	HESPERIDEAE
			Hesperidinae
IX	SCHIZOPETALEAE		Matthiolinae
			Euclidiinae
X	LEPIDIEAE		
	Brachycarpaeinae	VII	ARABIDEAE
	Lepidiinae		Cardaminae
	Notothlaspidinae		Arabidinae
	Isatidinae		
	Tropidocarpinae		
	Physariinae	VIII	ALYSSEAE
	Iberidinae		Lunariinae
	Thlaspidinae		Alyssinae
	Lyrocarpinae		Drabinae
	Capsellinae		
	Cochleariinae	IX	LEPIDIEAE
	Subulariinae		Cochleariinae
			Physariinae
			Lyrocarpinae
XI	EUCLIDIEAE		Tropidocarpinae
			Notothlaspidinae
			Capsellinae
XII	STENOPETALEAE		Thlaspidinae
			Iberidinae
			Pugioniinae
XIII	LUNARIEAE		Lepidiinae
			Subulariinae
XIV	ALYSSEAE		
XV	DRABEAE	X	BRASSICEAE
			Moricandiinae
			Savignyinae
			Brassicinae
XVI	ARABIDEAE		Vellinae
			Cakilinae
			Raphaninae
			Zillinae
XVII	MATTHIOLEAE		

Schulz (1936)	Janchen (1942)
XVIII HESPERIDEAE	XI CHAMIREAE
XIX SISYMBRIEAE	XII SCHIZOPETALEAE
Alliariinae Sisymbriinae Pachycladinae Brayinae Arabidopsidinae Camelininae Descurainiinae	XIII STENOPETALEAE XIV HELIOPHILEAE
	XV CREMOLOBEAE
	Cremolobinae Menonvilleinae

Schulz's tribes Hesperideae and Matthioleae were united by Janchen under the former name because he did not consider the difference of incumbent (Hesperideae) versus accumbent (Matthioleae) radicles of sufficient importance to warrant separate tribes. He also amalgamated Schulz's Alysseae, Lunarieae and Drabeae under the first name because he did not believe that the details of cell structure in the septum were adequate for recognition of 3 independent tribes. In several cases he transferred genera into new tribes: *Isatis* and its allies were placed, not in the Lepidieae, where Schulz had them, but in the Sisymbrieae—on account of the incumbent radicles! Janchen also, as the table shows, changed the sequence of the tribes with, as far as the European ones are concerned, the Sisymbrieae at the beginning.

In this respect it is worth pointing out that the sequence both of the tribes and the genera in Schulz's account is that of the order in which they were keyed out. That is, within a particular tribe, the first genus to be keyed out bears the first number within the tribe and the last one, the last number within the tribe.

Status of the Tribes

One of the other main changes that Janchen proposed was the disbandment of the tribe Euclidieae. He placed the various constituent genera into his Sisymbrieae, Hesperideae and Lepidieae. There is no doubt that the Euclidieae *is* an extremely artificial tribe—recognized only by the single or few-seeded indehiscent nut-like fruits—and that phylogenetically its constituent members have little in common. But the problem really is where these genera *do* belong! They are, for the most part, anomalous where Janchen places them and this situation emphasizes the difficulty, which occurs throughout the family, of finding natural allies for those genera with a very reduced or advanced fruit form.

In contrast to the artificiality of the Euclidideae, the Brassiceae is a fairly natural tribe with more or less clear boundaries. Recognized by the longitudinally folded cotyledons and a fruit usually clearly divided into a so-called upper "stylar" and lower "valvar" section (though the latter character can be very indistinct), the Brassiceae has not had its generic contents much altered in the recent systems. There are, inevitably, some exceptions. Because of their angustiseptate-like fruits, Hooker (1862) placed *Psychine* and *Schouwia* in the equivalent of modern-day Lepidieae whereas since then they have usually been regarded as members of the Brassiceae. There are also some genera which although generally placed in the Brassiceae are anomalous there on a number of counts—as, for example, *Conringia* and *Sprygínia* (Botschantzev, 1966).

One aspect of the Brassiceae which deserves special mention is the obvious trend of reduction in the fruit throughout the tribe: from a long fruit with readily dehiscent valves and numerous seeds, to a short, more or less indehiscent and few or single-seeded silicule. Several authors such as Rytz (1936), Pobedimova (1963), Dvorák (1971) and Gómez-Campo (1972) have discussed this phenomenon and considered its evolutionary significance. Such trends of reduction are, however, not restricted to the Brassiceae but can readily be traced throughout the family in different tribes and it is often quite obvious within individual genera, as for instance in *Aethionema* where there are several species with single-seeded indehiscent silicules. In this genus, and in other unrelated genera, heterocarpy occurs where the infructescence consists both of dehiscent usually 2-seeded fruits and single-seeded indehiscent ones. These evolutionary trends, particularly the former, are a marked characteristic of the Cruciferae and numerous examples could be cited. Zohary (1948) has mapped out what he considers are the main lines of fruit reduction in the family.

Other than the Brassiceae, the only tribe which has much claim to be regarded as natural is the Lepidieae. In it, the fruit and ovary are strongly compressed at right angles to the false septum, i.e. angustiseptate, as opposed to the rest of the family in which the fruit is compressed parallel to the false septum, i.e latiseptate; there is, however, no basic difference between these two positions relative to the flowering axis or the position of the stamens. In comparatively few genera of the Lepidieae, such as *Cochlearia* and its allies, it is difficult to be sure whether the condition is angusti- or latiseptate. With very few exceptions, such as *Andrzeiowskia*, the fruit of the Lepidieae is a silicule.

As was the case with the Brassiceae, the limits of this tribe and its contents have changed but little in recent classifications. The cases of *Psychine*, *Schouwia* and *Isatis* have already been mentioned. One other, wrongly allocated, genus worth a mention is the monotypic *Physalidium* placed by Schulz in the Lepidieae on account of the angustiseptate fruit but which, as Poulter (1956) showed, is undoubtedly congeneric with *Graellsia* of Schulz's Drabeae. *Graellsia* is one of the very rare examples of a genus in which both latiseptate and angustiseptate species are to be found.

What the biological significance of an angustiseptate fruit as opposed to a latiseptate one is, is difficult to answer but it is remarkable that the difference between the two types is generally quite distinct and that such a large number of genera (c. 70) should have the character of a narrow septum with in only a few cases affinities with latiseptate genera.

However, if the Brassiceae and Lepidieae can be considered as relatively natural tribes—although, and this should be stressed, their constituent genera are united only by one or very few characters in common—many of the other tribes of Schulz are much less so. The unification of the Matthioleae and Hesperideae and the amalgamation of Alysseae, with Drabeae and Lunarieae, which Janchen proposed, certainly do seem to be warranted and are improvements on Schulz's system.

The current position with regard to the tribes, including the changes that Rollins (1942) and Al-Shehbaz (1973) have made in the New World, as follows:

1.	Thelypodieae	8.	Brassiceae
2.	Pringleeae	9.	Chamireae
3.	Sisymbrieae	10.	Schizopetaleae
4.	Hesperideae	11.	Stenopetaleae
5.	Arabideae	12.	Heliophileae
6.	Alysseae	13.	Cremolobeae
7.	Lepidieae		

In terms of generic content, the situation is of 2 monotypic tribes (Pringleeae and Chamireae), 5 oligotypic ones (± under 10 genera—Thelypodieae, Schizopetaleae, Stenopetaleae, Heliophileae and Cremolobeae) and 6 giant tribes.

Whether there is much reality to all the tribes cited above is a moot point. Tribes are useful reference points in any large family but frequently they are much less natural than we assume. This seems particularly true for the Cruciferae where the only clearly natural and homogeneous supra-generic groups are those of groups of allied genera. Throughout the family it is possible to recognize these generic groups; often they are few in content with perhaps less than 6 genera. Ideally, if we were to attempt a reconstruction of supra-generic groups, it should be based on these groups working upwards with them as the building bricks rather than defining tribes and working downwards.

STATUS OF THE GENERA

The situation with regard to genera is considerably more satisfactory than the tribal one although this is scarcely surprising since on average the number of species in each genus is less than ten!; this on a world basis. There are a few giant genera (i.e. over 100 species), such as *Draba, Sisymbrium, Alyssum, Erysimum, Lepidium* and *Cardamine* which are distributed in different tribes throughout the family, and numerous oligotypic or monotypic ones.

Many of the anomalies amongst Schulz's genera have now been rectified either by reduction to synonomy or by placing them closer to their natural allies. Often the artificialities of generic placings by Schulz resulted from too strict a definition and interpretation of tribes; if, for instance, a genus had incumbent radicles it would be placed in say the

Hesperideae whereas one with accumbent radicles would be put in the Matthioleae—even though on general characters the two genera were clearly allied. Although this is not the place to discuss in detail what constitute "good" or "bad" characters in the family one of the difficulties in classification at *all* levels is the fact that some characters may be very constant in one part of the family and very variable in another. Radicle position, for instance, is often an important feature throughout the family but in *Aethionema* incumbent, oblique and accumbent types occur; similarly, the structure and position of nectary glands can provide useful characters in for example the Brassiceae, but can be very variable in at least the Hesperideae (Snogerup, 1967) and Sisymbrieae (Shaw, 1965); likewise details of the cells of the septum may be important or else, even within the same species, be very variable and of little taxonomic worth (Stork, 1972; Al-Shehbaz, 1973). There are other convenient characters which should sometimes be treated with caution. Stipe length, for example, can vary greatly within a species as happens in *Thelypodium* or *Diplotaxis* —a genus in which both stipitate and non-stipitate species occur. Even fruit shape can be surprisingly variable within a species and can be much influenced by the number of ovules which mature into seeds (Hedge, 1960).

Finally, in this section mention must be made of the numerous new taxa that have been described in the last few decades particularly from south-west and central Asia. Most of these have been new species, often necessitating changes in the existing infra-generic classification, but a few new genera have also been discovered and described. For example, two of the most remarkable discoveries in the last ten years have been *Physocardamum* (Hedge, 1968) from eastern Anatolia and *Fabrisinapis* (Townsend, 1971) from Sokotra. The former belongs to the Lepidieae, the latter to the Brassiceae. In neither case, are their affinities at all obvious; it is quite clear which tribes they belong to but within them it is extremely difficult to suggest close allies. They are further additions to the very large number of monotypic or oligotypic genera so characteristic of the family.

DISTRIBUTION IN THE OLD WORLD

There are few regions of the world where Crucifers are totally absent although in some areas, particularly the tropics, the family is thinly represented but for introduced and established cosmopolitan weeds. The general picture in the Old World is of a great concentration of genera in temperate regions of the northern hemisphere, a thin and localised representation in the southern hemisphere and few or very few species in the tropics. The only localised genera in the tropics are the montane or alpine *Oreophyton* (monotypic, Ethiopia) and *Papuzilla* (two species in New Guinea). *Cardamine*, *Lepidium* and *Rorippa*, very widespread on a world scale, are some of the few genera that are represented on a wider basis in tropical regions.

That the family is a particularly successful one, despite the high total of monotypic genera, is emphasized by its penetration into almost every available kind of habitat and environment. Several species grow well into the arctic circle, almost as far north as flowering plants are found, others are found in very high latitudes of the southern hemisphere, many occur up to the altitudinal limits of vegetation (species of *Draba* are found at 5700 m in the Karakoram range) and several genera are well-developed in the most ecologically and climatically inhospitable deserts. In fact, one of the features of the family is that it has successfully evolved and established itself in some of the most difficult and specialized environments.

On the other hand, the range of habit variation is relatively small. There is probably an almost equal division between annual and perennial species and of the latter the vast majority are herbaceous though often with a woody rootstock. The woody habit is developed in many genera, in most though not all cases apparently derived from herbaceous ancestors, but only in a few are tall shrubs represented, such as the S. African *Heliophila glauca*, up to 2 m, and the N. African *Foleyola billotii* which grows up to 1.5 m in height and breadth. True climbers are almost unknown but *Heliophila scandens*, which reaches to 3 m, is one of the rare exceptions in the Old World, though this habit is also approached by species of the South American *Cremolobus*.

As already indicated the Cruciferae is best represented in the temperate zone of the northern hemisphere. In particular, the countries surrounding the Mediterranean basin, and those of south-west and central Asia contain a greater representation of genera than any other part of the world. As a result of the intensive floristic work that has been carried out in this area in recent years, particularly the appearance of such modern Floras as *Flora Europaea*, *Flora of Turkey*, *Flora Palaestina*, *Flora Iranica*, *Flore Afrique du Nord* and the many Soviet Floras, it is now possible to collate, with reasonable accuracy, various aspects of the Cruciferae in these important regions.

Accordingly it seemed an excellent opportunity to determine general patterns of distribution, areas of maximum morphological variation, possible evolutionary matrix areas and centres of endemism. Rather than conduct such a survey from the viewpoints of systematics (i.e. tribes or genera) or political areas, it seemed that a more profitable approach might be to consider the family as it occurs in the phytogeographical regions of this area. Clearly, such phytogeographical divisions are not to be thought of as anything too precise. It is unlikely that any two botanists would draw their lines in exactly the same places. However, there is a fair measurement of agreement about the regions designated as Mediterranean, Irano-Turanian and Saharo-Sindian (Fig 1). In the most general terms, they correspond with those of Zohary (1973) but the circumscriptions that, largely for convenience, I have taken for the two latter regions differ somewhat from those of Zohary. For example, I have included the Mauritanian steppe area of N. W. Africa in Mediterranean territory and not in the Irano-Turanian region with which Zohary associated it. Likewise, at the eastern end of the Irano-Turanian region I have defined its boundary as the limits of the area "Central Asia" as used in Komarov's *Flora URSS*. The map (Fig 1) gives the rough boundaries of the regions as considered here.

These three regions vary greatly not only in geographical extent but also in altitudinal range and ecological diversity. For example, the Saharo-Sindian territory is relatively uniform from an edaphic and ecological viewpoint whereas the Irano-Turanian is extremely diversified ecologically, altitudinally and geologically.

I have omitted any consideration of the family in two other phytogeographical regions where there is quite a high numerical representation of genera and species: the Euro-Siberian part of Europe, which contains a few endemic genera and a wide range of morphological variation; and, the Sino-Himalayan

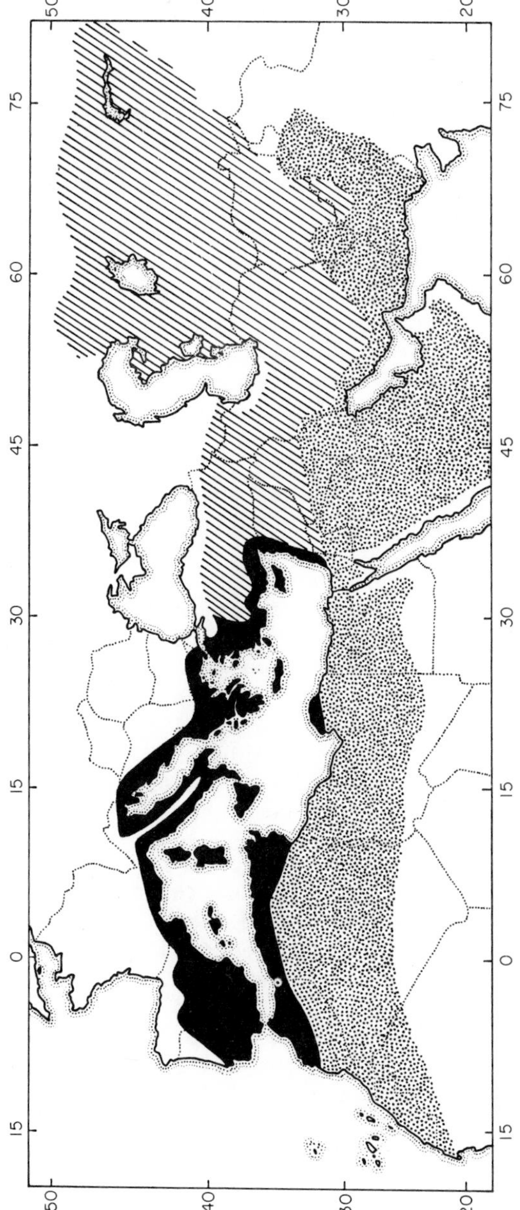

FIGURE 1. The approximate areas of the phytogeographical regions as used in this paper: black, Mediterranean; hatched, Irano-Turanian; stippled, Saharo-Sindian.

region, quite rich in endemic genera, usually at high altitudes, and an area much in need of a broad-based study of the family.

DISTRIBUTION IN THE NORTHERN HEMISPHERE OF THE OLD WORLD

The Mediterranean Region

In the Mediterranean region there are about 113 genera and over 600 species. Several of the genera are large, at least by the standards of the family, but in general their totals are made up by many closely related species as, for instance, in *Alyssum* (c. 80 species), *Biscutella* (c. 30 species), *Brassica* (c. 25 species), *Cardamine* (c. 30 species), *Erysimum* (c. 35 species), and *Thlaspi* (c. 33 species).

Specific endemism is 45 % which is somewhat lower than the 50 % which Zohary (p.83, 1973) has suggested as the overall total for the phanerogams of the region. Generic endemism is 17 % and is particularly interesting for two reasons: the distribution of the genera and the tribes to which they belong. All the endemic genera, which are listed in Table 2, occur in the west Mediterranean and none is found east of Italy; the greatest number are in N. W. Africa and S. Spain. Whether or not this concentration of endemic genera in the west and absence in the east is linked with past climatic history (e.g. the genera were at one time more widespread and have survived only in refugia) is not known but it is surprising that neither Greece nor Mediterranean Turkey has a single endemic genus; both areas are species-rich with numerous endemics.

This west/east division of the Mediterranean with a concentration of endemic genera in the west is also borne out when the figures of species endemism are considered. There are about 161 endemic species in the west—i.e. west of the line Tunisia, Sicily, southernmost Italy—and 114 in the east. Only 9 species clearly span both areas and are omni-Mediterranean endemics. These facts support the division of the region into east and west sectors as Zohary (cf. 1973) has already proposed.

The second interesting fact about generic endemism is that no fewer than 17 out of the 21 genera belong to one tribe—the Brassiceae. Most are quite distinct and isolated. They are, in general, *not* narrow taxonomic splits. The sub-tribe Raphaninae is especially rich in endemics with 10 genera out of its total of 18 restricted to this area. Many of the genera are very localized such as the saxatile *Hubera* and *Hemicrambe*, and many are found in disturbed environments as is the case of *Ceratocnemum* and *Rytidocarpus* which often occur

Table 2

Endemic Genera of Cruciferae in the Mediterranean Region

	Life duration	Tribe and sub-tribe	Number of species	Range
Bivonea	A	Lepid.-Thlasp.	1	Si Tun Ma Alg
Boleum	P	Brass.-Vell.	1	Hs
Ceratocnemum	A	Bra -Raph.	1	Ma
Cordylocarpus	A	Brass.-Raph.	1	Alg Ma
**Cossonia*	P	Brass.-Raph.	2	Alg Ma
Crambella	A	Brass.-Raph.	1	Ma
Euzomodendron	P	Brass.-Savig.	1	Hs
Fezia	A	Brass.-Raph.	1	Ma
Guiraoa	A	Brass.-Raph.	1	Hs
Hemicrambe	P	Brass.-Raph.	1	Ma
Hutera	AA/P	Brass.-Brass.	2	Ms
Ionopsidium	A	Lepid.-Thlasp	5	Lu It Si Hs Tun Alg Ma
Kremeriella	A	Brass.-Raph.	1	Alg Ma
Lycocarpus	A	Sisymb.-Sisymb.	1	Hs
Morisia	P	Brass.-Raph.	1	Co Sa
Otocarpus	A	Brass.-Raph.	1	Alg
Psychine	A	Brass.-Vell.	1	Alg Tun Ma
Rytidocarpus	A	Brass.-Vell.	1	Ma
Sisymbrella	A/P	Arabid.	2	It Si Ga Hs Lu Ma Alg
Succowia	A	Brass.-Vell.	1	Bl Co Hs It Sa Si Alg Ma
Trachystoma	A	Brass.-Brass.	3	Ma

A, annual; AA, biennial; P, perennial; Alg, Algeria; Bl, Balearic Islands; Co, Corsica; Ga, France; Hs, Spain; It, Italy; Lu, Portugal; Ma, Morocco; Sa, Sardinia; Si, Sicily; Tun, Tunisia.

* confined to the Mauritanian steppe area.

in cornfields. The fact that a large number of the Brassiceae in general are adapted to, or even restricted to, segetal or ruderal environments has been discussed by Rytz (1936) and Gómez-Campo (1972). Further aspects of the distribution of this tribe are considered below in the section dealing with the Saharo-Sindian region.

Of the other tribes in which endemic genera occur in the Mediterranean region, only the Lepidieae (2 genera), Arabideae (1 genus) and Sisymbrieae (1 genus) are represented. These genera are more widely distributed than those of the Brassiceae but as in that tribe are restricted to the west Mediterranean.

The wider question of floristic links between distant areas with a Mediterranean type of climate has not been considered in any detail but a quick survey would suggest that each of the five areas, two in the New World and three in the Old, has its own characteristic complement of Cruciferae which have evolved independently. This agrees with the general conclusions reached by Raven (1971) in a consideration of the phanerogams as a whole. There are several very widespread genera such as *Arabis*, *Draba*, *Cardamine*, *Descurainia* and *Lepidium*, which are well-represented in both the Mediterranean region and California, but the species in each area are different, with the obvious exception of introductions. *Lepidium* is also represented in southern Africa and in Australia but no real significance can be deduced from this as the genus is almost cosmopolitan—the most so, probably, in the whole family.

The Irano-Turanian Region

Although the greatest part of the Irano-Turanian region is indicated in Fig. 1, it is necessary to stress that parts of Tibet, Sinkiang and Mongolia should probably also have been included. However, because the eastern limits of the Irano-Turanian region have never been clearly defined and because of the difficulties in synthesizing information from these fringe areas, I have not, as already mentioned, included areas beyond 'Central Asia' as used in Komarov's *Flora URSS* (1939).

The Mediterranean basin has generally been thought of as the main centre of Cruciferae but, although it does contain a very large total of genera and species, the Irano-Turanian region has a greater claim to be considered as the cradle of the family, at least in the Old World. With c. 150 genera and almost 900 species it is a region of very great morphological variation. Not only is there a very high percentage of generic endemism (40 %) but many widely distributed genera, such as *Draba*, appear to have a matrix area here and have radiated from it.

Amongst the endemic genera, there are many characteristic patterns of distribution which are also found in other families (Wendelbo, 1971) as, for instance, that of the high alpine *Winklera* from Soviet Central Asia and Afghanistan; *Physoptychis* from the Elburz and Zagros mountains of Iran, N. Iraq and E. Anatolia; the Turanian genus *Lachnoloma* from the Caspian-Aral-E. Persian zone; and the distinctive *Veselskya* (syn. *Pyramidium*) from S. W. Afghanistan. In general terms there are considerably fewer endemic genera in the west of the Irano-Turanian region than the east; Turkey has only three endemics, *Tchihatchewia*, *Physocardamum* and *Pseudosempervivum* (marginally distinct from *Cochlearia*). As can be seen from Table 3, there are numerous genera with the distribution "Iran, Afghanistan, Central Asia"; over half of the overall total of genera are in Central Asia either partly or wholly. But in contrast to the Mediterranean region where a clear subdivision was recognizable on the basis of distribution patterns and endemism, no evidence came to light which suggested that the Irano-Turanian region could be sub-divided—although clearly it is a somewhat heterogeneous region (Zohary, 1973).

Table 3

Endemic Genera of Cruciferae in the Irano-Turanian Region

	Life duration	Tribe and sub-tribe	Number of species	Range
Acanthocardamum	P	Lepid.-Lepid.	1	Ir
Alyssopsis	P	Arabid.	1	Ir
Anchonium	P	Hesper.	2	Tu Ir Iran CA
Brossardia	P	Lepid.-Thlasp.	1	Ir Iran
Buchingera	A	Alyss.	1	Iran Afg CA
Calymmatium	A	Sisymb.	2	CA
Catenularia	A	Hesper.	1	CA
Chalcanthus	P	Brass.-Moric.	1	Iran Afg CA
Chartoloma	A	Lepid.-Isat.	1	CA

Chrysochamela	A	Sisymb.-Camel.	3	Le Tu
Cithareloma	A	Matth.	3	Afg CA
Clastopus	P	Alyss.	2	Ir Iran
Cryptospora	A	Hesper.	3	Iran Afg CA
Clausia	A/P	Hesper.	11	Iran Afg CA
Cymatocarpus	A	Sisymb.-Arabid.	3	Iran Afg CA
Cyphocardamum	P	Lepid.-Lepid.	1	Afg
Didymophysa	P	Lepid.-Physar.	2	Tu Ir Iran Afg CA
Dielsiocharis	P	Sisymb.	1	Ir
Diptychocarpus	A	Matth.	1	Ir Afg Pak CA
Douepia	P	Brass.-Moric.	1	Pak
Drabopsis	A	Arabid.	1	all areas
Elburzia	P	Drab.	1	Iran
Glastaria	A	Euclid.	1	Pa Le Tu Ir
Graellsia	P	Drab.	5	Tu Ir Iran Afg
Gynophorea	P	Hesper.	1	Afg
Hedinia	P	Lepid.-Capsell.	1	CA
Heldreichia	P	Lepid.-Iberid.	4	Le Tu Iran CA
Iskandera	P	Hesper.	1	CA
Irania	P	Alyss.	5	Ir Iran Afg
Koeiea	P	Matth.	4	Iran CA
Lachnoloma	A	Euclid.	1	Iran CA
Micrantha	P	Hesper.	1	Iran
Moriera	P	Lepid.-Iberid.	1	Iran Afg CA
Nasturtiicarpa	A	Sisymb.	1	Afg
Octoceras	A	Euclid.	1	Iran Afg Pak CA
Pachypterygium	A	Lepid.-Isat.	4	Iran Afg Pak CA
Parlatoria	A	Sisymb.-Alliar.	2	Tu Ir Iran
Peltariopsis	A	Lunar.	2	Tu Ir
Phaeonychium	P	Arabid.	2	Afg CA
Physocardamum	P	Lepid.-Physar.	1	Tu
Physoptychis	P	Alyss.	2	Tu Ir Iran
Prionotrichon	P	Matth.	4	CA
Pseudocamelina	AA/P	Matth.	7	Ir Iran
Pseudoclausia	P	Hesper.	1	CA
Pseudofortuynia	P	Brass.-Zill.	1	Iran
Pseudosempervivum	P	Lepid.-Coch.	3	Tu
Sameraria	A/AA	Lepid.-Isat.	11	Tu Iran Afg Pak CA
Sisymbriopsis	A/AA	Sisymb.-Bray.	1	CA
Sophiopsis	A/AA	Sisymb.-Desc.	4	Pak CA
Spirorrhynchus	A	Euclid.	1	Iran Pak CA
Sprygínia	A	Brass.-Moric.	6	Afg CA
Straussiella	P	Alyss.	1	Iran

Streptoloma	A	Sisymb.-Bray.	1	Iran Afg
Stroganowia	P	Lepid.-Coch.	16	Iran Afg CA
Stubendorffia	P	Lepid.-Lepid.	5	CA
Tchihatchewia	AA/P	Lunar.	1	Tu
Tetracme	A	Matth.	8	Iran Afg Pak CA
Trichochiton	A	Hesper.	1	CA
Veselskya	A	Matth.	1	Afg
Winklera	P	Lepid.-Lepid.	3	Afg Pak CA
Zerdana	P	Hesper.	1	Iran

A, annual; AA, biennial; P, perennial; Afg, Afghanistan; CA, Soviet Central Asia (sensu Komarov *Fl. URSS)*; Ir, Iraq; Le, Lebanon; Pak, Pakistan; Tu, Turkey.

In contrast to the previously mentioned genera which are restricted almost entirely to the confines of the Irano-Turanian region, there are many well-represented both in this region and that of the Mediterranean. There are many examples of these bi-regional genera such as *Alyssum*, *Isatis*, *Erysimum* and *Thaspi* and, in general, they give the impression of a main developmental area in the Irano-Turanian territories and a secondary one in the Mediterranean region.

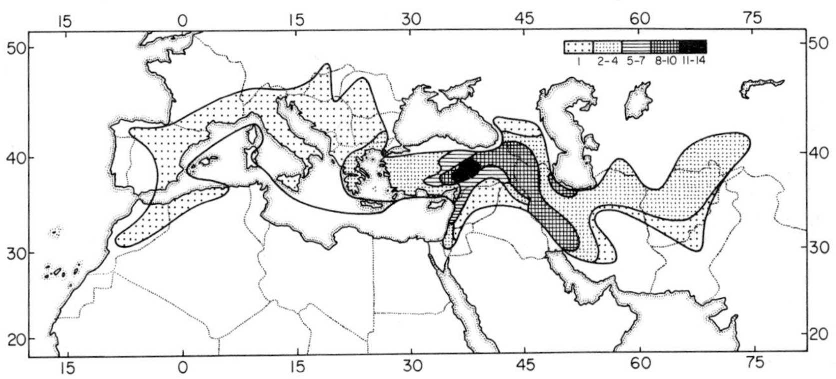

FIGURE 2. Species frequency and total distribution of *Aethionema*; a genus of c. 40 species with an area of maximum diversity in central eastern Anatolia.

There are also some genera which clearly have a main core in the Irano-Turanian region and a weak numerical representation of species in the Mediterranean. One such is *Aethionema*, a genus of about 40 species which, as the isoflor map (Fig. 2) shows, has its greatest number of species in central/eastern Anatolia and away from this matrix area the number of species decreases rapidly. One species, *A. saxatile*, is widespread in the Mediterranean and it is this one which occupies all the area of "1 species" in the west of the distributional zone. It is of interest to mention that the annual species are relatively taxonomically distinct and clear-cut whereas the perennials, considerably more numerous, give every indication of being in an active state of evolutionary diversification with many very closely related species difficult to separate from each other.

Another genus which apparently has a centre in the Irano-Turanian region but extends very far beyond it is *Smelowskia*. Unlike *Aethionema* it is at the eastern end of the region and, on account of its isolated taxonomic position and geographical disjunctions, gives every impression of being an ancient genus. Figure 3 shows the distribution of *Smelowskia*. *S. calycina*, a high alpine species from 3800 - 4600 m is found in N. E.

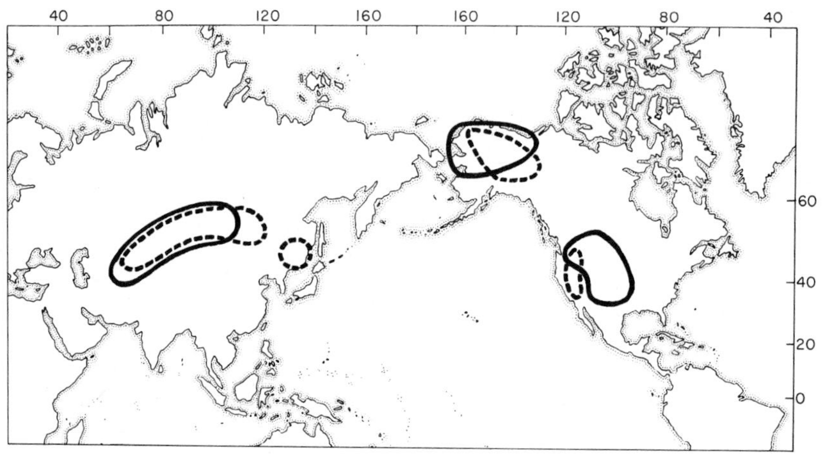

FIGURE 3. Total approximate distribution of *Smelowskia*: solid line, *S. calycina* (Steph.)C.A. Meyer; broken line, all other species of which there are 6 in Asia and 5 in northern America.

Afghanistan, Chitral, Soviet C. Asia and E. Siberia thence with a huge disjunction to another area in the northwest of N. America and, with another geographical gap, to a third, also alpine, area in western America. It varies but little throughout this range. The other species of *Smelowskia*, of which there are 6 in Asia (Botschantzev, 1968) and 5 in America (Drury and Rollins, 1952) show an almost exactly sympatric range. They give the impression of being local derivatives of *S. calycina* or at least are not profoundly different from it. These are very striking distribution patterns—particularly that of *S. calycina*. There are, however, several parallel situations in other families. *Crepis nana* (Compositae) extends continuously from C. Asia to N. E. Asia thence to northern America and southwards to western America (Babcock, Fig. 148, 1947); likewise, a closely inter-related group of eight alpine *Dracocephalum* species (Labiatae) extend vicariously across Asia from south-west to central to the extreme north-east, though not crossing into America (Hedge, 1967). Amongst other genera in the Cruciferae that have a comparable range may be cited *Braya* (Böcher, 1973) which also has an apparent matrix area in the mountainous central asiatic region with radiations from this centre.

Before leaving the Irano-Turanian region, brief mention should be made of two taxonomically interesting genera from Mongolia; an area which, as indicated earlier, should probably be considered in this phytochorion. The first is *Pugionium* with some of the most remarkable fruits found anywhere in the family (Fig. 4). Although placed in the Lepidieae, it is one

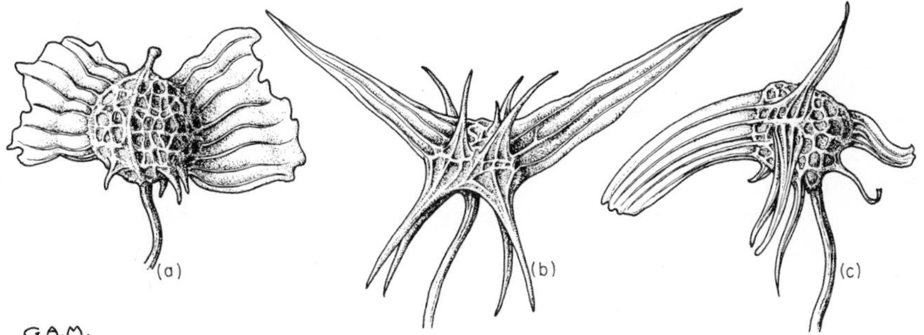

FIGURE 4. Fruits of *Pugionium:* a, *P. pterocarpum* Kom.; b, *P. cornutum* Gaertn.; c, *P. calcaratum* Kom. (after Komarov, 1932).

of the numerous examples of a genus without any obvious allies. The second is *Macropodium* with one species in Siberia and Mongolia (Grubov, 1955) and another in Ussuri and Sakhalin. This is often regarded, because of its simple spike-like inflorescence, ± sessile flowers and stipitate ovaries, as a very primitive genus (Komarov, 1939) and as having links, real or apparent, with the putatively primitive north American genera (Al-Shehbaz, 1973).

Although Mongolia and Tibet are not numerically rich in Cruciferae, they do contain a few interesting and problematical genera which would repay further study. As yet, however, adequate material from these countries is scarce.

Table 3 lists the endemic genera of the region; some of the recent narrow segregates from genera such as *Hesperis* (Dvorák, 1967) and *Thlaspi* (Meyer, 1973, who has split it into 12 independent genera) have not been cited but it must be admitted that some of those included may not merit independent generic status—such as *Gynophorea, Irania, Koeiea, Micrantha, Nasturtiicarpa* (Botschantzev, 1968) and *Trichochiton*.

The Saharo-Sindian Region

This region is characterized by the uniformity of its climatic, topographical and edaphic features. It includes the desertic regions of the Sahara, Arabia and Sind and covers a broad zone with a total east-west range of almost 5000 miles. Recently, Zohary (cf. 1973) has split the original Saharo-Sindian region of Eig (1931-32) into two independent regions—the western Saharo-Arabian and the eastern Sudanian—but at least for the purposes of this review I prefer to consider the area designated by the older term.

In addition to the uniformity of its environment the Saharo-Sindian region is also characterized by the poverty of its flora. At a fairly rough estimate the total of flowering-plant species is only about 1500; Ozenda (1958) gave a more accurate count of 1200 for the African part of the region. Many of the species are very widely distributed throughout the region and some genera which are well-developed within it contain vicarious species extending across the zone from west to east.

The Cruciferae are particularly well represented in the region and are, together with Chenopodiaceae, the fourth family in importance after the Gramineae, Compositae and Leguminosae. Genera characteristic for the whole or greater part of the region are: *Anastatica* (monotypic), *Nasturtiopsis*, *Notoceras*, *Pseuderucaria*, *Farsetia*, *Reboudia*, *Savignya* (monotypic), *Schimpera* (monotypic), *Zilla* (probably monotypic), *Schouwia* (probably monotypic), *Erucaria* and *Morettia*. As indicated above, some species are distributed throughout the whole area such as *Anastatica hierochuntica* (Fig. 5), *Zilla spinosa* and

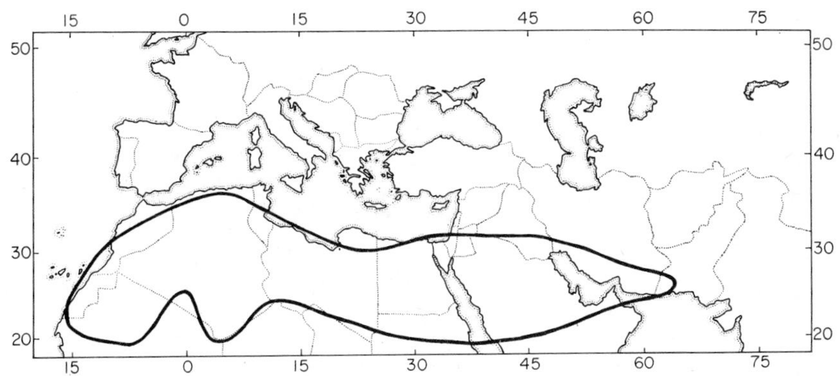

FIGURE 5. Total range of *Anastatica hierochuntica* L.; a typical Saharo-Sindian distribution with an east to west range total of almost 5000 miles.

Savignya parviflora and their ranges coincide almost exactly with that of the Saharo-Sindian region. A few others, such as *Notoceras bicorne* (Fig. 6) extend outwith the strict limits of the phytogeographical region and in this particular case the species grows on the Canary Islands and, at least in Israel, penetrates slightly into Irano-Turanian and Mediterranean territories.

Farsetia has about 8 species, all quite closely allied, in this its main area of variation and specific representation, but also occurs in eastern Africa as far south as N. Tanzania (Fig. 7). It provides an interesting example of an essentially Saharo-Sindian genus penetrating into Sudanian territory. In contrast to *Farsetia*, *Matthiola* is a genus with a main developmental area not in the Saharo-Sindian region,

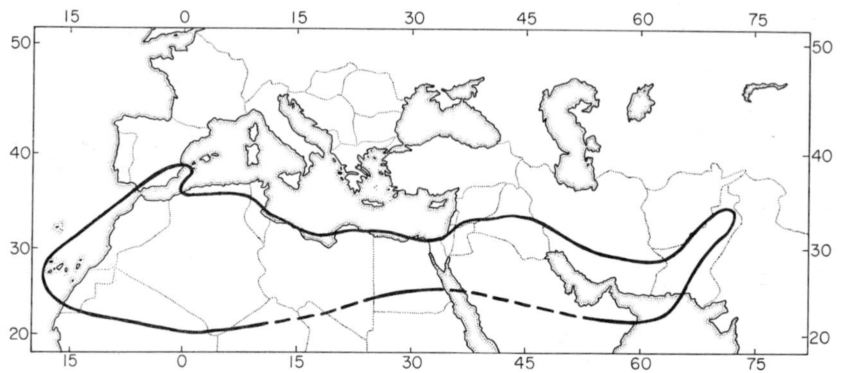

FIGURE 6. Total range of *Notoceras bicorne* (Ait.)Amo; a typical Saharo-Sindian distribution, also extending into Macaronesia and Mediterranean regions.

although represented there by a considerable number of species, several of them localised endemics. But in the same way as *Farsetia*, the distributional range of the genus extends southwards to eastern Africa; unlike it, however, *Matthiola* is also represented by one species in southern Africa (Fig. 8).

With regard to the endemic genera of the Saharo-Sindian region they clearly fall into two groups, the widespread and the localised. Several of the former have been mentioned above but of the localised endemics the majority are from N. Africa, particularly the Sahara. Only *Physorrhynchus* is from the eastern end of the Saharo-Sindian region and of the other two non-N. African-Saharan endemics, the anomalous *Horwoodia* grows in lower Iraq and *Stigmatella*, only marginally different from *Maresia*, in Israel.

Although all of the widespread Mediterranean-Asiatic tribes are represented in the Saharo-Sindian zone, several owe their inclusion to the occurrence of widespread weedy species. Only the Brassiceae, Euclidieae, Matthioleae, Alysseae and Hesperideae are numerically well-represented. The details of the endemic genera are shown in Table 4 but it is worth stressing here that no fewer than 11 out of the 19 belong to the

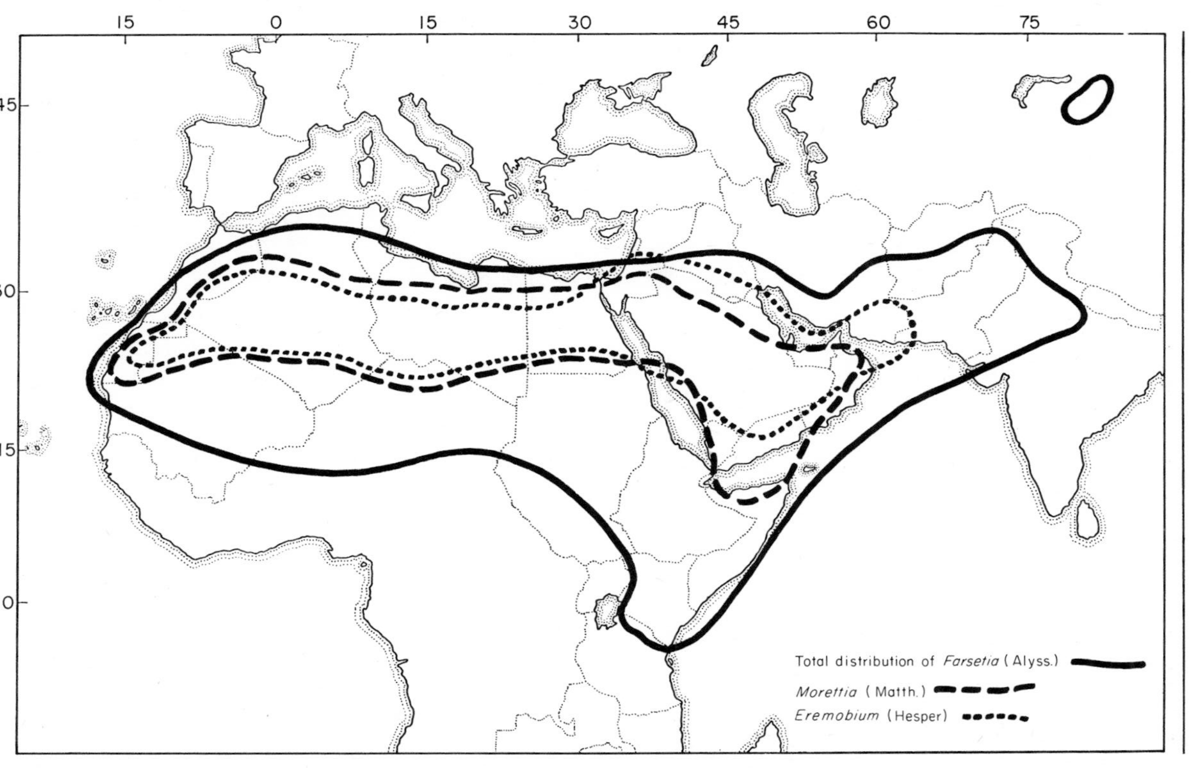

FIGURE 7. Approximate total distributions of *Farsetia*, *Morettia* and *Eremobium*.

Brassiceae and six out of its seven sub-tribes are represented.

The degree of generic endemism is 30 %; that of specific endemism is 34 %. The latter is a higher figure than the 25 % overall endemism indicated by Ozenda (1958) for the Saharan section of the region.

Table 4

Endemic Genera of Cruciferae in the Saharo-Sindian Region

	Life duration	Tribe and sub-tribe	Number of species	Range
Ammosperma	A	Brass.-Moric.	1	Sa
Anastatica	A	Euclid.	1	SS Sa Ho Eg Pa Ar Ir
Eremobium	A	Hesper.	3	Eg Pa Ir Pak
Eremophyton	A	Brass.-Raph.	1	SS Sa
Foleyola	P	Brass.-Moric.	1	SS Sa
Horwoodia	A	Lepid.	1	Ir Ar
Lonchophora	A	Matth.	1	Sa
Muricaria	A	Brass.-Raph.	1	Sa
Nasturtiopsis	A	Sisymb.-Bray.	2	Sa Eg Pa
Notoceras	A	Matth.	1	SS Sa Ho
Oudneya	P	Brass.-Savig.	1	SS Sa
Physorrhynchus	P	Brass.-Zill.	2	Iran Pak
Pseuderucaria	A	Brass.-Moric.	2	SS Sa Pa
Reboudia	A	Brass.-Brass.	2	SS Sa Eg Pa Ir
Savignya	A	Brass.-Savig.	2	SS Sa Pa Ar Ir
Schimpera	A	Euclid.	1	Eg Pa Ar Ir Iran
Schouwia	A	Brass.-Vell.	1	SS Sa Ho Eg Ar
Stigmatella	A	Hesper.	1	Pa
Zilla	P	Brass.-Zill.	2	SS Sa Ho Eg Ar Ir

A, annual; P, perennial; Ar, Arabia; Eg, Egypt; Ho, Ahaggar (Hoggar) Mtns.; Ir, Iraq; Pa, Palestine; Pak, Pakistan; Sa, Sahara (sensu Ozenda, 1958); SS, Spanish Sahara.

Although in most other families well-represented in the Saharo-Sindian region, there are close or derivative links with other phytogeographical regions, this is far from obvious with the Cruciferae. For example, the close links between Saharo-Sindian Chenopodiaceae and those of the Turanian area (Iljin, 1937), or the clear connections with southern Capparaceae, are not or scarcely complemented with examples in the Cruciferae. *Matthiola* and *Alyssum* to a degree provide an exception to this. Both these genera are basically Mediterranean-Irano-Turanian and the species in the Saharo-Sindian region, endemic or otherwise, are clearly derived from stocks from these areas.

Other examples at specific level could be cited but amongst the endemic genera there is considerable evidence of an autochthonous nucleus. Several, such as *Anastatica, Schimpera, Horwoodia* and *Zilla*—all with very advanced or reduced fruit structure—are without any close relatives; amongst the Brassiceae endemics which do have apparent relatives outside this region their links, only slender and distant, are with N.W. African-Mediterranean genera.

There is no real evidence to suggest which region—Mediterranean or Saharo-Sindian—supplied the other and the question is probably unanswerable. The important feature that emerges and needs to be stressed, however, is the very high concentration of the Brassiceae and its sub-tribes in the N.W. Africa - S. E. Spain area. Leaving aside phytogeographical regions the total number of localised endemic genera occurring here is 23 (Gómez-Campo, 1972). If all the Brassiceae genera that grow here are included, the total is 47; this out of a tribe total of c. 52. So there is no doubt where the present-day centre of the Brassiceae lies.

With 65 genera present in the Saharo-Sindian region and only 180 species, it is evident that none of the genera is large and in fact few, such as *Alyssum, Diplotaxis, Erucaria* and *Matthiola*, have more than 10 species.

Endemism in these Regions

The endemism in these three phytogeographical areas is given in Table 5.

Table 5

Generic and specific endemism in Cruciferae of the Mediterranean, Irano-Turanian and Saharo-Sindian Regions

	Genera : endemic	% endemism	Species : endemic	% endemism
Medit.	113 : 21	17	625 : 284	45
Ir.-Tur.	147 : 62	42	874 : 524	60
Sah.-Sind.	65 : 19	30	180 : 62	34

The figures serve to emphasise the importance of the Irano-Turanian region as a major centre of endemism both at generic and specific level. They also show the surprisingly high percentage for generic endemism in the Saharo-Sindian region; in contrast the figure for the Mediterranean region is considerably less than the other two regions.

The total number of genera represented in these three phytochoria is about 205 but only 36 are found in all three regions: *Aethionema, Alyssum, Arabidopsis, Arabis, Brassica, Calepina, Capsella, Cardaria, Carrichtera, Clypeola, Crambe, Descurainia, Diplotaxis, Eruca, Erucaria, Euclidium, Farsetia, Fibigia, Hutchinsia, Hymenolobus, Isatis, Lepidium, Lobularia, Malcolmia, Matthiola, Moricandia, Nasturtium, Neslia, Notoceras, Raphanus, Rapistrum, Rorippa, Sinapis, Sisymbrium, Thlaspi* and *Torularia.* Most of these genera are quite widespread occurring in other phytogeographical regions, such as the Euro-Siberian, Macaronesian or Sino-Himalayan; only a few, such as the essentially Saharo-Sindian *Farsetia, Notoceras* and *Moricandia*, are mainly confined to one region but spill out into the other two regions.

The number of genera which have endemic species in all three regions is six: *Alyssum, Crambe, Diplotaxis, Erucaria, Isatis, Matthiola.* Among them, only *Erucaria* scarcely occurs beyond the limits of the three regions.

The distribution of the endemic genera among the tribes is given in Table 6.

Table 6

Numbers of endemic genera in the tribes of Cruciferae of the Mediterranean, Irano-Turanian and Saharo-Sindian regions

	Mediterranean	Irano-Turanian	Saharo-Sindian
Brassicae	16	4	11
Lepidieae	2	15	1
Euclidieae	0	4	2
Lunarieae	0	2	0
Alysseae	0	4	0
Drabeae	0	2	0
Arabideae	1	3	0
Matthioleae	0	7	2
Hesperideae	0	9	2
Sisymbrieae	1	9	1

This shows even more convincingly than do the percentages of endemism in the previous table how the Irano-Turanian region —at least as far as the evidence of endemism is concerned— is a major area of diversification for the family in the Old World. It is the only region of the three in which all ten tribes have endemic genera. Also of special interest as far as this region is concerned is the large number of endemic genera in the Lepidieae and the Sisymbrieae; in the other regions only one or two endemic genera of these tribes are present. Too much, however, should not be read from this because on a world basis the Lepidieae and Sisymbrieae, as currently defined, have other major areas of development in North and South America; they are also represented in southern Africa and Australia.

Before turning to consider the general situation in the southern hemisphere it is interesting to compare the life-forms of the endemic genera in the three regions. In the Mediterranean region, there are 7 biennials/perennials and 14 annuals; in the Irano-Turanian, 38 biennials/perennials and 24 annuals; and in the Saharo-Sindian, 4 perennials and 15 annuals. Note the significantly different proportions in each region, with only in Irano-Turanian territories a higher number of perennials. Yet overall in the three areas there is an almost equal number of annuals to perennials: 51 to 49.

DISTRIBUTION IN THE SOUTHERN HEMISPHERE OF THE OLD WORLD

In the southern hemisphere of the Old World between 200 and 250 species are present; this is about one-tenth of the northern hemisphere total. Most of the total is made up by the species-representations in two areas—southern Africa and southern Australia.

Let us consider southern Africa first where the family has recently been revised for the *Flora of Southern Africa* (Marais, 1970). Here 15 genera and somewhat over 100 species are regarded as native; in addition there are about 18 genera and 40 species which occur as introduced weeds or escapes from cultivation, mostly from the Mediterranean region. Two of the tribes are restricted to southern Africa: Chamireae and Heliophileae. The former contains only one species, the anomalous *Chamira circaeoides*, an annual with unusually broad and persistent cotyledons. The other tribe, the Heliophileae, has as its main constituent member the genus *Heliophila*. This contains about 70 species mostly confined to the winter rainfall area of the Cape. Embracing a wide range of habit variation, a considerable variation in flower colour, including blue—a very unusual colour in the family—and both long and short fruit types. *Heliophila* provides an interesting example of explosive speciation in a small area—similar to, but not as spectacular as, *Erica* in the same region. The broad affinities of the tribe are unknown. The doubly transversely folded cotyledons, the chief characteristic of the tribe, apparently do not occur elsewhere in the family but it would be extremely interesting to investigate whether in other features there are links beyond southern Africa, either to the North with for example the Brassiceae, or with other southern hemisphere genera.

Although there are no external affinities amongst the endemic genera in southern Africa, two most interesting and significant links with the north are provided by *Matthiola* and *Erucastrum*. *Matthiola* is widespread in C. and S.W. Asia, the Mediterranean region, Macaronesia stretching southwards to eastern Africa and thence with a disjunction to southern Africa where it is represented by a single species—the widely

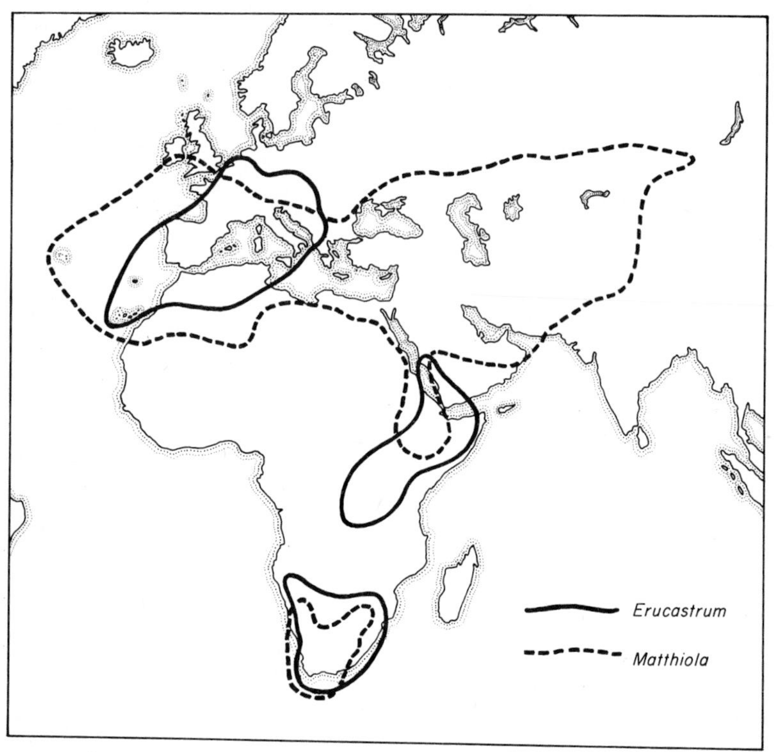

FIGURE 8. Approximate total distribution of *Erucastrum* and *Matthiola*.

distributed shrubby *M. torulosa*. Similarly, *Erucastrum* which is primarily a west Mediterranean genus, though also in western Europe and Macaronesia, has a second distributional area in E. Africa and a third in southern Africa where three species are found. The distributions of these two genera are shown in Fig. 8. There is little doubt that in both cases the main centre of diversity is in the north and that via the east African route (apparently non-montane, Burtt, 1971), they have reached southern Africa.

One of the most curious Crucifers of the southern hemisphere, and indeed of the whole world, is *Pringlea antiscorbutica*. Unusual both in its general facies, such as the dense spike-like unbranched racemes, and in technical characters, as for instance the thick spongy seed coat, *Pringlea* is the sole member of the tribe Pringleeae. It is equally odd in its distribution, being restricted to the remote islands of Kerguelen and Crozet. Taxonomically and geographically, it is extremely isolated.

In Australia there are between 50 and 60 endemic species variously assigned to the Lepidieae (such as *Cuphonotus* and *Phlegmatospermum*), Arabideae (*Cardamine*), the endemic monotypic tribe Stenopetaleae (*Stenopetalum*), Hesperideae (*Blennodia*) and the Sisymbrieae (*Arabidella*, *Drabastrum*, *Geococcus*, *Harmsiodoxa*, *Menkea*, *Pachymitus* and *Scambopus*). There are no obvious links with northern hemisphere or other southern hemisphere genera but likewise nobody has really studied this subject. There is relatively little range of morphological or habit variation (where there is a preponderance of ephemerals to perennials) but the prostrate *Geococcus pusillus* is a remarkable plant in that it is one of the very few species in the family exhibiting geocarpy—it buries its fruits in the ground as a result of the pedicels being sharply reflexed at fruiting time thus forcing the fruit into the soil. Several of the Australian species possess seeds that become mucilaginous on wetting and in a revision of some endemic genera, Shaw (1965) has used as a generic taxonomic character the type of mucilage produced. The presence or absence of mucilage exuded from the testa is regularly used throughout the family at generic (e.g. *Eremobium* v. *Blennodia*) or infrageneric level (*Alyssum*) but the *structure* of the mucus, for instance with or without spirally coiled threads, seems never previously to have been used as a character.

In New Zealand there are about eight genera. Only two, *Pachycladon* (Sisymbrieae) and *Notothlaspi* (Lepidieae) are endemic.

Papuzilla, the endemic New Guinea genus, shows no links between Asia and Australasia. It is a very close ally of the widespread *Lepidium* and may not be generically distinct from it (van Royen, 1964).

CONCLUSIONS

Taxonomy

The unsatisfactory state of the tribal classifications has already been stressed. Janchen made several improvements on Schulz's system but his proposals are not entirely satisfactory partly because he was considering the family primarily from a European viewpoint and not, as was Schulz, from a global aspect. The four main systems of classification have all had their adherents and this is reflected by the arrangements of major Floras. *Flora Europaea* follows Janchen; *Flora URSS*, a modified form of von Hayek; *Flora Kavkaza*, a form of Prantl; *Flora Iranica*, *Flore Afrique du Nord* and *Flora of Turkey*, are arranged to Schulz. Unfortunately, this means for example that the tribal name Arabideae is used by different authors in different senses and often it is not made clear in which sense it is being used.

A modern equivalent of Schulz's *Pflanzenfamilien* account is obviously a major desideratum but at present, in this era of Flora writing, it seems most unlikely that any botanical institute is going to take on such a daunting task. Information from numerous disciplines is accumulating at a great rate but few attempts are made to synthesize it.

One of the main problems facing the taxonomist is establishing relationships for the numerous monotypic genera of which, despite those that owe their existence to the zeal of taxonomists rather than to botanical reality, the majority *are* distinct.

There are several regions of the Old World where the family gives every impression of autochthonous development. In N. W.

Africa, both in the Mediterranean and Saharo-Sindian phytochoria, there is a marked concentration of the tribe Brassiceae, both with regard to localised endemic genera and to widespread ones. In southern Africa, to where the tribe Heliophileae is restricted, and in Australia, where the small tribe Stenopetaleae is endemic, there are very few traceable affinities with other geographically separated Cruciferae. Despite the existence of these areas of autochthonous development for particular tribes there is much evidence that the Irano-Turanian phytogeographical region, particularly its eastern C. Asiatic end, has been a major matrix and radiation centre for the family in general; here is the highest concentration of generic (42 %) and specific (60 %) endemism in any part of the Old World. In the other two phytogeographical regions which were evaluated, the percentages were lower; Mediterranean (17 % at generic level and 45 % at specific level) and Saharo-Sindian (30 % and 34 %). These two regions, however, are also important areas of diversity as, for instance, for the Brassiceae already mentioned.

The family is least well represented in the tropics and there is no existing evidence of it having originated there.

Primitive Characters and Relict Genera

Although it is possible to suggest, in some instances, what constitutes a primitive *character*, defining a primitive *genus* is fraught with hazards. Janchen (1942) defined a primitive Crucifer as having a long fruit with a broad septum, dehiscent valves, numerous seeds and without a beak, nectaries in a continuous ring, incumbent radicles, style $\pm$ spherical and hairs simple or mostly so. Others have considered that exserted stamens and a distinct gynophore are primitive characters because they are found in Capparaceae. Personally, I cannot agree with either definition or the implied assumption that the Cruciferae are derived from Capparaceae stock. If it is difficult to define accurately a primitive Crucifer, it is equally hard to translate theory into practice and propose which genera are primitive. *Pringlea, Thelypodium* and its allies in the New World, and *Macropodium* have variously been suggested as primitive genera but almost equally good cases could be put forward for any genus with a long fruit with many seeds and dehiscent valves, as for example many genera in the Sisymbrieae, Matthioleae or Arabideae. Heterobathmy—primitive and advanced characters occurring simultaneously—

is so frequent that the quest for a truly primitive Crucifer, as far as the family as a whole is concerned, is probably fruitless. Equally, there is no valid reason to suppose that tribes, genera or species with supposedly primitive characters are necessarily older than those with advanced characters.

Despite this, there are numerous genera that must be considered as relicts and presumably of some antiquity. These relicts, often very isolated morphologically and geographically, are found throughout the world in a variety of environments. Many of these such as *Pringlea* (Kerguelen), *Parolinia* (Canary Islands), *Veselskya* (Afghanistan), *Tchihatchewia* (Turkey) and *Foleyola* (Sahara) are probably survivors of extinct floras of widely different eras. Others such as the following so-called Tertiary relicts (a misleading term in that all plants today are relicts of Tertiary times!), *Pachyphragma* (N. E. Turkey), *Alliaria* and subgenus *Dentaria* of *Cardamine* (Europe) are possibly remnants of a similar and more recent flora.

Although the question of the allies of this family are beyond the scope of this review, it does seem clear that the Capparaceae, although not a progenitor of the Cruciferae, is quite a close relative. In particular, *Cleome* shares several points of similarity in characters of flower and fruit; furthermore, the short glandular tubercles that are so characteristic of *Cleome* are, at least superficially, the same as occur in such cruciferous genera as *Bunias*, *Anchonium* and *Matthiola*. There are, however, no really intermediate stages between the two families. One genus, *Dipterygium* was originally placed in the Cruciferae by Bentham and Hooker (*Genera Plantarum*) but has subsequently been placed in the Capparaceae, apparently correctly.

Evolutionary Trends

Several examples of the trends in fruit reduction, from a many-seeded, dehiscent long fruit to a few-seeded, indehiscent short fruit, have already been cited. This is a major trend throughout the family. A less widespread but equally interesting phenomenon is the occurrence of species which in vegetative and inflorescence characters are almost indistinguishable but in fruit are widely different. For example, *Turritis laxa* (Arabideae), *Sameraria armena* (Lepidieae), *Glastaria glastifolia* (Euclidieae), *Conringia orientalis* (Brassiceae) and *Peltaria alliacea* (Lunarieae) are all erect, glabrous, glaucous annuals with oblong-lanceolate clasping stem leaves and yellowish white flowers. In flower, they can be easily confused but in fruit they are obviously different.

There is enormous scope for tracing evolutionary trends within genera throughout the family. Rollins' precise biosystematic studies on the New World genera *Leavenworthia* (1963) and *Lesquerella*, with Shaw (1973), are excellent examples of what can be achieved. Relatively few genera in the Old World have been investigated in such depth but Snogerup's work on *Erysimum* in the Aegean (1967) and Titz's investigations on European *Arabis* (1971) are steps in the right direction.

In general terms the family gives every impression of being a highly adaptable one having evolved, and still evolving, in an unusually wide range of environments.

ACKNOWLEDGEMENTS

I am grateful to several colleagues at Edinburgh and Kew for information and useful discussions; in particular, I wish to thank those who helped greatly in the laborious task of extracting facts from the literature and the herbarium—Mrs A. Ballantyne, Miss J. M. Lamond and Miss G. A. Meadows, who also drew the text figures.

REFERENCES

Al-Shehbaz, I. A. (1973). *Contr. Gray Herb.* 204, 3 - 148.

Avetisian, V. E. (1964). *Bot.Inst.Akad.Nauk Armen SSR*, 14, 5 - 30.

Avetisian, V. E. (1974). *Bot.Inst.Akad. Nauk Armen SSR*, 27, 99 - 100.

Babcock, E. B. (1947). "The genus Crepis. Part 2." *Univ. Calif.Publ. Bot.* 22, 199 - 1030.

Böcher, T. W. (1973). *Ann.Bot.Fenn.* 10, 57 - 65.

Bonnet, E. (1896). *In* "Catalogue des Plantes Vasculaires de la Tunisie" (Bonnet, E. and Barratte, G.) pp. 13 - 36.

Botschantzev, V. P. (1966). *Bot.Mater.Gerb.Bot.Inst.Komarova Akad.Nauk SSSR,* 122 - 139.

Botschantzev, V. P. (1968). *Bot.Mater.Gerb.Bot.Inst. Komarova Akad. Nauk SSSR,* 140 - 146.

Botschantzev, V. P. and Vvedensky, A. I. (1955). *In* "Flora Uzbeckistanica" (A. I. Vvedensky, ed.) 3, 65 - 222. *Akad. Nauk Uzbek SSR, Taschkent.*

Burtt, B. L. (1971). *In* "Plant Life of South-West Asia" (P. H. Davis *et al.* eds) pp. 135 - 154. Botanical Society of Edinburgh.

Davis, P. H. (ed.) (1965). "Flora of Turkey", vol 1, pp. 248 - 495. Edinburgh University Press.

Davis, P. H. and Hedge, I. C. (1971). *Ann.Naturhist.Mus. Wien,* 75, 43 - 57.

Drury, W. H. and Rollins, R. C. (1952). *Rhodora* 54, 85 - 119.

Dvořák, F. (1967). *Repert.Spec.Nov.Regni Veg.*, 74, 139 - 144.

Dvořák, F. (1971). *Repert.Spec.Nov. Regni Veg.*, 82, 357 - 372.

Dvořák, F. (1973). *Österr.Bot.Z.*, 121, 155 - 164.

Eig, A. (1931 - 32). *Repert.Spec.Nov. Regni Veg.*, 63, 1 - 201.

Emberger, L. and Maire, R. (1941). "Catalogue des Plantes du Maroc" 4(suppl.), 1000 - 1015. Alger.

Gómez-Campo, C. (1972). *Biol.Cons.* 4(5), 355 - 360.

Grossheim, A. A. (1950). "Flora of the Caucasus" 2nd ed., vol 4, 108 - 251. *Akad. Nauk SSR, Leningrad.*

Grubov, V. (ed.) (1955). "Conspectus Flora Mongolian Peoples Republic" 148 - 159. *Akad. Nauk SSR, Leningrad.*

Hayek, A. von (1911). *Beih. Bot. Centralbl.*, 27, 127 - 335.

Hedge, I. C. (1960). *Notes Roy.Bot.Gard. Edinburgh*, 23, 173 - 174.

Hedge, I. C. (1967). *Notes Roy.Bot.Gard.Edinburgh*, 27, 149 - 173.

Hedge, I. C. (1968). *Notes Roy.Bot.Gard. Edinburgh*, 28, 293 - 296.

Hedge, I. C. and Rechinger, K. H. (1968). *In* "Flora Iranica" (K. H. Rechinger, ed.) 57, 1 - 372.

Heywood, V. H. (ed.) (1964). *In* "Flora Europaea" (T. G. Tutin *et al.*, eds) vol 1, 260 - 346. University Press, Cambridge.

Hooker, J. D. (1862). *In* "Genera Plantarum" (G. Bentham and J. D. Hooker) vol 1, pp. 57 - 102. Reeve and Co., London.

Iljin, M. M. (1937). *Sovetsk.Bot.* 95 - 109.

Jahandiez, E. and Maire, R. (1932). "Catalogue des Plantes du Maroc", vol 2 pp. 236 - 313.

Janchen, E. (1942). *Österr.Bot.Z.* 91, 1 - 28.

Komarov, V. L. (1932). *Izv.Imp.S.-Petersburgsk.Bot.Sada,* 30, 717 - 724.

Komarov, V. L. (ed.) (1939). *"Flora URSS",* vol 8, 13 - 469, *Akad. Nauk SSR, Leningrad.* English translation, Jerusalem 1970.

Loesener, Th. (1936). *Verh.Bot. Vereins Prov. Brandenburg,* 76, 157 - 166.

Maire, R. (1965). *In* "Flore de l'Afrique du Nord" (P. Quézel, ed.) 12, pp. 139 - 403. Paul Lechevalier, Paris.

Maire, R. (1967). *In* "Flore de l'Afrique du Nord" (P. Quézel, ed.) 13, pp. 1 - 365. Paul Lechevalier, Paris.

Marais, W. (1970). *In* "Flora of Southern Africa" (L. E.

Codd *et al.*, eds) vol 13, pp. 1 - 118. Government Printer, Pretoria.

Merxmüller, H. (ed.) (1969) "Prodromus einer Flora von Süd-westafrika". vol 48, pp. 1 - 11. Verlag von J. Cramer, Weinheim.

Merxmüller, H. and Leins, P. (1967). *Bot.Jahrb.Syst.* 86, 113 - 129.

Meyer, F. K. (1973). *Repert.Spec.Nov. Regni Veg.* 84, 449 - 470.

Ozenda, P. (1958). "Flore du Sahara septentrional et central" Centre National Recherche Scientifique, Paris.

Pavlov, N. V. (ed.) (1961). Flora of Kazakhstan, vol 4, 171 - 339. Akad. Nauk Kazakhst. SSR, Alma Ata.

Pobedimova, E. G. (1963). *Bot.Zhurn.SSSR*, 48(12), 1762 - 1775.

Poulter, B. A. (1956). *Notes Roy.Bot.Gard. Edinburgh*, 22, 85 - 93.

Prantl, K. (1890). *In* "Die natürlichen Pflanzenfamilien" (A. Engler and K. Prantl, eds) vol 3, part 2, pp. 145 - 208. Wilhelm Engelmann, Leipzig.

Quézel, P. (1954). Monographies régionales, 2. Institut de recherches sahariennes de l'Université d'Alger, 1 - 64, Alger.

Quézel, P. and Santa, S. (1962). "Nouvelle Flore de l'Algerie" vol 1, 387 - 436. Centre National Recherche Scientifique, Paris.

Raven, P. H. (1971). *In* "Plant Life of South-West Asia" (P. H. Davis *et al.*, eds) pp. 119 - 134. Botanical Society of Edinburgh.

Rechinger, K. H. (1964). "Flora of Lowland Iraq" 278 - 323. Verlag von J. Cramer, Weinheim.

Rollins, R. C. (1942). *Contrib. Dudley Herb.* 3, 217 - 226.

Rollins, R. C. (1963). *Contr. Gray Herb.* 192, 1 - 98.

Rollins, R. C. and Shaw, E. (1973). "The genus Lesquerella (Cruciferae) in North America". Harvard Univ. Press, Cambridge, Mass.

Rytz, W. (1936). *Ber.Schweiz.Bot.Ges.* 46, 517 - 544.

Schulz, O. E. (1919). *In* "Das Pflanzenreich" (A. Engler, ed.) Part 70, pp. 1 - 290. Wilhelm Engelmann, Leipzig.

Schulz, O. E. (1923). *In* "Das Pflanzenreich" (A. Engler, ed.) Part 84, pp. 1 - 100. Wilhelm Engelmann, Leipzig.

Schulz, O. E. (1924). *In* "Das Pflanzenreich" (A. Engler, ed.) Part 86, pp. 1 - 388. Wilhelm Engelmann, Leipzig.

Schulz, O. E. (1927a) *In* "Das Pflanzenreich" (A. Engler, ed.) Part 89, pp. 1 - 396. Wilhelm Engelmann, Leipzig.

Schulz, O. E. (1927b). *Notizbl.Bot.Gart.Berlin-Dahlem,* 9, 1057 - 1095.

Schulz, O. E. (1936). *In* "Die natürlichen Pflanzenfamilien" (A. Engler and H. Harms, eds) 2, vol 17b, pp. 227 - 658.

Shaw, E. A. (1965). *Trans.* & *Proc.Roy.Soc. South Australia* 89, 145 - 253.

Snogerup, S. (1967a). *Opera Bot.* 13, 1 - 70 and 14, 1 - 86.

Snogerup, S. (1967b). *Taxonomy, variation and evolution in Erysimum sect. Cheiranthus,* 1 - 8. University of Lund.

Stork, A. L. (1971). *Svensk Bot. Tidskr.*, 65, 283 - 292.

Stork, A. L. (1972). *Opera Bot.,* 33, 1 - 118.

Sunding, P. (1973). "Check-list of the Vascular Plants of the Cape Verde Islands" Botanical Garden, Univ. of Oslo.

Täckholm, V. (1956). *In* "Students' Flora of Egypt", 335 - 363.

Takhtajan, A. (1969). "Flowering plants. Origin and dispersal" Oliver and Boyd, Edinburgh.

Titz, W. (1971a). *Ber.Deutsch.Bot.Ges.* 84(11), 697 - 704.

Titz, W. (1971b). *Ann.Naturhist.Mus.Wien,* 75, 235 - 240.

Townsend, C. C. (1971). *Hooker's Icon.Pl.* 7, 4: tab 3673.

Van Royen, P. (1964). *Nova Guinea (Botany),* 19, 427 - 433.

Wendelbo, P. (1971). *In* "Plant Life of South-West Asia" (P. H. Davis *et al.*, eds) pp. 29 - 41. Botanical Society of Edinburgh.

Zohary, M. (1948). *Palestine J.Bot., Jerusalem Ser.,* 4, 158 - 165.

Zohary, M. (1966). *In* "Flora Palaestina", vol 1, pp. 246 - 329. Israel Academy of Sciences and Humanities, Jerusalem.

Zohary, M. (1973). "Geobotanical foundations of the Middle East". 2 vols. Gustav Fischer Verlag, Stuttgart.

CLASSIFICATIONS OF CRUCIFERAE

BENTHAM & HOOKER (1862)

I ARABIDEAE

II ALYSSINEAE

III SISYMBRIEAE

IV CAMELINEAE

V BRASSICEAE

VI LEPIDINEAE

VII THLASPIDEAE

VIII ISATIDEAE

IX CAKILINEAE

X RAPHANEAE

PRANTL
(1890)

I THELYPODIEAE

Stanleyinae
Cremolobinae
Heliophilinae
Chamirinae

II SINAPEAE

Lepidiinae
Cochleariinae
Alliariinae
Sisymbriinae
Vellinae
Brassicinae
Cardamininae

III SCHIZOPETALEAE

Schizopetalinae
Physariinae

IV HESPERIDEAE

Capsellinae
Turritinae
Erysiminae
Alyssinae
Malcolmiinae
Hesperidinae
Moricandiinae

HAYEK
(1911)

I THELYPODIEAE

II ARABIDEAE

Sisymbriinae
Erysiminae
Cardamininae
Arabidinae
Parlatoriinae
Isatidinae
Buniadinae

III ALYSSEAE

Hesperidinae
Brayinae
Euclidiinae
Lunariinae
Alyssinae
Drabinae

V LEPIDIEAE

Lepidiinae
Iberidinae
Thlaspidinae
Capsellinae
Subulariinae

VI SCHIZOPETALEAE

Tropidocarpinae
Physariinae
Stenopetalinae
Lyrocarpinae
Schizopetalinae

VII PRINGLEEAE

IV BRASSICEAE

Brassicinae
Raphaninae
Vellinae
Savignyinae
Moricandiinae

VIII HELIOPHILEAE

IX CREMOLOBEAE

X CHAMIREAE

SCHULZ
(1936)

I PRINGLEEAE

II STANLEYEAE

III ROMANSCHULZIEAE

IV STREPTANTHEAE

Euklisiinae
Caulanthinae

V CREMOLOBEAE

Crenolobinae
Menonvilleinae

VI CHAMIREAE

VII BRASSICEAE

Brassicinae
Raphaninae
Cakilinae
Zillinae
Vellinae
Savignyinae
Moricandiinae

VIII HELIOPHILEAE

IX SCHIZOPETALEAE

X LEPIDIEAE

Brachycarpaeinae
Lepidiinae
Notothlaspidinae
Iberidinae
Thlaspidinae
Lyrocarpinae
Capsellinae
Cochleariinae
Subulariinae

XI EUCLIDIEAE

XII STENOPETALEAE

XIII LUNARIEAE

XIV ALYSSEAE

XV DRABEAE

XVI ARABIDEAE

XVII MATTHIOLEAE

XVIII HESPERIDEAE

XIX SISYMBRIEAE

Alliariinae
Sisymbriinae
Pachycladinae
Brayinae
Arabidopsidinae
Camelininae
Descurainiinae

Isatidinae
Tropidocarpinae
Physariinae

JANCHEN
(1942)

I STANLEYEAE

II PRINGLEEAE

III ROMANSCHULZIEAE

IV STREPTANTHEAE

Euklisiinae
Caulanthinae

V SISYMBRIEAE

Thelypodiinae
Sisymbriinae
Descurainiinae
Alliariinae
Arabidopsidinae
Pachycladinae
Brayinae
Chrysochamelinae
Parlatoriinae
Isatidinae
Buniadinae

VI HESPERIDEAE

Hesperidinae
Matthiolinae
Euclidiinae

VII ARABIDEAE

Cardaminae
Arabidinae

VIII ALYSSEAE

Lunariinae
Alyssinae
Drabinae

IX LEPIDIEAE

Cochleariinae
Physariinae
Lyrocarpinae
Tropidocarpinae
Notothlaspidinae
Capsellinae
Thlaspidinae
Iberidinae
Pugioniinae
Lepidiinae
Subulariinae

X BRASSICEAE

Moricandiinae
Savignyinae
Brassicinae
Vellinae
Cakilinae
Raphaninae
Zillinae

XI CHAMIREAE

XII SCHIZOPETALEAE

XIII STENOPETALEAE

XIV HELIOPHILEAE

XV CREMOLOBEAE

Cremolobinae
Menonvilleinae

CYTOTAXONOMIC STUDIES OF *BRASSICA* AND RELATED GENERA

D. J. HARBERD

Department of Agriculture, The University, Leeds, England

INTRODUCTION

The studies summarised in this paper were initiated in an attempt to bridge the gap between the workers of two disciplines, taxonomy and plant breeding, so far as the Cruciferae is concerned. That there should be a gap at all is perhaps inevitable when the aims are so divergent—plant breeders are concerned with generating commercially viable populations with no regard to taxonomic status; and taxonomists traditionally abhor any material with a cultivated taint. Nevertheless, it is regrettable that the exponents of two different yet related disciplines should work, sometimes on similar materials, with so little intercourse. As an instance, in the current plant breeding scene workers are turning more and more to wild species as a source of new genetic variability for incorporation into existing crops. To be efficient in this endeavour they need guidance of a quasi-taxonomic nature—which wild species are sufficiently related to crop plants to be of potential value?—and this guidance is essentially lacking.

The Cruciferae *in toto*, with well over 2,000 species, is a large family. Forty years ago it was possible for Professor Manton, with characteristic vigour, to "review" the cytology of the whole family—consisting mainly of her own newly published data—and that paper still stands us in remarkedly good stead (Manton, 1932). I doubt whether any worker will ever have the courage to attempt anything quite so superhuman again. By contrast, the economically important members are relatively few in number, such that they form a group of manageable proportions; furthermore, they have naturally attracted a considerable amount of experimental attention, so that their cytological relationships are much more fully understood. In the next few pages an attempt is made to summarise this information for this very small portion of the family, and also to assess to what extent the picture that emerges might be representative of the family as a whole.

Firstly then, to define our portion of the Cruciferae: it is defined biologically rather than taxonomically and by applied biology at that! It encompasses those species and genera which are sufficiently related to the crop Brassicas to be potentially capable of exchanging gene material with them i.e. that coenospecies, sensu Turesson, that includes the crop Brassicas. The boundaries of such a group must vary as the work proceeds but it appears that it corresponds almost, but not exactly, with the sub-tribe Brassicinae of Schulz (1919). Thus *Reboudia*, which Schulz included in the Brassicinae, does not belong but all other genera of the sub-tribe do; and in addition a few of the genera from the sub-tribe Raphininae, notably *Raphanus* and *Enarthrocarpus*, must be included. The total number of species in this coenospecies varies according to taxonomic treatment; a consideration of our present evidence in conjunction with Schulz's monograph suggests that he would have recognised 108 species. These species are mainly European and North African in distribution. In fact, 62 of Schulz's species are reported as occurring within the territory covered by Flora Europaea, 1964, but Flora Europaea lists only 57 species in our group. The difference is accounted for by the facts that 11 of Schulz's species are demoted in rank by Flora Europaea, which in turn recognises 6 new species. By and large these changes suggest an essentially stable taxonomy, with relatively minor changes of interpretation.

INTRASPECIFIC CHROMOSOMAL POLYMORPHISM

In our experience the species within the group obey the unwritten law—"one species, one chromosome number"—faithfully. So faithfully in fact that one tends to look twice at a report suggesting chromosome inconstancy, seeking an explanation. Foremost among explanations we must consider the possibilities of errors in reports; and errors are essentially of three types. Firstly, these species are difficult taxonomically, and easily confused, so that a worker could make a mistake in identification. Gómez-Campo (1969) reports that seed of the family supplied by Botanic Gardens can be 10 % in error nomenclaturally at the genus level, with a 20 % in error at the species level; and our experience within the group is similar. Secondly, the material is difficult cytologically so that erroneous counts can be published more frequently than in some other families. Thirdly, aberrant individual plants with atypical chromosomes occur as they do in most species and these could have been reported as valid species counts. We have found 3 such aberrants so far.

Careful scrutiny of the 238 published species counts for species of our group listed in Bolkhovskikh's Atlas (1970) suggests that 17 of these (7.1 %) may be in error). Generally it is not possible to make any suggestion about the nature of the error, but in 4 cases it appears to be taxonomic, and in 5 cases cytological.

However, errors cannot account for all the cases of chromosomal polymorphism reported in our species. There are, for instance, a few cases of intraspecific polyploidy, presumably autopolyploidy, in which the polyploids occur as established populations. This happens in *Erucastrum nasturtiifolium* (Poiret)O.E. Schulz and in the genus *Rhynchosinapis*. In both cases we have so far only found diploid and tetraploid populations. *Erucastrum abyssinicum* (A.Rich)O.E. Schulz can also be cited, though in this case only the tetraploid race has so far been identified. No doubt further work will locate more examples of this type of change in chromosome number within species. Elsewhere in the Cruciferae it is already well documented, with some instances of much lengthier chromosome series, e.g. *Arabis holboellii* Hornem., (Böcher, 1951, 1954), *Biscutella laevigata* L., (Manton, 1937), *Sisymbrium irio* L., (Khoshoo, 1959). I can make no claim to being a taxonomic authority, but nevertheless I have every sympathy with taxonomists for not making species distinctions in some of these cases.

By contrast, the situation regarding intraspecific aneuploidy seems to be quite different. Two cases can be cited within our group, both in the genus *Brassica* as treated by Schulz. The species *B. integrifolia* (West)O.E. Schulz, contains two chromosome races, n = 17 and n = 18, and these are now known to be cross-sterile. They are normally treated nowadays as separate species, the latter as a taxon within *B. juncea* (L.)Czern. & Coss., and the former as *B. carinata* A. Braun. Consequently, as a result of later, and presumably better taxonomy, this instance of intraspecific aneuploidy disappears. The other case concerns *B. barrelieri* (L.)Janka, which similarly includes two chromosome races, $n = 9$ and $n = 10$, again cross sterile. There is a precedent for separating the 9 chromosome race as a species, *B. oxyrrhina* Coss., but this does not gain normal recognition—it is not followed either in Flora Europaea or in Maire's *Flore de l'Afrique du Nord*. In my opinion however, it should be adopted. I would not go so far as to suggest that stable population intraspecific aneuploidy must always indicate a need for taxonomic splitting, but certainly it would be wise to be suspicious.

Turning to the family as a whole there are several reports of intraspecific aneuploidy, but in most cases there is insufficient evidence to interpret it. What is very striking is that those cases that are most clearly documented—*Cardamine pratensis* L. (Guinochet, 1946; Lövkvist, 1947; Berg, 1967) and *Erophila verna* (L.)Chevall. (Winge, 1933, 1940; Tischler, 1934)—include both aneuploidy and polyploidy, and this coincidence is probably significant. In each case the chromosome numbers show modal frequencies around a long polyploid series, with aneuploids getting commoner, and more extreme in deviation, at the higher levels of polyploidy. This suggests that these cases are to be treated primarily as a polyploid series, possibly not meriting taxonomic splitting, on which is superimposed a secondary aneuploidy tolerated only in the higher numbers of the series when the imbalance is relatively less serious, and thus having little significance either biologically or taxonomically.

SPECIATION WITHOUT GENOME DIFFERENTIATION

Although each species has a characteristic chromosome complement, the chromosomes of different species are not necessarily dissimilar. In other words, taxonomists have frequently recognised more than one species (and sometimes more than one genus) corresponding to a particular genome. In many cases this is no doubt fully justified, but in some cases the multiplicity of species names and the frequency of occurrence of intermediates of uncertain status might suggest that the cause of biology would be better served by recognising fewer and more variable species and by reducing many of the taxa to subspecific rank. I can appreciate only too well the taxonomists problem here when some of the species groups do not fall into either of the extreme "easy" situations, i.e. clear discontinuity deserving specific recognition, or complete continuity best treated as a very variable species. Two very good examples here are the genus *Rhynchosinapis* and the "sea cabbages" (i.e. the species closely akin to *Brassica oleracea* L.). In both of these cases certain of the taxa are so uniform, so distinctive and so easily recognised that specific recognition seems natural and inevitable. However, in both cases this leaves a central core of material which is much more variable but without very clear discontinuities. It seems wrong to aggregate all of this miscellany into a single composite species so different in variability from the others, yet it is equally wrong to force it into a series of specific compartments. At this point I am glad that I am not a taxonomist, because to the cytologist the solution is simpler. All of the different taxa that share a common chromosome complement, no matter how many species, or even genera, nor how much variability (genetic, ecological, etc.) they encompass; all of them belong to a single *cytodeme*. They are identical by descent to a certain point in their evolution, already clearly differentiated from other such cytodemes, and their later divergence is a much more peripheral phenomenon. To the student of evolution the cytodeme is the important unit rather than the species.

Complete identity of chromosome complement can of course never be proved; nor is it necessary to go to such lengths. If two populations have a common chromosome number, are easily crossed to give a hybrid which is neither obviously weak in vigour nor of low fertility, then they belong to the same cytodeme. By contrast different cytodemes (which sometimes have the same chromosome number) are (a) difficult to cross, or (b) give a weak hybrid, or (c) have a sterile hybrid, and frequently exhibit all three criteria. We are perhaps fortunate in our group that such crude criteria are sufficient to decide a case. However, the fact that workers in other families might have greater difficulties of delimitation is no reason for us to fail to take advantage of our fortune. Of all of the many hundreds of crosses we have made only two cases have the slightest variation from this pattern. In the genus *Raphanus*, section Raphanis, all of the species apparently have the same complement of chromosome material, organised into 9 chromosomes, but there are two sets, differing by an interchange. Hybrids for the interchange are easily made and vigorous, and their fertility, though greatly reduced, can under no circumstances be taken to approach sterility. This is interpreted as a single cytodeme, including two "sub-cytodemes". The other case is essentially the same—two "sub-cytodemes" in the genus *Hirschfeldia* (n = 7) differing by an interchange, again easily crossed and producing a vigorous but subfertile hybrid (Harberd and McArthur, 1972). Neither of these cases is sufficient to disturb to any serious extent the principle that in the Brassicinae the material is easily grouped into sharply differentiated cytodemes.

Comparison of our results to date with Schulz's treatment suggests that he recognised an average of approximately 2 species per cytodeme (91 species are equivalent to 44 cytodemes). However, the division is by no means uniform. Only 6 cytodemes apparently do have 2 species each, a large number (24) contain only the single species and a very few (3 to date) include more than 6 species each, notably *Rhynchosinapis* (including *Hutera*), *Raphanus* and the "sea cabbages".

THE CYTODEMES

The lowest chromosome number so far located among the *Brassica* allies is of n = 7, and it appears that this number is characteristic of five distinct cytodemes (see Table 1). If 7 is indeed the lowest number then tetraploids would have a gametic number of at least 14, and therefore all cytodemes of n = 13 or less should be diploid. There is so far only one cytodeme of n = 13 known (including *Diplotaxis harra* and *D. crassifolia)* and though this may be tetraploid—for instance by allotetraploidy between a cytodeme of n = 7 and an unrecorded one of n = 6, or by aneuploid loss from a tetraploid of n = 14—provisionally it is classed as a diploid.

Cytodemes with 14 or more gametic chromosomes are not necessarily by virtue of that number bound to be polyploid, though in fact all cases investigated to date do have this property. The only known high chromosome numbers which have not yet been shown to be derived by polyploidy are *Erucastrun elatum* (n = 15) and *Brassica balearica* (n = 16).

Table 1

Provisional list of known basic diploid cytodemes among the *Brassica* allies. (Harberd, 1972, with additions and amendments.)

No.	*n*	Principal species, and comments
1	7	*Diplotaxis acris* (Forsk.)Boiss. Provisional. Count by Amin, 1973, but untested for cytodeme.
2	7	*D. erucoides* (L.) DC.
3	7	*Erucastrum virgatum* Presl.
4	7	*Hirschfeldia incana* (L.)Lagrèze-Fossat.
5	7	*Raphanus aucheri* Boiss. Provisional. Count by Harberd, unpub., but untested for cytodeme.
6	8	*Brassica fruticulosa* Cyr. including *B. maurorum* Dur. and *B. spinescens* Pomel, counted and tested by Harberd, unpub.
7	8	*Brassica nigra* (L.)Koch.
8	8	*Erucastrum nasturtiifolium* (Poiret)O.E. Schulz and *E. leucanthemum* Coss. & Dur.
9	8	*Erucastrum abyssinicum* (A. Rich)O.E. Schulz (diploid not yet to hand)[1].
10	8	*Trachystoma* spp. all species of the genus so far examined.
11	9	*Brassica oleracea* L. including many crops, also *B. rupestris* Raf., *B. insularis* Moris, *B. cretica* Lam. etc., (but excluding *B. balearica* Pers. and *B. scopulorum* Coss. & Dur. (syn. *B. spinescens* Pomel) included in error in Harberd, 1972.)
12	9	*Brassica oxyrrhina* Coss.
13	9	*Diplotaxis assurgens* (Del.)Gren.
14	9	*Diplotaxis catholica* (L.) DC.
15	9	*Diplotaxis tenuisiliqua* Del.

[1] At the meeting Dr. Bengt Jonsell informed me that he has found diploid populations of this species and he has since sent seed to verify his claim.

16	9	*Diplotaxis virgata* (Cav.) DC.
17	9	*Erucastrum canariense* Webb & Berthr., *E. cardaminioides* (Webb)O.E. Schulz.
18	9	*Raphanus* spp. all species of section Raphanis so far tested.
19	9	*Sinapis arvensis* L., *S. turgida* (Pers.) Del., *S. allioni* Jacq.
20	9	*Sinapis pubescens* L.
21	10	*Brassica barrelieri* (L.) Janka.
22	10	*Brassica campestris* L. including many crops (*B. chinensis* L., *B. rapa* L., etc.)
23	10	*Brassica tournefortii* Gouan.
24	10	Brassicaria section of the genus *Brassica* including *B. saxatilis* (Lam.) Amo, *B. rapanda* (Willd.) DC. and provisionally *B. gravinae* Ten. counted (Harberd, unpub.) but untested for cytodeme.
25	10	*Diplotaxis siifolia* G. Kunze, provisionally including *D. berthautii* Br.Bl. & Maire, counted but untested.
26	10	*Diplotaxis viminea* (L.) DC.
27	10	*Enarthrocarpus* spp. all species so far tested.
28	10	*Sinapodendron* spp. all species so far tested.
29	11	*Brassica amplexicaulis* (Desf.) Pomel (syn *B. souliei* (Batt.) Batt.).
30	11	*Brassica elongata* Ehrh.
31	11	*Diplotaxis tenuifolia* (L.) DC., *D. cretacea* Kotov. and provisionally *D. pitardiana* Maire, counted (Harberd, unpub.) but untested.
32	11	*Eruca* spp. all species so far tested.
33	12	*Rhynchosinapis* spp. and *Hutera* spp. including all species of both genera so far tested.
34	12	*Sinapis alba* L., *S. dissecta* Lag.
35	12	*Sinapis flexuosa* Poiret.
36	13	*Diplotaxis harra* (Forsk.) Boiss., *D. crassifolia* (Raf.) DC.

If this analysis is correct then at least 36, and probably not more than 45, basic diploid genomes are involved in the *Brassica* coenospecies. Every number between 7 and 13 inclusive is represented and there is a mode at 9 and 10 which between them account for 18 (i.e. 50 %) of the known cytodemes. Such a lengthy aneuploid series seems to be quite atypical of the Cruciferae. Elsewhere in the family aneuploid relations between species are known of course, but they are infrequent and close to the basic number. Thus the Arabideae are almost constant on $x = 8$, with a very few cases of $x = 7$ and fewer of $x = 6$.

By contrast the *Brassica* coenospecies is apparently very restrained in its polyploidy. Thus in the Arabideae polyploidy is reported to go as high as 32-fold (in *Dentaria*, Montgomery, 1955; Easterly, 1963), but no natural *Brassica* (or other member of the coenospecies) exceeds the tetraploid level. Furthermore, only eleven or twelve of the ca fifty cytodemes are tetraploid.

It is difficult to compare the results of this analysis with the situation in other tribes because the information available outside the Brassicinae is for chromosome numbers of species and not of cytodemes, but it does seem likely that both the frequency and the level of polyploidy are significantly lower than in the rest of the family.

Among the tetraploids, investigations are still proceeding but five are known to be allotetraploids (Table 2) and five

Table 2

Allotetraploid cytodemes, and their diploid progenitors

Allotetraploid	Diploids	Reference
Brassica carinata A.Braun	*B. oleracea* *B. nigra*	Morinaga, 1933
Brassica juncea (L.) Czern. & Coss.	*B. campestris* *B. nigra*	Morinaga, 1934
Brassica napus L.	*B. oleracea* *B. campestris*	U, 1935
Diplotaxis muralis (L.) DC.	*D. tenuifolia* *D. viminea*	Harberd and McArthur, 1972
Erucastrum gallicum (Willd.) DC.	*E. leucanthemum* and another unknown	Harberd and McArthur unpub.

are bivalent-forming autotetraploids (Table 3). This latter category has already been reported elsewhere in the Cruciferae (Mulligan, 1967) and even further afield, e.g. in the ferns (Lovis, 1964), yet it is sufficiently novel to consider in a little more detail. Four of the five autotetraploids have known diploid forms (Table 3) and in these cases the triploid hybrid behaves as a typical trivalent-forming triploid (Harberd and McArthur, 1972 and unpub.). More strikingly the triploid hybrid between the autotetraploids and unrelated diploid cytodemes form a constant number of bivalents which could only come by autosyndesis within the tetraploid chromosomes—this

Table 3

Bivalent forming autotetraploid cytodemes, and their diploid homologues

Tetraploid	Diploid
Brassica cossoneana Boiss. & Reut.	*B. fruticulosa*
Erucastrum abyssinicum (A. Rich)	unknown
Erucastrum laevigatum (L.)O.E. Schulz	*E. virgatum*
Erucastrum nasturtiifolium (Poiret) O.E. Schulz	diploid form of the same species
Rhynchosinapis spp.	diploids of the same genus

has been observed in eight different hybrids involving the autotetraploid *Erucastrum abyssinicum* (Harberd and McArthur, unpub.). Finally, two hybrids between autotetraploids have complete bivalent formation, and though subfertile must be classed as allotetraploids (Harberd, unpub.).

HYBRIDS BETWEEN CYTODEMES

By the criteria listed above hybrids between cytodemes are difficult to make; nevertheless such hybrids are required in order to continue investigations into the relationships between the cytodemes. Indeed since by definition only species with potential for gene exchange with crop Brassicas are to be included in the group, only cytodemes which can be crossed are to be considered. Early in our investigations it became apparent that in many interspecific crosses which never set seed the early stages of hybridisation were apparently normal, with pollen tube growth, fertilisation and the start of embryogenesis. Frequently the first visible sign of abnormality was a shrunken appearance of the young ovule, apparently caused by a shortage of endosperm, and this was quickly followed by abortion. This led to studies of embryo culture as a means of salvaging hybrids before they reached the abortion stage (Harberd, 1969) and ultimately to the routine employment of an embryo culture technique in all attempts to cross cytodemes. As a result well over 100 hybrids have been raised to date.

The crop Brassicas themselves include 6 cytodemes (3 basic diploid, and 3 derived allotetraploids) and 44 of the hybrids involve one of these as one parent, with the second parent from a list of 24 other cytodemes (Table 4). There is undoubtedly some potential here for exchanging gene material with the crop Brassicas. A further 6 cytodemes (*Brassica elongata,* the Brassicaria section of *Brassica, Trachystoma, Diplotaxis harra, D. viminea* and *Enarthrocarpus)* have not yet been crossed successfully with crop Brassicas, though all of them do have hybrids with species in the list of 24 other cytodemes of Table 4. Thus even if the direct hybrid with a crop Brassica does prove impossible in these cases, there is a possibility here for indirect gene exchange. The remaining cytodemes in the collection have not yet been involved successfully in any hybrid combination—but in most cases it seems likely that this is merely a reflection of the fact that insufficient experiment has yet been conducted. Possibly some of these cytodemes which are provisionally included in our group will need ultimately to be excluded; for the time being we are retaining an interest in all of the other species of those genera which have at least one species clearly included. In this we are perhaps indicating an excessive confidence in orthodox taxonomy! Nevertheless, it is beginning to look as though some of these species have very slender claims to our continued attention. As an example we might quote *Brassica amplexicaulis*. It is intriguing that this species should be classed as a member of our central genus *Brassica* because judging from our crossing evidence alone it is very isolated from all of our other material: we have been unsuccessful in attempts to cross it with 34 other cytodemes.

Table 4

Hybrids prepared involving crop Brassicas

	oleracea	*napus*	*campestris*	*juncea*	*carinata*	*nigra*
Brassica fruticulosa	+				+	+
B. cossoneana		+	+	+		
B. barrelieri				+		
B. oxyrrhina	+		+			
B. tournefortii			+			
Sinapodendron spp.			+	+		+
Erucastrum virgatum	+					+
E. canariense	+					
E. nasturtiifolium			+			
E. abyssinicum	+		+			
E. gallicum	+				+	
Rhynchosinapis	+		+			
Sinapis arvensis					+	
S. pubescens	+	+		+	+	
S. alba	+		+			
Hirschfeldia incana		+				
Diplotaxis tenuifolia	+					
D. erucoides		+	+	+		
D. assurgens					+	
D. tenuisiliqua					+	
D. virgata				+	+	
D. muralis	+		+			
Eruca spp.	+				+	
Raphanus spp.	+					

Chromosome pairing in hybrids. When a genome is present twice in a hybrid, as in the triploid hybrid between an allotetraploid and one of its constituent diploids, or in the triploid between an autotetraploid and an unrelated diploid, this fact is recognised fairly easily by examination of meiotic chromosome pairing. The characteristic features are firstly the *high* bivalent frequency and secondly the *constant* bivalent frequency from cell to cell, the frequency corresponding of course to the chromosome number of the genome in common. However, there are occasional disturbances in these two features, and a more reliable clue seems to be a third feature, namely the *appearance* of the bivalents themselves. Cytologically the Brassicinae are difficult, with small chromosomes and a too-easily staining cytoplasm. The appearance referred to is of a compact bivalent, clearly differentiated from the cytoplasm, and frequently with a shape which indicates that chiasmata have been formed on both sides of the centromere.

In striking contrast are hybrids which do not have a genome repeated. The pairing is then very variable, both from cell to cell, and from hybrid to hybrid, but generally low in frequency, while the loose open bivalents, rather poorly differentiated from the cytoplasm, obviously cannot have more than one chiasma each. In a very few cases, notably in the hybrid between *Brassica oleracea* and *B. campestris*, the pairing in a few cells may involve nearly all of the chromosomes, though on average it is much lower; more generally very few bivalents are present.

ORIGIN OF THE CYTODEMES

We tend to believe that genomes have differentiated from each other by a slow process of evolution, through the gradual incorporation of chromosome changes, both of structure and of number. At first the interchange in *Raphanus*, and again in *Hirschfeldia*, appears to be an example of the first step along these diverging paths. There can be no doubt that each of these cases do represent a step in differentiation, but on reflection it is apparent that the genomes with which we deal could not have arisen merely by an accumulation of many such steps. Apart from these two cases that have scarcely got started on their diverging paths we have no examples of partially differentiated genomes. Only four or five steps of this kind are needed for hybrid sterility: that is to produce an isolation mechanism of sufficient strength to enable separate evolution; and a hybrid of this kind should be easily recognised cytologically. If this is how the genomes arose we have to explain the curious anomaly that evolution went far beyond the necessary limits incorporating more and more chromosome changes presumably long after they had any selective advantage. (It is well to recall here that speciation took place in this group without any change of genome in many cases.) A much more plausible explanation of genome differentiation is that the chromosome pairing is restricted not so much by changes of chromosome structures as by changes in the meiotic mechanism. Thus a single change of spindle harmony could give effective isolation without any structural change in the chromosomes. Beyond being dissatisfied with chromosome structural change as a sufficient explanation of genome differentiation, we have little evidence of just what is involved. However, the bivalent forming autotetraploids give us some clues. In these cases each chromosome is present four times, but at meiosis they conjugate regularly as two pairs. This is not accomplished by a reduction in chiasma frequency—the bivalents are normal looking for the tribe and generally have at least one chiasma on each side of the centromere. That would be sufficient in a normal autotetraploid for some multivalent formation and indeed this is observed in autotetraploids synthesised by chromosome doubling in the tribe (e.g. Howard, 1939 on autotetraploid *Brassica oleracea;* Yakuwa, 1944, on autotetraploid *Brassica chinensis,* of the campestris cytodeme). There is therefore in the natural autotetraploids a mechanism which restricts association to pairs, and presumably to special pairs by suppressing cross pairing. Thus structurally similar chromosomes (which will pair autosyndetically in suitable species hybrid combinations)are prevented from pairing in their normal environment by some extrachromosomal mechanism.

If a change of this kind could occur at the diploid level a large number of incipient species would be generated under suitable circumstances more or less simultaneously. Most of these might succumb, but some could survive and diverge. A series of such abrupt origins and subsequent modifications seems a very plausible interpretation for our group.

UNILATERAL INCOMPATIBILITY

In common with many other plant genera we have observed that success in hybridisation frequently depends on the direction of the cross, i.e. which of the two species is used as pollen and which as seed parent or "unilateral incompatibility", (Harrison and Darby, 1955). Early on we used the fluorescent pollen tube technique (Martin, 1959) to determine the fate of pollen of one species on a foreign stigma, and we soon discovered that in many cases crosses in one direction were positive to the point of getting good pollen tube growth in the foreign style, whereas the reciprocal cross was negative. In crosses between cytodemes successful pollen tubes are normally succeeded by fertilisation, and then by abortion of the hybrid embryo, so that foreign pollen tubes frequently lead to a partial sterilisation of the ovaries. Thus, whereas crosses in neither direction yielded hybrid seed, the one sterilised the flower to any later pollination, whereas the other left it unaffected. More significant is the fact that there is a pattern between the species in this behaviour such that they may be approximately ranked from one extreme reaction to the other (Table 5).

At the top of the list are such species as *Brassica oxyrrhina*, *B. tournefortii*, *Erucastrum abyssinicum*, *Eruca* spp. and *Sinapodendron* spp., which are normally only successfully crossed, with respect to pollen tube growth, when used as female parents. Their stigmas are very unselective in that pollen of nearly all of the species germinated and grew into the style. By contrast the pollen of these species is most unsuccessful at germinating on the stigmas of other species.

At the bottom of the list are *Brassica juncea*, *B. cossoneana*, *B. fruticulosa* and *Sinapis pubescens*, which are usually only successful in hybridisation if used as pollen parents. The stigmas of these species are very highly selective so that pollen of very few other species will germinate on them. However, these species produce pollen that germinates freely on stigmas of other species.

Species at an intermediate position on the list tend to have these properties: that their pollen will germinate on the stigmas of species above them on the list, but not on species below them; and that their stigmas will germinate pollen from species below them in the list, but not from species above them. These rules only apply of course to those cases where there is a unilateral compatibility; many species pairs can be crossed in either direction, or sometimes in neither. This pattern has been observed in other genera, notably *Nicotiana* (Pandey, 1968) and may be called the step-like pattern.

Table 5

Approximate crossing series among Brassica cytodemes. Species more successful as female parents at the top of the list, with species more successful as males at the bottom.

Erucastrum abyssinicum
Brassica oxyrrhina
Eruca spp.
Brassica tournefortii
Sinapodendron spp.
Enarthrocarpus spp.
Diplotaxis erucoides
Diplotaxis tenuifolia
Brassica barrelieri
Diplotaxis muralis
Diplotaxis harra
Erucastrum virgatum
Brassica carinata
Diplotaxis catholica
Brassica napus
Erucastrum canariense
Brassica oleracea
Sinapis alba
Erucastrum gallicum
Brassica campestris
Hirschfeldia incana
Brassica nigra
Sinapis arvensis
Raphanus spp.
Trachystoma spp.
Sinapis pubescens
Brassica juncea
Brassica cossoneana
Brassica fruticulosa

Different species of the same cytodeme generally behave in the same way, but sometimes there are differences. However, differences have only been observed on the female side—all pollens of one cytodeme behave in the same way regardless of their specific or population origin, but the stigmas of one cytodeme may vary such that a single pollen sample may germinate on the stigma of one population but not on that of another. Again this parallels *Nicotiana*, (Pandey, 1968). There is a simple Darwinian explanation of this phenomenon. There can be no selective advantage in the capacity of a stigma to allow pollen of another species to germinate, whereas rejection of a foreign pollen may be vital to survival if the risk of cross pollination is high. Consequently the change must be from the positive to the negative reaction, and it must come about in the stigma, and in response to a contamination risk, so that some geographically isolated populations may remain positive. These conclusions fit with our observations. Thus stigmas of *Brassica carinata* of Ethiopian origin germinate the pollen of *Sinapis arvensis* freely, whereas a single population of the same cytodeme from Sicily rejects it; and *S. arvensis* is abundant in Sicily, but apparently not in Ethiopia. We can see too that we should not expect any change in reaction on the part of the pollen—any pollen which arrives on a foreign stigma is already lost to its own species so that no variation in its reaction could be selective.

These same principles probably apply throughout the group of cytodemes. Since all are presumably derived ultimately from a common ancestor, then were it not for changes of reaction all pollens would germinate on all stigmas; and every negative reaction observed implies a change in the stigma to exclude an unaltered pollen. Certain geographically isolated cytodemes would be exposed to very little contamination risk, and might therefore reject the pollen of few other cytodemes: thus *Sinapodendron*, confined to the Atlantic Islands along with very few other Brassica group species, comes high on our list.

Another group that might be expected to be highly unselective with regard to foreign pollens would be those species that are habitually self pollinated at an early flower stage. In these any foreign pollen is normally unlikely to arrive in time to compete with the self pollen, so that there might be no selective pressure to exclude it. *Brassica tournefortii* and *Erucastrum abyssinicum* are both habitual self pollinators and high on our list. Many of the out-pollinated Brassicas are self incompatible of course so that this observation fits too with the well known rules for crossing between self compatible and self incompatible species (Lewis and Crowe, 1958) though my interpretation is quite different.

Yet another factor which might be expected to influence the selection for cross incompatibility is the relative abundance of two species in mixed stands: we should expect the selection pressure for rejection of the foreign pollen to be greater in the rarer species.

There is some comfort in the fact that these suggestions do seem to fit with our ranked list of species. They are however, insufficient to explain the basic underlying pattern of the list: that is the tendency as one passes down the list for the species simultaneously and progressively to lose in their capacity to act as female parents of crosses and to gain in their capacity to act as males. The suggestion is now made that the list is in fact largely chronological—in that the more recent species would tend to lie below their closest ancestors in the list. This comes about because "new" species initially should have the same pattern of stigma-pollen reactions as their forebears; and then change as more negative reactions are acquired. The most important change will frequently be that with the most immediate ancestor, which will often be the most serious threat to the continued existence of the new species. By contrast the new species while still very rare will constitute little threat to the older and much more abundant one so that we might expect a unilateral incompatibility, the stigma of the newer rejecting the pollen of the older, and not vice versa. Such a process repeated many times, and without any modification would give the simple step like pattern. It would rank the most ancient species, so long as they remained abundant, towards the top of the list. However, ancient species on becoming relict, though not isolated, might rapidly acquire negative reactions to the pollens of many more recent species. Such ancient relicts might therefore be negative in reaction both as pollen and as seed parents, and as such would not fit neatly into our ranking list. In *Brassica amplexicaulis* we have a species perhaps fitting this specification.

CONCLUSION

There are about 100 wild species of the Cruciferae (including 12 genera from the subtribes Brassicinae and Raphaninae) which are sufficiently related to the 6 cultivated species of *Brassica* to be capable of experimental hybridisation with them (i.e. the *Brassica* coenospecies). Most of these species have a single chromosome complement (occasionally both in diploid and autotetraploid races), characteristic of that species but not necessarily confined to it. Grouping species with common chromosome complements into cytodemes, there are about 40 diploid cytodemes in the coenospecies, ranging in chromosome number from $n = 7$ to $n = 13$, and about 12 derived tetraploid cytodemes (including auto- and allotetraploids).

Two cytodemes each include two sub-forms involving chromosome interchanges, but otherwise the cytodemes are both constant internally and highly differentiated from one another. It is argued that they could not have arisen from ancestral cytodemes by a gradual evolutionary process, and that therefore the origin of new cytodemes from ancestral ones is essentially abrupt, complete and independent.

Crossing between cytodemes rarely leads to hybrid formation except by employing an embryo culture technique, and even then is frequently only successful in the one direction because the pollen will not germinate in the reciprocal. The cytodemes can be ranked approximately in a series such that the chances of crossing any two successfully are greater if the species which appears higher in the series is used as the female parent. The evolutionary significance of this series is thought to be both Darwinian and chronological.

ACKNOWLEDGEMENTS

Thanks are due to Professor J. H. Western, Professor of Agricultural Botany in the University of Leeds throughout the major period of these investigations for his continued support and encouragement. Much of the evidence quoted was collected by my colleagues, Dr. Myra Chu Chou, Dr. E. D. McArthur and Miss Carol Bostock, all working with Agricultural Research Council grants, and thanks are due both to them and to the Council for their support. Thanks are also due to Sigma Xi for a travel grant enabling Dr. McArthur to travel from America to work on the Brassica Programme.

REFERENCES

Amin, A. (1972). *In* IOPB Chromosome Number Reports XXXVIII. *Taxon* 21, 679.

Berg, C. C. (1967). *Act.Bot.Neer.* 15, 683 - 689.

Böcher, T. W. (1954). *Svensk.Bot.Tidskr.* 48, 31 - 46.

Bolkhovskikh, Z., Grif, V., Matvejeva, T. and Zakharyeva, O. (1969). "Chromosome numbers of flowering plants". Izdatel' stvo "Nauka", Leningrad.

Easterly, N. W. (1963). *Castanea* 28, 39 - 42.

Gómez-Campo, C. (1969). *Plant Introduction Newsletter* F.A.O. Rome. 22, 25 - 32.

Guinochet, M. (1946). *Compt.Rend.Acad.Sci.(Paris)* 222, 1131 - 1133.

Harberd, D. J. (1969). *Euphytica* 18, 425 - 429.

Harberd, D. J. (1972). *Bot.J.Linn.Soc.* 65, 1 - 23.

Harberd, D. J. and McArthur, E. D. (1972). *Heredity* 28, 253.

Harberd, D. J. and McArthur, E. D. (1972). *Heredity* 28, 254 - 257.

Harberd, D. J. and McArthur, E. D. (1972). *Watsonia* 9, 131 - 135.

Harrison, D. J. and Darby, L. (1955). *Nature* 176, 982.

Howard, H. W. (1939). *Cytologia* 10, 77 - 87.

Khoshoo, T. N. (1959). *Caryologia* 11, 297 - 333.

Lewis, D. and Crowe, L. K. (1958). *Heredity* 12, 233 - 256.

Lovis, J. D. (1964). *Nature* 203, 324 - 325.

Lövkvist, B. (1947). *Hereditas* 33, 421 - 422.

Lövkvist, B. (1956). *Symbolae.Bot.Upsaliensis* 14, 1 - 131.

Maire, R. (1965). "Flore de l'Afrique du nord, Vol. 12" Paul Lechevalier, Paris.

Manton, I. (1932). *Ann.Bot.* 46, 509 - 556.

Manton, I. (1937). *Ann.Bot.* 1, 439 - 462.

Martin, F. W. (1959). *Stain Technol.* 34, 125 - 128.

Montgomery, F. H. (1955). *Rhodora* 55, 161 - 173.

Morinaga, T. (1933). *Jap.J.Bot.* 6, 467 - 476.

Morinaga, T. (1934). *Cytologia* 6, 62 - 67.

Mulligan, G. A. (1967). *Can.J.Bot.* 45, 183 - 188.

Pandey, K. K. (1968). *Amer.Nat.* 102, 475 - 489

Schulz, O. E. (1919). Cruciferae-Brassiceae, Part 1: Brassicinae and Raphaninae. *In* "Das Pflanzenreich, Vol IV, Part 105" (A. Engler, ed.) Engelmann, Leipzig.

Tischler, G. (1934). *Bot.Jarhrb.* 67, 1 - 36.

Tutin, T. G., Heywood, V. H., Burges, N. A., Valentine, D. H., Walters, S. M. and Webb, D. A. (eds) (1964). "Flora Europaea" Vol 1. University Press, Cambridge.

U, M. (1935). *Jap.J.Bot.* 7, 389 - 452.

Winge, O. (1933). *Hereditas* 18, 181 - 191.

Winge, O. (1940). *Compt.Rend.Trav.Lab.Carlsberg.* Ser. Physiol. 23, 41 - 74.

Yakuwa, K. (1944). *Cytologia* 13, 162 - 163.

TRENDS IN THE BREEDING AND CULTIVATION OF CRUCIFEROUS CROPS

P. CRISP

National Vegetable Research Station, Wellesbourne, Warwick

INTRODUCTION

The Cruciferae contains a considerable number and diversity of crop plants. This, however, does not place it in the same league of agricultural importance as those other families which contain high numbers of crop plants—the Gramineae and the Leguminosae. Most cruciferous crops are grown for food, but nowhere do these form a substantial part of staple diets in the same sense as do the cereals or the pulses. Thus, many cruciferous species have been described as being eaten (Table 1), but most of these are condiments and garnishes to the main supplies of nutrients. Often these are local delicacies, and are usually collected from the wild rather than being cultivated, and a few more are in permanent cultivation as salads, vegetables, oil-seed and condiment crops, and animal feeds. This account deals principally with these species comprising the economically important Crucifers, which are subject to attempts at agronomic and genetic improvement.

Many of the cruciferous crops, especially within the genus *Brassica*, have been in cultivation for substantial lengths of time. As such they have often been widely disseminated by man. For example, *Brassica juncea*[1] is grown as a polymorphic series of cultivars in China, which led Sun (1970) to suggest that China is the gene centre for this species. *B. juncea* is believed to be an amphidiploid, the parental species of which are *B. campestris*[1] and *B. nigra* Koch. (Frandsen, 1943). However, the latter species does not occur in China. Sun (*loc.cit.*)

---

[1]*B. juncea* is taken to include all of the n = 18 *Brassica* species; and *B. campestris* to include all of the n = 10 *Brassica* species (Olsson, 1954). They are referred to as such throughout this article.

Table 1

Genera of the Cruciferae which are used as crop plants (excluding ornamentals).
Data are drawn largely from Bailey (1949), Hedrick (1972) and Herklots (1972).

Genus	Oils	Condiments and Garnishes			Raw Salads			Cooked Vegetables			Other Uses
	seed	seed	leaf	root	leaf	stem	root	leaf	stem	root	
Armoracia Gilib.			x	10	x			x			root as flour
Barbarea R.Br.					x						
Berteroa DC.					x						
Brassica L.	1	2			3			4	5	6	flowers as cooked vegetables 7 leaves (mainly) as pickles 8 stems and leaves as animal fodder 9
Bunias L.					x				x		
Cakile Miller					x						root as flour
Camelina	x										stem as fibres
Capsella Medicus								x			
Cardamine L.					x		x				
Caulanthus S.Wats.								x			
Chorispora R.Br.					x						
Coronopus Haller					x			x			
Crambe L.	x			x	11		x	x		x	
Eruca Miller					x						
Eutrema R.Br.				x							
Heldreichia Boiss.				x							
Isatis L.								x			leaf yields dye (woad)
Lepidium L.		x		x	12			x			
Lunaria L.		x					x			x	
Matthiola R.Br.								x			
Nasturtium R.Br.					13			13			
Peltaria Jacq.					x						
Pringlea Anders.				x	x						
Raphanus L.	x	x	x	x	x	14		x	14		seed pods eaten raw, cooked, or pickled animal fodder 15
Sinapis L.	x	2			x						as green manure
Sisymbrium L.		x			x			x			
Thlaspi L.					x						
Zilla Forsk.								x			

Numbers refer to economically important taxa and their products: 1 mustard oil, rape seed oil, etc.; 2 mustard; 3 chinese cabbage, etc.; 4 cabbage, kales, Brussels sprouts, etc.; 5 kohl rabi; 6 turnip, swede, etc.; 7 cauliflower, broccoli, chinese cabbage, etc.; 8 sauerkraut, etc.; 9 kales, rapes, etc.; 10 horse-radish; 11 sea-kale; 12 cress; 13 watercress; 14 radish; 15 fodder radish.

therefore suggested that the "raw" *B. juncea* was probably imported by migrating tribes from the Middle East. More recent introductions of cruciferous crops include all those now grown in America and Australia, which were introduced from Europe and Asia and those crops now established in many countries, especially in Europe, since the seventeenth century as a consequence of alterations to farming practice, notably crop rotation.

Many indications of the early distributions of those crops persist. The most striking is the "parallel evolution" of forms of *Brassica* in Europe and Asia. *B. oleracea* L. is a European crop species which has been selected to give a wide range of crop types. Vegetables have been developed where leaves, terminal buds, axillary buds, swollen stems, or floral tissues develop precociously and are harvested (Table 2). *B. napus* L. occurs in Europe as a vegetable or animal feed with swollen roots (the swede) or as an oil-seed crop. A similar pattern can be seen with *B. campestris* and *B. juncea* in Asia. Asiatic *B. campestris* contains vegetable forms which have been selected for large terminal buds, swollen stems, swollen roots, or large inflorescences. *B. juncea* includes forms with swollen stems or swollen roots. Both species have also been developed as leafy vegetables analogous to the kales of *B. oleracea,* and as oil-seed crops analogous to that of *B. napus.*

All of the important cruciferous crops are propagated from seed, but a few minor crops—watercress (*Nasturtium* spp.), horse radish (*Armoracia rusticana* Gaertner, Meyer & Scherb., syn. *Cochlearia armoracia* L.) and sea-kale (*Crambe maritima* L.)—are vegetatively propagated. The seed-propagated crops can be categorised into three types:

1. seed crops for oils and mustard condiments,
2. forage and fodder crops for animal feeds,
3. vegetables and salads for human consumption.

Many species contain crops in more than one of these categories (Table 3). This a feature of the Cruciferae, with close similarities between species and a diversity of horticultural types which man has selected within local species in particular geographical areas. As breeding objectives differ considerably between these crop types, breeding strategies may be quite different within each species. Thus, for review purposes it is more valid to consider the crop types than the crop species within the Cruciferae.

Table 2

A brief outline of the taxonomy (after Helm, 1963) and the main morphological differences between the agriculturally important taxa of *Brassica oleracea*

SPECIES	CHARACTER		CONVAR.	CHARACTER		VAR.	COMMON NAME	PRINCIPLE EDIBLE PORTION
Brassica oleracea	much axillary development		*oleracea*	stems much branched		*ramosa*	thousand-head kale, etc.	leaves*
				axillary buds develop more or less synchronously up stem		*gemmifera*	Brussels sprouts	axillary buds
	stem more or less unbranched	leaves stalked	*acephala*	stem enlongated	large number and/or size of leaves	*acephala* *sabellica* *selensia* *palmifolia*	kales, collards, borecole, etc.	leaves
					stem thickened	*medullosa*	marrow-stem kale	stem*
				stem bulbous		*gongylodes*	kohl rabi	stem
		apical bud large; leaves sessile; stem compressed	*capitata*	head compact	head very compact	*capitata*	cabbage	terminal bud
					leaves wrinkled	*sabauda*	savoy cabbage	terminal bud
				head lax; midrib prominent		*costata*	Portuguese cabbage	leaves
		large terminal inflorescence develops more or less synchronously	*botrytis*	some axillary development		*italica*	sprouting broccoli, calabrese	floral tissue
				no axillary buds; precocious development of pre-floral tissue		*botrytis*	heading broccoli, cauliflower	floral tissue

* animal feed

Table 3

The products of the most important crop species in the family Cruciferae
(Major products are within the thickened lines)

SPECIES	CHROMOSOME NUMBER n =	PRODUCTS		
		OIL-SEED AND SEED-BASED CONDIMENTS	VEGETABLES	ANIMAL FEEDS
Brassica oleracea L.	9	-	kale, cabbage, broccoli, etc.	kale, etc.
B. campestris sensu lato	10	oil seed turnip rape, toria, sarson, etc.	turnip, Chinese cabbage, etc.	turnip, turnip rape
B. nigra Koch.	8	oil seed, mustard	-	-
B. napus	19	oil seed rape, colza	swede (rutabaga)	swede, swede rape, kale-rape
B. juncea sensu lato	18	mustard oil (raya), mustard	Chinese and Indian leaf mustard, etc.	-
Raphanus sativus L.	9	oil seed	radish	fodder radish
Sinapis alba	12	oil seed, mustard	-	-
Eruca sativa (Miller) Thell.	11	oil seed (taramira)	salad rocket	-
Crambe maritima L.	15 30	oil seed	sea kale	-
Armoricacia rusticana Gaertn.,Mey.& Scherb.	16	-	horse radish	-
Nasturtium spp.	16 24	-	water cress	-
Lepidium sativum L.	8	-	cress	-
Camelina sativa	20	oil seed	-	-

VEGETATIVELY PROPAGATED CRUCIFEROUS CROPS

Only sea-kale, horse-radish and watercress are propagated vegetatively to give commercial cruciferous crops. Sea-kale is of very minor importance, and is usually propagated by cutti segments from rhizomes of established plants and using these to develop new crowns, although it can also be grown from seed.

In the horse-radish the swollen tap root develops subsidiary roots which form the propagants for the next crop when the main root is harvested. Many horse-radish strains now in cultivation are seed-sterile (Stokes, 1955), and little, if any, effective breeding work has been reported. A problem with many vegetatively propagated crops is the build up of virus infections. Usually these viruses are not transmitted in the seed, and can be controlled by propagating new vegetative material from seed to replace infected stocks. Horse-radish can become seriously infected with virus and so attempts have been made in the U.S.A. to produce seed-fertile horse-radish by crossing with Bohemian material (Yarnell, 1956). An alternative approac is to regenerate virus-free plants from aseptically cultured meristems of infected plants, and this technique has now succes fully been applied to horse-radish (Paludan, 1971; Mori, 1971).

Watercress is now largely propagated from seed, the crop being grown in water beds which simulate the streams of the species' natural habitat. Cuttings or whole plants can also be used to inoculate fresh beds, which remain productive for about three years, being harvested up to ten times a year. The sterile triploid hybrid *Nasturtium officinale* R.Br. (n = 16) x *N. microphyllum* (Boenn.)Reichenb. (*uniseriatum* Howard & Manton) (n = 32)—"brown cress"—was originally grown extensively, but problems due to the fungal disease crook root, and virus infection resulted in *N. officinale*—"green cress"—replacing the hybrid during the 1950's. *N. officinale* is fertile and so can be propagated from seed; the virus is not seed-borne (Tomlinson 1957), and thus uninfected stocks can be raised. In addition, *N. officinale* is more resistant than the hybrid to crook root (Spencer and Glasscock, 1963). Selection within *N. officinale* has been towards stocks with later flowering (Bleasdale, 1964), rapid growth, and lack of bitterness (Sansom, 1948).

Autotetraploid *N. officinale* (n = 32) has been produced and possessed several advantages over the diploid, being more succulent and later flowering, and possessing more Vitamin C (Howard 1952). However, this cress had a reduced seed yield and the necessity of vegetative propagation might have raised problems of virus elimination. These preliminary results suggest that a more intensive effort at producing autotetraploids, or even allotetraploid or allohexaploid *N. officinale* x *microphyllum* (J.C. Haigh, unpublished), and breeding from them for improved seed yield and agronomic qualities could result in greatly improved strains.

Considerable developments are being made with the mechanical harvesting of watercress. In France about 20 % of the watercress crop is harvested with rotating scythes which travel along the beds, the product being marketed as a loose pack of unsorted leaves and stems. Developments in the U.K. include similar machines, one of which selectively sorts and bundles the watercress to give packs in the traditional hand-picked fashion. Attempts are also being made in Britain to grow watercress in more controllable conditions under cover (NAAS, 1969; E. C. Herwin, personal communications). In France developments include growing the cress hydroponically, or in beds with greatly reduced water flow (Coïc *et al.*, 1972); and in Asia the cress is grown in damp soils and is eaten as a boiled vegetable which reduces its bitterness (Herklots, 1972).

SEED-PROPAGATED CRUCIFEROUS CROPS

The commercially important cruciferous crops are produced as annuals or biennials from seed. Outside of the three categories already defined (oil-seed and mustard crops, animal feeds, and vegetables) only a few crops of limited importance are seed based, such as *Isatis* for the dye woad, and *Sinapis* for green manure.

Oil-Seed and Mustard Crops

The principal traditional uses for oil from cruciferous seeds are cooking, illumination, and as a food preservative and condiment. More recently such oils, especially from the rapes—*Brassica campestris* and *B. napus*—have found uses as industrial lubricants and in processed human foodstuffs, notably margarine.

Oil-Seed Crops

Cruciferous seeds contain substantial amounts of oil, and several species are grown as a source of this oil (see Table 3). Cruciferous oil-seeds now rank about fifth in importance behind soya beans, cotton seed, groundnuts and sunflower seed (Ohlson, 1972). The main emphasis is on *Brassica campestris* (oil-seed turnip rape, toria, sarson), but *B. juncea* (raya) is of importance in Asia, and *B. napus* (oil-seed rape, colza) in temperate Europe and Canada.

Both self-compatible and self-incompatible forms occur in the two main oil bearing types of *B. campestris*, var. *toria* and var. *sarson*, and in *B. juncea*. Various components of yield have been found to be subject to heterotic vigour in both *B. campestris* (Rajan, 1970; Rao, 1970b) and *B. juncea* (Singh and Singh, 1972), and strongly suggest that hybrid cultivars based on self-incompatible material should be produced in place of the present mass-selected varieties.

In Europe and North America the cruciferous oil crops retain some of the traditional importance of the cruciferous forage crops in general husbandry as a component in crop rotation, especially with cereals. They become more important economically as labour costs increase, because drilling of seed and harvesting can be automated. Additionally, they supply an alternative to mineral and animal oils as lubricants and as constituents of human foodstuffs, mainly margarine. The economic and political dependence that this affords has led to increasing interest being taken in oil crops in general, and the cruciferous oil crops in particular in temperate countries, to which they are better adapted than other oil-seed crops.

Four main types of oil-seed crucifers are grown in the temperate areas—the annual and biennial types of both *B. campestris* and *B. napus*. In Europe, emphasis is placed on the biennial *B. napus*, but in the shorter, more continental growing season of Canada, about 80 % of the oil crop is the fast growing annual *B. campestris* (Bunting, 1969). As with mustard, a frequent harvesting method is to flatten the crop in order to encourage seeding, and then to combine harvest it. In addition to these *Brassica* crops, small acreages of *Sinapis alba* are grown in Sweden, and *Camelina sativa* is still grown as a traditional crop in various parts of Europe (Lööf, 1960; Bunting, 1969). Breeding in Europe and Canada has had large emphasis placed on the composition of the oil, as high erucic acid levels lead to physiological disorders in mammals. Erucic acid-free types of both *B. napus* (Stefansson *et al.*, 1961) and of *B. campestris* (Downey, 1964, 1966) have been found in Canada in fodder forms of these species and have been incorporated into both annual and biennial oil-seed forms in Canada and in Europe (Jönsson, 1973). The relatively easy transfer of the erucic-free character by back crossing indicates a fairly simple genetic control. Jönsson (*loc.cit.*) reported that effective selection could also be made within *B. campestris* cultivars with normal high levels of erucic acid to reduce these levels, and his results strongly suggest that the genes controlling this character are additive in nature.

Conversely, high erucic acid levels may be required for industrial use of rapeseed oil, and moderately successful attempts have been made to raise the erucic acid levels of various oil-seed crucifers by breeding (Appelqvist and Jönsson, quoted in Lööf and Appelqvist, 1972).

Cotyledonary oil content of these taxa is determined by the genotype of the embryo (Dorrell and Downey, 1964), and plants can be grown on from seeds which have had a cotyledon removed and assessed for oil content. Progress with these breeding programmes has been greatly assisted by gas chromatographic analyses of oil content of these single cotyledons (Thies, 1971).

Of secondary importance is breeding for reduced linolenic acid, which causes chemical instability of the oil when used as a lubricant; and for increased linoleic acid, low levels of which may lead to physiological disorders (Röbbelen, 1971). Röbbelen (*loc.cit.*, quoting the work of W. Thies and his colleagues) reported that attempts at breeding material with decreased linolenic acid and increased linoleic acid were unsuccessful, and screenings of about 500 *Brassica* cultivars and 500 crucifer species revealed no useful deviations from a 2:1 ratio of linoleic:linolenic acids. He suggested that breeding for these characters may be impossible because of physiological limitations of changing this ratio. More recently, however, Rakow (1973) has reported forms with induced mutations which had linoleic:linolenic acid ratios of about 4:1 and 1:1 due to heritable changes in the linolenic acid content. These results suggest that the two fatty acids may at some stage in their formation be under independent genetic control.

Mustard

Brassica juncea (brown mustard) and *Sinapis alba* (white mustard) are the principle sources of the seed used in mustard manufacture, which is now an established industry in several European countries and in Canada. *B. nigra* (black mustard) was until the 1950's an important constituent of mustard, but since that time has been more or less completely replaced by *B. juncea*, which is more suitable for mechanical harvesting because the siliquas do not shatter as readily as in *B. nigra*. Old-established growing areas for mustard were determined by regional culinary requirements, and small acreages of the crop can be found in many parts of the world. However, the rapid growth of the crop allows it to be produced in areas with short growing seasons, and Canada is now the major growing area for mustard.

Cultivation of the crop is highly mechanised on a large scale. Seed is broadcast or drilled directly into the field, and its rapid growth rate usually prevents any requirement for herbicide or insecticide treatment. In general, seed is now collected by combine harvesting the mature crop. This may be preceded by swathing down the growing crop in order to encourage seed ripening before frosts appear, as is the practice in Canada.

S. alba is an outbreeder, being wind or insect pollinated. *B. juncea* by contrast is an inbreeder. Breeding progress in both species is by selection and progeny testing, but whereas in *B. juncea* lines can be established by single plant selection, in *S. alba* inbred lines have to be established on the basis of sib crossing in order to avoid inbreeding depression (J. S. Hemingway, personal communication).

Animal Feeds

Cruciferous crops supply animal feeds as silage, as seed meal left over after extraction of oil, as forage crops grazed *in situ* in the field, and as stored root fodder used as winter feeds.

The production of silage from crucifers is of small importance, in part due to problems of animal disorders acknowledged to be associated with intensive feeding on crucifer material (Kay, 1971; Greenhalgh, 1971). However, there are indications that the process of ensilaging may reduce the glucosinolate content which is presumed to be responsible for these disorders; and, again, that progress may be made with reducing glucosinolate content in *B. oleracea* by breeding (Josefsson *et al.*, 1972).

Seed meal is a relatively unimportant by-product of oil production, and had received little attention in its own right except as an incidental to the attempts at changing fatty acid contents in the oil. Recently, however, *B. napus* with low glucosinolate content has been identified and this character is being incorporated into oil seed forms so that the seed meal may become of higher agricultural value (Lööf and Appelqvist, 1972).

The use of cruciferous species as forage and fodder crops is largely restricted to those countries, such as Britain, Holland and New Zealand, which specialise in small scale intensive farming of ruminants. A wide range of species is used; forage crops include *Raphanus sativus* (fodder radish), *Brassica oleracea* (kale, cabbage), *B. campestris* and *B. napus* (rapes); fodder crops consist of those with swollen stem or root storage organs—*B. oleracea* (kohl rabi), *B. campestris* (turnip) and *B. napus* (swede). Improvements to farming practice should result in an increase in the importance of these crops, which had been showing a general decline for the last century. These improvements include suitable herbicides, strip grazing with moveable electric fencing, direct precision drilling of seed, selective mechanical thinning (Pascal, 1971), and mechanical harvesting and feeding of stored fodder. It is of interest to note that one of the traditional uses of brassicas—as a "cleaning" crop to reduce weed populations in rotation farming, has now decreased in importance due to the advent of herbicides (Elliot, 1971). The future importance of these crops may lie in part with reassessments of crop rotation in the light of damage done by continuous cereal production. In addition, in terms of productivity of protein and starch per unit area, in general they outyield the grain and silage graminaceous crops (Kay, 1971).

Most of the forage crucifer cultivars are open-pollinated and are the products of mass selection. However, an appreciation of the breeding system in the brassicas and the advantages of heterotic vigour has led to hybrid kales being produced. For example, Johnston (1963) and du Crehu (1969) showed that F_1 hybrid kales greatly outyielded open-pollinated cultivars, but the depressed seed yield of the inbred parents made these an unattractive proposition. Consequently, emphasis has been laid on the production of double cross hybrids, using four inbred parental lines (Johnston, 1964, 1965; du Crehu, 1969, 1970, and triple cross hybrids, using six inbred lines (Thompson, 1964). The principle behind the production of these hybrids is to use parental lines each of which possesses a different self-incompatibility allele. These are crossed to give F_1 hybrids, which are vigorous and give good seed yields. The F_1 hybrids are crossed together, or with any unpaired parental lines, and so on until a single seed population is produced. The main problem with this procedure is that because of the biennial nature of kale, for the triple crosses it takes eight years from the inbreds being crossed together to the crop being grown in the field (Thompson, 1964). The first product of this approach has been a double cross hybrid, the marrow-stem kale cv. Maris Kestrel. This will be superseded by a triple cross Maris Kestrel by 1975 (Thompson, 1971). Maris Kestrel exemplifies the breeding of forage crucifers for modern husbandry, having been specifically bred to fit into the requirements of strip grazing (NSDO, 1973a).

Other developments with forage crops include the incorporation of race-specific resistance to clubroot (*Plasmodiophora brassica)* into rapes from resistant swedes and turnips (Lammerink, 1970; NSDO, 1973b). Another important development has been the production of "stubble turnips", principally in Holland. These are drilled into unploughed land after overwintering crops have been harvested, to give a quick-growing forage crop. The Dutch cultivars are the product of the development of synthetic and open-pollinated populations from inbred lines with resistance to clubroot, high dry matter content, and low glucosinolate content (Toxopeus, 1970). Also, new types of cruciferous species are being assessed as forage crops. In particular, fodder radish, which is resistant to clubroot and grows very quickly is almost certain to increase in importance; and synthetic rape *B. napus* (from *B. oleracea* x *B. campestris)* cultivars with increased stem edibility have been released in Sweden.

Vegetables

Crucifers form substantial proportions of the vegetable acreage in Europe and Asia. Indeed, several European countries have more than 30 % of their vegetable acreages down to crucifers, compared with about 6 % in the U.S.A. (Nieuwhof, 1969). The distribution of particular Crucifer vegetables differs considerably: the *Brassica campestris* vegetables in Asia and the *B. oleracea* vegetables in Europe are almost mutually exclusive but a number of other differences are apparent, reflecting national tastes rather than geographic origins of crops or their economic status. Thus, Brussels sprouts are very much a British crop, with as much grown in the U.K. as in the rest of Europe put together, and about ten times as much as in the U.S.A. (Nieuwhof, *loc.cit.*). Similarly, cauliflowers are principally a European crop, their place being largely taken by calabrese in the U.S.A. As standards of living improve, a decrease in the consumption of cabbages and kales is accompanied by an increase of the milder flavoured brassicas: cauliflowers, calabrese and Brussels sprouts. This is despite the fact that cabbages produce at least five times more edible weight per unit area than the three milder flavoured brassicas and are much cheaper to the consumer.

Apart from yield and consumer preferences, the main requirement of cruciferous vegetables in the developed countries is plant to plant uniformity. Crops which mature uniformly can be harvested in one or a few cuts, with a consequent reduction in costs, and crops which can be marketed within one quality grade command higher prices. Many of the developments in vegetable production have been prompted by this requirement for uniform crops. Direct drilling of seed of cruciferous vegetables such as cabbages, cauliflowers, calabrese and Brussels sprouts has been developed neither because it reduces the risks or even the costs of plant establishment, nor because it greatly increases yield or quality, but primarily because it decreases variability.

Other attempts at inducing uniformity in crops by physiological means have included giving young cauliflower plants a period of cold treatment before being transplanted to the field. This synchronises the vernalisation process which results in the formation of the curds, and may substantially reduce the spread of maturity within the treated crop (Salter and Ward, 1972). The growing of calabrese at very close spacing, say with 15 cm. between plants instead of the customary 60 cm., can also result in a uniform crop of terminal inflorescences which can be harvested with a single cut (Rubatsky and Hall, 1970). Salter (1971) extended this approach to cauliflowers, producing effectively a new crop ("mini-cauliflowers") where each plant bore a cauliflower curd of 4 - 8 cm. in diameter, in contrast to the curds of conventionally grown plants, which normally exceed 10 cm.

Increased uniformity within individual plants bearing several marketable portions has been attained by removing the apical bud from the plant. This is now a standard practice with Brussels sprouts, and leads to increased uniformity of maturity of the sprouts on the stem. The same method has now been extended to calabrese; removal of the terminal bud can result in uniform laterals being produced (Palevitch and Pressman, 1973).

Breeding for uniformity has resulted, notably, in the production of F_1 hybrids. The first reported commercial production of F_1 Crucifers was a cabbage cultivar in Japan in 1938 (Sakata, 1973). This was based on self-incompatible parental material maintained vegetatively by cuttings rather than as inbred lines. Since that time F_1 vegetables have come to dominate the Japanese crucifer seed trade. In *B. oleracea* the Japanese produce F_1 hybrids of calabrese, Brussels sprouts, cabbage, cauliflower, horticultural kale, and kohl rabi. Similarly, in *B. campestris* various Chinese cabbages and, recently, horticultural turnips are now produced as F_1's. F_1 cultivars of radish are also available.

Interest in Europe and the U.S.A. in F_1 brassicas started in the 1950's and has resulted in a wide range of European F_1 Brussels sprouts and cabbages, and American F_1 cabbages and calabreses.

Progress with F_1 and other hybrid Crucifers has been highly dependent on a knowledge of the breeding system, and this work was, until recently, restricted to vegetables. Many of the more recent developments have revolved around the identification of different incompatibility alleles using the method of van Hal and Verhoeven (1968) whereby compatibility could be assessed by pollen tube growth in styles rather than by seed set.

Two problems are associated with the production of F_1 seed. Firstly, parental material may have low seed yields due to inbreeding depression. This is, perhaps, relatively unimportant in the vegetables, where each seed (in terms of the plant grown from it) is worth several times that of an oil-seed or animal-feed crop. Secondly, the procedure of breeding an inbred parent may result in considerable inadvertent selection in favour of self-fertile material within that inbred line.

This results in self- rather than cross-fertilisation between lines when used as parents for an F_1. Appreciable quantities of selfed rather than hybrid seed in the F_1 can considerably reduce its value when grown as a crop, due to the depressed yield of the parental types (Johnson, 1966).

These problems have given rise to a number of different approaches to breeding uniform vegetables, principally by producing other types of hybrids. Several inbred lines may be hand-crossed together to give small quantities of F_1's which are then open-pollinated to give commercial bulk seed, termed a synthetic cultivar. This approach has been taken with cauliflower (Dixon, 1971, 1973; P. Crisp, unpublished; M. Buiatti, personal communication), and Brussels sprouts, cabbage and calabrese (A. G. Johnson, personal communication). Similarly, in all of these crops three-way and four-way (or double cross) hybrids utilising, respectively, three or four inbred lines are being investigated or produced by commercial seed firms in America, Asia and Europe.

Alternative methods of producing F_1 and other hybrids lie in maintaining male-sterile or self-incompatible parental material not as recurrently seeding inbred lines, but as vegetative clones. The original F_1 hybrid cabbage produced in Japan is believed to have had one vegetatively maintained, highly self-incompatible parent which was pollinated by a less incompatible parent maintained by seeding. The same technique was advocated for F_1 cabbage in the U.S.A. (Odland and Isenberg, 1950). Very recently an American seed firm has apparently vegetatively propagated a male-sterile cabbage on a large enough scale to give 40 acres of seeding crop intended for F_1 production (A. G. Johnson, personal communication), but further details of this are not yet available.

Usually, however, F_1 and other hybrids are produced from inbred lines. The main advantage of using lines is that a much higher number of parents can be generated from seed than by vegetative means, and thus the F_1 seed yield is considerably increased. This limitation need not apply if only small quantities of seed from inbred parents are required, as in synthetic cultivars. As an example, winter cauliflowers grown in the relatively frost-free areas of South West Britain may be quoted. About 7500 acres are grown of cultivars supplying a continuity of harvests between December and May. The quantity of seed required each year for each cultivar is therefore quite small and can be supplied from one or two acres of seeding plants. These plants, in turn, can be propagated by seeding together a few dozen parental plants. The system employed is that parental plants are vegetatively propagated and are mass seeded together through two generations to give the commercial generation of seed (Haine, 1955). Maintenance of the same parental plants as clones from year to year ensures that the seed released to growers always has a similar genetic constitution. These clones are maintained by taking curd or stem cuttings, which allows a multiplication rate of perhaps ten per year. An advance on this rate of multiplication has been afforded by aseptic propagation methods. The cauliflower is particularly suited to this technique as the surface of the curd is composed of thousands of apical meristems (Crisp and Walkey, 1974). In nutrient, aseptic conditions these meristems give rise to leafy shoots, which allow a multiplication rate tens or even hundreds of times greater than earlier methods. This technique cannot, with similar ease, be extended to most of the other Crucifers because of the unique presentation of masses of meristems in the cauliflower. However, careful dissection may yield large numbers of meristems in other crops; for example, some hundreds of meristems are available within the "buttons" of a single plant of Brussels sprouts, and within the developing head of calabrese.

Another possibility is that clones can be regenerated from aseptically maintained callus tissues. Such methods have been employed for cauliflower (Margara, 1969; Buiatti *et al.*, 1973; M. Buiatti, personal communication), marrow-stem kale (Lustinec and Horak, 1970), and *Sinapis alba* (Bajaj and Bopp, 1972), although none of these reports has apparently resulted in commercial applications. One problem with regenerating plants from callus is the increased likelihood of regenerating genetically aberrant plants, which would be highly undesirable in a breeding programme; indeed, Horak *et al.* (1971) noted the presence of polyploids in some of their regenerated marrow-stem kale material.

A problem with most material which is vegetatively propagated by taking cuttings is the build-up of virus infection. Usually these viruses are not transmitted in the seed, and can be controlled by propagating new vegetative material from seed to replace infected stocks. Such a procedure cannot, however, be applied to stocks of breeding material which must maintain their genetic identity, as is the case with the cauliflower clones already mentioned. The procedure of regeneration of plants from aseptically cultured meristems can be used to eliminate virus infection. This has now been used to regenerate virus-free cauliflowers (Walkey *et al.*, 1974).

The production of inbred cultivars is of restricted importance in the vegetable crucifers. Most summer cauliflower cultivars are self-compatible, and are usually bred from very restricted genetic bases—even from single plants. This approach is used in most of the main growing regions of this crop such as India, Italy, and North West Europe, although in Japan F_1 hybrid summer cauliflowers are produced. Other self-compatible cruciferous vegetables such as those included in *Brassica juncea* and *B. napus* are, at present, usually bred as mass selected cultivars from wider genetic bases.

BIOLOGICAL FEATURES OF THE CRUCIFERAE IN RELATION TO BREEDING SEED-PROPAGATED CROPS

The Production of Homozygous Lines

Lines of material possessing degrees of homozygosity are used in crucifer breeding to ensure greater genetic similarity within a crop than in more heterozygous mass selected crops. The assumption behind their use is that genetically similar crops will tend to be phenotypically similar. Thus, inbred lines may be used themselves as cultivars, or as parental material for F_1 and other hybrid cultivars.

These inbred lines are produced by self-pollination of selected plants; and this procedure may entail "bud pollination" (Pearson, 1929), whereby the self-incompatibility of the parent is avoided by pollinating while the flower is in the bud stage and the histochemical reaction resulting in self-incompatibility is not yet operative. It may take five or six generations of inbreeding for material to reach the degree of homozygosity which the breeder requires. Progeny testing of each generation may be necessary and, as many Crucifers are biennials, the production of inbreds becomes a lengthy business.

Concern about the time spent on producing inbreds has resulted in attention being directed towards less conventional methods of producing homozygous material. In particular, a number of workers have investigated the potential of doubling the haploid chromosome complement of gametophytes, female and male, to give "instant inbreds" which, by definition, should be completely homozygous.

The production of offspring resembling the maternal parent has been reported when attempts have been made at wide species crosses, involving *B. oleracea* x *B. campestris* (Olsson *et al.*, 1955), and *Brassica* x *Raphanus* (Tokumasu, 1970a, 1970b). These offspring have been termed matromorphs, and a possibility was that they were the product of a doubling of the female gametophyte chromosome complement. However, Mackay (1972) quoted his own work and that of S. Tokumasu and T. Haruta, which showed that if these matromorphs were selfed, their progenies showed segregation for various genetic markers, and could not have been homozygous. Mackay considered that they were more likely to be the product of diploid parthenogenesis. Almost certainly the matromorphs were the product of recombination within the female sexual apparatus. In accord with Mackay's findings within *Brassica*, Tokumasu (1970b) reported that three matromorphic products of *Brassica* x *Raphanus* crosses included one aneuploid and all three differed morphologically from one another. Agamospermic reproduction has been recorded as an alternative to the normal sexual process in several non-crop genera of the Cruciferae, including *Draba, Arabis, Erysimum* and *Parrya* (Mulligan and Findlay, 1970). It was not certain in any of these latter cases if recombination of genetic material had been involved in the production of maternals. It appears, therefore, that despite its initial promise, this technique offers little to plant breeding, either as a method of producing "instant inbreds" or of producing genetically identical clones from selected plants.

There has been a report of one haploid being produced by crossing *B. campestris* with *B. nigra* (Prakash, 1973a), and several of haploids arising spontaneously in *B. napus* (Olsson and Hagberg, 1955; Thompson, 1969; Stringham and Downey, 1973). A considerable increase in the rate of production of haploids, and its applicability to other genotypes may be necessary before this could be considered as a reliable technique for general use in producing homozygotes by doubling of the chromosome complement of the haploid. Differences between *B. napus* cultivars in their tendencies to produce haploids probably reflect a genetic control of this character

(Stringham and Downey, *loc.cit.)*. This raises problems that use of this character in breeding programmes may result in unacceptably high levels of haploid production when diploid breeding is resumed. However, very recently an erucic-free oil-seed cultivar of *B. napus* (Maris Haplona) has been bred using spontaneously formed haploids as bases for homozygous lines, and problems have not been encountered with haploid production in the cultivar (K. F. Thompson, personal communication).

The production of haploids from pollen is currently a potentially attractive alternative to inbreeding to produce homozygotes. This involves the aseptic culturing of pollen or anthers on a suitable medium, with the regeneration of a haploid plant from an embryo-like structure which develops to include one of the nuclei of the pollen grain (Sunderland, 1971). Successes with this technique appear to reflect clear-cut taxonomic groupings, and at present are largely restricted to the Solanacae (see, for example, Nitsch, 1970) and other families with binucleate pollen (Brewbaker, 1957). Reported successes within the Cruciferae, which has trinucleate pollen, include that with pollen from *B. oleracea* and a *B. oleracea* x *B. campestris* hybrid (Kameya and Hinata, 1970a), and with *Arabidopsis* (Gresshoff and Doy, 1972). These, however, have involved regeneration of plants from callus derived from pollen, rather than directly from pollen grains. This means that the rate of haploid production is, at present, considerably less than in, say, *Nicotiana* (Sunderland, 1971) or barley (Clapham, 1971), where several dozen individual haploids, presumably with distinct genotypes, can be derived from each anther.

The Breeding System

The incompatibility system of the Cruciferae has been thoroughly investigated, and has been shown to be sporophytically controlled at or near the pollen/stigma interface (Bateman, 1955; Thompson, 1957; Sampson, 1964; Ockendon, 1972). It has been utilised extensively in the production of hybrids, especially in the vegetable crops, but even here its utilisation could be extended. Hybrids produced by controlled pollinations and marketed by Japanese seed companies, include some, such as summer cauliflower, which are usually considered as being too self-compatible for hybrid production. The lesson to be learnt is that self-incompatible lines can be selected from the range of variability present in material which over-all is substantially self-compatible. It should be feasible, and our own work supports this, to select self-incompatible lines for a wide range of cauliflower types (P. Crisp and A. R. Gray, unpublished). Singh (1959) isolated self-incompatible lines from *Brassica juncea*, which is also usually self-compatible.

The converse is also possible, that self-compatible lines can be selected from material which is substantially self-incompatible, such as kales (Thompson, 1966; Thompson and Taylor, 1971), and autumn and winter cauliflowers (L. E. Watts, unpublished; P. Crisp, unpublished). Less emphasis has been placed on the development of inbred cultivars by the seed trade because of the commercial advantages of hybrids, especially F_1's. These include the proven practical advantages of F_1's in yield and uniformity, as well as the fact that, because of segregation in the F_2, seed cannot be saved from an F_1 crop with the hope of raising a similar crop.

Utilisation of the incompatibility system goes further. As biometrical investigations of the crucifer crops continue to yield data on optimum population structure (for example, see Zeevaart, 1955; Johnston, 1968; Crisp and Gray, 1973), the breeding system becomes of increasing significance. In broad terms, appreciable degrees of heterotic vigour for agronomic characters require that cultivars be composed of strongly self-incompatible but cross-compatible material. Conversely, if gains can be made by exploiting additive genetic variation, then cultivars should consist of inbred material containing self-compatible alleles.

Inbreeding depression is perhaps a small price to pay for increased uniformity in many of the vegetable crops. Quite apart from the processors' requirements, which may put maximum sizes on vegetables, there is a tendency for the fresh market to require smaller cabbages, cauliflowers and so on. Decreases in yield per plant caused by inbreeding depression should, therefore, be of limited importance in these crops, and they largely could be compensated for by closer spacing of these smaller plants.

The overall picture within the vegetable Crucifers is, therefore, that hybrids can be produced in a wide range of vegetable crops, but so could inbreds, and the probable trend is for hybrids and inbreds to supersede the existing open-pollinated cultivars, especially if the latter are not the product of progeny-tested material (Farthing, 1972).

The production of F_1 hybrid cultivars by controlled pollination may be too expensive if the value of individual plants is less than that for vegetables, even if substantial heterosis can be demonstrated. Other types of hybrid cultivars based on the performance of the incompatibility system are, however, feasible if the rate of seed multiplication is high enough to justify the maintenance of parental material as inbred lines. The hybrid forage kale cv. Maris Kestrel has already been described, where four or six inbred lines are maintained as parents. Oil-seed and mustard crops are selected for high seeding rates, and useful inbred parents should, by definition, have good seed yielding capacities, which would alleviate some problems with seed production. Synthetic populations of *Sinapis alba* intended for mustard production have already been produced (J. S. Hemingway, personal communication), and the same progress could almost certainly be made with oil seed *B. campestris*.

The value of inbreds as varietal populations is far less in animal feed and oil-seed crops than it is in vegetables, where reductions in yield may be compensated for by increased uniformity. The exceptions are where the material is self-compatible, as in the polyploid species *B. juncea* and *B. napus*, where inbred lines can be established easily and with little danger of inbreeding depression.

Male Sterility

Male sterility is an alternative to the incompatibility system as a method of producing hybrid cultivars. Two basically different types of male sterility are used in plant breeding, effected respectively by nuclear and by cytoplasmic factors.

Genetic Male Sterility

Male sterility (*ms*) determined by single genes has been identified in several cruciferous crop species. In *Brassica napus* (oil rape) Takagi (1970) induced a recessive *ms* gene with gamma irradiation and Koch and Peters (1953) reported genetic male sterility in the same crop. In *B. campestris*, non-allelic *ms* genes were found in self-incompatible and self-compatible cultivars of var. *sarson* and var. *toria* (Anon, 1967). In *B. oleracea ms* genes have been found in cabbage (Rundfeldt, 1960; Nieuwhof, 1961) in Brussels sprouts (Johnson, 1958; North, 1961; Nieuwhof, 1968), in cauliflower (Jensma, 1957; Nieuwhof, 1961, 1968; Borchers, 1966) and in calabrese (Cole, 1957; Sampson, 1966, 1970; Dickson, 1970; Borchers, 1971). Tokumasu (1951) found an *ms* gene in *Raphanus sativus* (radish).

At least five of these *ms* genes in *B. oleracea* are non-allelic (Dickson, 1970). If just four of these were accumulated as homozygotes in one line, then crossing with pollen from a line heterozygous for these genes would give over 90 % male-sterile offspring (Nieuwhof, 1968). This method could be used to bulk up the male sterile parents of an F_1 hybrid.

In one case an *ms* gene was linked with a seedling pigmentation marker in calabrese (Sampson, 1966). This might allow efficient rogueing out of male-fertile plants at the seedling stage from plants intended as female parents of an F_1. Another possibility is that environmental factors might govern the gene so that the male sterility might be effected when required. High temperature has been shown to activate the expression of male sterility with two of these genes in *B. oleracea* (Dickson, 1970; Nieuwhof, 1968). However, treatments have not been found that are applicable on a field scale, either to induce or repress male sterility. For example various plant hormones and metabolic inhibitors sprayed on to a male-sterile cauliflower failed to restore fertility (Borchers, 1966). Attempts at producing male sterility by using gametocides, although giving partial success, also appear to be of no use on a field scale (Ruebenbauer and Binek, 1969; G. J. Faulkner and T. H. Thomas, personal communication).

Male-sterile material could be bulked up by vegetative propagation, and the feasibility of this method has been shown for cauliflower using aseptic propagation (Crisp and Walkey, 1974); and for cabbage using conventional propagation (A. G. Johnson, personal communication).

Cytoplasmic Male Sterility

Cytoplasmic male sterility is potentially the most useful method of producing male-sterile lines. By this method (used, for example, for the commercial production of F_1 hybrid cultivars of onion, and carrot) cytoplasmic factors controlling male sterility are maintained in breeding material by using the male-sterile parent as a female. Crosses made by another parent onto this male-sterile stock give F_1 hybrids, which are also male-sterile. The male sterility of these progenies does not matter, of course, unless the crop in question is being grown for seed, as is the case with the oil and mustard crops. If this is the case then the male parent must carry a factor—usually a nuclear gene—restoring fertility to the F_1 hybrid. Cytoplasmic male sterility has apparently only seldom been found in the cruciferous crops. Ogura (1968) reported it in radish and this factor is in the process of being transferred into commercially suitable stocks (Bonnett, 1970). Cytoplasmic male sterility has also been found as the product of crossing *Brassica oleracea* and *B. nigra* (Pearson, 1972). Material derived from Pearson's stocks is being incorporated into a number of breeding programmes with *B. oleracea*, mainly calabrese, in the U.S.A. (A. G. Johnson, personal communication). Only one other report of the phenomenon has been made—in *B. napus* (Yamaguchi and Kanno, 1963), but this has not apparently had a commercial application.

Polyploidy

Polyploidy can be employed in plant breeding towards a number of ends: as a method of obtaining changes such as increased dry matter content, frost hardiness, and size of particular organs and also as a method of regulating genetic recombination and expression. In the cruciferous crop plants these "physiological" and "genetic" changes closely correspond to attempts at making respectively autopolyploids and allopolyploids.

Autopolyploids

Polyploidy is of limited importance where the oil-seed crucifers are concerned because of probable reduction in seed yield due to partial sterility. However, it has been reported that colchicine treatment of *Brassica juncea* gave rise to high yielding autopolyploid derivatives which had the additional bonus of possessing non-shattering siliquae (Anon, 1967). Also, Chowdhury *et al.* (1967) reported that autotetraploid forms of *Brassica campestris* var. *sarson* were more self-compatible and gave a higher seed set than their self-incompatible diploid parents. Kadota and Ito (1952) noted the same phenomenon with *B. campestris* var. *pekinensis*, although this is not an oil crop. Low initial seed sets following autopolyploidisation could be selectively improved, as Tyagi and Das (1970) did with *sarson*, and Parthasarathy and Rajan (1953) did with *toria*. However, in general it seems improbable that autopolyploidisation of the cruciferous oil crops could supply advances which breeding at the diploid level could not. Problems with seed set are more likely to be solved by using a proper appreciation of the breeding system of the diploid than by attempting to circumvent this system with autopolyploids, with the attendant problems caused by meiotic disturbances.

Amongst the cruciferous vegetables autopolyploidy is again of limited importance. Problems in the vegetables tend to centre on uniformity, and multiple copies of genes would make selection of homozygous material much more difficult. Thus, within the vegetables autopolyploidy has seldom been used, and then only towards specific ends, such as increasing organ size, and success in these ventures has apparently been restricted to radish. Several reports have been made from Asia of the overall superiority of tetraploid radishes (Tatuno, 1947; V"lkova, 1971; Lutkov, 1966). The tetraploids apparently have reduced bolting tendencies, higher root[2] weight, and greater cold tolerance (Nishijama, 1942, 1947; Savos'kin, 1967; Rud', 1970). Nishijama (1947) also claimed that autotetraploids exhibited no clubroot infection, in contrast to the diploids, and Rud' (1970) showed that some autotetraploids had vitamin C contents 50 - 60 % higher than the diploids.

The overall tendencies of the autopolyploids are to have greater yields of vegetative matter which may include greater dry matter content; and to have reduced seed set and reduced response to selection. The advantageous characters reach their full importance in the forage and fodder crops, and it is here that most work has been done with autopolyploid Crucifers. Barr and Newcomer (1943) showed that autotetraploid cabbage had more sugar, vitamin C and colloidal nitrogen than the diploid, although the diploid had more soluble nitrogen, a higher ash content, and more vitamin C when at maturity.

---

[2] strictly speaking, the swollen "root" of the radish is the hypocotyl.

Frydrych (1970) showed that autotetraploid kohl rabi had a greater chlorophyll content and dry weight, and was more photosynthetically active in shaded conditions than the diploid. Olsson (1963) noted that autotetraploid turnip matured later than the diploid, and considerably outyielded the diploid when both were at maturity. Reports essentially supporting these findings for autotetraploid turnip have been made by several workers (Joseffson, 1955; de Roo, 1962; Anon, 1973). Autotetraploid thousand-head kale, and autotetraploid fodder radish had lower yields than the diploids, although the radish may compensate for this by flowering later (McNaughton, 1971). Conversely, Mackiewicz (1969, 1970) reported that autotetraploid kales outyielded the diploid, and that the F_1 triploid produced by crossing the diploid and the tetraploid also showed substantial increases in yield. The potential of triploids cannot, apparently, be extended to *Sinapis alba* (Olsson and Rufelt, 1948) or to radish (Inomata, 1970), where crossing diploid and autotetraploid resulted in small or abortive triploid seeds.

An essential feature of autopolyploids appears to be that there may be "physiological" differences from their parental diploid, resulting in different growth characteristics which could allow them to fulfill slightly different agronomic requirements. Thus to compare autotetraploids directly with their diploid progenitors may not reveal the real potential of the polyploid.

To date, the only successful introduction of an autotetraploid forage crucifer cultivar has been a marrow-stem kale from Sweden (Åkerberg, 1970).

Allopolyploids

Since the classic work of Karpechenko (1924) in crossing *Brassica* and *Raphanus*, considerable efforts have been made to elucidate taxonomic and cytological problems in the Cruciferae by using interspecific and intergeneric hybridisation (U, 1935; Sasaoka, 1930; Morinaga, 1929a, b, 1931, 1933, 1934; Sikka, 1940; Frandsen, 1947; Olsson, 1956; Harberd, 1974).

Interspecific hybridisation has applications in the production of cruciferous crop plants in several respects. The incorporation of cytoplasmic male sterility into calabrese following a *Brassica nigra* (n = 8) x *B. oleracea* (n = 9) cross by Pearson has already been discussed. Pearson (1970b) also reported that the amphidiploid from this cross, which is analogous to *B. carinata (n* = 17) could be back crossed to *B. oleracea* to yield fertile types resembling calabrese and cabbage. The possibility is that desirable genes could be introgressed from different species into crop plants by using this method of back crossing from the species' hybrid or its amphidiploid. Such a scheme has been advocated for the transfer of clubroot resistance from *B. campestris (n* = 10) to *B. oleracea (n* = 9) (Honma and Heeckt, 1960) and McNaughton (1971) reported attempts at transferring leaf characteristics of *B. campestris (n* = 10) to *B. napus (n* = 19) via their synthetic allopolyploid *B. napocampestris (n* = 29). Such schemes, however, are necessarily long term because of the initial problems with sterility barriers, and so more emphasis has been placed on increasing the range of variability of existing polyploid crops, or of synthesising new ones. Thus, Prakash (1970, 1973b) has produced variable amphidiploids from *B. campestris (n* = 10) x *B. nigra (n* = 8) with the object of improving the oil crop *B. juncea (n* = 18). Stable amphidiploids selected from this programme had higher oil content and yield than existing *B. juncea* types, and had resistance to *Albugo*, *Peronospora* and *Erysiphe*. Most interspecific hybrids have been aimed at improving forage crops. Swedes and swede-rapes (*B. napus*, *n* = 19) have been resynthesised by crossing various *B. oleracea (n* = 9) and *B. campestris (n* = 10) types (see, for example, Rudorf, 1950; Olsson *et aï.*, 1955; Olsson, 1960; McNaughton, 1971). Problems of embryo inviability in the early stages of such programmes have been alleviated by the use of *in vitro* techniques for culturing embryos, such as those of Nishi *et al.*(1959) and Harberd (1969). In the future wide species crosses may be made using *in vitro* fertilisation, as Kameya and Hinata (1970b)demonstrated with *B. campestris*, or protoplast fusion, as Kameya and Takahashi (1972) attempted with *B. oleracea* and *B. campestris*.

The polyploid species *B. napocampestris (n* = 29) has also been synthesised as an oil-seed crop (Olsson, 1963); as a root fodder (Frandsen and Winge, 1932); and as leafy forage (McNaughton, 1971). However, in general none of these forms was superior to existing types of *B. napus*, due to inferior seed quality in the oil-seed forms, and lower dry matter content in the fodders and forages. One promising line of research is that being pursued by McNaughton (1973) to produce forage *B. napocampestris* using a form of *B. campestris*—ssp. *nipposinica*—which has a large number of laciniate leaves and little stem, which may result in forms with improved edibility.

Raphanus x *Brassica* hybrids are possible alternatives to fodder radish, which themselves may offer some advantages in yield over fodder rape (Johnston, 1962). Hybrid material based on *R. sativus* x *B. oleracea* may yield winter hardy, *Plasmodiophora*-resistant types with delayed flowering and high soluble carbohydrate contents (McNaughton, 1971). Hybrids between *R. sativus* and other *Brassica* species, *B. campestris* and *B. napus*, are possible (Terasawa, 1932; Chopinet, 1944; McNaughton, 1971) but have not been incorporated into breeding programmes.

The *Brassica* x *R. sativus* hybrids are also being considered as vegetables for human consumption in the U.S.S.R. One particularly interesting development is that reported by Moskov (1970), where derivatives from cabbage x radish crosses growing under continuous light in cabinets yielded 21 crops a year with a yield of 120 kg of green matter per m^2 per year—and the roots as well as the leaves were edible! F_1's produced by crossing this material with Chinese cabbage (*B. campestris*) gave 400 kg/m^2/year of edible material, which is about 50 - 100 times the yield of a cabbage crop. Presumable applications of this process are in space-ships and similar systems.

Mutation

The usual application of mutation breeding is for changing single genes. Most of the characters being bred for in the Cruciferae, such as yield, quality and uniformity are under polygenic control, and the problems tend to lie more with reducing genetic variability by breeding than with inducing more variability by mutation. However, particularly within the Asiatic oil crops, and where specific characters under fairly simple genetic control are involved, mutation breeding has been attempted with some success.

Among the products of irradiated oil-seed *B. campestris*, Khan and Zamir-ul-Islam (1965) reported increases in growth rates, and Basu, Srivastava and Sahni (1970) reported an increase in earliness. Wilczowska (1970) reported increased seed and oil yield in irradiated *B. napus*, *B. campestris* and

Camelina sativa. Hagberg and Åkerberg (1962) stated that a *Sinapis alba* cultivar derived from mutation breeding outperformed other cultivars in oil yield. Some successes have also been had with the reduction of linolenic acid in oil-seed *B. napus* by mutagenic treatment (Racow, 1973).

FUTURE TRENDS IN THE CRUCIFEROUS CROPS

Economic considerations

Most of the herbicides and insecticides used for vegetable crops were developed as a result of screening chemicals for the major crops, such as cereals and cotton. A similar pattern is emerging with systemic fungicides and bactericides. Even for the major crops the rapidly increasing costs of screening and developing new chemicals, as well as an increasing awareness of the dangers of pollution, ensure that future emphasis will be directed towards the integration of chemical treatments with improved husbandry practices, including the cultivation of improved cultivars, particularly those with resistance to pests and diseases.

If the breeding of Crucifers is to become more important, where will the breeders priorities lie, and what new research tools will he employ? Apart from overall increases in yield, priorities will almost certainly remain different for the various crops: uniformity and predictability of vegetables; composition of oil; and digestibility of animal foods.

In the near future there is little likelihood of great increases or decreases in the importance of vegetables relative to other crops, or of cruciferous vegetables relative to other vegetables. Current general tendencies may be maintained. For example, in Europe cabbages tend to decrease as cauliflowers and Brussels sprouts increase in acreage. We should also see an increase in the Crucifers being grown specifically for the vegetable processing industry, such as calabrese and "minicauliflowers". Longer term predictions are more difficult to make: even such dogmas as the eventual mechanisation of the growing crop may not become realities if the relative cost of manual labour does not maintain its present rate of increase.

Oil crops will almost certainly increase in importance due to decreasing or erratic supplies of mineral and animal oils.

The cruciferous oil crops are particularly suitable for temperate, even sub-Arctic regions. It is not unreasonable to foresee an expansion of oil-seed rape and similar crops in North and West Europe in the next decades on a scale greater than that in Scandinavia during the World War II years (Bunting, 1969). This expansion besides encouraging greater breeding efforts within existing cruciferous crops, may also involve evaluation of different cruciferous species, and may extend to mutation breeding. Hybridisation of different types of plants, and polyploidisation are unlikely to be used as methods of increasing seed yield because of the higher degree of sterility which usually result from these treatments.

Intensive agricultural methods have resulted in recent increases in the productivity of non-ruminant animals (pigs and poultry), but a serious limitation to a continuing increase of these animals is that they compete with humans for their food. Ruminants (cattle and sheep), however, flourish on food which is not necessarily utilisable directly by humans, and these include the fodder Crucifers. Productivity per unit area of these Crucifers in terms of utilisable energy and protein is higher than for cereals. On the basis of these arguments the most efficient use of available land would be as a very broad generalisation, to produce cereals for humans, fodder for ruminants, and to reduce non-ruminant production. These predictions may be seriously upset by the large-scale production of cheap milk and meat analogue foods, based, for example, on protein derived from yeast grown on mineral hydrocarbons (Raymond, 1971). But even so, it is unlikely that such products would immediately dominate the market. A more probable pattern would be, as with margarine vs. butter, a build up of the analogue food after many years to a state of equilibrium. This being the case, it is reasonable to suppose that animal feed Crucifers will be of use for decades to come, and their importance may well increase. Research will almost certainly centre around the production of material with higher yields in terms of what the animals can eat, and in reducing levels of goitrogenic and other disease-inducing substances. The high cost of machinery and transport may mean that such crops will be primarily developed for grazing *in situ*. The value of cruciferous crops in rotation with cereals and other non-cruciferous crops is another important factor in their probable retention in farming systems.

Possible Research Developments

It is particularly valid within the context of this article to consider those features which are common to the Cruciferae, and if they can be more generally applied within the Cruciferous crops. The breeding system, is, of course, of fundamental importance, and considerable progress has been made in the vegetables and some animal feeds by using F_1 and other hybrids. The principles of hybrid production could be extended to other animal feed crops, and to the oil-seed crops. Progress with altering the contents of erucic acid and other constituents in oil-seed *B. napus* and *B. campestris* could also be extended to other cruciferous oil crops. Crucifer breeders may also find useful techniques in the work which is carried out on the "plant *Drosophila*", *Arabidopsis thaliana*. Apart from the large volume of data presented on the genetics of this species, there are a number of studies which may have wider applications within the Cruciferae, notably the possibility of obtaining "instant homozygotes" from *Arabidopsis* (Gresshoff and Doy, 1972), and the incorporation of genetic material from bacteria into the *Arabidopsis* genome (Ledoux *et al.*, 1971) with the prospect of generating crucifer crops carrying genetic material from, say, nitrogen-fixing bacteria.

One foreseeable development within the Cruciferae is the use of new species as existing crops, or indeed the synthesis of new crops. Wild and cultivated types which may become important as oil-seed crops include *Crambe* spp. (Meier and Lessman, 1973; White and Higgins, 1966), *Conringium orientalis* (Runer, 1970), and *Sisymbrium brassicaeforme* (Burnasheva *et al.*, 1973). *B. carinata* is grown on a small scale as a vegetable in Ethiopia; unselected material grown as a vegetable in the U.S.A. compared favourably for yield and flavour with collards (*B. oleracea)* and mustard greens (*B. juncea)*(Stephens *et al.*, *loc.cit.)*. We have only to consider the replacement of *Nasturtium officinale* x *microphyllum* by *N. officinale*, and of *Brassica nigra* by *B. juncea* in the mustard industry, both within the last 20 years, to realise that precedents exist for new crucifer species finding places in our agriculture.

The newly synthesised allopolyploidys are also likely to increase in importance. We already have "synthetic" *B. napus* cultivars from hybridising *B. oleracea* and *B. campestris*. *B. juncea* has been resynthesised on several occasions by crossing

B. campestris and *B. nigra;* and some non-homologous recombinants resulting from irregular meioses in the synthetic *B. juncea* have had very high seed yields (Prakash, 1973b). *B. napocampestris,* a combination of *B. napus* (= *B. oleracea* x *campestris)* x *B. campestris* may be of use as a forage crop (McNaughton, 1973). Will we see synthetic *B. carinata (= B. nigra* x *oleracea)?* What will be the results of the various *Raphanus* x *Brassica* breeding programmes? One interesting development is that of producing interspecific F_1 hybrids. By utilising the self-incompatibility of the turnip (*B. campestris,* 2*n* = 20) as the female, and rape (*B. napus,* 2*n* = 38) as the pollinator, Mackay (1973) produced sesquidiploids (2*n* = 29) which were very vigorous as forages, and considerably outyielded the parents.

Also of potential importance are hybrids produced between types within species. These include such vegetables as the "caulicab"—a derivation of calabrese x cabbage cross which according to sowing date was reported to give cabbage or calabrese heads (van Clute, 1952). "Green Ball" is a cultivar derived from crossing calabrese and cauliflower (Honma and Heecht, 1971). The red Brussels sprouts (e.g. cv. Rubine) are believed to have originated in Brussels sprouts x red cabbage crosses (M. Nieuwhof, in litt.). None of these, or other hybrid derivatives, have as yet been commercially successful. Attempts are also being made to improve forage crops by intraspecific hybridisation: these include marrow-stem kale x Brussels sprouts hybrids (Thompson, 1971), and derivatives from kohl rabi x kale (Simon, 1966).

One further use of intra- and inter-specific hybridisation is in the transfer of heritable disease resistance. Varietal differences have been recorded for resistance in cauliflower to *Alternaria* (Braverman, 1971) and *Xanthomonas* (Mazzucchi, 1968; Cameranes *et al.,* 1970); in cabbage to *Xanthomonas* (Mazzucchi, 1968; Williams and Staub, 1971), *Fusarium* (Anon, 1969; Tiščenko and Zajceva, 1969); and *Peronospora* (Minkov and Nakov, 1969); and in a swede and turnip rapes (*B. napus* and *B. campestris)* to *Peronospora* (Anon, 1970a). Considerable investigations have also been carried out into resistance to clubroot, *Plasmodiophora brassicae.* These have shown varietal differences within cabbages (Walker and Larson, 1951; Nieuwhof and Wiering, 1962; Anon, 1969, 1970b; Chiang and Crete, 1970), and within *Brassica napus* and *B. campestris* (Anon, 1970a, 1970b; Lammerink, 1970; Johnston, 1970).

These reports of new crop species, new synthetic crops, and disease resistance factors within the Cruciferae give strong support to a policy of gene conservation within the family. Suggestions such as that of Watson and Baker (1969) that gene centres for resistance to clubroot may occur in the west Mediterranean, indicate that conservation work on wild species and primitive cultivars (Gómez-Campo, 1972) are unlikely to be wasted. The same argument applies for cultivars of oil-seed Crucifers (Venclavovic *et al.*, 1969; Rai *et al.*, 1970) and vegetables (Creech, 1970). In the vegetables, in particular, the advent of F_1 hybrids has led to rapid, recent disappearances of relatively unselected types. The breeders' raw material is genetic variability, and nowhere is this more relevant than in the Cruciferae, where similarities between species, and diversity within species offer considerable scope for inventive use of this variability.

REFERENCES

Åkerberg, E. (1970). *Sver.Utsädesför.Tidskr.* 80, 11 - 35. *Pl.Breed.Abstr.* 41, 357 (1971).

Anon (1967). *Ann.Rep.Ayub Agric.Res.Inst., Lyallpur for 1966/67. Pl.Breed.Abstr.* 40, 2292 (1970).

Anon (1969). *Res.Rep.Canada Dept.Agric. for 1968. Pl.Breed. Abstr.* 41, 4549 (1971).

Anon (1970a). *Sver.Utsädenför.Tidskr.* 80, 71 - 139. *Pl. Breed.Abstr.* 41, 357 (1971).

Anon (1970b). *Res.Rep.Canada Dept.Agric. for 1969. Pl. Breed.Abstr.* 42, 1809 (1972).

Anon (1973). *Rep.Scott.Pl.Breed.Stn. 1972*, 32. Pentlandfield, Scotland.

Bailey, D. H. (1949). "Manual of cultivated plants most commonly grown in the continental United States and Canada". 2nd edition. Macmillan, New York.

Bajaj, Y. P. S. and Bopp, M. (1972). *Z.Pflanzenphysiol.* 66, 378 - 381.

Barr, C. G. and Newcomer, E. H. (1943). *J.agric.Res.* 67, 329 - 336.

Basu, A. K., Srivastava, Y. C. and Sahni, V. M. (1970). *Proc. Indian Sci.Congr.* 57, 522.

Bateman, A. J. (1955). *Heredity, Lond.* 9, 53 - 68.

Bleasdale, J. K. A. (1964). *J.hort.Sci.* 39, 277 - 283.

Bonnett, A. (1970). Eucarpia Conference Report "Male Sterility in horticultural crops". Versailles, France.

Borchers, E. A. (1966). *Proc.Amer.Soc.hort.Sci.* 88, 406 - 410/

Borchers, E. A. (1971). *J.Amer.Soc.hort.Sci.* 96, 542 - 543.

Braverman, S. W. (1971). *Pl.Dis.Reptr.* 55, 454 - 457.

Brewbaker, J. L. (1957). *J.Hered.* 48, 271 - 277.

Buiatti, M. Baroncelli, S. and Bennici, A. (1973). Verbal communication at Eucarpia conference on "Aseptic culture methods in plant breeding", Leeds, England.

Bunting, E. S. (1969). *Fld.Crop Abstr.* 22, 215 - 223.

Burnasheva, S. N., Kambarova, D. D. and Umarov, A. U. (1973). *Chem.Nat.Compd.* 6, 362.

Cameranes, L., Mazzucchi, U. and Toderi, G. (1970). *Riv. Agron.* 4, 260 - 264.

Chiang, M. S. and Crete, R. (1970). *Can.J.Genet.Cytol.* 12, 253 - 256.

Chopinet, R. (1944). *Revue hort.* 29, 98 - 100.

Chowdhury, J. B. and Das, K. (1967). *Indian J.Genet.Pl.Breed.* 27, 284 - 288.

Chowdhury, J. B., Pawan, K. and Ghai, B. S. (1967). *Indian J.Genet.Pl.Breed.* 27, 457 - 460.

Clapham, D. (1971). *Z.Pflanzenzuchtg.* 65, 285 - 292.

Coic, Y., Cook, C. and Lesaint, C. (1972). *C.r.Seanc.(Agric.)* 58, 101 - 106. *Hort.Abstr.* 43, 1988 (1973).

Cole, K. (1957). *Proc.Gen.Soc.Can.* 2, 44.

Creech, J. L. (1970). "DR.-159, Recent plant introductions", New York State Agric. Exp. Stat., Beltsville.

Crisp, P. and Gray, A. R. (1973). *Rep.natn.Veg.Res.Stn. (1972)*. 33 - 34. Wellesbourne, England.

Crisp, P. and Walkey, D. G. A. (1974). *Euphytica* 23, 305 - 313.

de Roo, R. (1962). *Rev.Agric.Brux.* 15, 897 - 899.

Dickson, M. H. (1970). *J.Amer.Soc.hort.Sci.* 95, 13 - 14.

Dixon, G. E. (1971). *Rep.natn.Veg.Res.Stn. (1970)*, 45. Wellesbourne, England.

Dixon, G. E. (1973). *Rep.natn.Veg.Res.Stn. (1972)*, 35. Wellesbourne, England.

Dorrell, D. C. and Downey, R. K. (1964). *Can.J.Pl.Sci.* 44, 499 - 504.

Downey, R. K. (1964). *Can.J.Pl.Sci.* 44, 295.

Downey, R. K. (1966). *L.Qual.Plant et Mat.Veget.* 13, 171 - 180.

du Crehu, G. (1969). *C.r.Acad.Sci.Paris* 4, 736 - 741.

du Crehu, G. (1970). *In* Proc.Eucarpia Fodder Crops Conference pp. 85 - 94. Lusignan, France.

Elliott, J. G. (1971). *In* "The future of brassica fodder crops". (Greenhalgh, J. F. D. and Hamilton, M. eds), pp. 26 - 30. Occ. Publ. Rowett Inst. No. 2. Aberdeen, Scotland.

Farthing, B. (1972). *Commercial Grower* 3983, 723.

Frandsen, H. N. and Winge, O. (1932). *Hereditas* 16, 212 - 215.

Frandsen, K. J. (1943). *Dansk.bot.Ark.* 11(4), 1 - 17.

Frandsen, K. J. (1947). *Dansk.bot.Ark.* 12(7), 1 - 16.

Frydrych, J. (1970). *Photosynthetica (Praha)* 4, 139 - 145.

Gómez-Campo, G. (1972). *Biol.Conserv.* 4, 355 - 360.

Greenhalgh, J. F. D. (1971). *In* "The future of brassica fodder crops". (Greenhalgh, J. F. D. and Hamilton, M. eds), pp. 56 - 64. Occ. Publ. Rowett Inst. No. 2. Aberdeen, Scotland.

Gresshoff, P. M. and Doy, C. H. (1972). *Aust.J.biol.Sci.* 25, 259 - 264.

Hagberg, A. and Åkerberg, E. (1962). "Mutations and Polyploidy in Plant Breeding". Heinemann, London.

Haine, K. E. (1955). *In* Rep. XIV Int.hort.Congr. 479 - 483. Wageningen, Netherlands.

Harberd, D. J. (1969). *Euphytica* 18, 425 - 429.

Harberd, D. J. (1975). *In* "The Biology and Chemistry of the Cruciferae" (Vaughan, J. G. *et al.*, eds). Academic Press, London.

Hedrick, U. P. (1972). (ed.) "Sturtevant's Edible Plants of the World". Dover Publ. Inc., New York.

Helm, J. (1963). *Kulturpflanze* 11, 92 - 210.

Herklots, G. A. C. (1972). "Vegetables in South-East Asia". George Allen and Unwin, London.

Honma, S. and Heeckt, O. (1960). *Euphytica* 9, 243 - 246.

Honma, S. and Heeckt, O. (1971). Mich.agric.Exp.Stn. Report No. 135.

Horak, J., Landa, Z. and Lustinec, J. (1971). *Phyton (Buenos Aires)* 28, 7 - 10.

Howard, H. W. (1952). *J.Hort.Sci.* 27, 273 - 277.

Inomata, N. (1970). *Jap.J.Genet.* 45, 173 - 182.

Jensma, J. R. (1957). Medel.Inst.Hort.Pl.Breed. Wageningen Report No. 96.

Johnson, A. G. (1958). *Nature (Lond.)* 182, 1523.

Johnson, A. G. (1966). *Euphytica* 15, 68 - 79.

Johnston, T. D. (1962). *Rep.Welsh Pl.Breed.Stn. (1961)*, 59 - 60. Aberystwyth, U.K.

Johnston, T. D. (1963). *Euphytica* 12, 198 - 204.

Johnston, T. D. (1964). *Euphytica* 13, 147 - 152.

Johnston, T. D. (1965). *Euphytica* 14, 120 - 123.

Johnston, T. D. (1968). *Euphytica* 17, 63 - 73.

Johnston, T. D. (1969). *In* "Grass and Forage Breeding", (L. Phillips and R. Hughes, eds), pp. 83 - 87. Brit.Grassl. Soc.Occas.Symp. No. 5.

Johnston, T. D. (1970). *Pl.Path.* 19, 156 - 158.

Jönsson, R. (1973). *Z.Pflanzenzuchtg.* 69, 1 - 18.

Josefsson, A. (1955). *Hereditas* 41, 285 - 287.

Josefsson, E., Ellestrom, S. and Sjodin, J. (1972). *Z. Pflanzenzuchtg.* 67, 353 - 359.

Kadota, T. and Ito, K. (1952). *Jap.J.Breed.* 1, 198. *Pl. Breed.Abstr.* 23, 1526 (1953).

Kameya, T. and Hinata, K. (1970a). *Jap.J.Breed.* 20, 82 - 87.

Kameya, T. and Hinata, K. (1970b). *Jap.J.Breed.* 20, 253 - 260.

Kameya, T. and Takahashi, N. (1972). *Jap.J.Genet.* 47, 215 - 217.

Karpechenko, G. D. (1924). *J.Genet.* 14, 375.

Kay, M. (1971). *In* "The future of brassica fodder crops". (Greenhalgh, J. F. D. and Hamilton, M., eds), pp. 49 - 55. Occ.Publ.Rowett Inst. No. 2. Aberdeen, Scotland.

Khan, S. A. and Zamir-ul-Islam. (1965). Proc. 17th Pakistan Sci.Conf.Karachi 1965, Pt. III, Abstract No. A99. *Pl. Breed.Abstr.* 41, 471 (1971).

Koch, H. and Peters, R. (1953). *Wiss.Z.Martin-Luther-Univ. Halle-Wittenb.* 2, 363 - 367.

Lammerink, J. (1970). *N.Z.J.agric.Res.* 13, 105 - 110.

Ledoux, L., Huart, R. and Jacobs, M. (1971). *In* "The way ahead in plant breeding". Proc.6th.Congr.of Eucarpia, (Lupton, F. G. H., Jenkins, G. and Johnson, P., eds), pp. 165 - 184. Plant Breeding Institute, Cambridge, England.

Lööf, B. (1960). *Fld. Crop Abstr.* 13, 1 - 7.

Lööf, B. and Appelqvist, L.-Å. (1972). *In* "Rapeseed", (Appelqvist, L.-Å. and Ohlson, R., eds), pp. 101 - 122. Elsevier, Amsterdam, Netherlands.

Lustinec, J. and Horak, J. (1970). *Experientia* 26, 919 - 920.

Lutkov, A. N. (1966). *In* "Experimental polyploidy in plant breeding", pp. 7 - 34. Nauka, Novosibirsk. *Pl.Breed.Abst.* 40, 6909 (1970).

Mackay, G. R. (1971). *J.Univ.Newcastle upon Tyne agric.Soc.* 24, 16 - 20.

Mackay, G. R. (1972). *Euphytica* 21, 71 - 77.

Mackay, G. R. (1973). *Euphytica* 22, 495 - 499.

Mackiewicz, H. O. (1969). *Genet.Pol.* 10, 119 - 123.

Mackiewicz, H. O. (1970). *TagBer.dt.Akad.Landwiss, Berl.* 101, 293 - 298.

McNaughton, I. H. (1971). *In* "The future of brassica fodder crops", (Greenhalgh, J. F. D. and Hamilton, M., eds), pp. 39 - 47. Occ. Publ. Rowett Inst. No. 2, Aberdeen, Scotland.

McNaughton, I. H. (1973). *Euphytica* 22, 301 - 309.

Margara, M. J. (1969). *Acad.Sci.Paris Sér.D.* 268, 686 - 690.

Mazzucchi, U. (1968). *Inptore fitopatol.* 18, 1 - 4. *Pl. Breed. Abstr.* 41, 4058 (1971).

Meier, V. D. and Lessman, K. J. (1973). *Crop Sci.* 13, 237 - 240.

Minkov, I. and Nakov, B. (1969). *((Sci.Trans.V.Kolarov.high. agric.Inst.Hort.)Plovdiv)* 18, 135 - 142. *Pl.Breed.Abstr.* 40, 8690 (1970).

Mori, K. (1971). *Jap.agric.Res.Quarterly* 6, 1 - 7.

Morinaga, T. (1929a). *Cytologia* 1, 16 - 27.

Morinaga, T. (1929b). *Jap.J.Bot.* 4, 277 - 280.

Morinaga, T. (1931). *Cytologia* 3, 77 - 83.

Morinaga, T. (1933). *Jap.J.Bot.* 6, 467 - 475.

Morinaga, T. (1934). *Cytologia* 6, 62 - 67.

Moskov, B. S. (1970). *Vestn.sel'skohoz.Nauk.* 4, 99 - 101. *Pl.Breed.Abstr.* 41, 622 (1971).

Mulligan, G. A. and Findlay, J. N. (1970). *Can.J.Bot.* 48, 269 - 270.

NAAS (1969). "10th Progress Rep. of Exp.Hort., Farms and Stations", pp. 122. National Agricultural Advisory Service, London.

Nieuwhof, M. (1961). *Euphytica* 10, 351 - 356.

Nieuwhof, M. (1968). *Euphytica* 17, 202 - 206.

Nieuwhof, M. (1969). "Cole Crops". Leonard Hill, London.

Nieuwhof, M. and Wiering, D. (1962). *Euphytica* 11, 233 - 239.

Nishi, S. *et al.* (1959). *Jap.J.Breed.* 8, 215 - 222.

Nishijama, I. (1942). *Botany Zool., Tokyo.* 10, 57 - 58.

Nishijama, I. (1947). *Seiken, Ziho.* 3, 104 - 118.

Nitsch, J. P. (1970). *Phytomorphology* 19, 389 - 404.

North, C. (1961). 8th.Ann.Rep.Scott.Hort.Res.Inst., pp. 34 - 36. Dundee, Scotland.

NSDO (1973a). Leaflet 4/73/3069 "Maris Kestrel" available from National Seed Development Organisation Ltd., Newton Hall, Newton, Cambridge, U.K.

NSDO (1973b). Leaflet 5/73/3155 "Nevin Rape" available from National Seed Development Organisation Ltd., Newton Hall, Newton, Cambridge, U.K.

Ockendon, D. J. (1972). *New Phytol.* 71, 519 - 522.

Odland, M. L. and Isenberg, F. M. R. (1950). *Proc.Amer.Soc. hort.Sci.* 56, 372 - 376.

Ogura, H. (1968). *Memoire Fac.Agric.Univ.Kogoshima* 6, 40 - 75.

Ohlson, R. (1972). *In* "Rapeseed", (Appelqvist, L.-Å. and Ohlson, R., eds), pp. 9 - 35. Elsevier, Amsterdam.

Olsson, G. (1951). *Lantmannen* 35, 377 - 399.

Olsson, G. (1954). *Hereditas* 40, 398 - 418.

Olsson, G. (1960). *Hereditas* 46, 351 - 386.

Olsson, G. (1963). *In* "Recent plant breeding research", (Åkerberg, E. and Hagberg, A., eds), pp. 179 - 192. John Wiley and Sons, London.

Olsson, G. and Hagberg, A. (1955). *Hereditas* 41, 227 - 237.

Olsson, G., Josefsson, A., Hagberg, A. and Ellerstrom, S. (1955). *Hereditas* 41, 241 - 249.

Olsson, G. and Rufelt, B. (1948). *Hereditas* 34, 351 - 365.

Palevitch, D. and Pressman, E. (1973). *HortScience*, 8, 411 - 412.

Paludan, N. (1971). *Tidsskr.PlAvl.* 75, 387 - 410.

Parthasarathy, N. and Rajan, S. S. (1953). *Euphytica* 2, 25 - 30.

Pascal, J. A. (1971). *In* "The future of brassica fodder crops", (Greenhalgh, J. F. D. and Hamilton, M., eds), pp. 14 - 25. Occ. Publ. Rowett Inst. No. 2. Aberdeen, Scotland.

Pearson, O. H. (1929). *Proc.Amer.Soc.hort.Sci.* 26, 24 - 38.

Pearson, O. H. (1970a). *HortScience* 5, 343.

Pearson, O. H. (1970b). *HortScience* 5, 343.

Pearson, O. H. (1972). *J.Amer.Soc.hort.Sci.* 97, 397 - 402.

Prakash, S. (1970). *Sver.Utsädesför.Tidskr.* 80, 58.

Prakash, S. (1973a). *Euphytica* 22, 613 - 614.

Prakash, S. (1973b). *Genet.Res.* 21, 133 - 137.

Rai, J. N., Tewari, J. P., Singh, R. P. and Sazena, J. C. (1969). "Indian oleiferous and wild crucifers, a study in their morphology, range of variations and diseases". Botany Department, Lucknow Univ., India.

Rajan, S. S. (1970). *In* Proc. International conference on oil rape, Paris, May 1970, pp. 193 - 194. Centre Technique Interprofessionel des Oleagineux Metropolitains, Paris.

Rakow, G. (1973). *Z.Pflanzenzuchtg.* 69, 62 - 82.

Rao, T. S. (1970a). *Radiat.Bot.* 10, 569 - 575.

Rao, T. S. (1970b). *Euphytica* 19, 539 - 542.

Raymond, W. F. (1971). *In* "The way ahead in plant breeding", (Lupton, F. G. H. *et al.*, eds), pp. 221 - 228. Plant Breeding Institute, Cambridge, England.

Röbbelen, G. (1971). *In* "The way ahead in plant breeding", (Lupton, F. G. H. *et al.*, eds), pp. 207 - 214. Plant Breeding Institute, Cambridge, England.

Rubatsky, V. E. and Hall, H. L. (1970). *HortScience* 5, 353 - 354.

Rud', V. D. (1970). *Vestn.sel'skohoz.Nauk* 119 - 121. *Pl. Breed.Abstr.* 40, 8669 (1970).

Rudorf, W. (1950). *Z.Pflanzenzuchtg.* 29, 35 - 54.

Ruebenbauer, T. and Binek, A. (1967). *Hodowla Rosl.Aklim. Nasienn.* 11, 91 - 101.

Rundfeldt, H. (1960). *I.Zetis.Pflanzenzuchtg.* 44, 30 - 62.

Rüner, Ü. and Honkanen, E. (1972). *In* "Rapeseed", (Appelqvist, L.-Å. and Ohlson, R., eds), pp. 249 - 273. Elsevier, Amsterdam.

Sakata, (1973). "Seed Catalogue for 1973/4". Sakata Seed Co., Japan.

Salter, P. J. (1971). *Agriculture, Lond.* 78, 231 - 235.

Salter, P. J. and Ward, R. J. (1972). *J.hort.Sci.* 47, 57 - 68.

Sampson, D. R. (1964). *Can.J.Genet.Cytol.* 6, 435 - 445.

Sampson, D. R. (1966). *Can.J.Pl.Sci.* 46, 703.

Sampson, D. R. (1970). *Can.J.Genet.Cytol.* 12, 677 - 684.

Sansom, C. H. (1948). "Cultivation of watercress". Bull. Min.Agric. No. 136. H.M.S.O., London.

Sasoka, T. (1930). *Jap.J.Genet.* 6, 20 - 32.

Savos'kin, I. P. and Rud', V. D. (1967). *In* "Experimental polyploidy in plant breeding", pp. 201 - 204. Nauka, Novosibirsk, 1966. *Pl.Breed.Abstr.* 40, 4504 (1970).

Sikka, S. M. (1940). *J.Genet.* 40, 441 - 509.

Simon, J. (1966). *St.Statky 1966*, 12 - 14. *Pl.Breed.Abstr.* 40, 3296 (1970).

Singh, D. (1959). *Indian Oilseeds J.* 3, 95 - 99.

Singh, S. P. and Singh, D. (1972). *Can.J.Genet.Cytol.* 14. 227 - 233.

Spencer, D. M. and Glasscock, H. H. (1953). *Pl.Path.* 2, 19 - 21.

Stephens, T. S., Saldana, G. and Griffiths, F. P. (1970). *J.Amer.Soc.hort.Sci.* 95, 3 - 5.

Stefansson, B., Hougen, F. W. and Downey, R. K. (1961). *Can.J.Pl.Sci.* 41, 218 - 219.

Stokes, G. W. (1955). *J.Hered.* 46, 15 - 21.

Stringam, G. R. and Downey, R. K. (1973). *Can.J.Pl.Sci.* 53, 229 - 231.

Sun, V. G. (1970). *J.agric.Ass.China* 71, 42 - 52.

Sunderland, N. (1971). *Sci.Prog.* 59, 527 - 549.

Takagi, Y. (1970). *Z. Pflanzenzuchtg.* 64, 242 - 247.

Tatuno, S. (1947). *Jap.J.Genet.* 22, 31 - 32.

Terasawa, Y. (1932). *Jap.J.Genet.* 7, 183 - 193.

Thies, W. (1971). *Z.Pflanzenzuchtg.* 65, 181 - 202.

Thompson, K. F. (1957). *J.Genet.* 55, 45 - 60.

Thompson, K. F. (1964). *Euphytica* 13, 173 - 177.

Thompson, K. F. (1966). *Rep.Pl.Breed.Inst. (1965/6),* 7 - 34. Cambridge, U.K.

Thompson, K. F. (1969). *Heredity, Lond.* 24, 318 - 319.

Thompson, K. F. (1971). *In* "The future of brassica fodder crops", (Greenhalgh, J. F. D. and Hamilton, M., eds), pp. 31 - 38. Occ.Publ. Rowett Inst. No. 2. Aberdeen, Scotland.

Thompson, K. F. and Taylor, J. P. (1971). *Heredity, Lond.* 27, 459 - 471.

Tiscenko, A. P. and Zajceva, L. A. (1969). *(Trans.Volograd. Exp.Sta.All-Union Inst.Plant Industry)* 6, 85 - 96. *Pl.Breed.Abstr.* 41, 4060.

Tokumasu, S. (1951). *Sci.Bull.Fac.Agric.Kyushu Univ.* 13, 83 - 89.

Tokumasu, S. (1970a). *Mem.Ehime Univ.VI Agric.* 14, 285 - 302. *Pl.Breed.Abstr.* 41, 4052 (1971).

Tokumasu, S. (1970b). *Jap.J.Breed.* 20, 15 - 21.

Tomlinson, J. A. (1957). *Rep.natn.Veg.Res.Stn. 1956,* 61. Wellesbourne, U.K.

Toxopeus, H. (1970). *In* Proc. Eucarpia Fodder Crops Conference, pp. 73 - 83. Lusignan, France.

Tyagi, A. P. and Das, K. (1970). *Indian J.Genet.Pl.Breed.* 30, 476 - 480.

U, N. (1935). *Jap.J.Bot.* 7, 389 - 452.

V''lkova, Z. (1971). *Genet. and Sel.* 4, 257 - 265.

van Hal, J. G. and Verhoeven, W. (1968). *In* Proc. Eucarpia Brassica Crops Conference (G. E. Dixon, ed.), pp. 32 - 33. Wellesbourne, England.

Venclavovic, F. S. *et al.* (1969). *(Trans.appl.Bot.Genet. Plant Breed.)* 41, 173 - 177. Pl. Breed. Abstr. 40, 8204 (1970).

Walker, J. C. and Larson, R. H. (1951). *Phytopathology* 41, 51.

Walkey, D. G. A. *et al.* (1974). *J.hort.Sci.* in press.

Watson, A. G. and Baker, K. F. (1969). *Econ. Bot.* 23, 245 - 252.

White, G. A. and Higgins, J. J. (1966). Res.Rep. No. 95. U.S. Dept. Agric., Beltsville, U.S.A.

Wilczkowska, J. (1970). *Biul.Inst.Hodowli i Aklimatyzacji Roslin* 1/2, 55 - 68. *Pl.Breed.Abstr.* 43, 2128 (1973).

Williams, P. H. and Staub, T. (1971). *Phytopathology* 61, 917 .

Yamaguchi, T. and Kanno, C. (1963). *Bull.Ist.agron.Div. Tokai-Kinki agric.Exp.Stat.* 9, 162 - 182.

Yarnell, S. H. (1956). *Bot.Rev.* 22, 81 - 166.

Zeevaart, J. A. D. (1955). *Euphytica* 4, 127 - 132.

SEED STUDIES IN THE CRUCIFERAE

J. G. VAUGHAN

Biology Department, Queen Elizabeth College, London, England

JOAN R. PHELAN

Biology Department, St. Mary's College, Twickenham, England

K. E. DENFORD

Botany Department, University of Alberta, Edmonton, Canada.

INTRODUCTION

The seed is a plant structure which provides the botanist with many areas of investigation (Kozlowski, 1972). Early anatomical work with seeds revealed variation of great value to the taxonomist (Netolitzky, 1926). The use of the scanning electron microscope at the present time is providing new and useful information in systematics (Heywood, 1971). Seed development as studied by the light and electron microscopes, also certain biochemical techniques, is an important aspect of morphogenesis (Corti and Sarfatti, 1973). To the biochemist and plant physiologist, the phenomena of seed germination and dormancy pose many problems and, in the sphere of plant utilisation, seeds and their residues form an important part of human food and animal feed.

The Cruciferae contain a large number of species; many of which are of economic importance. In the range of investigations described in the previous paragraph, the seeds of cruciferous plants have often been utilised. The present paper deals with the seeds of the Cruciferae where studies of structure and certain chemical constituents have provided information of taxonomic value.

SEED STRUCTURE

External Structure and Gross Morphology

A number of investigations of the external structure of Cruciferous seeds in relation to taxonomy have been carried out with reference to colour, shape and other surface features (e.g. Francois, 1937; Plitt, 1941; Musil, 1948; McCugan, 1948; Cernohorský, 1950; Murley, 1951). An outstanding feature of gross internal structure used in systematics has been the relative position of radicle and cotyledons and the absence or degree of folding of the cotyledons. These internal characters (Fig. 1) were used as long ago as 1824 by De Candolle in his initial classification of the Cruciferae and have subsequently been used in most systems of classification of the family. In a study of the seeds of some 90 genera and some 200 species of the Cruciferae (Vaughan and Whitehouse, 1971), surface and gross features such as shape, colour, size, production of mucilage, presence or absence of a wing, hilum characters and embryo folding were utilised. The scanning electron microscope assists greatly in resolving the surface of the testa (Fig. 2). For the identification of the residues of cruciferous oil and weed seeds in animal feeds the appearance of fragments of the testa as seen in surface view with the light microscope is of great value in quality control (Vaughan, 1970).

Internal Structure

Without a doubt, variation in the testa structure of the cruciferous seed provides a great amount of taxonomic information and many workers have employed this character in studies of systematics (e.g. D'Arbaumont, 1890; Gram, 1894, 1898; Pammel, 1897; Pieters and Charles, 1901; Ritter, 1909; Viehoever *et al.*, 1920; Fedosseyeva, 1936; Cernohorský, 1946; McCugan, 1948; Vaughan, 1956, 1959; Binet, 1958; Vaughan *et al.*, 1963; Singh, 1964). The testa may consist of: (i) an

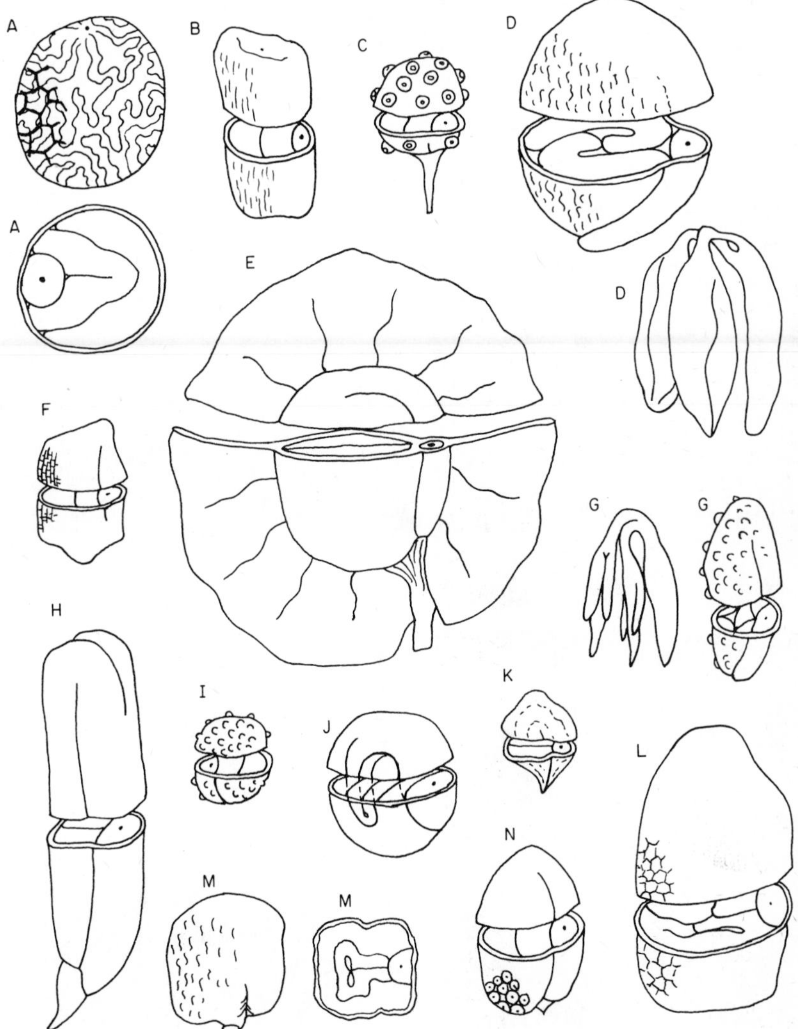

FIGURE 1. Cruciferous seeds (whole and in T.S.) of some representative types, x 5. A, *Succowia balearica;* B, *Alliaria petiolata;* C, *Aethionema arabicum;* D, *Cardamine eneaphyllos;* E, *Fibigia clypeata;* F, *Orychophragmus violascens;* G, *Lepidium sativum;* H, *Stubendorffia aptera;* I, *Ionopsidium acaule;* J, *Bunias erucago;* K, *Thlaspi alpestre;* L, *Cardamine heptaphylla;* M, *Calepina irregularis;* N, *Conringia orientalis.*

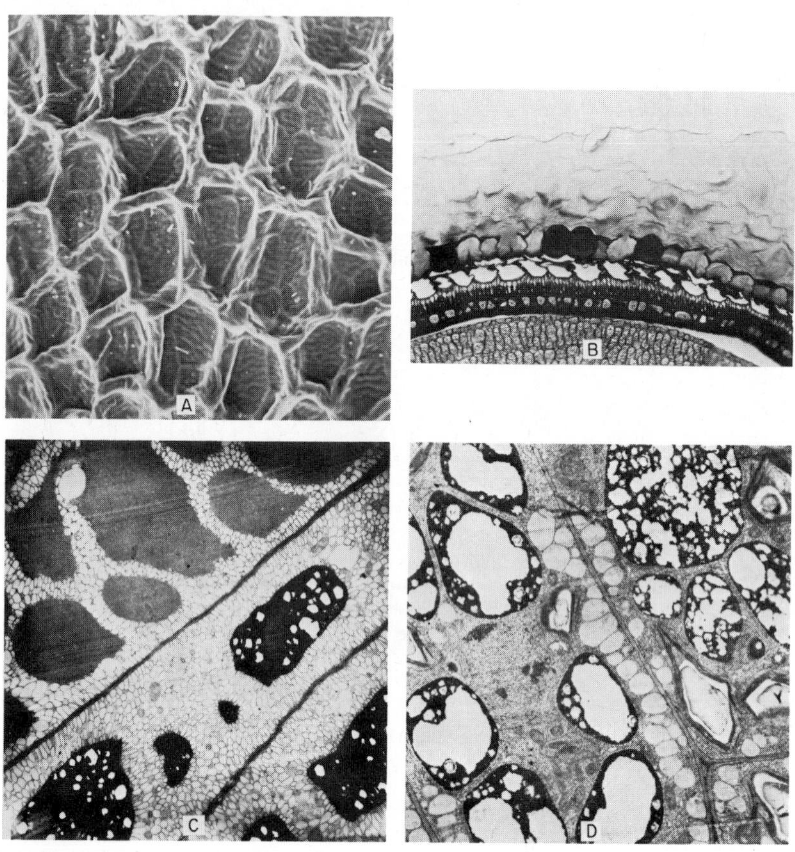

FIGURE 2. A, Surface of *Brassica nigra* testa as seen with the scanning electron microscope, x 105; B, T.S. *Sinapis alba* testa, x 65; C, aleurone and myrosin grains of *S. alba* seed, x 2,000; D, development of myrosin grains from vacuoles in *S. alba* seed, x 3,750.

epidermal layer, one cell thick, which may be mucilaginous; (ii) a subepidermal layer; (iii) a palisade layer, one cell thick, the walls of which may be thickened and pigmented; (iv) a layer of parenchyma cells, some of which may contain pigment. Associated with the testa is the aleurone layer, the remains of the endosperm. Of these layers, the epidermis, subepidermis and palisade layer are most useful in taxonomic studies (Figs 2 and 3).

Generally speaking studies of the microscopic structure of the cruciferous embryo help little towards an understanding of the taxonomy of the family. However, Netolitzky (1926) reports blue aleurone grains and chloroplasts in the embryo epidermis of *Matthiola* and small oxalate crystals in the embryo cells of *Alyssum calycinum*. Of most interest is the distinction of the protein ergastic bodies into aleurone and myrosin grains (Fig. 2). Cells containing myrosin grains were first described as distinct from those containing aleurone grains by Heinricher (1884) because they stained more intensely with Millon's reagent. Spatzier (1893) reported that the myrosin grains, compared with the aleurone grains, are more variable in size, have no inclusions (globoids) and are highly refractive. Variation in the distribution of myrosin cells in cruciferous embryos was noted by Netolitzky (1926).

The seed characters described in the previous paragraphs have been used in taxonomic studies of the family by Cernohorský (1947) and Vaughan and Whitehouse (1971), the latter study dealing with the greater number of taxa. Vaughan and Whitehouse used the following microscopic characters in their survey (Figs 2 and 3).

Testa epidermis: Fifteen basic types were distinguished, (1) Compressed cells (2) Mucilaginous cells, mucilage with or without striations (3) Mucilaginous cells, mucilage forms reticulations (4) Mucilaginous cells of different sizes (5) Mucilaginous cells with thickening on outer tangential wall. In water, the mucilage expands to form a definite shape with a "halo" at its apex (6) As (5) but the mucilage does not swell sufficiently in water to break through the cell wall (7) Non-mucilaginous cells with a large swelling which protrudes into the lumen, almost filling it (8) Mucilaginous cells with inner tangential walls thickened (9) Mucilaginous cells with a large solid column on the inner tangential wall,

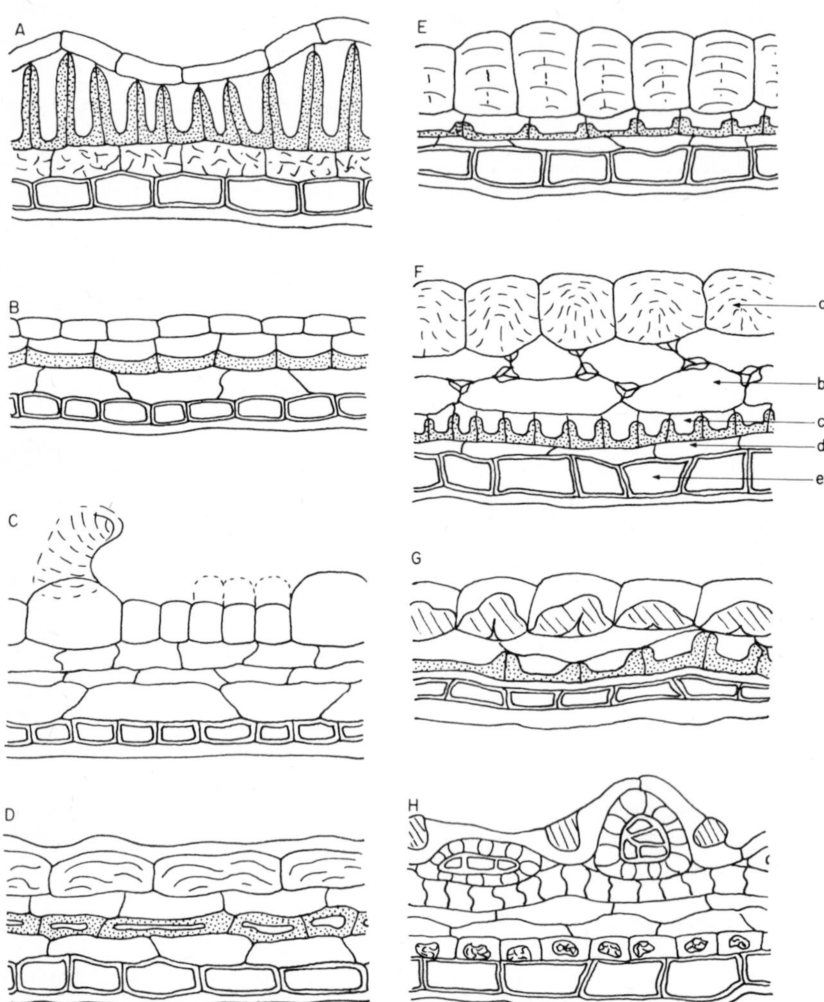

FIGURE 3. T.S. testa, x 50. A, *Raphanus raphanistrum* subsp. *raphanistrum*; B, *Cakile maritima*; C, *Aethionema saxatile*; D, *Sameraria* sp.,; E, *Eruca vesicaria* subsp. *sativa*; F, *Sinapis alba*; G, *Ptilotrichum spinosum*; H, *Ricotia lunaria*.

a, epidermal layer; b, subepidermal layer; c, palisade layer; d, parenchyma; e, aleurone layer.

protruding into the cell lumen (10) Mucilaginous cells with a ridged column on the inner tangential wall (11) Mucilaginous cells with a large hollow column on the inner wall (13) As (12) but the column is markedly flattened at the top end and has a wide hollow centre (14) Mucilaginous cells with thin wrinkled "walled" hollow columns (15) Thick-walled non-mucilaginous cells.

Testa subepidermis: Three basic types were distinguished, (1) Parenchyma, either of one or two layers of small flattened cells or one layer of "giant" cells (2) Collenchyma (3) Stone cells.

Testa palisade layer: Eight basic types were distinguished, (1) All walls thin (2) Inner tangential walls thickened and thickening flat or concave (3) Inner tangential walls thickened and thickening strongly convex (4) Inner tangential and lower half of radial walls thickened and radial thickening bulging (5) Inner tangential and whole radial walls thickened. Radial thickening bulging and cells tangentially elongated (6) as (5) but cells more or less isodiametrical or radially elongated (7) Outer walls thickened (8) All walls thickened.

As stated earlier the testa inner parenchyma and endosperm are of little value in taxonomy. Vaughan and Whitehouse (1971) found that, as regards the embryo, only the distribution of the myrosin cells was of systematic interest. Where present in the embryo, myrosin cells were scattered throughout the tissue or concentrated around the procambial strands.

The variation in the anatomy of cruciferous seeds was shown by Vaughan and Whitehouse to be of value at different taxonomic levels, particularly for genera and species. A number of authorities on the Cruciferae (e.g. De Candolle, 1824; Schulz, 1936; Tutin *et al.*, 1964) have found it convenient to divide certain genera into sections. Again, knowledge of seed anatomy assists at the infrageneric level. Most of the systems of classification of the Cruciferae (De Candolle, 1824; Endlicher, 1839; Hooker, 1862; Pomel, 1883; Schulz, 1936; Manton, 1932; Janchen, 1942) have grouped genera into tribes. In their studies of seed anatomy, Vaughan and Whitehouse (1971) found little or no support for the tribal division within the Cruciferae.

Seed Development

Proper understanding of mature structure often requires a knowledge of development. Descriptions of the development of the cruciferous seed from the ovule have been given by Berg (1865), Brandza (1891), Guignard (1892), Netolitzky (1926), Thompson (1933) and Klykhen (1937). The majority of these workers have indicated that the outer layers of the testa, including the palisade layer, are formed from the outer integument of the ovule while the inner integument forms the inner parenchymatous layer of the seed coat. During seed development, the nucellus disintegrates but some endosperm persists as a well formed aleurone layer which is intimately connected with the testa.

The development of epidermal mucilage in a large number of cruciferous species was studied by Abraham (1885), D' Arbaumont (1893), Winton and Winton (1932) and Dale and Scott (1943). All these workers agreed that the mucilage formed from starch grains in the immature cells but there was disagreement on the mode of formation of the column, where present. Some workers suggested that the column developed from the mucilage, others that it is part of the cell wall.

Recent studies of seed development have utilised the transmission electron microscope. Schulz and Jensen (1968) investigated early embryogenesis in *Capsella* up to the heart-shaped embryo stage. Rest and Vaughan (1972) traced the development of protein and oil bodies in *Sinapis alba* from the heart-shaped embryo to the mature seed.

In the latter study, it was shown that in cotyledon cells of developing embryos, numerous small vacuoles coalesce to produce one large vacuole which itself later subdivides. Each of these subdivisions becomes filled with protein resulting in a single protein grain (Fig. 2). Differences were observed between the development of myrosin and aleurone grains. In the developing myrosin cells, at 24 days from petal fall, the contents of the rough endoplasmic reticulum cisternae, which surround the vacuoles, are relatively well stained and resemble the contents of the myrosin grains as seen in later stages. The myrosin grains develop within the vacuoles in a homogenous manner. In the developing aleurone cells, the reserve protein is first observed within the tonoplast as lumps of electron dense material while the cisternae contents of the surrounding endoplasmic reticulum stain only slightly. By reference to work on other taxa, this lumping effect seems to be correlated with the presence of globoid inclusions (Englemann, 1966; Horner and Arnott, 1965; Vigil, 1970).

Oil bodies of *S. alba* were first seen in the cytoplasm some 18 days after petal fall. Frey-Wyssling *et al.* (1963), also working with *S. alba*, suggested that the oil bodies arose directly from the endoplasmic reticulum. The study by Rest and Vaughan (1972) did not support this. These authors also suggested the possibility that the oil bodies were surrounded by a monomolecular layer of phospho-lipid which prevented the bodies coalescing. No evidence was found for a 3-layered unit membrane.

CHEMOTAXONOMIC STUDIES INVOLVING SEEDS

Chemical Constituents and Methods Utilised in Taxonomic Studies

In chemotaxonomic studies of higher plants, much use has been made of the seed as a source of compounds. One very good reason for this has been the need, in systematic comparisons of taxa, for organs of a fixed physiological age. The seed is ideal for this purpose.

As regards the Cruciferae, certain of the seed constituents have been widely in taxonomic studies. The glucosinolates are somewhat peculiar to the family and consequently have been used in investigations of a large number of taxa within the family (Ettlinger and Kjaer, 1969). Because of the economic importance of *Brassica* and *Sinapis*, much attention has been paid to taxa within these genera. Lipid analysis has provided useful information (Appelqvist, 1968). The present paper deals particularly with protein separation methods as applied to *Brassica* and *Sinapis* taxonomy. Some reference will be made to glucosinolates.

In this work the protein separation methods have involved serological (double diffusion and immunoelectrophoresis) and electrophoretic techniques (including isoenzyme staining). These techniques had not previously been used in studies of *Brassica* and *Sinapis* taxonomy and therefore the earlier investigations were concerned with their applicability to the genera stated.

A serological investigation (Vaughan *et al.*, 1966) was carried out into the taxonomic relationships of *B. nigra* (*n* = 8), *B. oleracea* (*n* = 9) and *B. campestris* (*n* = 10). These taxa are often regarded as the "basic" *Brassica* species, and on cytological and plant breeding evidence (Fig. 4), are

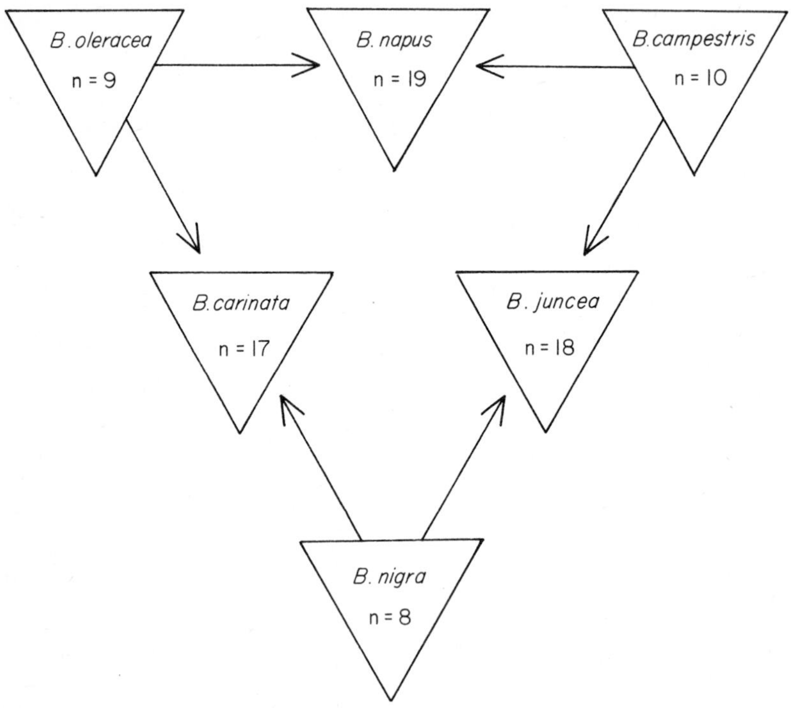

FIGURE 4. Cytological relationships of *Brassica* species.

thought to be the putative parents of *B. carinata* (*n* = 17), *B. juncea* (*n* = 18) and *B. napus* (*n* = 19). The gel diffusion methods employed in the investigation separated the three species and also indicated that *campestris* and *oleracea* are closer to each other than either is to *nigra*. This serological finding is in keeping with the morphological work of Schulz (1919) who placed *campestris* and *oleracea* in the section *Brassicotypus* and *nigra* in the section *Melanosinapis*.

Vaughan and Denford (1968) investigated the seed albumins of some ten *Brassica* and *Sinapis* taxa by means of acrylamide

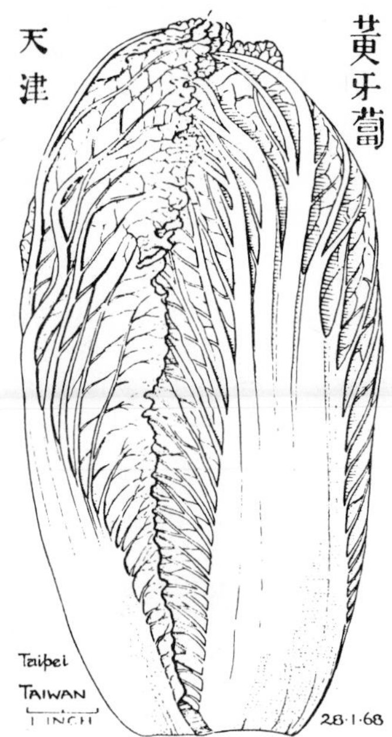

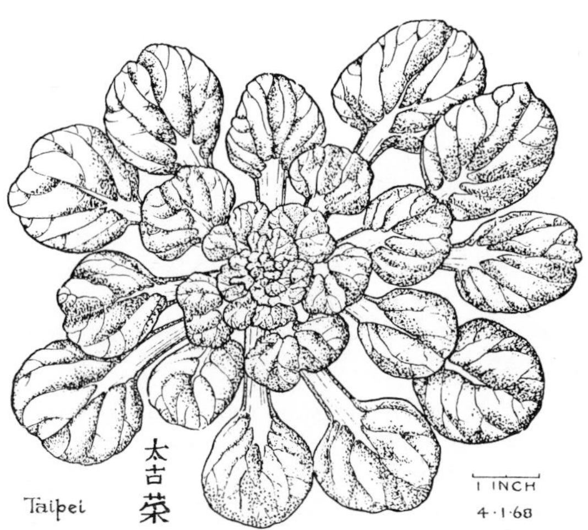

FIGURE 5. *Brassica pekinensis*, Petsai (Top figure)
Brassica chinensis, Pak choi(Bottom figure)
(both figures by permission of G. A. C. Herklots)

gel electrophoresis. Taxonomic assessment was based on a percentage similarity of Rp values and the results presented in the form of a three-dimensional model. The investigation provided useful information for an interpretation of generic and specific status.

Isoenzyme staining assists in the detection of the homologous relationship between proteins separated in gels. Vaughan and Waite (1967a) investigated the -galactosidases, -glucosidases and esterases of certain *Brassica* and *Sinapis* taxa. In addition to confirming the relationship of *B. campestris*, *B. oleracea* and *B. nigra* referred to in a previous paragraph, evidence was presented which supported the generic distinction between *Brassica* and *Sinapis*.

It is felt that the chemotaxonomic methods stated are of value in systematic studies of *Brassica* and *Sinapis* taxa and therefore should provide useful information when applied to some difficult taxonomic situations within the genera.

The Ten Chromosome Complex Comprising *B. campestris* L., Its Allies and *B. tournefortii* Gouan (Denford, 1970).

This group of plants shows a wide range of polymorphy (Fig. 5) and hence rather special problems concerning the establishment of specific characters relating to its taxonomy. The main taxa within the complex are as follows, the nomenclature being that of Musil (1948).

- *B. campestris* L. (Annual Turnip-Rape), an oil seed plant.
- *B. campestris* L. (Wild Turnip), regarded by Linnaeus (1753) as a weed or ruderal.
- *B. campestris* L. var. *autumnalis* DC. (Biennial Turnip-Rape), an oil seed plant.
- *B. campestris* var. *rapa* Prain (Garden Turnip), a root crop.
- *B. campestris* var. *sarson* Prain (Indian Colza), an annual oil seed crop of the Indian sub-continent. Prain (1898) also described another Indian oil seed variety—*toria*.

Workers who have been prominent in investigations of the systematics of the previous taxa are Linnaeus (1753), De Candolle (1821), Prain (1898), Schulz (1919) and Bailey (1922, 1930). A survey of the publications of these workers reveals considerable confusion in respect of nomenclature and rank for the taxa so far stated. Indeed, it might be better to call the members of the *campestris* complex by their common names (turnip, turnip rapes and wild turnip) and, as Musil (1948), treat the taxa as varieties of *campestris*.

B. pekinensis Rupr. (Petsai), a vegetable or salad plant of the Orient, introduced into European and New World Countries in the early part of the 20th century (Bailey, 1930).
B. chinensis L. (Pak choi), utilization and origin similar to that of *pekinensis*.
B. perviridis Bailey (Tender green), utilization and origin similar to that of *pekinensis*.

These three Oriental plants are well recognised but again the nomenclature is confused and there are many horticultural forms (Bailey, 1922, 1930; Herklots, 1972). *B. tournefortii* Gouan (Wild Turnip), endemic to Europe but has been introduced into the U.S.A. and Australia (where it is a prevalent weed). This taxon seems to be morphologically distinct from the other members of the 10 chromosome complex on characters of the leafage (Schulz, 1919).

Some aspects of the taxonomy of the complex have been investigated from the point of view of seed morphology (Musil, 1948; Vaughan, 1959) and cytogenetics (Sikka, 1940; Olsson, 1954) but, on these criteria, the group is still difficult to interpret. For this reason Denford (1970) reinvestigated the situation using the seed proteins and the methods already described in this article.

Denford investigated a large collection of seed accessions (about 150). The protein spectra of the seeds was compared by means of acrylamide gel electrophoresis involving general protein staining and the identification of eleven different kinds of isoenzymes. Some serological analysis involving the double diffusion technique, was also carried out. The interpretation of the data was as in Vaughan and Denford (1968). In addition it was necessary to utilise a computer programme method to process the large amount of information obtained.

In the accessions investigated, there appeared to be comparatively few seed albumins as estimated by general protein staining and Rp value. Of the 32 protein bands recognised, two of them were unique to *B. tournefortii*, never being found in any of the other taxa. Also there were certain albumins, absent from *tournefortii*, but present in the other taxa.

The distribution of isoenzymes provided further taxonomic information. It was found that the following units had unique enzyme patterns:- (1) Turnip (2) Annual Turnip-Rape, Biennial Turnip-Rape, Wild Turnip *(B. campestris)* (3) *Sarson* (4) *Toria* (5) Petsai (6) Pak choi (7) Tendergreen (8) *B. tournefortii*. Consequently the "Wild" *B. campestris* appears to be conspecific with the cultivated Turnip-Rapes.

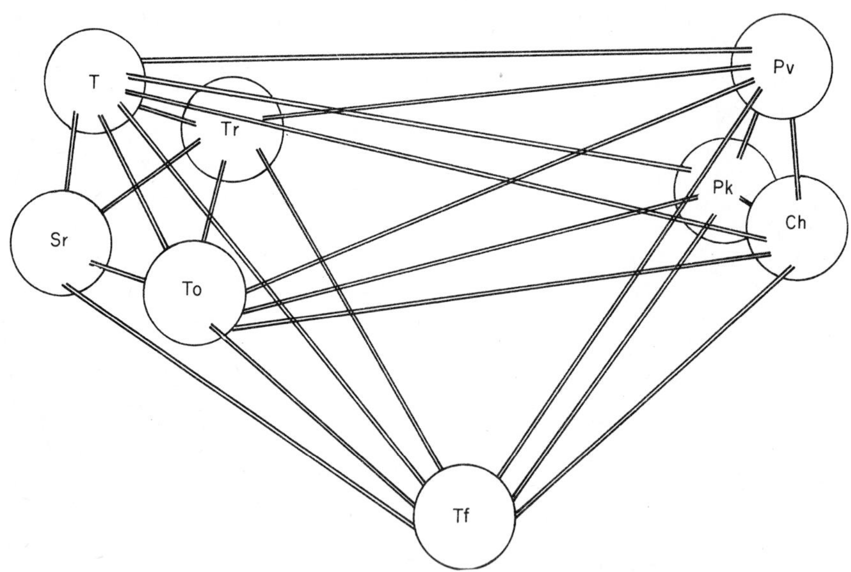

FIGURE 6. Three dimensional representation of the *Brassica* ten chromosome taxa based on isoenzyme studies (Denford, 1970).

T, Turnip; Tr, Turnip Rape; Sr, *Sarson;* To, *Toria;* Pv, Tendergreen; Pk, Petsai; Ch, Pak-choi; Tf, *Brassica tournefortii*.

If the percentage similarity of the isoenzyme distribution is used to form a three-dimensional diagram (Fig. 6) then the following group is achieved:

1 Turnip, Turnip-Rape, Wild Turnip (*B. campestris), Sarson, Toria*
2 Petsai, Pak-choi, Tendergreen
3 *B. tournefortii*.

As there was a unique pattern of isoenzyme distribution for the eight taxa as described in a previous paragraph, so the three groups now indicated had unique enzymes.

The separation of *B. tournefortii*, a plant which grows wild in the Mediterranean region, from the other 10 chromosome taxa on protein data is well supported by morphological and genetic information (Schulz, 1919; Olsson, 1954).

Sun (1946) suggested that there are two races of *B. campestris*:- Eastern (Petsai, Pak-choi, Tendergreen) and Western (Turnip, Turnip-Rape). The protein work of Denford (1970) supports this distinction and includes the Indian *Sarson* and *Toria* in the Western group. If one accepts the Eastern/ Western distinction then the taxonomic rank of the groups is open to discussion. Sun (1946) included all taxa under the one species—*B. campestris* but Denford (1970) preferred different specific status for each of the Eastern and Western groups.

The Nine Chromosome Complex Comprising *B. oleracea* L. and *B. alboglabra* Bailey (PHELAN, *personal communication)*

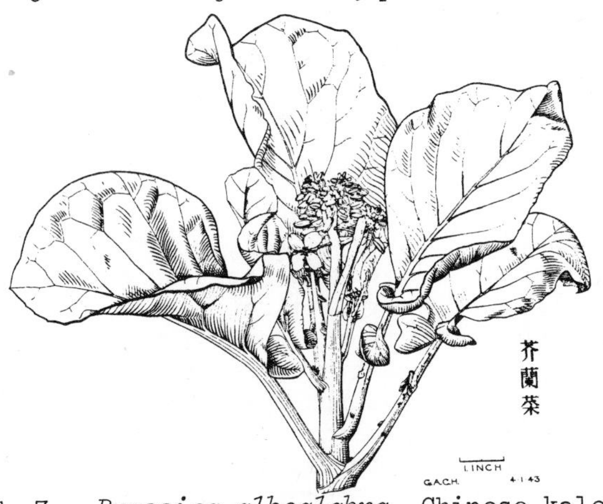

FIGURE 7. *Brassica alboglabra*, Chinese kale (by permission of G. A. C. Herklots)

There are two taxa in the genus *Brassica* with $n = 9$, namely *B. oleracea* L. and *B. alboglabra* Bailey. Crosses between these two plants are easily made (Sinskaja, 1928).

B. oleracea was first described by Linnaeus in his *Species Plantarum* (1753) as the wild native plant of West and South Europe and he listed all the cultivated forms as varieties of the wild species, suggesting that they were derived from it. There have been several classifications of the cultivated varieties since then (De Candolle, 1824; Schulz, 1919; Bailey, 1922, 1930; Mansfeld, 1959) based on general morphology.

B. alboglabra, usually described as Chinese Kale, was first described by Bailey in 1922 and distinguished from *B. oleracea* by its white flowers, ovoid leaf blade with auricles, long petiole and absence of thickened parts (Fig. 7). This separation has been queried by several authors (Sinskaja, 1928; Burkill, 1930; Hu, 1962; Sun, 1946; Yarnell, 1956). For example, Sun (1946) suggests that there are two varieties of kale:- yellow flowered *B. oleracea* var. *acephala* and white flowered *B. oleracea* var. *albiflora (alboglabra)*. However, Herklots (1972) mentions that there are in fact white, red and yellow flowered cultivars of the Chinese kale. Vavilov (1949) accepted the separate specific status for *oleracea* and *alboglabra*, suggesting that the former originated in the Mediterranean area, the latter in Japan and East China. Morphological studies have thus presented a confusing picture regarding the taxonomic status of Chinese kale. In an attempt to clarify the situation, Phelan (*personal communication*) has investigated the seed glucosinolates and proteins of the 9 chromosome complex.

Phelan, in her study of the volatile oils produced by the seed glucosinolates (Fig. 8) found the information of interest regarding the relative taxonomic position of *oleracea* and *alboglabra*. *Alboglabra* was distinct in terms of the amount of 3-butenyl isothiocyanate produced. This distinction does not necessarily support a separate specific status for *alboglabra*. However, it does support a taxonomic distinction between the Eastern *alboglabra* and the Western *oleracea* varieties which provides an interesting parallel with the study of Denford (1970) on the 10 chromosome taxa. In terms of the amount of allyl isothiocyanate produced, Phelan found a good correlation between this chemical information and the usually accepted *oleracea* varieties.

Denford based his distinction of the 10 chromosome *Brassica* plants into Eastern and Western groups on protein data. In

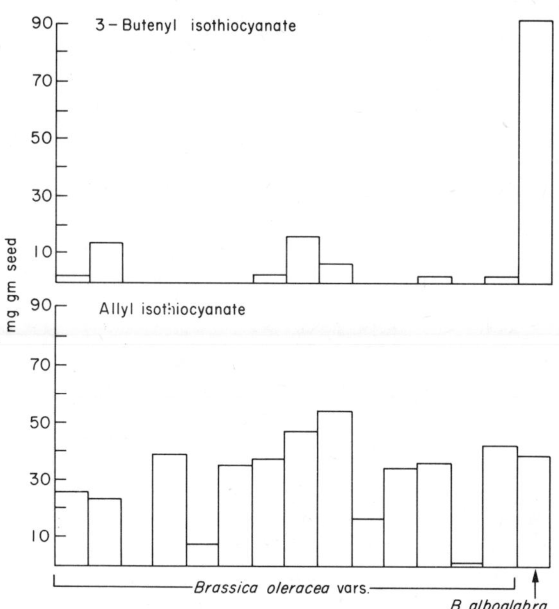

FIGURE 8. Volatile mustard oils in *Brassica alboglabra* and varieties of *Brassica oleracea*.

addition to the isothiocyanate studies, Phelan investigated the seed albumins and certain isoenzymes of the 9 chromosome complex. Her results showed as much variation within the varieties of *B. oleracea* as between varieties. Also, no distinction could be made between *B. oleracea* and *B. alboglabra*. Therefore, in this case, the glucosinolates provided the most interesting chemotaxonomic information. A similar situation was reported for *B. juncea* (Vaughan and Gordon, 1973).

The Generic Status of *Brassica* and *Sinapis*

With reference to the cultivated species, there has been some debate concerning the generic distinction between *Brassica* and *Sinapis*. Most European publications (e.g. Tutin *et al.*, 1964) accept the distinction but North American works normally include Charlock (*S. arvensis* L.) and White Mustard (*S. alba* L.) in the genus *Brassica* (Bailey, 1922; Musil, 1948). In the publications referred to, taxonomic relationship is based on morphological criteria.

Vaughan and Waite (1967a) and Vaughan and Denford (1968) reinvestigated the situation with a serological and electrophoretic study of the seed proteins. There appeared to be a clear distinction between White Mustard/Charlock and the other taxa which would support the separate generic status referred to in the previous paragraph. This distinction is also supported by seed lipid studies (Appelqvist, 1968).

Studies of Amphidiploidy within the Genus *Brassica*

One of the most interesting aspects of *Brassica* crop taxonomy has been the suggestion that certain species evolved as amphidiploids (Fig. 4). This suggestion was based originally on cytological work (Morinaga, 1934; U, 1935) but evidence has also been forthcoming from plant breeding work (Frandsen, 1943, 1947; Ramanujam and Sriniviaschar, 1943; Olsson, 1960a, 1960b), studies of comparative anatomy (Berggren, 1962), volatile oil production (Vaughan *et al.*, 1963) and leaf phenolics (Dass and Nybom, 1967). Because of the successful application of protein separation methods to problems of *Brassica* taxonomy, it was decided to investigate amphidiploidy using these methods.

It has often been claimed that the protein pattern of a hybrid represents an addition of some or all the proteins of the putative parents (Alston and Turner, 1963). As confirmation or otherwise of this claim, Vaughan *et al.* (1970) investigated the seed proteins of synthesised *B. napus* with respect to its parents, namely *B. campestris* and *B. oleracea*. Analysis by serological and electrophoretic methods revealed no new proteins, including certain enzymes, in the newly established hybrid. This supported the addition concept of protein spectra for hybrids. Similar information was obtained for the other presumed hybrids, *B. juncea* and *B. carinata* (Vaughan and Waite, 1967b).

Detailed studies have been carried out into the taxonomy of *B. juncea* (Vaughan *et al.*, 1963; Vaughan and Gordon, 1973). *B. juncea* is a mustard of great economic importance. It is an ancient crop in the Far East where it has been grown mainly as a vegetable and in the northern part of the Indian subcontinent where it is an important oil seed plant. In fairly recent times *B. juncea* has been introduced into Europe and

North America and grown for seeds which have provided oil and been used in condiment mustard. Both studies (Vaughan *et al.*, 1963; Vaughan and Gordon, 1973) provided good evidence for two geographic races of the plant:- (1) A Far Eastern or Oriental race where the seed shows a marked mucilaginous epidermis and produces more allyl isothiocyanate than 3-butenyl isothiocyanate (2) An Indian race where the seed does not have a marked mucilaginous epidermis and where more 3-butenyl isothiocyanate is produced than allyl isothiocyanate. An investigation of seed proteins did not support this distinction.

The existence of two geographic races poses interesting problems concerning the origin of *B. juncea*. If one accepts that the plant originated as a hybrid between *B. campestris* and *B. nigra* then, on the seed characters described, the Indian race resembles *B. campestris* more than *B. nigra*. The reverse is true for the Oriental race. One is therefore faced with at least two possible situations. *B. juncea* may have evolved in two independent centres or human selection may account for the marked distinction described.

FUTURE INVESTIGATIONS

It is felt that the chemotaxonomic investigations described have provided much useful information regarding the taxonomy of *Brassica* crops and therefore might be extended to other taxa within the genus and indeed to the Cruciferae as a whole. A consideration of the descriptions of *Brassica* and *Sinapis* in Tutin *et al.* (1964) reveals many aspects of the taxonomy of wild species which are by no means clear. Chemotaxonomic studies might assist here. Regarding the hybrid origin of certain *Brassica* crops little effort has been made to ascertain the distribution of the putative parents in the presumed areas of origin. It is suggested that such studies combined with the chemotaxonomic techniques which have now been successfully developed would provide much useful information concerning the origin of these important plants.

REFERENCES

Abraham, M. (1885). *Jb.wiss.Bot.* 16, 599 - 637.

Alston, R. E. and Turner, B. L. (1963). "Biochemical Systematics". Prentice-Hall, N.J.

Appelqvist, L.-Å. (1968). *Acta Univ.Lund. Sectio II No.7*, pp. 1 - 25.

Bailey, L. H. (1922). *Gentes Herb.* 1, 53 - 108.

Bailey, L. H. (1930). *Gentes Herb.* 2, 211 - 267.

Berg, O. (1865). "Anatomischer Atlas zur pharmacentischen Warenkunde". Berlin.

Berggren, G. (1962). *Sv.Bot.Tidskr.* 56, 65 - 135.

Binet, P. (1958). *Revue gén.Bot.* 65, 129 - 185.

Brandza, M. (1891). *Revue gén.Bot.* 3, 1 - 32, 71 - 84, 105 - 126, 150 - 165, 229 - 240.

Burkill, I. H. (1930). *Gdns'Bull.* 5, 99 - 117.

Cernohorský, Z. (1946). *Cslky Zemel.* 19, 162 - 169.

Cernohorský, Z. (1947). *Op.bot.Cech.* 5, 7 - 92.

Cernohorský, Z. (1950). *Bull.Intern.Cl.Sci.Math.Nat.Med. Acad. Tcheque Sci.* 47, 5 - 10.

Corti, E. F. and Sarfatti, G. (1973) (eds). "From Ovule to Seed: Ultrastructural and Biochemical Aspects". *Cytologia* Supplement, 25, 1 - 314.

Dale, W. T. and Scott, L. I. (1943). *Proc.Leeds phil.lit. Soc.* (Science Section) 4, 111 - 122.

D'Arbaumont, J. (1890). *Bull.Soc.bot.Fr.* 37, 251 - 257.

D'Arbaumont, J. (1893). *Annls. Sci.nat.* (ser.7, Bot.) 11, 125 - 181.

Dass, H. and Nybom, N. (1967). *Can.J.Genet.Cytol.* 9, 880 - 890.

De Candolle, A. P. (1821). Regni Vegetabilis Systema Naturale. Vol. II, pp. 1 - 745. Paris.

De Candolle, A. P. (1824). Prodomas Systematis Naturalis Regni Vegetabilis. Vol. I, pp. 131 - 236. Paris.

Denford, K. E. (1970). "A Study of the Seed Proteins of Certain *Brassica* Species using Electrophoretic and Serological Techniques". Ph.D. thesis, London University.

Endlicher, S. (1839). "Genera Plantarum Secundum Ordines Naturales Disposita". pp. 861 - 888. Vienna.

Englemann, E. M. (1966). *Amer.J.Bot.* 53, 231 - 237.

Ettlinger, M. G. and Kjaer, A. (1968). *In* "Recent Advances in Phytochemistry". (T. J. Mabry *et al.*, eds), Vol. I., pp. 60 - 144. Appleton-Century-Crofts, New York.

Fedosseyeva, A. (1936). *Acta Univ.voroneg.* 9, 64 - 82.

Francois, L. (1937). *Annls Epiphyt.* 3, 8 - 21.

Frandsen, K. J. (1943). *Dansk Botanisk Arkiv.* 11, 1 - 17.

Frandsen, K. J. (1947). *Dansk Botanisk Arkiv.* 12, 1 - 16.

Frey-Wyssling, A. *et al.* (1963). *J.Ultrastruct.Res.* 8, 506 -516.

Gram, B. (1894). *Bot.Tidsskr.* 19, 116 - 142.

Gram, B. (1898). *Landwn VersStnen.* 50, 449 - 481.

Guignard, L. (1892). *Bull.Soc.bot.Fr.* 39, 392 - 395.

Heinricher, E. (1884). *Ber.dtsch.bot.Ges.* 2, 463 - 466.

Herklots, G. A. C. (1972). "Vegetables in South-East Asia". George Allen and Unwin, London.

Heywood, V. H. (ed.) (1971). "Scanning Electron Microscopy". Academic Press, London and New York.

Hooker, J. D. (1862). *In* "Genera Plantarum". (G. Bentham and J. D. Hooker, eds), Vol. I, pp. 57 - 102. Lovell Reed, London.

Horner, H. T. and Arnott, H. J. (1965). *Amer.J.Bot.* 52, 1027 - 1038.

Hu, C. C. (1962). *China Hort.* 8, 1 - 19.

Janchen, E. (1942). *Ost.bot.Z.* 91, 1 - 28.

Klykhen, P. (1937). *Nytt.Mag.Naturvid.* 77, 201 - 215.

Kozlowski, T. T. (ed.) (1972). "Seed Biology". Vol. I, pp. 1 - 416. Academic Press, New York and London.

Linnaeus, C. (1753). "Species Plantarum". Vol. II, pp. 561 - 1200.

Mansfeld, R. (1959). "Die Kulturpflanzen". Vol. II, pp. 1 - 659. Academic-Verlag, Berlin.

Manton, I. (1932). *Ann.Bot.* 46, 509 - 556.

McCugan, J. M. (1948). *Can.J.Res.* 26, 520 - 587.

Morinaga, T. (1934). *Cytologia, Tokyo.* 6, 62 - 67.

Murley, M. R. (1951). *Am.Midl.Nat.* 46, 1 - 81.

Musil, A. F. (1948). "Distinguishing the Species of *Brassica* by their Seeds". *U.S. Dep.Agric.Misc.Publ.* No. 643.

Netolitzky, F. (1926). "Anatomie der Angiospermen - Samen". *In* "Handbuch der Pflanzenanatomie". (K. Linsbauer, ed.), Vol. IX, pp. 1 - 360.

Olsson, G. (1954). *Hereditas* 40, 398 - 418.

Olsson, G. (1960a). *Hereditas* 46, 171 - 222.

Olsson, G. (1960b). *Hereditas* 46, 351 - 386.

Pammel, L. H. (1897). *Am.mon.microsc.J.* 18, 205, 269, 312.

Pieters, A. J. and Charles, V. K. (1901). *Bull.Div.Bot.U.S. Dep.Agr.* 29.

Plitt, T. M. (1941). *Pl.Physiol.* 16, 422 - 424.

Pomel, A. (1883). "Contribution à la classification méthodique des Crucifères". Paris University.

Prain, D. (1898). *Agric.Ledger* 5, 1 - 80.

Ramanujam, S. and Srinivaschar, D. (1943). *Indian J.Genet.* 3, 73 - 88.

Rest, J. A. and Vaughan, J. G. (1972). *Planta* 105, 245 - 262.

Ritter, G. (1909). *Beih.bot.Zbl.* 26, 132 - 156.

Schulz, O. E. (1919). Cruciferae-Brassiceae, Part I: Brassicinae and Raphaninae. *In* "Das Pflanzenreich, Vol. IV, Part 105" (A. Engler, ed.) Engelmann, Leipzig.

Schulz, O. E. (1936). *In* "Die Natürlichen Pflanzenfamilien". (H. G. A. Engler and K. A. E. Prantl, eds), Vol. IIb, pp. 227 - 658.

Schulz, R. and Jensen, W. (1968). *J.Ultrastruct.Res.* 22, 376 - 392.

Sikka, S. M. (1940). *J.Genet.* 40, 441 - 509.

Singh, B. (1964). *Bull.natn.bot.Gdns.Lucknow* No. 89.

Sinskaja, E. N. (1928). *Bull.Appl.Bot.Genet. and Pl.Breed.* 19, 1 - 648.

Spatzier, W. (1893). *Jb.wiss.Bot.* 25, 39 - 79.

Sun, V. G. (1946). *Torrey Bot.Club Bul.* 73, 244 - 281, 370 - 377.

Thompson, H. C. (1933). *J.agric.Res.* 47, 215 - 232.

Tutin, T. G., Heywood, V. H., Burges, N. A., Valentine, D. H., Walters, S. M. and Webb, D. A. (1964)(eds) *In* "Flora Europaea" Vol. I, pp 260 - 346. University Press, Cambridge.

U, N. (1935). *Jap.J.Bot.* 7, 389 - 452.

Vaughan, J. G. (1956). *Phytomorphology* 6, 363 - 367.

Vaughan, J. G. (1959). *Phytomorphology* 9, 107 - 110.

Vaughan, J. G. (1970). "The Structure and Utilization of Oil Seeds". Chapman and Hall, London.

Vaughan, J. G. and Denford, K. E. (1968). *J.exp.Bot.* 19, 724 - 732.

Vaughan, J. G. and Gordon, E. I. (1973). *Ann.Bot.* 37, 167 - 18

Vaughan, J. G. and Waite, A. (1967a). *J.exp.Bot.* 18, 100 - 109

Vaughan, J. G. and Waite, A. (1967b). *J.exp.Bot.* 18, 269 - 276

Vaughan, J. G. and Whitehouse, J. M. (1971). *J.Linn.Soc. Lond.(Bot.)* 64, 383 - 409.

Vaughan, J. G., Denford, K. E. and Gordon, E. I. (1970). *J. exp.Bot.* 21, 892 - 898.

Vaughan, J. G., Hemingway, J. S. and Schofield, H. (1963). *J.Linn.Soc. Lond.(Bot.)* 58, 435 - 447.

Vaughan, J. G., Waite, A., Boulter, D. and Waiters, S. (1966). *J.exp.Bot.* 17, 332 - 343.

Vavilov, N. I. (1949). *Chron.Bot.* 13, 1 - 364.

Viehoever, A., Clavenger, F. and Ewing, C. O. (1920). *J. agric.Res.* 20, 117 - 140.

Vigil, E. L. (1970). *J.Cell.Biol.* 46, 435 - 454.

Winton, A. L. and Winton, K. B. (1932). "The Structure and Composition of Foods". Vol. I, pp 1 - 710. John Wiley, New York.

Yarnell, S. H. (1956). *Bot.Rev.* 22, 81 - 166.

TRICHOMES IN STUDIES OF THE CRUCIFERAE

R. C. ROLLINS and U. C. BANERJEE

Gray Herbarium, Harvard University, U.S.A.

INTRODUCTION

Trichomes have been depended upon as a taxonomic character at every level in the classification of the Cruciferae. Their frequent presence as a quickly read surface feature of all or nearly all aboveground parts of the plant ranks them in importance with many other external features for taxonomic purposes. They are widely present among taxa of the family but there are many species and fewer whole genera that are completely glabrous. Some of the classifications of the Cruciferae, notably that of Prantl (1891), utilized trichomes as taxonomic characters to an unusual degree and thereby produced a system that is quite artificial in many respects, especially at the tribal level. At a lower hierarchical level, the judicious use of trichome characters along with other kinds of taxonomic characters leads to a satisfying arrangement of the species and genera. However, in the present paper, we are interested in the use of trichomes in studies of interspecific relationships, evolution and the adaptedness of species to certain climatic areas and edaphic situations.

For this purpose, we have examined, with the aid of the scanning electron microscope (SEM), all sixty-nine species of the genus *Lesquerella* that occur in North America. These plants range from annuals, found mostly in the middle western part of the United States, to herbaceous or subligneous perennials that occur from the Arctic through the Cordilleran region of western North America to the state of Puebla in

Mexico. Without exception, the species of *Lesquerella* are densely clothed with trichomes. The surfaces of the leaves, stems, and other structures of many species are silvery from the crust of trichomes with radiating arms which overlap in one to several layers. The only exterior parts of the plants ever free of trichomes are the petals, stamens, and siliques. But in many species the siliques are also covered with trichomes.

The diversity shown by these structures among the species of *Lesquerella* native to North America is very substantial and has attracted the attention of several botanists. Vanatta (1907) examined 21 species and placed them in five groups based on the type of trichome they possessed. In his monograph of *Lesquerella*, Payson (1922) laid stress on the trichomes as indicators of species relationships and in a more recent treatment of the genus involving one of us (Rollins and Shaw, 1973) the differences in the trichomes of the species were utilized in their delineation and classification within the genus.

As in all the Cruciferae, the trichomes are single-celled and they mature very early in the ontogeny of the surface where they occur. On leaves, for example, long before they are fully expanded, the trichomes have become dead cells and exist as cell walls with whatever endodeposited material that has taken place. In *Lesquerella ovalifolia*, Lanning (1961) found that the depositional material was primarily calcium carbonate laid down on the cell wall interior in the form of calcite. Thus in working with trichomes on mature parts of the plant, we are dealing with single dead cells present for the most part on the surface but with a portion of the cell imbedded in the epidermal layer (Plate 1, Fig. 3). There is scarcely any tendency for them to be shed or even rubbed off from specimens because they are both tightly held and of a tough resistant material. The trichome cells are differentiated as part of the epidermal layer where they tend to increase to full size very rapidly. In early stages of development such organs as the leaf, bud or ovary are densely covered with trichomes which form a protective coat over these fast-growing parts of the plant.

The density of the trichomes on the mature plant surfaces tends to be species-specific with some variation dependent upon the edaphic factors affecting plant growth. However, there is a broad correlation between a high density, often with several overlapping layers of trichomes (Plate 5, Fig. 29) and high moisture stress situations such as arid areas or high elevations and high latitudes where strongly desiccating winds occur. The sites occupied by *Lesquerella* plants in the arid region of western North America are most often open, high light intensity situations which are at the same time exposed to winds of considerable velocity. It is on the plants which characteristically occupy such sites that the trichome covering is densest. In contrast to this, species of *Lesquerella* occurring in areas of greater rainfall and a more generally humid climate have a comparatively sparse covering of trichomes (Plate 5, Fig. 30). This broad correlation between climate and species with a dense or spaced trichome covering is a significant feature of the geography of members of the genus.

The detailed taxonomic and evolutionary study of *Lesquerella* just completed (Rollins and Shaw, 1973) provides the framework for further studies in the genus. It is now possible to look at structure or system in terms of its overall organization. Some appropriate questions are: how does trichome diversity mesh with patterns of species relationship that were determined largely on the basis of other characters? What evolutionary patterns do the trichomes themselves reveal? Remembering that the trichomes are single cells, it is intriguing to inquire as to how far the differentiation and diversity of these single cells in their manifested state have gone in mirroring the species relationships and evolutionary patterns within the genus.

SPECIES RELATIONSHIPS

In the 1973 monograph, we placed the 69 species into ten groups based on what we considered to be the intragroup affinities of the species. These are as follows:

Group 1. *Lesquerella angustifolia, L. argyraea, L. densiflora, L. filiformis, L. gordonii, L. gracilis, L. lindheimeri, L. recurvata, L. sessilis, L. tenella, L. thamnophila.*

Group 2. *Lesquerella fendleri, L. hitchcockii, L. rubicundula.*

Group 3. *Lesquerella johnstonii, L. mcvaughiana, L. purpurea.*

Group 4. *Lesquerella arctica, L. calderi, L. engelmannii, L. ovalifolia, L. pinetorum, L. pruinosa.*

Group 5. *Lesquerella inflata, L. mexicana, L. mirandiana, L. pueblensis, L. schaffneri, L. wyndii.*

Group 6. *Lesquerella aurea, L. gooddingii.*

Group 7. *Lesquerella alpina, L. arenosa, L. arizonica, L. calcicola, L. cinerea, L. globosa, L. intermedia, L. lata, L. ludoviciana, L. montana, L. rectipes, L. valida.*

Group 8. *Lesquerella carinata, L. douglasii, L. fremontii, L. garrettii, L. macrocarpa, L. multiceps, L. occidentalis, L. paysonii, L. prostrata, L. utahensis, L. wardii.*

Group 9. *Lesquerella cordiformis, L. hemiphysaria, L. kingii, L. palmeri, L. peninsularis.*

Group 10. *Lesquerella auriculata, L. densipila, L. grandiflora, L. lescurii, L. lyrata, L. perforata, L. stonensis.*

Three unlike species of uncertain affinity, *Lesquerella argentea, L. berlandieri* and *L. lasiocarpa,* were not placed in any of the 10 groups.

Table 1 gives some of the trichome characteristics of the *Lesquerella* species. The arrangements of the species are alphabetical in different categories of trichome types. These arrangements show a remarkable correspondence to the groups of species in some instances. For example, those species with simple or stalked trichomes, as opposed to sessile trichomes, correspond exactly to Group 10 of our monograph. Another arrangement in which all of the species with the rays webbed more than one-half their lengths incorporates the species of Group 5 plus others. A third arrangement with a ratio of one ray to two distal ray endings and free trichome branches consists of 6 species of Group 1. Other arrangements show less correspondence to the groups of our monograph but it is clear that the trichomes are a critical source of information and by themselves have enough information content to show up species affinities in *Lesquerella*.

TRICHOME DIVERSITY

The trichomes of each species were analyzed with respect to a series of characteristics as shown in Table 1. An index of branching complexity ranging from 1, the least complex, to 4, the most complex, was determined as a ratio of the number of primary to ultimate trichome branches per trichome. This was done by counting the number of primary branches near the center of the trichome and the number of ultimate branch endings. Index 1 is a ratio of one primary to one ultimate branch per trichome; Index 2 is a ratio of one primary to roughly two ultimate branches; Index 3 is a ratio of one primary to roughly three ultimate branches; Index 4 is a ratio of one primary to roughly four ultimate branches.

In the trichomes with a more or less central point of cell insertion into the epidermal layer, and where the branches radiate from this central axis, the branches are often called rays. This is a true stellate trichome, exemplified in a simple form in Plate 2, Fig. 7, and in a complex form in Plate 2, Fig. 11. Intermediate types are illustrated in Plate 2, Figs. 8 - 10. Stellate trichomes predominate in all but seven species where the trichomes are simple or dendritic or both. Trichomes with a stalk and with branches arising along this vertical axis are known as dendritic trichomes. Species with this type of trichome, exemplified in Plate 1, Figs. 2, 3 and 5 were placed under Index 1 because there is no further complexity of branching other than that represented by the simple branch itself.

There is a transition from dendritically branched types of trichomes to the stellate form in which the branches radiate from a central point. Trichomes approaching the fully radiating condition, illustrated in Plate 2, Fig. 8, have the radiating branches incomplete around the central attachment point leaving an open gap in a fan-like arrangement. In some species, the gap is fairly wide as in *Lesquerella grandiflora* (Plate 1, Fig. 2) while in others such as *L. johnstonii* (Plate 1, Fig. 6) the gap is nearly closed. A slightly more widened gap is shown in *L. gooddingii* (Plate 1, Fig. 4). These appear to represent transitional forms which ultimately lead to the truly stellate type of trichome.

Table 1

Trichome characters of *Lesquerella* species

Species	Branches	Tubercles	Umbo	Cover	Group
		Simple or Stalked			
auriculata	free	not present	not present	spaced	10
densipila	free	not present	not present	spaced	10
grandiflora	free	not present	not present	overlapping	10
lasiocarpa	free	inconspicuous	not present	spaced	10 (?)
lescurii	free	not present	not present	spaced	10
lyrata	free	not present	not present	spaced	10
perforata	free	not present	not present	spaced	10
stonensis	free	not present	not present	spaced	10
		Stellate, rays simple, webbed 1/2 to >3/4			
Species	**Branches**	**Tubercles**	**Umbo**	**Cover**	**Group**
argentea	simple	prominent	present	contiguous	5 (?)
fendleri	simple	prominent	present	overlapping	2
inflata	simple	inconspicuous	present	contiguous	5
mcvaughiana	simple	prominent	present	overlapping	3
mexicana	simple	inconspicuous	present	overlapping	5
mirandiana	simple	prominent	present	contiguous	5
pueblensis	simple	prominent	present	overlapping	5
schaffneri	simple	prominent	present	overlapping	5
wyndii	simple	prominent	present	overlapping	5

Table 1 continued

Index 1. Roughly 1:1 ratio of center to distal arms, branches free

Species	Branches	Tubercles	Umbo	Cover	Group
argyraea	simple	prominent	not present	spaced	1
aurea	s & f*	inconspicuous	not present	overlapping	6
densiflora	s & f	inconspicuous	not present	spaced	1
filiformis	forked	prominent	not present	contiguous	1
globosa	s & f	inconspicuous	not present or present	overlapping	7
gooddingii	s & f	inconspicuous	not present	contiguous	6
johnstonii	s & f	prominent	not present	overlapping	3
purpurea	s & f	inconspicuous	not present	overlapping	3

Index 2. Roughly 1 center ray to 2 distal ray endings, branches free

Species	Branches	Tubercles	Umbo	Cover	Group
gordonii	forked	inconspicuous	not present	spaced	1
gracilis	forked	inconspicuous	not present	spaced	1
lindheimeri	forked	prominent	not present	contiguous	1
recurvata	f & b**	prominent	not present	spaced	1
sessilis	forked	inconspicuous	not present	spaced	1
tenella	forked	prominent	not present	spaced	1

* simple and forked

** forked and branched

Table 1 continued

Index 2. Roughly 1 center ray to 2 distal ray endings, branches <1/4 fused

Species	Branches	Tubercles	Umbo	Cover	Group
alpina	forked	prominent	not present	overlapping	7
arenosa	forked	inconspicuous	not present	contiguous	7
arizonica	forked	prominent	present	overlapping	7
cinerea	f & b	prominent	not present	overlapping	7
engelmannii	s & f	prominent	present	overlapping	4
fremontii	forked	prominent	not present	contiguous	8
hemiphysaria	branched	prominent	not present	overlapping	9
kingii	forked	prominent	not present	overlapping	9
ludoviciana	forked	prominent	not present	overlapping	7
montana	forked	prominent	not present	overlapping	7
occidentalis	forked	prominent	not present	overlapping	8
rectipes	f & b	prominent	not present	overlapping	7

Index 3. Roughly 1 center ray to 3 distal ray endings, branches <1/4 fused

Species	Branches	Tubercles	Umbo	Cover	Group
angustifolia	branched	prominent	not present	spaced	1
arctica	f & b	prominent	present	overlapping	4
carinata	branched	prominent	not present	contiguous	8
cordiformis	f & b	prominent	not present	overlapping	9
kingii	f & b	prominent	present	overlapping	9
lata	f & b	inconspicuous	not present	overlapping	7
multiceps	branched	prominent	present	overlapping	8
palmeri	branched	prominent	not present	overlapping	9

Table 1 continued

paysonii	forked	not present	present	contiguous	8
peninsularis	branched	prominent	not present	overlapping	9
prostrata	f & b	prominent	present	overlapping	8
rubicundula	f & b	not present	not present	overlapping	2
wardii	branched	prominent	not present	overlapping	8

Index 3. Roughly 1 center ray to 3 distal ray endings, branches 1/4 to 1/2 fused

Species	Branches	Tubercles	Umbo	Cover	Group
arctica var. *scammanae*	forked	prominent	present	contiguous	4
calcicola	f & b	prominent	present	overlapping	7
carinata	branched	prominent	not present	contiguous	8
intermedia	f & b	prominent	not present	overlapping	7
kingii 3 subsp.	f & b	prominent	present	overlapping	9
ovalifolia	f & b	prominent	present	overlapping	4
valida	branched	prominent	not present	overlapping	7

Index 4. Roughly 1 center ray to 4 distal ends, branches 1/4 to 1/2 fused

Species	Branches	Tubercles	Umbo	Cover	Group
calderi	branched	prominent	present	overlapping	4
garrettii	f & b	not present	not present	overlapping	8
hitchcockii	branched	inconspicuous	present	overlapping	2
pinetorum	f & b	prominent	not present	overlapping	4
pruinosa	branched	prominent	not present	overlapping	4
thamnophila	branched	prominent	not present	overlapping	1
utahensis	branched	inconspicuous	present	overlapping	8

The most advanced species of *Lesquerella* have trichomes that are most complex either because of the branching, the sculpturing on the trichomes, or the webbing between the rays or a combination of these

Branching Complexity

The stellate type of trichome with radiating rays may have these in a wholly simple form as shown in *Lesquerella argyraea* subsp. *diffusa* (Plate 2, Fig. 7). A forking of the rays may occur near the center of the trichome as illustrated by *L. recurvata*, or the forking may occur at some distance from the center as shown by the trichomes of *L. tenella* (Plate 2, Fig. 8). The next stage in branching complexity on a rising scale is that shown in *L. occidentalis* subsp. *cinerascens* (Plate 2, Fig. 10) where the rays are twice forked. As the number of rays and branches increase, and there is some complication of ray fusion where they come together, an added dimension to the complexity is present. This is shown in two forms by the trichomes of *L. thamnophila* (Plate 2, Fig. 11) and *L. ovalifolia* (Plate 2, Fig. 12).

Ray fusion.

The basal fusion of the thickened rays is sometimes extensive, producing a peltate scale-like structure (Plate 6, Fig. 36). This type of ray fusion is very different from the type of fusion involving webbing between the rays. The distinction can readily be seen by comparing the trichomes in Fig. 15, Plate 3, with that of Fig. 36, Plate 6. In the latter, the tubercles forming the sculptured surface extend over the entire fused area whereas in the former, the sculptured area is over the rays only. Here the webbing between the rays is devoid of sculpturing.

Other than branching, important trends of modification are seen in the amount of fusion and the amount of webbing between them in the stellate trichomes. The rays may be free to the base as shown in *Lesquerella tenella* (Plate 2, Fig. 8). The range in ray fusion extends from slightly fused as in *L. occidentalis* subsp. *cinerascens* (Plate 2, Fig. 10) to about one-half fused as in *L. hitchcockii* (Plate 6, Fig. 36). In respectto ray fusion, the trichomes of each species were scored as to whether the rays were fused less than one-quarter or one-quarter to one-half of the total diameter. This permitted the grouping of the species roughly according to the amount of fusion present among the rays of their trichomes. Thirty-one of the species, the largest number, fall into the category of trichomes only slightly fused up to one-quarter of their diameter. The next largest group with stellate trichomes, 15 species, have the rays free. In eight species the trichomes have the rays fused one-quarter to one-half their lengths.

Species with trichomes having fused rays that are branched are more closely related to each other than they are to species with either unfused branched or unfused unbranched trichomes or those with webbing between the rays. The species with fused rays tend to be concentrated in the western plains and Rocky Mountain region and northward to the Arctic.

Increased webbing

The barest suggestion of webbing is found in the trichomes of *Lesquerella douglasii* (Plate 3, Fig. 13) but this is a branched trichome and the species is unrelated to the others possessing webbed trichomes. Nevertheless, it does show clearly that the webbing material is strikingly different from the material of the ray itself. The trichome of *L. mirandiana* (Plate 3, Fig. 14) shows definite webbing and the relatively large number of rays are simple. If this is compared with the trichome of *L. argyraea* subsp. *diffusa* (Plate 2, Fig. 7) which has little or no webbing and fewer simple rays, the tie-in of the webbed trichome type with the non-webbed thpe becomes clear. Increased webbing is illustrated in the trichome of *L. pueblensis* (Plate 3, Fig. 15) and a further increase is shown in *L. inflata* (Plate 3, Fig. 16). The ultimate in webbing is present in the trichomes of *L. mexicana* (Plate 3, Figs 17 and 18). Here the webbing material extends virtually to the tips of the ray.

A parallel feature to the increasing extensiveness of webbing is an increase in the number of rays. This trend may be seen in the figures mentioned above. From the phylogenetic point of view, those plants with webbed trichomes are interrelated forming a series of allopatric species extending from southwestern Texas to the state of Puebla in Mexico. Comparing the trichomes with fused rays with those showing webbing, it is clear that the trend has been from trichomes with free rays toward those with maximally fused rays as one series, and from trichomes with free rays toward those with maximum webbing in another series.

Presence or absence of an umbo

The trichomes of some species have a definite mound at the center formed either by an unsculptured wall or by a combination of the wall and a concentration of tubercles

(Plate 4, Fig. 21 and Plate 2, Fig. 12). This mound, or convex elevation, we have called an umbo. It is present on the trichomes of 20 of the 69 North American species of *Lesquerella* and absent or obscure in the other 49. In some instances, it is a very conspicuous feature, in others it is a low mound. In at least one species, *L. globosa* (Plate 5, Fig. 26), there is a prominent umbo on the trichomes of the understory but the trichomes of the outer layer do not have this feature. Besides being smooth or sculptured, the umbo of trichomes of different species may be different in size, shape, and degree of irregularity.

Surface Sculpturing

The trichome surfaces range from completely smooth as in *Lesquerella garrettii* (Plate 4, Fig. 24) to densely tuberculate. In some instances the center portion of the trichome is smooth and the tubercles are present on the rays as in *L. gracilis* (Plate 4, Fig. 23). But other trichomes of this same species may be tuberculate throughout. The density of the tubercles varies between species and the uniformity of size differs also. Several figures of Plate 4 bring these points out graphically. In quite a few species, the largest tubercles are at or near the center of the trichome and they taper down in size outward on the rays. This may be seen in *L. johnstonii* (Plate 1, Fig. 6), *L. douglasii* (Plate 3, Fig. 13) and *L. ovalifolia* (Plate 5, Fig. 28) among others. On the other hand, the tubercles may be relatively uniform over the center portion and outward on the rays as illustrated by *L. recurvata* (Plate 4, Fig. 19) and *L. globosa* (Plate 5, Fig. 26). The tubercles do not occur to any extent on the webbing material between the rays in any of the trichomes observed. This may be seen in *L. pueblensis* (Plate 3, Fig. 15).

The nature of the tubercle is difficult to determine. They are certainly a feature of the outer cell wall surface but how they originate is not known. Some tubercles have a minute hole-like depression in the center and others appear to be without such a hole. It may be noted that the seven species that are distinctive because they possess auriculate instead of cuneate-based cauline leaves also have spaced, stalked, and smooth trichomes with free branches. The trichomes of these species, *Lesquerella auriculata, L. densipila, L. lasiocarpa, L. lescurii, L. lyrata, L. perforata* and *L. stonensis*, are distinctive when compared to the trichomes of the other species of the genus.

Irregularity of rays.

In most trichomes of *Lesquerella*, the rays are straight or nearly so. However, in some species crooked, distorted and irregular rays are a characteristic feature. This is true in *L. kingii* subsp. *bernardina* (Plate 6, Fig. 32), *L. fremontii* (Plate 6, Fig. 31) and a number of other species. The same kind of irregularity shows up among species with webbed trichomes as illustrated by *L. schaffneri* (Plate 6, Fig. 33).

GEOGRAPHICAL DISTRIBUTION

Species possessing a certain trichome form tend to occupy the same or contiguous geographic areas. For example, those species that have trichomes with numerous simple rays and extensive webbing between the rays occupy an area from western Texas southward through Mexico to the state of Puebla. Only one of the nine species, *Lesquerella fendleri*, has a much wider range than the others and extends much to the north and west of the region indicated. Another example is that of species possessing a stalked or simple trichome. These occur in Tennessee and Alabama and in Oklahoma and Texas on the eastern edge of the total range of *Lesquerella*.

The large number of species occupying the Cordilleran region of western North America tend to have trichomes of a similar type. This is exemplified in Plate 4, Figs. 22 and 24; Plate 6, Figs. 31, 32 and 34. It is a highly branched stellate trichome type which also characterizes species that reach the far north, namely *L. arctica* and *L. calderi*, and is found exclusively on the plants of the South American species present in Bolivia, Argentina and Uruguay.

Payson (1922) put forward the hypothesis that *Lesquerella* started its evolutionary diversification in the region of central Texas and suggested that radiating in all directions there was an increased specialization and complexity found among the species. The more remote species were thought ultimately to have been evolved from those occurring at or near the center of origin in central Texas. In testing this hypothesis against the pattern of trichome diversity found in *Lesquerella*, one comes out with much the same general pattern if certain assumptions are made. The first assumption is that the primitive trichomes were stalked. The second is that the evolutionary direction went toward exclusively simple trichomes as in *Lesquerella lyrata* in one direction and more importantly toward sessile radiately branched trichomes of widely diversified forms, as indicated above, in the other.

The major trends of trichome specialization can be traced geographically using the central Texas area as a starting point. To the west, northwest and north the stellate type trichome on the whole becomes increasingly massive with thicker and more highly divided rays. To some extent, the total number of rays tends to increase in parallel. Toward the south and southwest, the major trend is in the direction of increased webbing between the rays. Also, there is a definite trend toward more numerous rays. On the other hand, the rays remain unbranched. Northeastward from the Texas center, the trend is toward unbranched trichomes although some species with both unbranched and dendritic trichomes occur.

Other geographically correlated trends of trichome types are less marked. What emerges when the trichomes are considered from a geographical point of view is that they do mark evolutionarily related species which tend to occupy the same or contiguous areas.

TRICHOME DENSITY

From the eastern portion of the geographical range of *Lesquerella* in the United States, species occur in which the trichomes are spaced away from each other. This is the mesic area of the overall range. As one proceeds westward into the drier region, the density and extent of overlapping of trichomes increases dramatically. In the driest and most exposed sites, the trichomes form a crust over the leaf-surface. One can scarcely escape the speculation that increased trichome density is associated with the needs of the plants to conserve water and to reflect high light intensities. The selective pressure provided by the harsh sites where *Lesquerella* often occurs certainly is demanding of the plants that grow there. It appears that in the case of *Lesquerella*, an important response has been the elaboration of protective layers of trichomes.

REFERENCES

Lanning, F. C. (1961). *Science* 133, 380.

Payson, E. B. (1922). *Ann.Mo.Bot.Gard.* 8, 103 - 236.

Prantl, K. (1891). *Cruciferae. Die Natürlichen Pflanzenfamilien* 3(2), 145 - 206.

Rollins, R. C. (1955). *Rhodora* 57, 241 - 264.

Rollins, R. C. and Shaw, E. A. (1973). "The Genus Lesquerella (Cruciferae) in North America". Harvard University Press, Cambridge, Mass.

Vanatta, E. G. (1907). *Proc.Acad.Nat.Sci.Phila.* 59, 247 - 248.

EXPLANATION OF PLATES

PLATE 1

Increase in branching complexity; transition from stalked dendritic trichome to sessile radiate trichome type. Fig. 1. *Lesquerella densipila*, x 100. Fig. 2. *L. grandiflora*, x 100. Fig. 3. *L. lasiocarpa* subsp. *berlandieri*, x 500. Fig. 4. *L. gooddingii*, x 250. Fig. 5. *L. lasiocarpa* subsp. *berlandieri*, x 250. Fig. 6. *L. johnstonii*, x 100.

PLATE 2

Increase in branching complexity among sessile radiate trichomes. Fig. 7. *Lesquerella argyraea* subsp. *diffusa*, x 100. Fig. 8. *L. tenella*, x 250. Fig. 9. *L. recurvata*, x 100. Fig. 10. *L. occidentalis* subsp. *cinerascens*, x 100. Fig. 11. *L. thamnophila*, x 100. Fig. 12. *L. ovalifolia*, x 100.

PLATE 3

Development and increase of webbing between the rays. Fig. 13. *Lesquerella douglasii*, x 250. Fig. 14. *L. mirandiana*, x 250. Fig. 15. *L. pueblensis*, x 250. Fig. 16. *L. inflata*, x 100. Fig. 17. *L. mexicana*, x 100. Fig. 18. *L. mexicana*, x 50.

PLATE 4

Presence, distribution and absence of tubercles. Fig. 19. *Lesquerella recurvata*, x 250. Fig. 20. *L. calderi*, x 100. Fig. 21. *L. calderi*, x 500. Fig. 22. *L. kingii* subsp. *diversifolia*, x 100. Fig. 23. *L. gracilis*, x 250. Fig. 24. *L. garrettii*, x 100.

PLATE 5

Presence or absence of an umbo; spaced relationships of trichomes. Fig. 25. *Lesquerella macrocarpa*, x 100. Fig. 26. *L. globosa*, x 250. Fig. 27. *L. schaffneri*, x 100. Fig. 28. *L. ovalifolia*, x 50. Fig. 29. *L. pruinosa*, x 100. Fig. 30. *L. recurvata*, x 50.

PLATE 6

Irregular rays; thickened radiate types. Fig. 31. *Lesquerella fremontii*, x 250. Fig. 32. *L. kingii* subsp. *bernadina*, x 50. Fig. 33. *L. wyndii*, x 100. Fig. 34. *L. pinetorum*, x 250. Fig. 35. *L. rubicundula*, x 250. Fig. 36. *L. hitchcockii*, x 250.

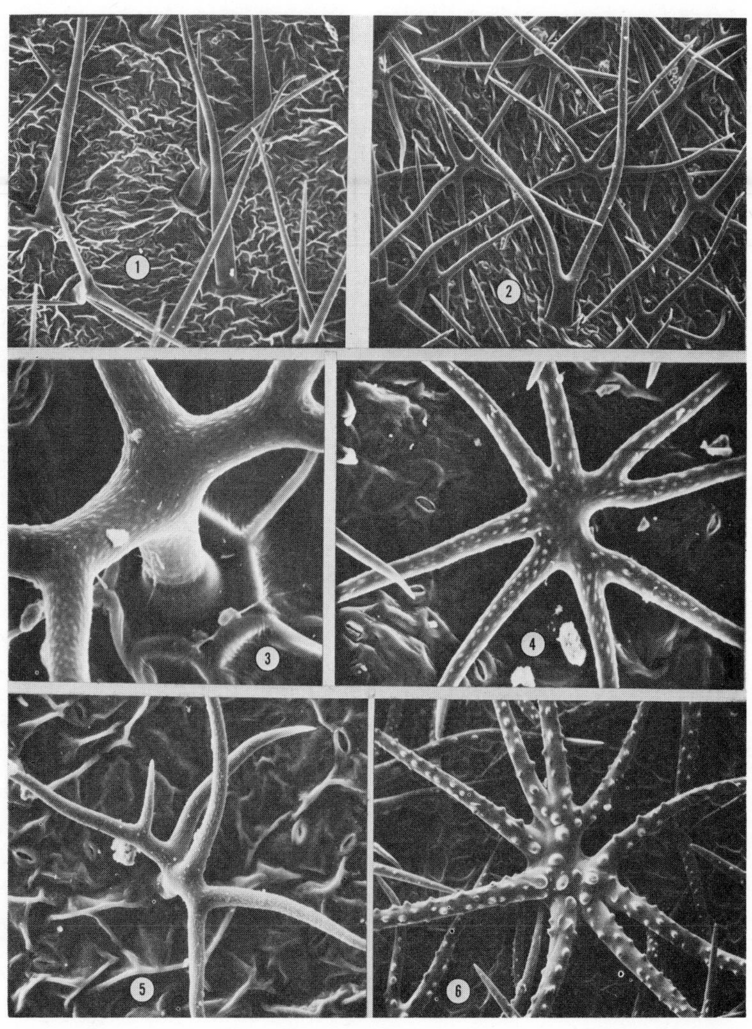

PLATE 1

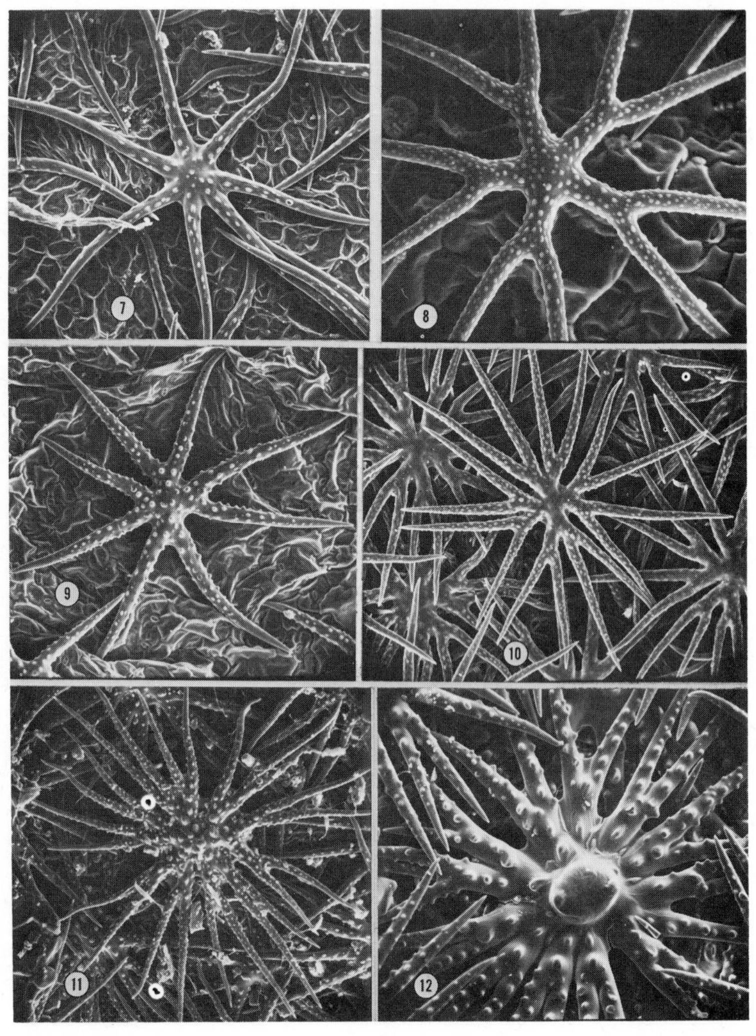

PLATE 2

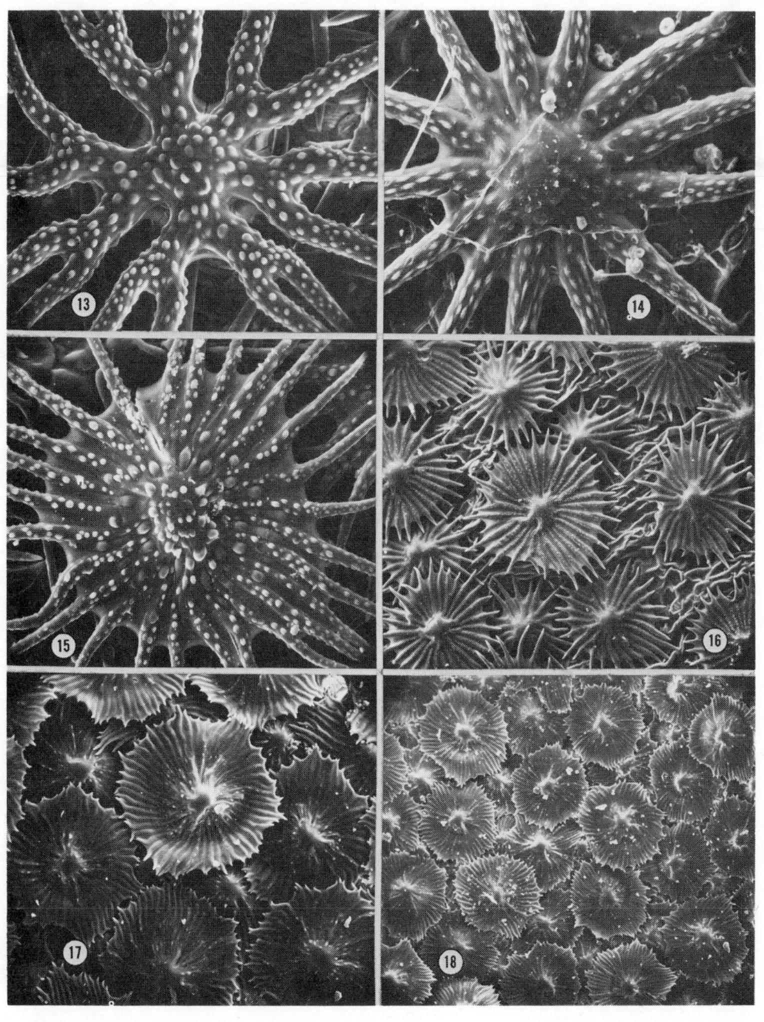

PLATE 3

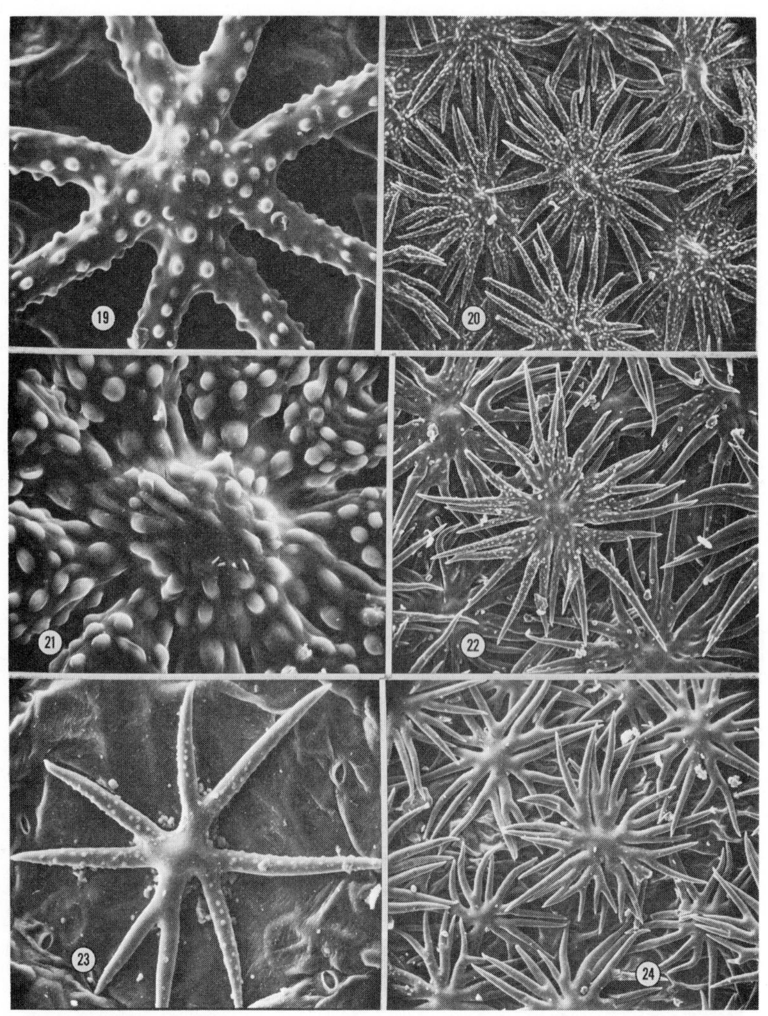

PLATE 4

PLATE 5

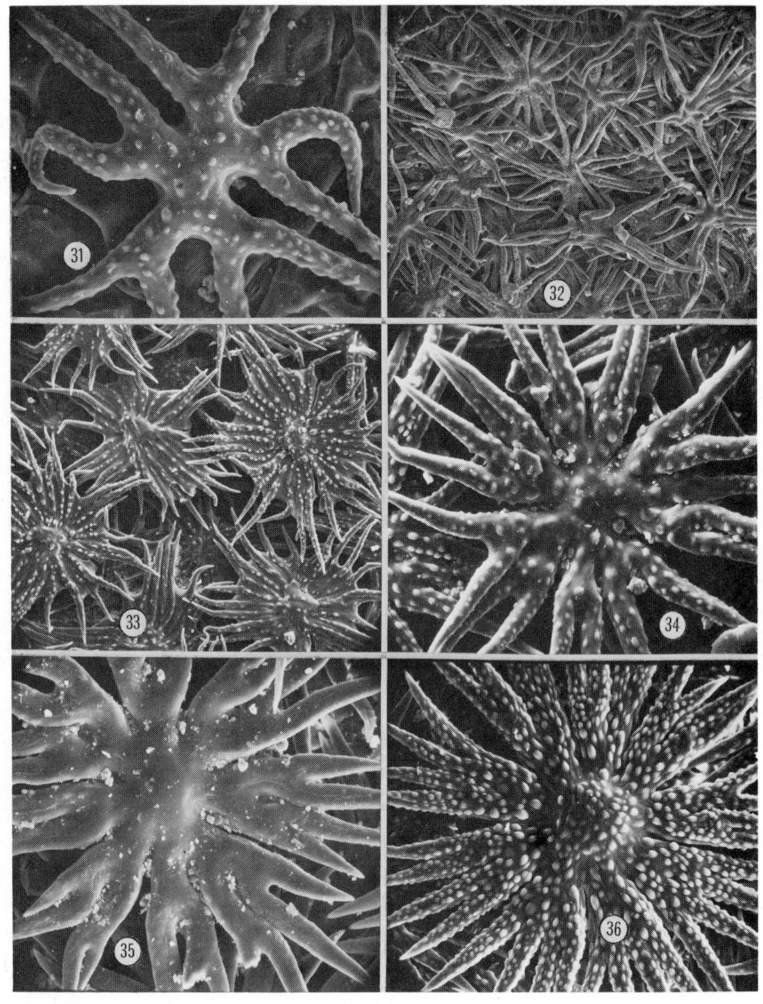

PLATE 6

VARIATIONS IN NATURAL POPULATIONS OF *ARABIDOPSIS THALIANA* (L). HEYNH

M. J. LAWRENCE

Department of Genetics, University of Birmingham, England

INTRODUCTION

Arabidopsis thaliana (Fig. 1) is a small, annual, self-compatible crucifer with a chromosome number of $2n = 10$ that belongs to the tribe Sisymbrieae (Clapham *et al.*, 1962). It occurs throughout Europe, the Mediterranean, East Africa, Asia and Japan and has been introduced into North America, South Africa and Australia (Redei, 1970). In the British Isles, it has been recorded in nearly all vice-counties, though the more detailed information available from the B.S.B.I. survey suggests that it is generally less common in the north and west of the mainland and much less common in Ireland (Fig. 2).

Arabidopsis thaliana is best known, of course, as a laboratory organism. It's suitability for this purpose was first pointed out thirty years ago by the German botanist, Laibach (1943), who founded a collection of geographical races with this use in mind. Being a small plant, it is possible to raise a large number of individuals in a small space. Furthermore, certain races of the species can be brought into flower within three weeks and will set seed within six weeks of being sown when raised in suitable conditions of light and temperature. It is possible, therefore, to raise several generations of this species per annum. Lastly, though individual plants will set seed by self-pollination without human intervention, seed can be obtained by cross-pollination, by hand, without much difficulty.

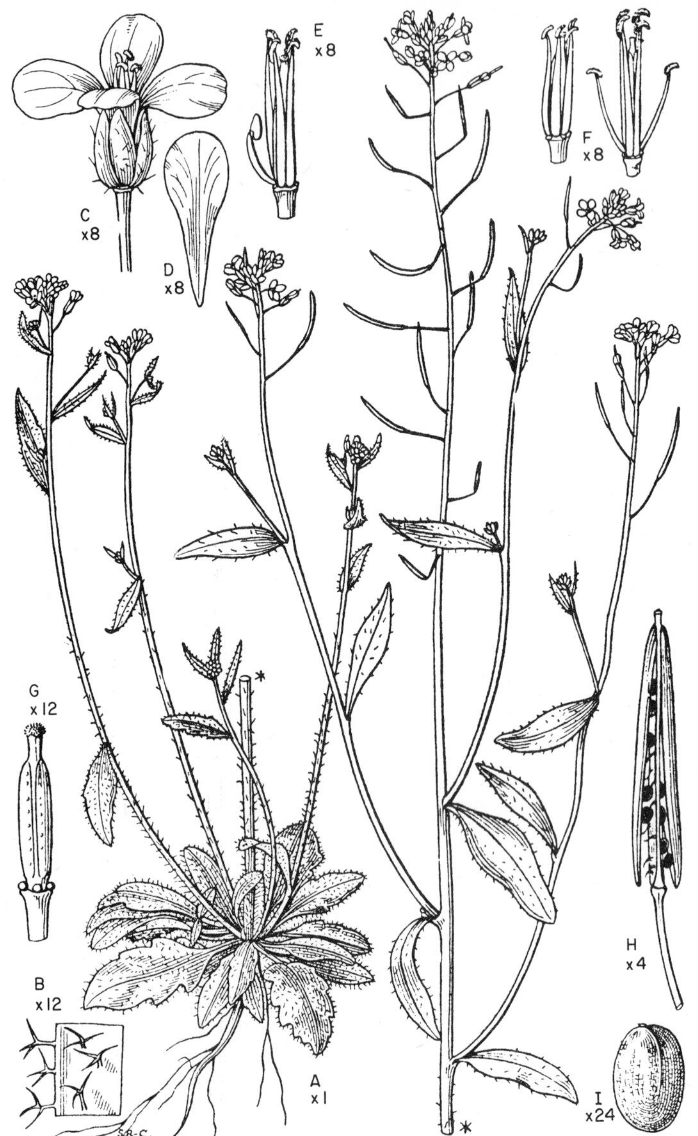

FIGURE 1. *Arabidopsis thaliana* (L.) Heynh. Reproduced with kind permission from Ross-Craig (1949).

A = plant; B = hairs on leaf; C = flower; D = petal; E, F and G = essential organs; H = fruit; I = seed.

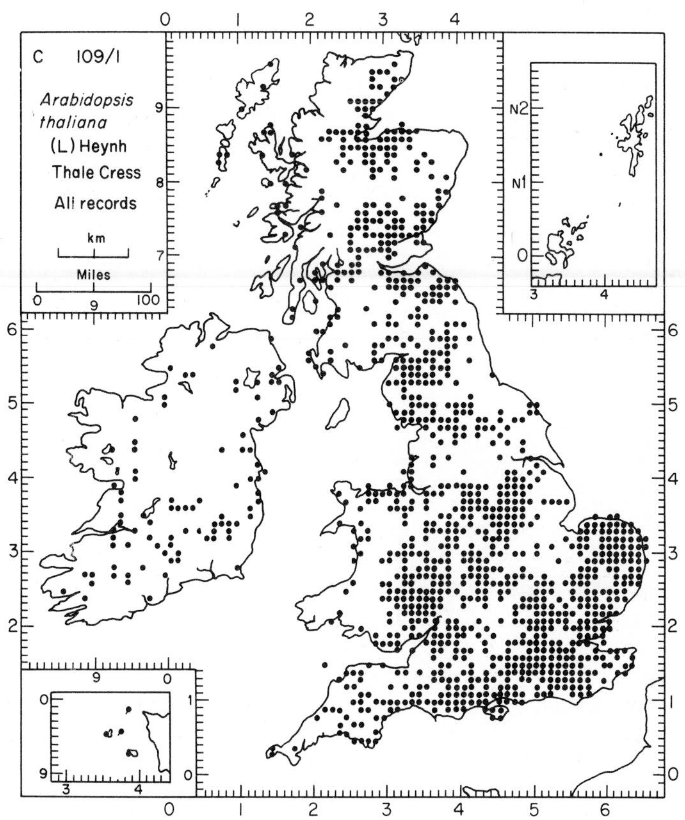

FIGURE 2. Distribution of *Arabidopsis thaliana* in the British Isles. Reproduced with kind permission from Perring and Walters (1962).

Because of these convenient properties, *A. thaliana* has been used in many different kinds of research over the past thirty years, among which are investigations concerning developmental genetics, the physiology of growth and development, metabolism and mutation. As a result of this work many different kinds of morphological, physiological, nutritional and chromosomal mutations have been described, stocks of which are readily available; and methods of growing the species in aseptic conditions on agar in test tubes have been developed (see the review by Redei, 1970 and the *Arabidopsis Information Service* newsletters for further details).

We now know, therefore, quite a lot about what might be called the formal biology of the species. However, we know much less about the natural history or population biology of *A. thaliana*, as is also the case, of course, with it's zoological counterpart, *Drosophila melanogaster*. It is with this aspect of the biology of the species that I wish to deal in the present article. We turn firstly to consider three aspects of its population biology, namely, the nature of the habitats in which it is found, the life cycle and the breeding system of the species.

THE NATURAL HABITAT OF THE SPECIES

Though *Arabidopsis thaliana* is found in most parts of the British Isles, it does not appear to be particularly common in any. It is, however, regularly found in three kinds of habitat. Firstly, *A. thaliana* is often found as a weed, together with *Capsella bursa-pastoris*, in the borders and on paths and walls in parks and gardens. Secondly, it was, in the recent past at least, found on abandoned railway tracks where, as one of several colonising species, it was frequently quite a prominent member of the flora. Neither of these kinds of habitat have, of course, a stable flora, for both are liable to change. However, thirdly, in the Derbyshire Dales, *A. thaliana* is one of several small crucifers which appear to belong to a persistent, stable flora. In this region, it is common on southward facing, freely draining limestone slopes together with *Cardamine hirsuta*, *Erophila verna* and *Draba muralis* (Ratcliffe, 1961). These three kinds of habitat appear to have little in common except that in each the ground cover is incomplete thus providing areas of bare soil on which *Arabidopsis* occurs. It is possible, therefore, that each habitat may be inhabited by a distinct race of the species.

THE LIFE CYCLE OF THE SPECIES

All of the races of the Laibach collection, from which most of the lines used in genetic research with *Arabidopsis thaliana* have originated, will come into flower within a few weeks of being sown, providing conditions of light and temperature are not limiting. Again, providing two weeks or so are allowed to elapse between time of harvest and time of sowing, the seed of the races from this collection germinates uniformly at a very high percentage. Neither of these statements is generally true of material sampled from natural populations. Thus, much material of British origin (e.g. from Derbyshire) will not flower at all unless either the germinating seed or the young plant is subjected to several weeks of low temperature treatment, prior to it being grown on in normal conditions of light and temperature (Jones, 1971c; Snape, 1973). Since non-flowering individuals are not observed in populations from which such material has been sampled, it is clear that in these habitats germination takes place in the autumn, the seed or the young plant being subsequently vernalised by the low temperatures which prevail in winter. In these circumstances,therefore, there is not much doubt that the species behaves as a winter annual.

Not all British material requires a period of low temperature before it will flower, however, which raises the question as to whether in the natural populations from which such material is obtained the species behaves as a summer annual by germinating in the spring and thereby completing it's life cycle in a single calendar year. Indeed, some workers have classified races of *Arabidopsis thaliana* into winter and spring annuals on the basis of whether they require a period of low temperature before they will flower or not (Cetl, Dobrovolna, and Effmertova, 1965, 1967; Cetl and Dobrovolna, 1968). There is, however, some controversy about this matter (Redei, 1970) which is difficult to resolve on the present evidence, partly because the seed from some populations exhibits a very considerable degree of innate dormancy; partly because the seed of the species is quite long-lived both in the laboratory and in the field (Ratcliffe, personal communication); but chiefly because we have as yet very little information about the behaviour of the species in it's natural habitat. For example, if, because of dormancy, seed is unable to germinate until autumn, flowering may not take place until the following spring because growth and development proceed at a low rate during the low temperatures and low light intensities of the intervening winter. The absence of a requirement for a period of low temperature before flower initiation takes place cannot, by itself, therefore, be taken as evidence that the race in question is of the summer annual type.

Apart from some park and garden populations, where *A. thaliana* can be found at all stages of it's life cycle at most times of the growing season, the species in Britain usually comes into flower early in the year during April and completes it's life cycle in early summer during June, that is, before the period of the year when, due to the high rate of insolation, the risk of drought is at its maximum for a species with a shallow root system.

THE BREEDING SYSTEM OF THE SPECIES

Arabidopsis thaliana was for a long time regarded as a wholly inbreeding species, largely on the evidence of its behaviour in the laboratory environment. Recently, the work of Jones (1968b, 1971a) in England, of Karbe and Robbelen (1968) in Germany and of Trojan (1971) and of Cetl, Manouskova and Relichova (1973)in Czechoslovakia has raised serious doubts about this view. All three groups of workers found that variation within a number of natural families was appreciably greater than that within inbred lines in experiments performed in the laboratory, where the variation in question concerned a number of metrical characters, chiefly, flowering time. This observation is most simply interpreted on the view that some outcrossing does in fact take place in natural populations of the species and that the resulting heterozygosity gives rise to segregation in these natural families with respect to the genes which determine the metrical character in question.

Snape and Lawrence (1971) have confirmed this view in a direct way by examining the progenies of a number of plants, each of which breed true for the recessive trait, glabrous leaves, and each of which was closely and completely surrounded by six other plants which bred true for the dominant trait at this locus, the normal, sparsely hairy leaves, typical of the species.

Now if these glabrous plants always set seed by self-pollination, all their progeny would have had glabrous leaves too. If, however, some of the seed has resulted from cross-pollination with the surrounding wild-type plants, some of the progeny will bear hairy leaves. A small proportion of the progeny of these glabrous plants did, in fact, have hairy leaves from which it was estimated that the frequency of natural outcrossing in this material was 1.73 %. There is no doubt, therefore, that *A. thaliana* is not, in fact, a wholly inbreeding species, though in view of this very low frequency of outcrossing, it is clearly a predominantly self-fertilising one.

The results of an experiment of essentially the same type as the one just described, that was carried out in the following season, throw some light on what causes cross-pollination in this species. In this experiment, half of the groups of plants were enclosed individually in insect-proof cages, the remaining half being left unenclosed as in the previous season. The average frequency of outcrossing of the enclosed glabrous plants was found to be only 0.35 %, whereas that of their unenclosed sister plants was 3.57 %. The exclusion of insects thus has resulted in a ten-fold reduction in the frequency of outcrossing in this material. Now bees have never been observed to visit the open flowers of *A. thaliana* but hover-flies (Syrphidae) have, both in the urban environment in which these experiments were performed and, particularly, in the natural habitat of the species. The most reasonable interpretation of these results is, therefore, that most of the outcrossing which takes place in populations of *A. thaliana* results from the foraging activities of hover-flies, only a small proportion arising from contact between the inflorescences of closely adjacent plants. The somewhat higher frequency of outcrossing obtained from the unenclosed plants of the second experiment (3.57 %) as compared with that obtained from the first experiment (1.73 %) is consistent with this view, for the second experiment was laid out in a more exposed location next to grassland which is known to be the larval habitat of several of the more common species of hover-fly in Britain.

VARIATION IN NATURAL POPULATIONS OF *ARABIDOPSIS THALIANA*

If a natural population of *Arabidopsis thaliana* is examined, either directly or by raising a sample of its progeny in a suitably designed laboratory experiment, we find that while much variation is in evidence, this is almost entirely of the metrical kind. Mutations of the major or discontinuously distributed kind, on which much of the laboratory work of *A.*

thaliana has depended, are for all practical purposes unknown in natural populations of this, or indeed, many other species of living organism. In considering variation in natural populations of the species therefore, we shall be concerned with variation with respect to such metrical characters as flowering time, height, siliqua number and after-ripening requirement.

Variation between Populations

We turn first to consider variation between populations, particularly variation between populations which occur in different habitats of the species. It will be recalled that earlier it was mentioned that in Britain *Arabidopsis thaliana* appears to occur in three distinct kinds of habitat, these being parks and gardens, disused railway tracks and the limestone slopes of the Derbyshire Dales. Furthermore, since these habitats appeared to have little in common, save that in all the ground cover was incomplete, it was surmised that the populations of *A. thaliana* found in these habitats might constitute more or less distinct ecological races. The results of an experiment reported by Jones (1971a) provides some support for this view. This experiment involved samples from six populations in all, four of which were taken from populations growing on disused railway tracks in Warwickshire and two from parks in Birmingham and London. In each population, seed was taken from five plants chosen at random so that 30 natural families were involved in all. The seed so obtained was sown in soil in a glasshouse in a randomised block experiment, ten plants being raised in each of the 30 families.

The mean flowering times of these population samples were as follows:-

Habitat	Population	Mean Flowering Time (days)
Railway track	1 Alcester	39.03
	2 Broom	61.32
	3 Luddington	54.69
	4 Henley-in-Arden	21.57
Park	5 Cannon Hill	7.58
	6 Ruislip	8.57

The first point worth making about these results is that, although there are considerable differences between the first four populations in respect of their average flowering time, the most striking difference concerns these, on the one hand, and the park populations, on the other. Indeed, the average flowering times of the latter are comparable to that of an early-flowering inbred line from the Laibach collection (2.33 days), which was included in this experiment as a control.

The second point worth making about the results of this experiment is that the park populations contain very much less variation in them than do the railway track populations (Fig. 3). Thus the family variances of the railway track populations are both large and heterogeneous, particularly those of population 2 and 4, while those of the park populations are small and relatively homogeneous. Indeed, since the latter are comparable to the variance of the inbred line used as a control, they raise the question of whether these populations contain any genetical variation. In a subsequent experiment, which concerned the selfed progeny of these park population plants, it was just possible to detect heritable variation among the progenies of population 5, but not among those of population 6 (Jones, 1971a). Thus park populations appear to be genetically as well as phenotypically homogeneous, a reflection perhaps of the relative homogeneity of the environment in this kind of habitat compared with that in others.

That the families of the railway track populations are so variable is less easy to account for in the absence of a detailed knowledge of the ecological characteristics of this kind of habitat. The heterogeneity of these family variances, however, leaves little doubt that part of this variation is a consequence of the occurrence of outcrossing in these natural populations for it cannot be accounted for in any other way.

The third and final point that emerges from the results of this experiment is that not all the plants came into flower within the duration of the experiment, even though this was in excess of four months. None of the plants were given a period of cold treatment, however. Thus, the presence of a minority of non-flowering individuals demonstrates that some of the genotypes in the experiment have a definite requirement for such treatment before they will flower. We notice, however, that these genotypes are confined to the first three railway

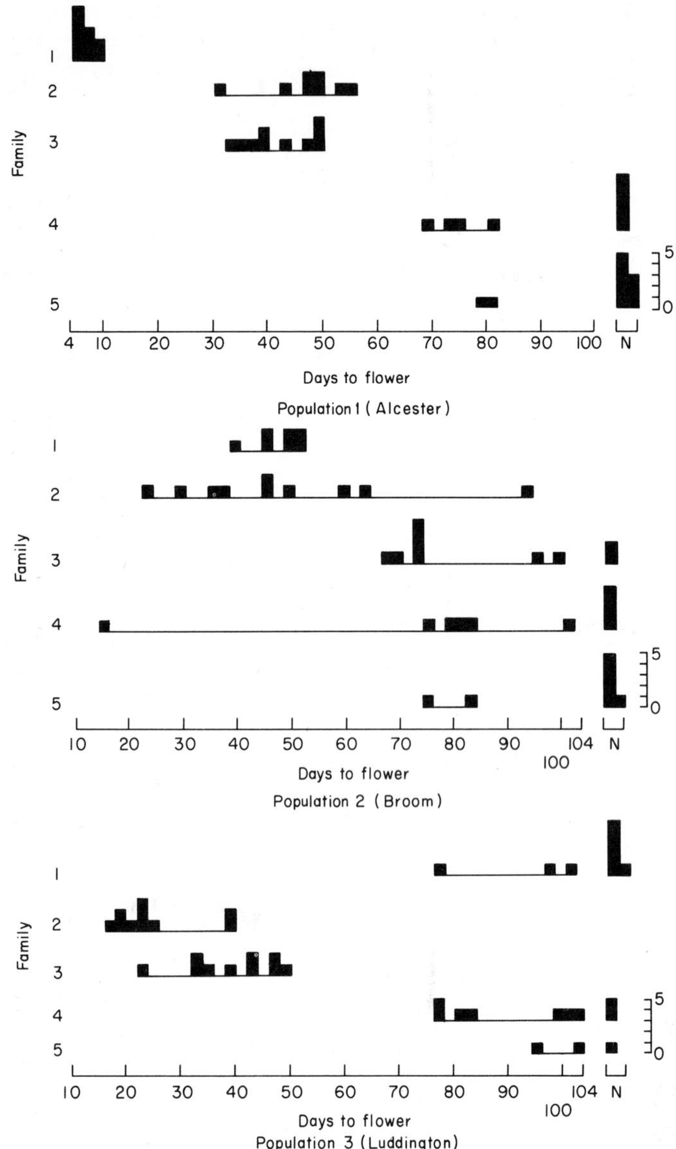

FIGURE 3. See legend opposite.

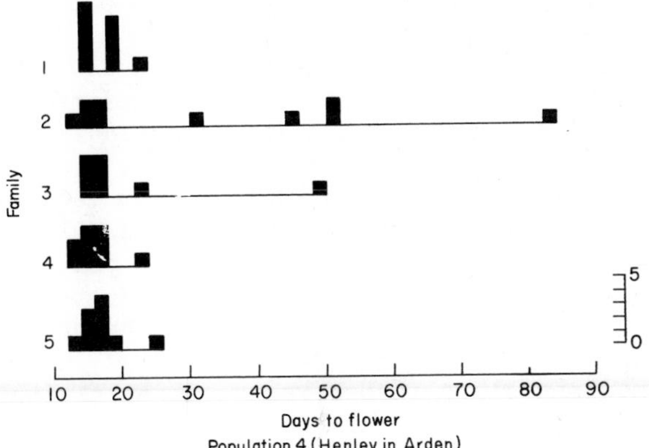

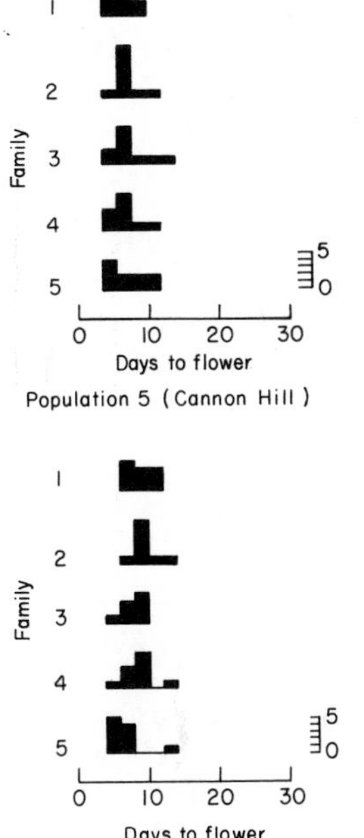

FIGURE 3. Distribution of flowering times in five natural families from each of six populations. The numbers of non-flowering individuals in each of the first three populations are shown in the right-most columns marked N. Reproduced with kind permission from Jones (1971a).

track populations; none are found in the park populations.

This relationship between low temperature requirement and habitat emerges more clearly from a later experiment carried out by Jones (1971c). This experiment involved the investigation of the effects of six different periods of low temperature treatment on 12 natural families from each of three populations. One of these populations, Cannon Hill, was the same as the park population, number 5, of the previous experiment. The second, Wixford, was another railway track population from the same general area as those of the previous experiment. The third population, Winnats Pass, was found on an exposed limestone slope in Derbyshire at an altitude of over 300 m. above sea-level. All three kinds of habitat in which *A. thaliana* is found are thus represented in this experiment.

The results obtained from this experiment are shown in Fig. 4. These graphs show the effect of the indicated period of cold treatment on the proportion of flowering plants and on the average flowering time of those plants which came into flower in each of the three populations.

As in the previous experiment, the material from Cannon Hill clearly has little or no requirement for low temperature treatment, for all plants in the experiment came into flower after as little as a single week of treatment. We note, however, that there is a small, but significant, effect of treatment on this material, plants coming into flower a little earlier after 5 or more weeks of treatment than they do with less.

Some of the genotypes of the Wixford railway track population, however, do have a definite requirement for a period of low temperature before they will flower, but we note that, as in the previous experiment, these are very much in a minority and that none appear to require more than 5 weeks of treatment. We again note that even those genotypes which have no requirement, nevertheless appear to respond to treatment, for the material which has been subjected to 11 weeks of low temperature treatment comes into flower earlier than any that has received less.

The effect of low temperature treatment, however, is most clearly seen on the material from Winnats Pass. In this

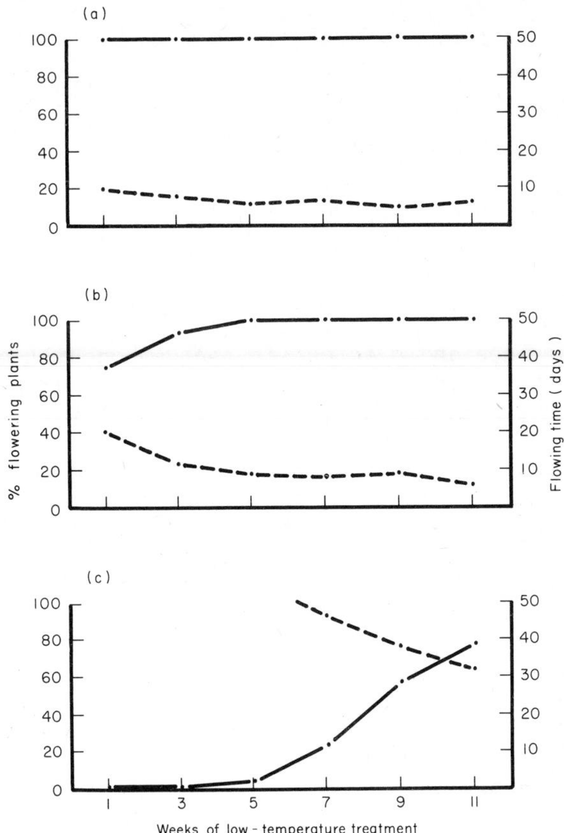

FIGURE 4. The effect of low-temperature treatment on flowering in *Arabidopsis*. The full lines show the percentages (left ordinate) and the broken lines the average flowering times (right ordinate) of those individuals which were induced to flower during the experiment. Material is from (a) Cannon Hill Park, Birmingham, (b) a railway track at Wixford, Warwickshire and (c) from Winnats Pass, Derbyshire.

population, no genotype will flower unless it has received at least 3 weeks of treatment and 23 % fail to come into flower after even 11 weeks of low temperature treatment. Indeed, subsequent experience with this population has shown that it is necessary to treat the germinating seed for not less than 16 weeks if all genotypes are to be brought into flower.

While there can be little doubt that the low temperature requirements of the material from these three populations reflects their diverse origin, it is less easy to account for these differences in a satisfactory way. For example, we note that the low temperature requirement appears to be related to average winter temperature, for it can hardly be doubted that, on average, winters are more severe on the exposed slopes of Winnats Pass than they are in the more sheltered habitat of Cannon Hill park in Birmingham. Yet if the chief purpose of a requirement for low temperature is to prevent flowering of a winter annual in an autumn mild enough to otherwise allow it, the need for such a requirement appears to be *least* in the Winnats Pass and *greatest* in the Cannon Hill park population; in other words, the converse of the situation we find in this British material.

Interestingly enough, some results from an investigation of cold requirement in a number of Czechoslovakian populations of *Arabidopsis thaliana* by Cetl, Dobrovolna and Effmertova (1965, 1967) appear to accord with this expectation, at least in part. Thus, these workers found that "winter annual" populations (those with a definite requirement for low temperature treatment) were found only in the warmer, drier lowlands (below 300 m above sea-level), whereas populations of the "summer annual" type occurred higher up in the hills of Western Moravia in colder, wetter habitats (above 400 m). Populations of the "mixed" type were found in an intermediate altitudinal position.

However, Effmertova (1967) further showed that the after-ripening requirement of a sample of the "summer annual" populations was less, on average, than that of the "winter annual" populations. If this observation is taken at its face value, it suggests that these Czechoslovakian populations of "summer annuals" are in fact populations of ephemerals whose seed is capable of rapid germination soon after it has been shed and in which, since the individuals have no cold requirement, are potentially capable of producing more than one generation per annum. Thus, interesting though these results from Czechoslovakian populations undoubtedly are, they nevertheless fall outside the scope of the argument that was advanced earlier about the purpose of cold requirement in populations of *A. thaliana* because, as we recall, this argument concerned differences between populations of *winter* rather than summer annuals.

The British material, on the other hand, does appear to be of the winter annual type. Thus, Jones (1968a), who examined the after-ripening requirement of seed from a pair of Derbyshire, a pair of railway track and a pair of park populations found that seed from the former would germinate sooner after harvest than that from the park populations (Fig. 5). Since the germination of the seed from these park populations was still less than 10 % even after more than two months from harvest, germination in the natural habitat would, on this evidence, be delayed until the early autumn at least when, because of the lower light intensities and temperatures, as well as the shorter day-lengths which obtain at this time of the year, flowering would not take place even though plants are otherwise capable of doing so.

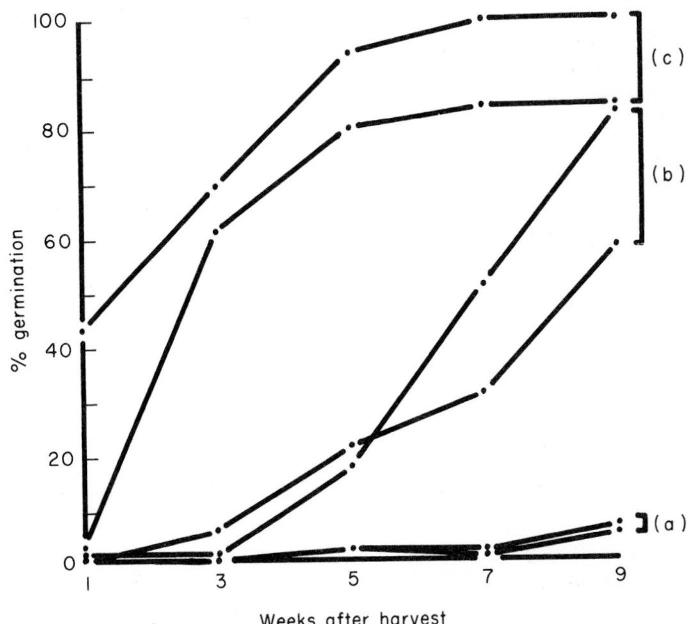

FIGURE 5. Germination and time after harvest. Material from (a) Cannon Hill Park and University Botanic Gardens, Birmingham, (b) railway tracks at Rubery and Hunnington, Worcestershire and (c) Millers Dale and Eaton, Derbyshire.

On the other hand, the seed from these Derbyshire populations appears to be able to germinate within a month of it being shed, for it has much less innate dormancy than seed from the park populations. However, observation of the behaviour of natural populations of *A. thaliana* in Derbyshire (Ratcliffe, 1961; Snape, 1973) shows that germination does not generally take place until early autumn. This further delay in germination is apparently brought about by an enforced dormancy of the seed. Though the factors which induce this dormancy are not well understood, it appears to enable seedlings to avoid the severe fluctuations in soil moisture which occur in summer in the thin soils which overlie these freely-draining limestone slopes. This enforced dormancy thus protects the population during a period of the year when its seedlings would otherwise be very clearly at risk.

This experiment of Jones' serves to emphasise the risk which attends any attempt to infer the properties of material in a natural population from the results obtained from laboratory experiments alone. As it happens, we should not have been seriously misled had we been unaware that germination is delayed in natural populations of *A. thaliana* in Derbyshire, because an earlier investigation had established that these were of the winter annual type on the basis of their need for a period of low temperature before flowers are initiated. However, this will not always be the case. For example, though Effmertova's experiments on the after-ripening requirements on the Czechoslovakian material were conducted in pots on soil in the open and not in Petri dishes, on filter paper, in an incubator as in Jones' experiment, it is possible that, in the natural habitats of her "summer annual" and "mixed" races, germination is delayed until autumn in the same way as it is in the Derbyshire populations. But if this were the case, all these Czechoslovakian races would germinate in the autumn and hence all would be regarded as winter annuals. In these circumstances, of course, the behaviour of these populations would be exactly as we expect on the argument that we advanced earlier, the function of a requirement for low temperature treatment being specifically related to the need to avoid the hazard of premature flowering in lowland habitats.

The behaviour of material from British populations of the species cannot in any way, of course, be squared with this view. Indeed, it is possible that a vernalisation requirement in Derbyshire material is but one aspect of a more general physiological adaptation to these exposed habitats, rather than a specific response to one aspect of the environment; this is clearly a matter for future investigation.

Be this as it may, and we are clearly unable to verify these speculations one way or another on the evidence presently available, there is little doubt that populations of *A. thaliana* that are found in different habitats show a particularly marked differentiation in respect of their properties.

Variation within Populations

Though we may as yet be unable to account, in a satisfactory way, for the differences we find between populations from different types of habitat, it can hardly be doubted that these differences have arisen as the result of the different effects of natural selection in the different environments in which we find this species. Selection, however, can produce such effects if, and only if, there are heritable differences between the individuals of a population with respect to traits of adaptive significance. It is appropriate, therefore, to conclude this review of variation in *Arabidopsis thaliana* with a discussion of the evidence of variation within natural populations of the species.

There is, of course, much evidence of heritable variation within many natural populations of *A. thaliana* . Thus Napp-Zinn (1964), Cetl (1965), Dobrovolna (1967) have shown that there is heritable variation within populations with respect to a number of developmental characters such as the percentage of generative plants in material which has a cold requirement but which has been given less than the amount required to induce all individuals in the sample to flower; the number of days to the appearance of flower primordia; rosette width and the number of rosette leaves. In this country, Jones (1968a, 1971a, b, c) and Snape (1973) have similarly demonstrated the presence of heritable variation in samples from natural populations from all three types of habitat with respect to a number of metrical characters such as flowering time, rosette width, basal leaf number, height at flowering time, number of siliquae, seed dormancy and response to cold treatment in both natural families as well as those produced by the systematic crossing of individuals in breeding experiments. There is thus no shortage of evidence to show that there is heritable variation within natural populations of *A. thaliana*. Furthermore, in the light of the evidence presented earlier concerning the breeding system of this species, it is clear that most of this heritable variation falls to differences between, rather than within, natural families of individuals. In other words, a population of this predominantly self-pollinating species consists of a heterogeneous collection of semi-inbred lines.

Now the chief purpose of this kind of experiment is to produce information with which to attempt to understand the action and hence the effects of natural selection in populations of this species. In some circumstances, it may be possible to ascertain the effects of selection directly by appropriate observation of the natural population in situ. In general, however, this will be a far from easy task, especially when variation, with respect to metrical characters, is the chief point of interest. However, Mather (1966) has proposed that it is possible to deduce the type of selection acting on a trait given a knowledge of the genetical architecture of this trait. Thus, a character that has been subject to directional selection, the type of selection where one or other of the extremes of the distribution is favoured, would be expected to manifest strong directional dominance and where non-allelic interaction were also present, that this would be expected to be of the duplicate type. Fitness traits, such as viability, fertility and fecundity, are obvious examples of traits which, in most circumstances, must be subject to directional selection.

On the other hand, a character subject to stabilising selection, where intermediate rather than extreme phenotypes are favoured, would display mostly additive genetical variation with little or no dominance, such dominance as is present being ambidirectional in nature. Furthermore, characters under stabilising selection are not expected to manifest much non-allelic interaction.

These predictions concerning the relationship between the genetical architecture of a character and the type of selection acting on it have now been confirmed in a number of cases (see, for example, Kearsey and Kojima, 1967). We may, therefore, examine such evidence as is available in *A. thaliana* with a view to attempting some conclusions about the type of natural selection which appears, on this argument, to be acting on characters in populations of this species.

Now, though the experiments on Czechoslovakian populations of Dobrovolna (1968, 1969) and of Cetl and Relichova (1971) were not of the type which permits the separation of additive from non-additive genetical effects, they nevertheless yielded estimates of heritability for number of days to flower primordia and number of rosette leaves which were of the order of 0.5, those of the first character being, on average, larger than those of the second. Heritabilities of this magnitude, particularly since some are estimates of narrow heritability, are not expected for traits subject to directional selection. Thus, though this evidence is incomplete, these traits appear to be subject to stabilising, rather than to directional, selection in these Czechoslovakian populations.

Jones (1968a) on the other hand, carried out a genetical analysis of variation in material from the Cannon Hill population by means of the diallel cross method, which does permit the partition of the total genetical variation into an additive and a non-additive proportion. She found that the character, flowering time (which is similar to number of days to the appearance of flower primordia), displayed strong unidirectional dominance for early flowering, which suggests that in this population the character is subject to directional selection for early flowering. This is an unusual outcome, for flowering time is usually found to display either little dominance, or dominance of the ambidirectional kind, both in this (see below) and many other species. However, late flowering individuals in this population might well be at risk because of seasonal cultivation by gardeners in this park, for many of the borders are replanted for the summer season a few weeks after *A. thaliana* comes into flower there.

Snape (1973), who investigated a Derbyshire population, found that all three of the characters that he studied, namely flowering time, basal leaf number and siliqua number, displayed ambidirectional dominance and appear, therefore, to be subject to stabilising selection. This is expected with flowering time, for in general plants which flower very early are at a greater risk from poor weather than are those which flower later, particularly in *A. thaliana*, which comes into flower earlier than most species in Britain and elsewhere. Conversely, individuals that flower very late may be unable to produce much seed before their growth and development are abruptly curtailed at the onset of drought in late spring.

Siliqua number, on the other hand, being clearly a component of fitness, is expected at first sight to be subject to directional selection and hence display strong, directional dominance. However, in general, selection cannot favour individuals that produce a very large number of siliqua if, in doing so, the quality of the seed is thereby impaired. In other words, it is possible that plants which produce most siliquae may not produce most seed. In these circumstances, the effects of selection would, of course, be of the stabilising type.

CONCLUSIONS

Now these conclusions about the type of selection which acts on the traits in question in the natural populations of this species take us only part of the way, of course, towards the goal of an understanding of the factors which maintain these metrical polymorphisms.

For example, the results we have been discussing concern experiments which have been carried out in a laboratory environment for the simple reason that it is not possible to perform any kind of genetical analysis with respect to metrical characters unless families of individuals can be recognised and the environment in which these individuals are reared is subject to statistical control. These requirements can be met only in the laboratory. Yet, as is well known, *Arabidopsis thaliana* is rather sensitive to a variable environment and not infrequently displays genotype-environment interaction (Griffing and Langridge, 1962; Pederson, 1968; Griffing and Zsiros, 1971; Westerman and Lawrence, 1970; Westerman, 1971a, b, c). Thus, while there is no doubt that individuals in natural populations differ in respect of, for example, their flowering time, height and siliqua number, in view of this evidence of fairly widespread genotype-environment interaction in the species, we cannot be certain that the genetical variation we detect in the laboratory is expressed in the same way in the natural environment of the species.

In the one case where this matter has been examined at all critically, Snape (1973) found that the relationship between performance in the laboratory and performance in the natural environment was positive in respect of flowering time; that there was no relationship in respect of two vegetative characters, basal leaf number and plant height; and that the relationship was actually negative in respect of siliqua number—despite the fact that all four traits display heritable variation in the laboratory (as it happens, this finding does not materially affect our earlier conclusions about the type of selection acting on siliqua number, though this could not, of course, be predicted in advance of this information).

Lastly, the results of these experiments do not tell us *why* it is advantageous for populations of *A. thaliana* to maintain these metrical polymorphisms, only that this apparently is the case. This is, of course, much the most difficult part of the problem to investigate and is, therefore, that part of the population biology of *A. thaliana* about which we know least. However, the experiments we have reviewed in the previous sections of this paper do at least have the merit of persuading us that, since the traits we have considered appear to be subject to selection, despite the effort required, it is worth attempting to identify the physical and biotic factors of the natural environment which maintain these polymorphisms.

REFERENCES

Arabidopsis Information Service Newsletter. (1964) ed. Röbbelen, G. Institut für Pflanzenbau und Pflanzenzüchtung der Universität, Göttingen. No. 1 onwards.

Clapham, A. R., Tutin, T. G. and Warburg, E. F. (1962). "Flora of the British Isles", Cambridge University Press.

Cetl, I. (1965). *In* "Arabidopsis Research", Rep Int.Symp., Göttingen, (G. Röbbelen, ed.), pp. 46 - 52.

Cetl, I. and Dobrovolná, J. (1968). *Arabidopsis Information Service* 5, 15 - 16.

Cetl, I., Dobrovolná, J. and Effmertová, E. (1965). *Arabidopsis Information Service.* 2, 3.

Cetl, I., Dobrovolná, J. and Effmertová, E. (1967). *Arabidopsis Information Service.* 4, 9 - 10.

Cetl, I., Dobrovolná, J. and Effmertová, E. (1973). *Arabidopsis Information Service.* 10, 35 - 36.

Cetl, I. and Relichová, J. (1971). *Arabidopsis Information Service.* 8, 4.

Dobrovolná, J. (1967). *Arabidopsis Information Service.* 4, 6 - 7.

Dobrovolná, J. (1968). *Arabidopsis Information Service.* 5, 17.

Dobrovolná, J. (1969). *Arabidopsis Information Service.* 6, 20.

Effmertová, E. (1967). *Arabidopsis Information Service.* 4, 8 - 9.

Effmertová, E. and Cetl, I. (1968). *Arabidopsis Information Service.* 5, 16.

Griffing, B. and Langridge, J. (1962). *In* "Statistical Genetics and Plant Breeding". Nat.Acad.Sci. and Nat.Res. Council Publ. No. 982, pp. 368 - 394. Washington.

Griffing, B. and Zsiros, E. (1971). *Genetics* 68, 443 - 455.

Karbe, C. and Röbbelen, G. (1968). *Arabidopsis Information Service.* 5, 13 - 15.

Kearsey, M. J. and Kojima, K. (1967). *Genetics* 56, 23 - 37.

Jones, M. E. (1968a). "Biometrical studies of variation in wild populations of *Arabidopsis*". Ph.D. thesis, University of Birmingham.

Jones, M. E. (1968b). *Arabidopsis Information Service.* 5, 11 - 13.

Jones, M. E. (1971a). *Heredity* 27, 39 - 50.

Jones, M. E. (1971b). *Heredity* 27, 51 - 58.

Jones, M. E. (1971c). *Heredity* 27, 59 - 72.

Laibach, F. (1943). *Bot.Arch.* 44, 439 - 455.

Mather, K. (1966). *Proc.Roy.Soc.B.* 164, 328 - 340.

Napp-Zinn, K. (1964). *Beiträge zur Phytologie, Festschrift H. Walter,* (K. Krub, ed.), pp. 33 - 49. Ulmer, Stuttgart.

Pederson, D. G. (1968). *Heredity* 23, 127 - 138.

Perring, F. M. and Walters, S. M. (eds) (1962). "Atlas of the British Flora". Nelson, London for the B.S.B.I.

Ratcliffe, D. (1961). *J.Ecol.* 49, 187 - 203.

Redei, G. P. (1970). "Arabidopsis thaliana (L.) Heynh. A review of the genetics and biology". Bibliographia Genetica XX, No. 2. Martinus Nijhoff, The Hague.

Ross-Craig, S. (1949). "Drawings of British Plants. Part III. Cruciferae". Bell, London.

Snape, J. W. (1973). "Population and biometrical genetics of Arabidopsis thaliana: A study of a single population". Ph.D. thesis, University of Birmingham.

Snape, J. W. and Lawrence, M. J. (1971). *Heredity* 27, 299 - 302.

Trojan, R. (1971). *Arabidopsis Information Service.* 8, 5.

Westerman, J. M. (1971a). *Heredity* 26, 93 - 106.

Westerman, J. M. (1971b). *Heredity* 26, 373 - 382.

Westerman, J. M. (1971c). *Heredity* 26, 383 - 395.

Westerman, J. M. and Lawrence, M. J. (1970). *Heredity* 25, 609 - 627.

PROPERTIES AND FUNCTION OF PLANT MYROSINASES

R. BJÖRKMAN

Pharmacia Fine Chemicals AB, Uppsala, Sweden

INTRODUCTION

Myrosinases are a group of enzymes which for a long time have been known to split the naturally occurring mustard oil glucosides, for example sinigrin, into pungent mustard oils. The International Union of Biochemistry has recommended the name thioglucoside glucohydrolase, E.C. 3.2.3.1.

The enzyme was discovered by Bussy as early as in 1839. In a report about the formation of mustard oils he described the isolation of a substance with properties similar to those of albumin, which he called myrosyn. This substance was involved in the hydrolysis of sinigrin (Bussy, 1840).

In 1897 Gadamer suggested a structure for the substrate sinigrin. The formula was derived from the discovery that when black mustard seeds were crushed in the presence of water, allyl isothiocyanate, glucose and potassium bisulphate were formed:

$$CH_2{=}CH{-}CH_2{-}N{=}C\begin{matrix}\diagup S{-}C_6H_{11}O_5\\ \diagdown O{-}SO_3K\end{matrix} + H_2O \longrightarrow CH_2{=}CH{-}CH_2{-}NCS + KHSO_4 + C_6H_{12}O_6$$

This formula was considered valid until 1956 when Ettlinger and Lundeen proved that the correct formula for sinigrin should be:

$$CH_2{=}CH{-}CH_2{-}C\begin{matrix} \diagup S{-}C_6H_{11}O_5 \\ \diagdown\!\!\diagdown N{-}O{-}SO_3K \end{matrix}$$

They suggested that the isothiocyanates are formed by a Lossen rearrangement initiated by enzymic removal of the glycosyl group. This structure has later been verified by chemical synthesis of various mustard oil glucosides (Ettlinger and Lundeen, 1957) and by X-ray crystallography (Waser and Watson, 1963).

The question as to whether the hydrolysis of glucosinolates is carried out with a single enzyme or with a mixture of two entities, a sulphatase and thioglucosidase, has been discussed for several years. The two-enzyme hypothesis was first proposed by von Euler and Erikson in 1926. A few years later Neuberg and von Schoenebeck (1933) claimed that they had separated the two enzymes. The latest report that the myrosinases had been separated into two enzymes was published by Gaines and Goering (1960, 1962). However, their results could not be reproduced by later investigators (Calderon *et al.*, 1966). This view is in contrast to the single enzyme mechanism postulated by Ettlinger and Lundeen (1956). Since then several investigators have tried, in vain, to separate the sulphatase and the thioglucosidase by various chromatographic methods. Today it is considered quite clear that the myrosinase is a single enzyme, a thioglucosidase in the sense of Ettlinger and Lundeen.

Another feature of the myrosinase action was the discovery by Nagashima and Uchiyama (1959) that the enzyme is strongly activated by ascorbic acid.

OCCURRENCE

As mentioned previously myrosinase and glucosinolates were first discovered in mustard seed. Today we know that they are present in a variety of plants. The enzyme appears always to be accompanied with one or more glucosinolates. They occur in all Cruciferae species examined, but have also been found in Resedaceae, Capparidaceae, Tropaeolaceae (Snowden and Gaines, 1969), Limnantraceae and Caricaceae (Tang, 1973). Enzymes with myrosinase activity have also been found in fungi (*Aspergillus sydowi*)(Reese *et al.*, 1968, Ohtsuru *et al.*, 1969), bacteria (*Paracorobactrum aerogenoides*)(Oginsky *et al.*, 1965), in mammalian tissues (Goodman *et al.*, 1959), and in the cabbage aphid (*Brevicoryne brassicae*)(MacGibbon and Allison, 1968).

The amount of myrosinase activity found in *Sinapis alba* and some *Brassica* species and cultivars has been investigated by Henderson and McEwen (1972) and by Björkman and Lönnerdal (1973). The results from the two groups were rather similar. We thus found that the activity was about ten times higher in *S. alba* than in *B. napus* and *B. campestris*. A certain variation was also found between the various varieties of the latter species (Fig. 1).

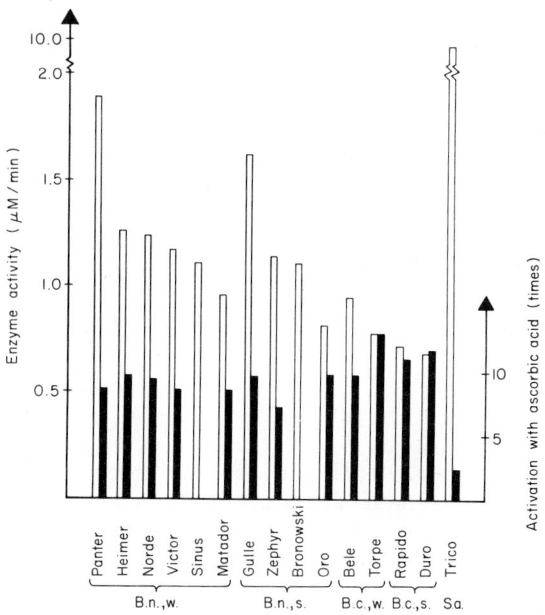

FIGURE 1. Myrosinase activity (unfilled staples) and relative degree of ascorbic acid activation (filled staples) in seed extracts of *Sinapis alba* (S.a.) and various cultivars of *Brassica napus* (B.n.) and *B. campestris* (B.c.). w = winter type; s = summer type. The assays were carried out with 0.12 mM sinigrin at pH 5.5 and 23°C. Assays on the degree of activation of myrosinases in Sinus and Bronowski were not included in this investigation. (From Björkman and Lönnerdal, 1973)

The cytochemical localization of myrosinase in the root tips of *S. alba* was demonstrated by Iversen (1970) with electron microscopic methods. He incubated the tissue with sinigrin in the presence of Pb^{2+} ions. The sulphate liberated from the sinigrin by the enzyme formed the insoluble electron dense $PbSO_4$ which he could localize mainly to the dilated cisternae of the endoplasmic reticulum, but also to some extent to the mitochondria.

ISOENZYMES

The existence of multiple forms of myrosinase has been shown in many plants. By analytical gel electrophoresis various authors have demonstrated the separation of several myrosinase isoenzymes. MacGibbon and Allison (1970) also found different patterns depending on whether the extracts were made from leaf, stem, root or seed. The immunoelectrophoretic experiments performed by Vaughan and Gordon (1969) also indicate the existence of serologically different forms of myrosinases.

Recent experiments performed on a preparative scale in Uppsala (Björkman and Janson, 1972, Lönnerdal and Janson, 1973) and in Kyoto (Ohtsuru and Hata, 1972) describe the complete isolation and some characterization of different myrosinase isoenzymes from *S. alba*, *B. napus* and *B. juncea*. This existence of several multiple forms or isoenzymes of myrosinase may be very useful in chemotaxonomic studies.

ASCORBIC ACID

In 1961 Ettlinger *et al.* in Houston reported that they had separated two myrosinase isoenzymes from yellow mustard seed (*S. alba*) by an extraction procedure. The enzyme activity of one of the components was indifferent to ascorbic acid. The other myrosinase, on the other hand, required ascorbic acid for activity. The activity was thereby enhanced about 400 times.

About six years later Tsuruo *et al.* (1967) in Kyoto reported a chromatographic separation of two myrosinases from *B. juncea* on TEAE-cellulose ion exchanger. They found, however, that both components were identical with respect to ascorbic acid activation, mechanism (i.e. both were pure β-thioglucosidases) and other enzymic properties.

In 1972 several reports, partly contradictory, on the ascorbic acid activation of myrosinase isoenzymes were published independently. Vose (1972) described the separation of two myrosinases from yellow mustard seed (*S. alba*). The fractionation was carried out on a LKB-electrofocusing column. He found that one of the myrosinases was only slightly affected by ascorbic acid while the other was greatly stimulated by this agent. He also found differences in their response to increased reaction temperatures. When he performed the fractionation according to Tsuruo *et al.* (1967) with DEAE- and TEAE-cellulose columns he also obtained two myrosinase fractions, but contrary to Tsuruo *et al.* he found that one of the myrosinases was strongly activated while the other was slightly inhibited by ascorbic acid.

Björkman and Janson (1972) reported the separation of three myrosinases from yellow mustard seed (*S. alba*) by ion exchange chromatography, gel filtration and preparative isoelectric focusing. Experiments on their activation by ascorbic acid showed that they were all activated by ascorbic acid concentrations up to 1 mM. The activity of the major component was increased about four times while the activities of the other two components were increased about twenty and forty times respectively.

In 1972 Henderson and McEwen reported the effect of ascorbic acid on myrosinase isoenzymes from various oilseeds. The experiments were performed in an analytical scale using polyacrylamide gel electrophoresis. The enzyme activity was developed both in the absence and presence of ascorbic acid. Concerning the yellow mustard seed (*S. alba*) enzyme preparation they found that one of the components was unaffected by ascorbic acid but at least one was activated. In rapeseed (*B. napus*) they also found several isoenzymes which all gave positive response to ascorbic acid.

Ohtsuru and Hata (1972) in Japan described the purification of four myrosinase isoenzymes from mustard seed powder. The activity of one of them was reported to be increased about fifty times and the other three about a hundred times by ascorbic acid. It is, however, difficult to compare figures on the activity from one report to another since the degree of activity obtained also depends on the concentration of substrate used in the assay.

ISOLATION AND PURIFICATION

The complete isolation of a protein is a prerequisite for the determination of its structure and several of its physicochemical and chemical properties.

Partially purified myrosinase preparations were obtained by the use of cellulose ion exchange columns by Gaines and Goering (1962), Tsuruo *et al.* (1967) etc. In 1972 some authors independently reported the complete isolation of myrosinases. Björkman and Janson (1972) obtained a completely purified myrosinase from *S. alba* by a combination of ion exchange chromatography on DEAE-cellulose, gel filtration on Sephadex G-200 and isoelectric focusing in a density- and pH-gradient. The enzyme was found to be homogeneous with all the analytical methods used, viz. electrophoresis on polyacrylamide gel at pH 2.5 and 10, isoelectric focusing on polyacrylamide gel, free zone electrophoresis according to Hjertén and ultra centrifugation. Besides the myrosinase described, another two myrosinase isoenzymes were separated by the ion exchange step. These were, however, obtained in a less pure state.

Ohtsuru and Hata (1972) reported the complete purification of four myrosinase isoenzymes from mustard powder. They used ion exchange chromatography on DEAE-Sephadex A-50 at pH 7 and 8.5, CM-Sephadex at pH 5 and gel filtration on Sephadex G-200. All the isoenzymes were found to be homogeneous on disc electrophoresis on polyacrylamide gels and ultracentrifugation.

Recently another report from Uppsala (Lönnerdal and Janson, 1973) described the complete isolation of a myrosinase from rapeseed (*B. napus)*. Essentially the same methods as described earlier for the *S. alba* myrosinase were used. In this work the separation of another three isoenzymes was obtained.

PHYSICO-CHEMICAL DATA AND STRUCTURE

Physico-chemical characterisation of pure myrosinase preparations from different plant sources show a small but significant variation among the myrosinase isoenzymes. All myrosinases investigated were found to be glycoproteins containing from about 9 to 23 % of carbohydrates, with a molecular weight from about 125,000 to over 150,000. Their isoelectric points vary between 4.6 and 6.2.

The myrosinase isolated from yellow mustard seed (*S. alba*) (Björkman and Janson, 1972) had an isoelectric point at pH 5.08 and a molecular weight of 151,000. The molecule contained 18 % carbohydrates, principally hexoses. The only aminosugar detected was glucosamine. Molecular sieving in 6 M guanidinium hydrochloride after complete reduction and alkylation of the enzyme indicated that the molecule was composed of two identical subunits, each having a molecular weight of about 62,000 with reference to amino acids. The other two myrosinases from the same source had their isoelectric points at pH 5.45 and 5.9 respectively, and the molecular weights were found to be approximately 145,000 and 135,000 respectively, as determined by gel filtration on Sephadex G-200.

Lönnerdal and Janson (1973) in Uppsala isolated a myrosinase from rapeseed (*B. napus*) with a molecular weight of 135,000, containing about 14 % of carbohydrates. Reduction and alkylation, with subsequent molecular sieving on Sepharose 6 B in 6 M guanidinium hydrochloride indicated that the molecule was composed of two polypeptide chains each having a molecular weight of about 65,000. The carbohydrate part was shown to be shared between the two polypeptide chains. This enzyme could be separated into three isoenzymes with similar isoelectric points, viz. 4.96, 4.99 and 5.06. This disparity is probably due to a variation in carbohydrate content and composition. The three isoenzymes contained 9.3, 15.2 and 17.4 % respectively of carbohydrates. They also found three more myrosinases in *B. napus* having the isoelectric points 6.2, 5.6 and 4.9. These isoenzymes were, however, not purified completely and characterized further.

The four myrosinases isolated by Ohtsuru and Hata (1972) from mustard powder were also found to be glycoproteins, containing 15.8, 17.8, 22.5 and 8.6 % of hexoses. Of these the first three were very similar with respect to molecular weight, sedimentation coefficient and isoelectric point, which were 153,000, 6.8 and 4.6 respectively. Also the amino acid compositions were very similar. The fourth myrosinase with a hexose content of 8.6 % was a smaller enzyme with a molecular weight of about 125,000, a sedimentation coefficient of 5.8 and an isoelectric point at pH 4.8. The amino acid composition showed significant deviations from those of the other three. The number of subunits for the four enzymes was determined by analytical electrophoresis in SDS-polyacrylamide gel. The authors found the molecular weights of the subunits to be about 40,000 and 30,000 respectively, and claim that the enzymes will thus contain at least four subunits. This finding disagrees with the results obtained in Uppsala. Unfortunately, the authors do not specify which species of mustard seed they had used in their investigation. Such information would have been of great value for a comparison of the results. In any case, this discrepancy in the results concerning the number of subunits is not satisfactory if the isoenzymes are considered to have a common genetic origin. Table 1 shows some physico-chemical data for a few myrosinases.

Table 1

Physico-chemical data for purified myrosinases

	*S. alba**	*B. napus***	Mustard powder***	
Molecular weight	151,000	135,000	152,000	125,000
Number of subunits	2	2	4	4
Subunits m.w.	62,000	65,000	40,000	30,000
Carbohydrates %	18	14	15.8/17.8/22.5	8.6
Isoelectric point	5.08	5.0	4.6	4.8

* Björkman and Janson, 1972.
** Lönnerdal and Janson, 1973.
*** Ohtsuru and Hata, 1972

ENZYMIC PROPERTIES

The most widely used substrate in the study of the enzymatic properties of myrosinases is sinigrin. But, of course, also the other 60 naturally occurring glucosinolates can act as substrates. A comparative study of the relative activities on six different glucosinolates with myrosinase isoenzymes from *S. alba* and *B. napus* was presented by Björkman and Lönnerdal (1973). The six glucosinolates examined here, listed with decreasing activity, were glucotropaeolin, sinigrin, glucocheirolin, progoitrin, glucosinalbin and glucocapparin (Fig. 2).

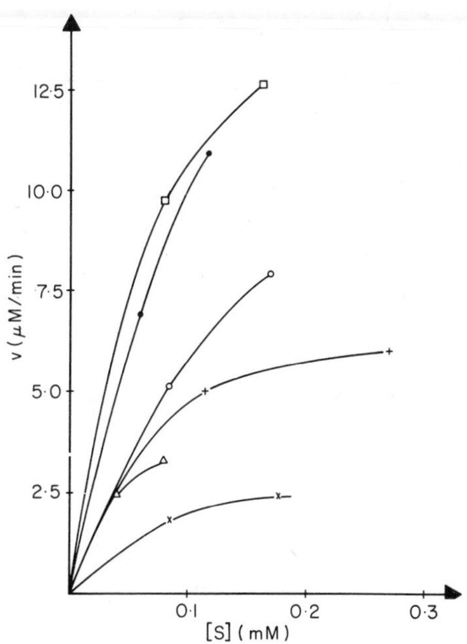

FIGURE 2. Activity of myrosinase from *S. alba* on various glucosinolates (pH 5.5, 23°C). □ = glucotropaeolin, ● = sinigrin, ○ = glucocheirolin, + = progoitrin, Δ = glucosinalbin, x = glucocapparin. (From Björkman and Lönnerdal, 1973).

No significant variation was found between the isoenzymes. Thus, the myrosinases from different seeds are not specifically adapted to a particular set of glucosinolates. Many authors have tested several other non-glucosinolate glucosides as substrates for the myrosinase. Among these only *p*-

nitrophenyl glucoside (*p*-NPG) and *o*-nitrophenyl-β-galactoside were hydrolysed by myrosinase (Reese *et al.*, 1958).

The enzymatic hydrolysis of sinigrin yields the volatile mustard oil, allyl isothiocyanate. The major glucosinolate in rapeseed and some other species is called progoitrin. It has an hydroxyl group in 2-position from the central carbon atom. When progoitrin is enzymically hydrolysed it also forms an isothiocyanate, the 2-hydroxy-3-butenyl isothiocyanate. This compound is, however, unstable and cyclizes spontaneously to form L-5-vinyl oxazolidine-2-thione, also called goitrin due to its goitrogenic properties.

The data for the pH optima for the enzymes vary from one report to another, but generally figures between 4 and 7 are reported. Some investigators have found rather sharp maxima, while others have obtained a broad plateau. Those differences are probably partly due to differences in the conditions in the reaction mixture, such as concentration, ionic strength, kind of buffer, temperature, substrate, etc. and partly due to differences in purity and origin of the enzyme. At our laboratory we obtained different pronounced pH optima for different isoenzymes from *S. alba* and *B. napus*, all between pH 4 and 5.5 in citrate buffer (Björkman and Lönnerdal, 1973).

The reaction rate increases with temperature until about 60 - 65°C. Above this temperature denaturation of the enzyme starts. Vose (1972) however, found differences in the temperature dependence between two isoenzymes. One had its maximum at 75°C and the other, which required ascorbic acid for activity, at 45°C. This difference may, however, be due to effects from the ascorbic acid present, in one way or another.

The effect of ascorbic acid has been investigated by several authors, since 1959 when Nagashima and Uchiyama found that ascorbic acid acted as a cofactor for myrosinase. It is today clear that different myrosinase isoenzymes have different responses to ascorbic acid, while the activities of others are increased by factors up to several hundred.

When ascorbic acid is added both the K_m and the V_{max} are increased, i.e. the affinity of the enzyme for the substrate (sinigrin) is decreased while the maximal reaction rate is increased. This is not the normal behaviour of a positive effector.

The mechanism for the ascorbic acid action is still not fully known. The optimal concentration of ascorbic acid has been found to be about 1 mM for all isoenzymes tested. When larger amounts are added it acts as an inhibitor. In ascorbic acid concentrations of about 5 - 10 mM the enzymic activity has been found to be essentially absent (Fig. 3).

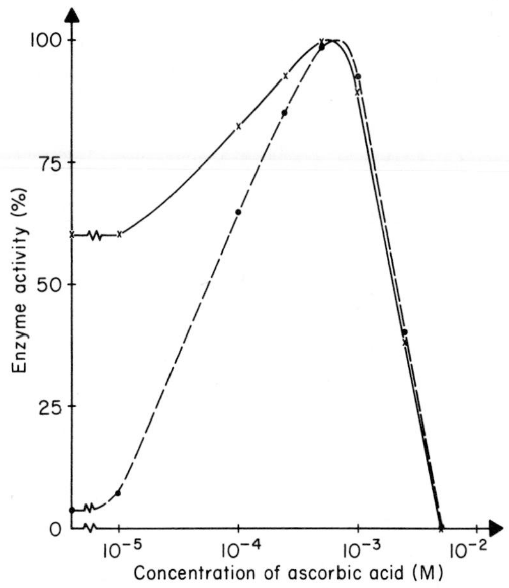

FIGURE 3. The effect of ascorbic acid concentration on the activation of myrosinase. The assays were carried out at 23°C with 0.12 mM sinigrin at pH 5.5. X = myrosinase from *S. alba*; ● = myrosinase from *B. napus*. (From Björkman and Lönnerdal, 1973).

Equilibrium dialysis experiments indicated that an unusually large amount of ascorbic acid molecules can be bound to the myrosinase molecule. The equilibrium constant was determined to be about 50 000 M^{-1}, shared by as much as 22 ligands (Björkman and Lönnerdal, 1973).

The effect of ascorbic acid on myrosinase is not considered to be due to the oxidation-reduction properties of ascorbic acid. Ettlinger *et al.* (1961) investigated the effect of several ascorbic acid analogues. They found that many of the analogues, for example 2-O-methyl-L-ascorbate, also acted as coenzymes, however, with smaller activation factors than L-ascorbate itself. The results of later investigators also support the theory that the activation is not an oxidation-reduction phenomenon. Recently Ohtsuru and Hata (1973b) published results which showed that the effect of ascorbic acid is not due to a dissociation-association mechanism of the enzyme subunits either. They conclude that the activation is due to a slight conformational change of the protein.

Reese *et al.* (1958) showed that *p*-nitrophenyl-β-glucoside (*p*-NPG) can act as a substrate for the myrosinase. Later Tsuruo and Hata (1968) found that this sytem was not activated by ascorbic acid. With high ascorbic acid concentrations, however, an inhibitory effect was observed and also when *p*-NPG was used as a substrate.

These results contributed to the hypothesis for enzyme action, put forward by Tsuruo and Hata in 1968. They postulated the presence of one site of action for the substrate, and two sites for the effector. The substrate site has two moieties, one for the glycone and one for the aglycone part of the glucosinolate. The conformation of the glycone moiety is altered when the ascorbic acid site is occupied, so that the glucosinolate fits better in its site. Higher concentrations of ascorbic acid have an inhibiting effect on the enzyme because the second ascorbic acid site is the same as the substrate site (glycone moiety). When *p*-NPG is used as a substrate it is not affected by moderate concentrations of ascorbic acid, since it does not occupy the aglucone moiety of the site.

Investigations on the functional groups have shown that the enzyme is a so called SH-enzyme. Complete inactivation has been obtained with the SH-reagents *p*-mercuri-benzoate (PCMB) and 5-5′-dithio-bis(2-nitrobenzoic acid), also called Ellmans reagent. Ohtsuru and Hata (1973a) found that two of the four SH-groups present in the molecule are necessary for activity. They have also investigated the inhibitory effect of certain specific amino acid reagents and found that amino groups and a histidyl residue may be in the active centre of the enzyme. They state that "activation by ascorbate may be assigned to the conformational changes of myrosinase caused by ascorbate: Even a slight conformational change of myrosinase caused by ascorbate may cause the surface exposition of the amino groups".

REFERENCES

Björkman, R. and Janson, J.-C. (1972). *Biochim.Biophys.Acta* 276, 508 - 518.

Björkman, R. and Lönnerdal, B. (1973). *Biochim.Biophys.Acta* 327, 121 - 131.

Bussy, A. (1840). *Ann.Chem.u.Pharm.* 34, 223 - 230.

Calderon, P., Peterson, C. S. and Mattick, L. R. (1966). *J.Agr.Food Chem.* 14, 665 - 666.

Ettlinger, M. G. and Lundeen, A. J. (1956). *J.Am.Chem.Soc.* 78, 4172 - 4173.

Ettlinger, M. G. and Lundeen, A. J. (1957). *J.Am.Chem.Soc.* 79, 1764 - 1765.

Ettlinger, M. G., Dateo Jr., G. P., Harrison, B. W., Mabry, T. J. and Thompson, C. P. (1961). *Proc.Natl.Acad.Sci.* 47, 1875 - 1880.

von Euler, H. and Erikson, St. E. (1926). *Fermentforschung* 8, 518.

Gadamer, J. (1897). *Ber.chem.Ges.* 30, 2322 - 2327.

Gaines, R. D. and Goering, K. J. (1960). *Biochem.Biophys. Res.Comm.* 2, 207 - 212.

Gaines, R. D. and Goering, K. J. (1962). *Arch.Biochem. Biophys.* 96, 13 - 19.

Goodman, I., Fouts, J. R., Bresnick, E., Menegas, R. and Hitchings, G. H. (1959). *Science* 130, 450 - 451.

Henderson, H. M. and McEwen, T. J. (1972). *Phytochemistry* 11, 3127 - 3133.

Iversen, T.-H. (1970). *Protoplasma* 71, 451 - 466.

Lönnerdal, B. and Janson, J.-C. (1973). *Biochim.Biophys. Acta* 315, 421 - 429.

MacGibbon, D. B. and Allison, R. M. (1968). *N.Z.Jl.Sci.* 11. 440 - 446.

MacGibbon, D. B. and Allison, R. M. (1970). *Phytochemistry* 9, 541 - 544.

Nagashima, Z. and Uchiyama, M. (1959). *Bull.Agr.Chem.Soc. Japan* 23, 555 - 556.

Neuberg, C. and von Schoenebeck, O. (1933). *Naturwissenschaften* 21, 404 - 405.

Oginsky, E. L., Stein, A. E. and Greer, M. A. (1965). *Proc. Soc.Exp.Biol.Med.* 119, 360 - 364.

Ohtsuru, M. and Hata, T. (1972). *Agr.Biol.Chem.* 36, 2459 - 250

Ohtsuru, M. and Hata, T. (1973a). *Agr.Biol.Chem.* 37, 269 - 275.

Ohtsuru, M. and Hata, T. (1973b). *Agr.Biol.Chem.* 37, 1971 - 1972.

Ohtsuru, M., Tsuruo, I. and Hata, T. (1969). *Agr.Biol.Chem.* 33, 1309 - 1314.

Reese, E. T., Clapp, R. C. and Mandels, M. (1958). *Arch. Biochem.Biophys.* 75, 338 - 353.

Snowden, D. R. and Gaines, R. D. (1969). *Phytochemistry* 8, 1649 - 1654.

Tang, C.-S. (1973). *Phytochemistry* 12, 769 - 773.

Tsuruo, I. and Hata, T. (1968). *Agr.Biol.Chem.* 32, 1425 - 1431.

Tsuruo, I., Yoshida, M. and Hata, T. (1967). *Agr.Biol.Chem.* 31, 18 - 26.

Vaughan, J. G. and Gordon, E. I. (1969). *Phytochemistry* 8, 883 - 887.

Vaughan, J. G., Gordon, E. I. and Robinson, D. (1968). *Phytochemistry* 7, 1345 - 1348.

Vose, J. R. (1972). *Phytochemistry* 11, 1649 - 1653.

Waser, J. and Watson, W. H. (1963). *Nature* 198, 1297 - 1298.

GLUCOSINOLATES IN THE CRUCIFERAE

A. KJÆR

Department of Organic Chemistry, The Technical University of Denmark, Lyngby, Denmark

INTRODUCTION

Were one to name any single type of chemical compound as particularly characteristic of the family Cruciferae, the glucosinolates, a collection of organic anions with the uniform structure 1, would be an obvious choice. To these can be attributed the potential pungency of most crucifers, including several species esteemed, for this reason, as condiments, potherbs, and remedies through the ages (mustard, horseradish, cress, etc.). They seem partly responsible also for the undesirable toxic manifestations occasionally observed as a result of the use of crucifer materials in animal, or human, nutrition (e.g. rape, cabbage). Hence, vast economic interests are associated with our understanding of the chemical nature, biosynthetic origin, and botanical distribution of the glucosinolates (1) within the large and important crucifer family.

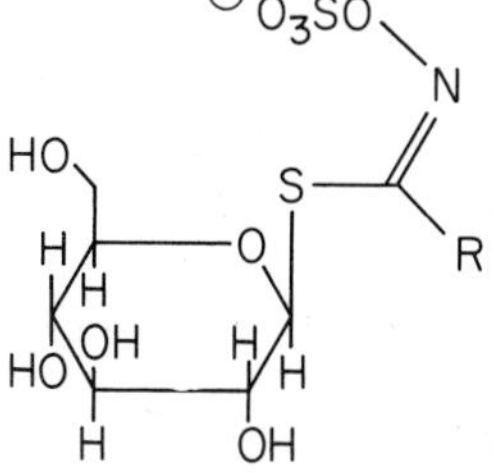

$^{\ominus}O_3SO$ N HO S H O R H OH H HO H H OH

1

For a detailed background of the subject, the reader is directed to earlier reviews: an account of the historical development along with a survey of the individual crucifer species studied up to 1959 for their contents of glucosinolates (Kjær, 1960), supplemented with a more recent and penetrating discussion (Ettlinger and Kjær, 1968), should provide a comprehensive account of the state of affairs by the end of 1967. Information about the chemical structure of novel glucosinolates and, notably, more recent developments in our knowledge of their *in vivo* synthesis has been compiled (Kjær and Olesen Larsen, 1973), and the potential merits of glucosinolates in molecular taxonomy has recently been discussed (Kjær, 1973).

It is the purpose of the present chapter to discuss, on a basis of the extant knowledge, some problems of importance for continued studies within this field.

GLUCOSINOLATES

Chemistry

The class of glucosinolates (1) identified thus far as constituents of higher plants, encompasses more than 70 individual compounds, remarkably uniform in structure, varying solely in the character of the side-chain R. Distributionally, the Cruciferae constitutes a centre of gravity, with more than 60 glucosinolates represented within the family.

Acid hydrolysis of a glucosinolate (1) affords, as expected, hydroxylamine, sulphate, moieties from the thioglucosidic linkage, and the carboxylic acid $R.CO_2H$. On the other hand, hydrolysis, catalyzed by a group of enzymes (myrosinases), separately deposited but invariably accompanying the glucosinolates in the living plant sources, takes a different course. In most cases, enzyme-induced detachment of glucose, producing the aglucone (2) or its tautomer, is followed by molecular rearrangement of the latter yielding, with concomitant loss of sulphate, an isothiocyanate (mustard oil) 3 as the stable end-product.

Under certain circumstances, however, fragmentation of 2 to elemental sulphur and nitriles 4, rather than rearrangement, tends to become a competitive or even major reaction.

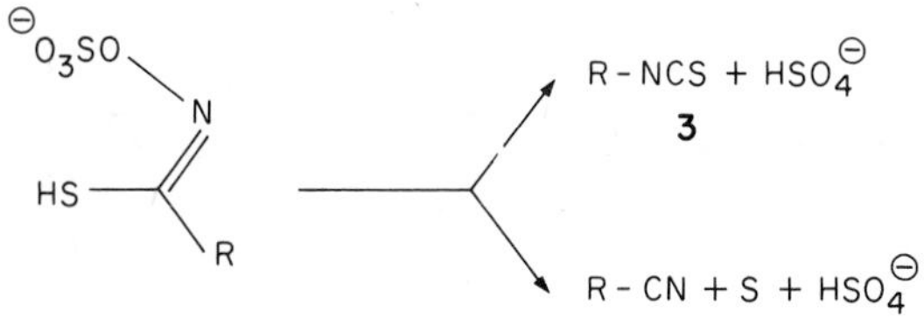

$^{\ominus}O_3SO$—N=C(SH)—R → $R-NCS + HSO_4^{\ominus}$ (3); $R-CN + S + HSO_4^{\ominus}$ (4)

2 3 4

An enzyme-catalyzed degradation within certain crucifers (e.g. *Thlaspi* and *Lepidium* species) of their native glucosinolates (1:R=CH_2:CH.CH_2 and Ph.CH_2, respectively) to produce, partly or entirely, thiocyanates, R.SCN, rather than isothiocyanates 3, remains enigmatic and deserves detailed investigation.

Mustard oils 3, deriving from natural glucosinolates, exhibit great variations as to stability, volatility, pungency, taste, etc. Often, conversion into thioureas, or substituted thioureas, upon reaction with ammonia or amines, has proved expedient in structure elucidation work or for the purpose of characterization. Glucosinolates, hydroxy-substituted in the 2- or 3-position of their side-chains, on enzymic hydrolysis afford isothiocyanates, which, mostly spontaneously, pass into stable, cyclic thionocarbamates, 5 or 6.

Several glucosinolates, including types that occur in important species of the Cruciferae, have been produced by chemical synthesis.

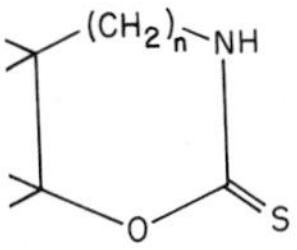

$(CH_2)_n$ NH O S

5 ; n = 0

6 ; n = 1

Occurrence

Authenticated sources of glucosinolates are limited to dicotyledonous angiosperms within which the distribution appears to be discontinuous and, in fact, restricted to a few loci. Foremost amongst these is the order Capparales *sensu* Cronquist (1968) or Takhtajan (1969), comprising, as the major families, the Capparaceae, Cruciferae and Resedaceae. The available evidence suggests that glucosinolates are ubiquitously present within all three families, though not entirely unknown outside the order. For a detailed discussion, recent reviews (Ettlinger and Kjær, 1968; Kjær, 1973) should be consulted.

Within the Cruciferae, generally accepted as a natural taxon composed of about 350 genera and 2500 species, an estimated 300 species have thus far been studied for their contents of glucosinolates. The results, scattered over a vast number of publications, can, to a considerable extent, be tracked down *via* various reviews (Kjær, 1960; Kjær and Olesen Larsen, 1973) and shall not be restated here.

Mostly, various parts of a given crucifer (roots, stems, leaves, inflorescences and fruits) qualitatively display the same pattern. Considerable variation may occur, however, in the absolute, and if as often more than one glucosinolate is present, also in the relative amounts.

For practical reasons, a substantial amount of work on crucifers has been limited to seed constituents. In such cases, especially, the botanical authentication requires critical attention. The Cruciferae constitutes a systematically difficult taxon, abounding in infraspecific complexes and artificial hybrids. Polyploids, amphiploids and cultivars are numerous, and the nomenclature frequently unwieldy and non-consistent. Precise botanical identification hence frequently becomes a problem requiring specialist assistance. Even so, however, different names may often be attached to the same specimen by different authorities, a situation liable to create confusion and calling for a degree of familiarity with biological variability on the part of the chemist. Regrettably, lack of understanding is frequently reflected in published reports wherein precise chemical identifications have been linked to dubious, or, at best, insufficiently defined biological entities. Routine deposition of herbarium vouchers, including plants derived from seeds subjected to chemical studies, could contribute enormously towards improved correlations between observed chemical patterns and biological identity. Extended application of this system must therefore, once again, be strongly recommended.

There is no crucifer, out of the several hundred species investigated, with a demonstrable incapability to synthesise glucosinolates. Considerable variation exists, however, as to the type of side-chains (R in 1) elaborated by a given species. The chemical nature of the individual glucosinolates and their possible relationships, not always apparent from simple side-chain inspection, is best discussed in terms of their biosynthetic origin.

Biosynthesis

General

From extensive experimental studies, presented and discussed in recent reviews (Ettlinger and Kjaer, 1968; Kjaer and Olesen Larsen, 1973), it is known that an *a*-amino acid 7, in the proper species, passes through a sequence of consecutive oxidations, accompanied by decarboxylation *en route*, followed by sulphuration, glucosylation, and, finally, sulphonation, to give the glucosinolate 1 as outlined in Scheme 1.

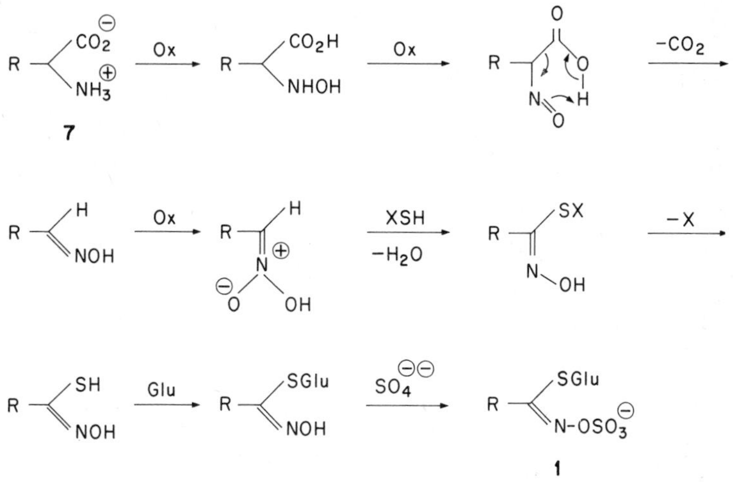

Scheme 1

All evidence on hand points to the general sequence, depicted in Scheme 1, as the only one operating in Nature, rendering *α*-amino acids 7 obligatory precursors for the *in vivo* synthesis of glucosinolates 1. Inspection of the side-chains of the known glucosinolates from natural sources immediately reveals that some of these are identical with the side-chains of ordinary protein amino acids whereas others, the majority, are obviously similar to, though without any direct counterparts in, the naturally occurring *α*-amino acids. We shall discuss the two classes of glucosinolates separately.

Glucosinolates derived directly from common Protein Amino Acids

(a) Aliphatic Side Chains. The parent glucosinolate (1, R = H), conceivably deriving from glycine (Scheme 1), is unknown and supposedly not a very stable compound. Methylglucosinolate (1, R = Me), the expected product from incorporation of alanine, is curiously absent from crucifers, as far as is known (Gmelin and Kjær, 1970), whereas it seems to constitute the predominant and most widely distributed glucosinolate within the Capparaceae.

Isopropylglucosinolate, arising from valine, is widely distributed within Cruciferae, virtually always accompanied by (*S*)-*sec*-butylglucosinolate, obviously deriving from *L*-isoleucine. The pair of branched side-chain glucosinolates has been encountered in several species representing genera such as *Cardamine, Cochlearia, Lunaria, Sisymbrium,* and others. The leucine counterpart, isobutylglucosinolate, is a recent addition to the series, recognized, so far, in *Conringia orientalis* (Underhill and Kirkland, 1972), two species of the genus *Thelypodium,* and in *Cochlearia officinalis* (Al-Shehbaz, 1973).

Glucosinolates 1 with side-chains R corresponding to those of the aliphatic protein amino acids glycine, serine, threonine, cysteine, methionine, lysine, arginine, aspartic acid, and glutamic acid (7), have not yet been encountered as natural products. Their future finding, however, would mostly occasion little surprise.

(b) Aromatic and Heterocyclic Side-Chains. Phenylalanine and tyrosine have their amino acid counterparts in benzyl- and *p*-hydroxybenzylglucosinolate. Although the former has been recognized in several species of widely varying familial relationship (Ettlinger and Kjær, 1968), its distribution within the Cruciferae seems rather restricted, with several *Lepidium* species as characteristic sources.

A somewhat similar limitation as to distribution apparently obtains for *p*-hydroxybenzylglucosinolate; here, the genus *Sinapis* seems to afford the richest source.

The analogue of tryptophan, 3-indolylmethylglucosinolate, stands out as a component seemingly limited in its occurrence to seedlings and young vegetative tissue of many species from a number of families including Cruciferae, within which, e.g. *Isatis tinctoria* and *Brassica* species are known as useful sources (Elliott and Stowe, 1971 and literature cited therein).

The histidine equivalent, 5-imidazolylmethylglucosinolate, has not yet been encountered in Nature. Attempts to disclose its existence should be encouraged.

Glucosinolates derived from modified Protein Amino Acids

(a) Homologization. A conspicuous feature of a list of glucosinolate side-chains known at the present (Kjær, 1973), is the abundance of arrays formally representing higher homologues, R. $(CH_2)_n$–, of those arising directly from protein amino acids <u>7</u> and discussed above. In fact, this derivation is a real one, supported by conclusive experiments proving the operation, in many crucifers, of the chain-elongating reaction sequence shown in Scheme 2.

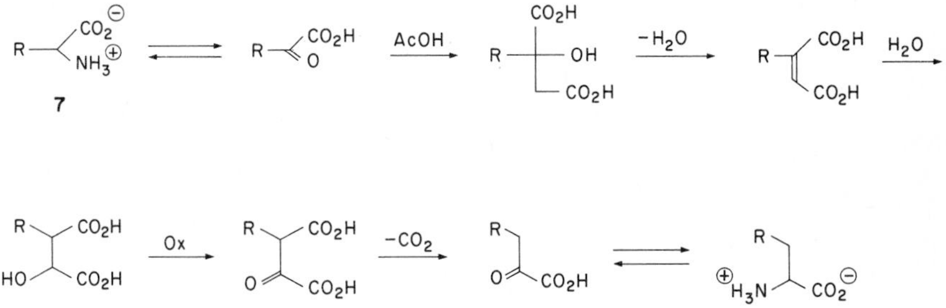

Scheme 2

Though experimentally tested in only a few cases, there is reason to believe that the sequence set out in Scheme 2 is a general one that, of course, can be traversed repeatedly. Several enzymes, of unknown substrate specificity, are involved in the various homologization steps. It remains a challenge for further studies to unravel the detailed nature of these. Only then can the full potentialities of the observed glucosinolates as "chemical markers", carrying useful information about phylogenetic relationships be truly assessed.

Ethylglucosinolate, theoretically derivable from alanine by a one-cycle homologization is known, but rare, as a natural product, a single *Lepidium* species being the sole reported source thus far (Kjær and Larsen, 1954). Analogously, 2(*S*)-methylbutylglucosinolate, with a proved cruciferous appearance in *Dentaria pinnata* (Delaveau and Kjær, 1963), most certainly derives from 2-amino-4-methylhexanoic acid which, in its turn, may result from chain elongation of isoleucine.

The sole natural glucosinolate containing a carboxylated side-chain, *viz.* $MeO_2C.[CH_2]_3-$, is restricted in its occurrence, as far as is known at present, to *Erysimum odoratum* Ehrh. (Gmelin and Kjær, 1969). In accord with expectation, α-aminoadipic acid and, still better, its δ-methyl ester was incorporated into the ester glucosinolate in an *Erysimum* species. Aspartic and glutamic acids, but surprisingly not acetate, were efficiently converted into the glucosinolate, in this case making amino acid homologization *via* the standard route of Scheme 2 less convincing (Chisholm, 1973).

In a group of crucifer glucosinolates, theoretically, but also actually deriving from methionine, the homologization principle has reached its culmination so far. Side-chains are exhibited which can collectively be expressed as $MeS.[CH_2]_n$, or the corresponding sulphoxides or sulphones, with n assuming every single value from 3 to 11. The side-chain with n = 2, arising from methionine itself, seems curiously absent from the natural collection of ω-methylthioalkylglucosinolates including their *S*-oxidized counterparts. The group appears to be virtually restricted to the Cruciferae, within which it is, however, represented in several genera. To what extent the observed patterns, i.e. the value of n, carry useful information as to generic relationship is not known. For details regarding occurrence of the individual homologues within the family, the reviews quoted above should be consulted.

Experimental evidence supports common origin of the ω-methylthioalkyl- and the ω-alkenylglucosinolates, with the side-chains CH_2:CH. [CH_2]$_n$, n = 1, 2, and 3 known so far, the latter group arising by terminal elimination of the sulphur function. Alkenylglucosinolates occur primarily, but not exclusively, in the genus *Brassica*. Again, more detailed information about the enzyme systems catalyzing the eliminations might be of considerable help in understanding true relationships.

Aromatic amino acids share the capacity to undergo homologization, reflected in the existence in many crucifers of glucosinolates with a 2-phenylethyl side-chain, the origin of which, through reactions outlined in Scheme 2, has been experimentally verified. Again, the recent reviews should be consulted for details.

(b) Oxidative Modifications. Additional to linear elongation, oxidation of side-chains arising from several protein amino acids (e.g. valine, leucine, isoleucine, methionine, phenylalanine, and tyrosine) must be invoked to account for the complete list of known glucosinolates (Kjær, 1973). Detailed information as to the nature of the enzymes involved, the actual substrates undergoing oxidation, the stereochemical course of the oxidations, the degree of reversibility, *etc.* is still lacking.

Some typical cases of oxidatively modified side-chains in glucosinolates of cruciferous origin are: 3-benzoyloxypropyl, encountered in *Malcolmia maritima*, conceivably derived by double homologization of serine, or by reduction of a 3-carboxypropyl chain, in both cases followed by benzoylation; (*R*)-1-hydroxy-2-propyl and (*R*)-1-hydroxy-2-butyl, and the corresponding benzoates, all found in *Sisymbrium austriacum*; 2-hydroxy-2-methylpropyl in *Conringia orientalis*; 3-hydroxylated 5-methylthiopentyl and 6-methylthiohexyl chains, as well as the corresponding sulphoxides and sulphones, in *Erysimum virgatum* Roth (Kjær and Schuster, 1970) and *E. rhaeticum* Schleich. ex DC. (Kjær and Schuster, 1973), respectively; 8-methylthio-3-oxo-octyl, and the corresponding sulphoxide, in *Arabis hirsuta* (L.)Scop. (Kjær and Schuster, 1972); (R) 2-hydroxy-3-butenyl in *Brassica* spp. and the corresponding (S)-enantiomer in *Crambe abyssinica*; and (*S*)-2-hydroxy-4-

pentenyl in *Brassica napus*. In the aromatic series, in addition to 4-hydroxybenzyl and its *O*-methyl derivative, both arising from tyrosine, benzyl groups hydroxylated, or methoxylated, in 3-, 3, 4-, and 3, 4, 5-positions have been encountered as side-chains in glucosinolates from crucifers (e.g. within the genera *Heliophila, Hesperis,* and *Lepidium*). In the elongated 2-phenylethyl side-chain, hydroxylation at the benzylic position is a known feature, yielding a carbinol centre with (*R*)-configuration, as in *Barbarea* spp., or with (*S*)-configuration as in *Sibara virginica* (L.)Rollins.

Significance and Application

Viewed,as above, against a background of two major principles governing their *in vivo* synthesis: (i) linear chain elongation, and (ii) oxidative modifications, the impressive, but disconcerting picture of more than 60 crucifer glucosinolates, recedes into an almost harmonious and pleasing unity of well-proportioned natural molecules. Profitable speculations on generic relationship between taxa at all levels: order, family, genus, species, and chemical races, on the basis of their glucosinolate patterns, hence must take our reasonably detailed knowledge about the biosynthetic pathways leading to the individual glucosinolates into account. Only then can we hope to see the existing, rather comprehensive knowledge about glucosinolate distribution, playing its full rôle as an assistant in the task of unravelling true, i.e. biologically conditioned, relationships.

FUTURE PROBLEMS

Glucosinolates are natural compounds with a long history. Before 1840, two crystalline representatives, the classical sinigrin and sinalbin, had been reported and their susceptibility to enzymic hydrolysis realised. Despite a number of significant contributions, the next century, however, did not bring about more than a moderately augmented knowledge within the field. With the advent of modern methods of separation and structure elucidation after World War II, an almost explosive development set in as reflected, for example, in the fact that of the more than 70 naturally occurring glucosinolates known today, only 8 date back further than 1952. A major achievement was the correct formulation of the general glucosinolate structure <u>1</u> by Ettlinger and Lundeen (1956), another the elucidation of the major biosynthetic pathways by Underhill and his associates, and others (see Kjær and Olesen Larsen, 1973 for references).

Today we are still faced with numerous problems within this field. Technically and economically important as they are, the glucosinolates will continue to draw attention on the part of the analytical chemist steadily searching for efficient methods of separation and quantitative determination. In this area novel techniques such as high-pressure liquid chromatography may conceivably become of great importance. Again, efforts to disclose the existence of novel glucosinolates and to map out the patterns characteristic for well-authenticated new sources will undoubtedly continue, hopefully even intensify, and should be encouraged as a prerequisite for an efficient utilization of glucosinolate patterns as an auxiliary character in systematic work. Promising attempts along such lines have already appeared, e.g. in studies of the systematics of the genera *Thelypodium* (Al-Shehbaz, 1973) and *Cakile* (Rothman, 1974). A fruitful cooperation between systematists and chemists, also in this area, is evident. In all likelihood the liaison is a lasting one that shall prove helpful in bringing about a better understanding of the many complex problems concerning relationship and origin within the Cruciferae, but hopefully also at levels of higher category.

It has been one purpose of this chapter to inform on salient points regarding the nature and origin of the glucosinolates in Cruciferae. Another, and equally important, to draw attention to a fascinating and still open field for continued studies. Anyone entering this area with devotion and understanding is likely to have a rich and rewarding harvest.

REFERENCES

Al-Shehbaz, I. A. (1973). *Contribut.Gray Herbar.* No. 204, p.66.

Chisholm, M. D. (1973). *Phytochemistry* 12, 605.

Cronquist, A. (1968). "The Evolution and Classification of Flowering Plants". Nelson and Sons, London.

Delaveau, P. G. and Kjaer, A. (1963). *Acta Chem.Scand.* 17, 2562.

Elliott, M. C. and Stowe, B. B. (1971). *Plant Physiol.* 47, 366.

Ettlinger, M. G. and Kjaer, A. (1968). *In* "Recent Advances in Phytochemistry" (T. J. Mabry *et al.*, eds) Vol. 1, pp. 59 - 144. Appleton-Century-Crofts, New York.

Ettlinger, M. G. and Lundeen, A. J. (1956). *J.Amer.Chem.Soc.* 78, 1952.

Gmelin, R. and Kjaer, A. (1969). *Acta Chem.Scand.* 23, 2548.

Gmelin, R. and Kjaer, A. (1970). *Phytochemistry* 9, 569.

Kjaer, A. (1960). *Fortschr.Chem.Org.Naturstoffe* 18, 122.

Kjaer, A. (1973). *In* "Chemistry in Botanical Classification" (G. Bendz and J. Santesson, eds) *Nobel Symposium No. 25*, pp. 229 - 234. Academic Press, New York and London.

Kjaer, A. and Larsen, I. (1954). *Acta Chem.Scand.* 8, 699.

Kjaer, A. and Olesen Larsen, P. (1973). *In* "Biosynthesis" (T. A. Geissman, ed.) Vol. 2, pp. 95 - 105. Specialist Periodical Reports. The Chemical Society, London.

Kjaer, A. and Schuster, A. (1970). *Acta Chem. Scand.* 24, 1631.

Kjaer, A. and Schuster, A. (1972). *Acta Chem. Scand.* 26, 8.

Kjaer, A. and Schuster, A. (1973). *Phytochemistry* 12, 929.

Rothman, J. E. (1974). *Contribut. Gray Herbar.* No. 205, pp. 34 - 60.

Takhtajan, A. (1969). "Flowering Plants. Origin and Dispersal". Oliver & Boyd, Edinburgh.

Underhill, E. W. and Kirkland, D. F. (1972). *Phytochemistry* 11, 2085.

LIPIDS IN THE CRUCIFERAE

L-Å. APPELQVIST

Department of Food Hygiene, Royal Veterinary College, Stockholm, Sweden

INTRODUCTION

Due to the fact that the Cruciferae embraces such a large number of species and that lipids include a wide array of different molecular structures, the present review will be limited to only certain aspects of the general subject. A restriction of the presentation to only those recent papers which treat this subject from an entirely phytochemical point of view would for various reasons not be appropriate. This survey will mainly present inter- and intra-generic, inter- and intra-specific variability in cruciferous seed fatty acid and sterol patterns. Also organ- and organelle-specificity in lipid patterns and aspects of the mode of control of fatty acid composition will be treated.

Since questions related to cropping and industrial utilization of the economically very important oil crops in the Cruciferae family, viz. rape and mustard seeds (*Brassica campestris, B. juncea* and *B. napus*) have been presented recently (Appelqvist, 1971b; Appelqvist and Ohlson, 1972), these aspects will only be touched upon briefly in this account.

Those familiar with the text of Hilditch (Hilditch and Williams, 1964) certainly associate erucic acid with Cruciferae. The presence of from 1 to ca 60 % erucic acid in the seed lipids of about 3/4 of all cruciferous species so far studied makes such associations natural, and consequently erucic acid is a key compound in this presentation. However, the story would be incomplete if some of the other unusual fatty acids found in the Cruciferae were not also discussed.

SEED LIPIDS

Gross Fatty Acid Patterns and Triacyl Glycerol Structure

The fatty acid patterns of acyl lipids of a tissue often differ qualitatively and quantitatively. Nevertheless, total fatty acid patterns will be used as a characteristic of seeds in the first part of this survey. This is justified since triacyl glycerol fatty acids predominate in seed tissue; see e.g. McKillican (1966). Also total fatty acid pattern is often the only information presented in studies on seed lipids. In a recent presentation of rapeseed lipids, the chemically more strict approach starting with lipid classes was used (Appelqvist, 1972a).

It is well known that palmitic, stearic, oleic, linoleic and linolenic acids are very widespread in the plant kingdom. Besides these "common" fatty acids, several "uncommon" fatty acids occur in seeds of the Cruciferae family and a major emphasis in this review will be on these "uncommon" acids although variability in content of the common fatty acids will also be considered.

Epoxylinoleic acid in Camelina sativa

A few percent of 15,16-epoxylinoleic acid (see Fig. 1) is reported to be present in *Camelina sativa* (Gunstone and Morris,

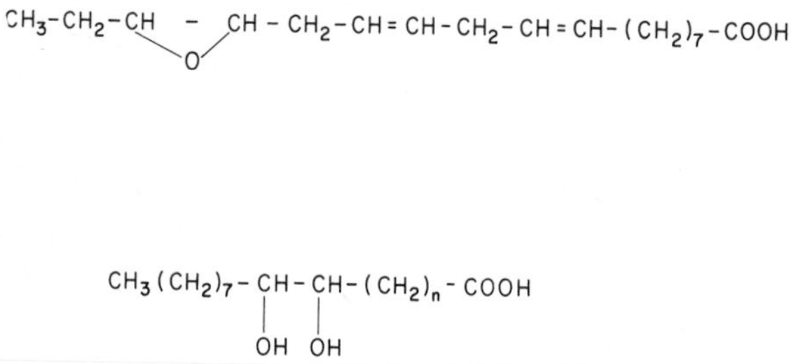

$$CH_3-CH_2-\underset{\diagdown O \diagup}{CH - CH}-CH_2-CH=CH-CH_2-CH=CH-(CH_2)_7-COOH$$

Epoxylinoleic acid

Camelina sativa

$$CH_3(CH_2)_7-\underset{|}{\overset{}{CH}}(OH)-\underset{|}{CH}(OH)-(CH_2)_n-COOH$$

Dihydroxy-saturated acids

Cardamine impatiens

n = 7, 9, 11, or 13

FIGURE 1.

1959). Whereas Mikolajczak *et al.* (1961) found no epoxy acid in a sample of this species, analyses of two samples available in our laboratory indicated low levels of the acid (Appelqvist, 1968a). Whether this discrepancy is due to the differences in analytical techniques used or signifies intra-specific variability can not be ascertained. As regards "common" fatty acids, *C. sativa* seed oils have ca 6 % palmitic acid, 2 % stearic acid, 11 % oleic, 15 % linoleic and 40 % linolenic acid. The erucic acid content is as low as ca 3 % whereas the eicosenoic acid content is ca 15 % (Appelqvist, 1968a). It would certainly be interesting to look for larger amounts of epoxy acids in related species. So far the minute amounts reported from *C. sativa* seems to be the only record of epoxy acids in the Cruciferae. Other families are known to contain species rich in epoxy acids (Wolff, 1966).

Dihydroxy acids in Cardamine impatiens

The genus *Cardamine* offers an interesting example of intrageneric variation in seed fatty acid patterns. Whereas seed oil from *Cardamine impatiens* L. contains ca 25 % of saturated long chain acids (18, 20, 22 and 24 carbons) with vicinal dihydroxy groups (Fig. 1)(Miller *et al.*, 1965), other species of this genus, *C. bellidifolia* (Appelqvist, 1971a), *C. enneaphylla* and *C. flexuosa* (Tallent, personal communication), *C. hirsuta* (Miller *et al.*, 1965) and *C. pratensis* (Appelqvist, 1971a) lack these unusual acids, at least to any substantial degree as observed on normal TLC or GLC analysis of the fatty acid methyl esters.

The dihydroxy acids all have the hydroxy groups in the 9 and 10 position calculated from the methyl end and are thus (n-9) and (n-10) acids (Mikolajczak *et al.*, 1965). The chain length distribution of the hydroxy-derivatives was 5 % C_{18}, 5 % C_{20}, 66 % C_{22} and 24 % C_{24}, whereas the total percentage for the non-hydroxy acid mono-enes was 15 % 18:1, 7 % 20:1, 33 % 22:1 and 6 % 24:1. This might be of interest to note, since a biosynthetic relationship has been suggested between mono-enes and dihydroxy acids (Mikolajczak *et al.*, 1968).

More recent studies at the USDA-lab in Peoria have revealed that the hydroxy acids are located at the outer positions of the triacyl glycerols and that one of the two hydroxy groups in each acid is acetylated. It appears that the (n-9) and (n-10) positions are acetylated to approximately equal extent. No di-acetylated or un-acetylated acids were found in the *Cardamine impatiens* seed oil analyzed (Mikolajczak *et al.*, 1968).

No detailed studies on the distribution of dihydroxy acid-containing-triacyl glycerols among the various aspects of the genus *Cardamine* seems to be reported.

Hydroxy acids in Lesquerella

In the genus *Lesquerella*, all of the 22 species (up to 1962 ca 70 were described according to Barclay *et al.*, 1962) studied within the "New Crops" program of the USDA (United States Department of Agriculture) contained substantial amounts of monohydroxy fatty acids with either 18 or 20 carbon atoms. (Barclay *et al.*, 1962, Mikolajczak *et al.*, 1962, Kleiman *et al.*, 1972, Barclay and Tallent, personal communication). The structure of the C_{20} acid called lesquerolic acid was deduced as 14-hydroxy-*cis*-11-eicosenoic acid (Smith *et al.*, 1961). The C_{16} hydroxy acids were found to be a mixture of ricinoleic acid (12-hydroxy-*cis*-9-octadecenoic acid) and densipolic acid (12-hydroxy-*cis*-9,cis-15-octadecadienoic acid)(Miller *et al.*, 1965). Figure 2 illustrates the chemical structures of these acids. All the oils of *Lesquerella* also contained a few per

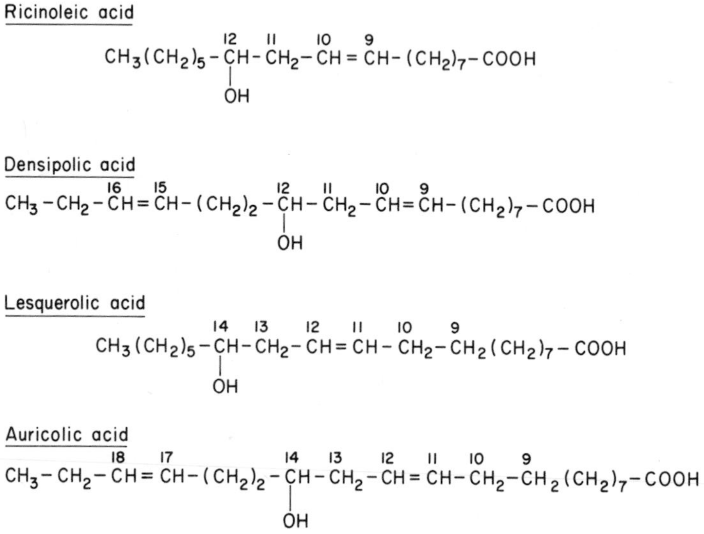

Ricinoleic acid

$$CH_3(CH_2)_5-\overset{12}{C}H(OH)-\overset{11}{C}H_2-\overset{10}{C}H=\overset{9}{C}H-(CH_2)_7-COOH$$

Densipolic acid

$$CH_3-CH_2-\overset{16}{C}H=\overset{15}{C}H-(CH_2)_2-\overset{12}{C}H(OH)-\overset{11}{C}H_2-\overset{10}{C}H=\overset{9}{C}H-(CH_2)_7-COOH$$

Lesquerolic acid

$$CH_3(CH_2)_5-\overset{14}{C}H(OH)-\overset{13}{C}H_2-\overset{12}{C}H=\overset{11}{C}H-\overset{10}{C}H_2-\overset{9}{C}H_2(CH_2)_7-COOH$$

Auricolic acid

$$CH_3-CH_2-\overset{18}{C}H=\overset{17}{C}H-(CH_2)_2-\overset{14}{C}H(OH)-\overset{13}{C}H_2-\overset{12}{C}H=\overset{11}{C}H-\overset{10}{C}H_2-\overset{9}{C}H_2(CH_2)_7-COOH$$

FIGURE 2. Monohydroxy acids found in various *Lesquerella* species.

cent of palmitic and stearic acids and variable amounts of oleic (10 - 29 %), linoleic (2 - 10 %) and linolenic acid (1 - 14 %).

Lesquerolic acid was the major fatty acid (45 - 72 %) in 17 of the 22 species studied, accompanied by minor amounts (traces to 11 %) of C_{18} hydroxy acids. In three species no C_{20} hydroxy acid was detected; these had 44 - 50 % C_{18} hydroxy acids with densipolic acid far exceeding ricinoleic in the samples reported.

Interesting taxonomic implications were previously drawn, when it was realized that all the species then known to be lacking C_{20} hydroxy acids were of the "auriculate-leaved" group (Barclay *et al.*, 1962). The two "auriculate-leaved" species which had C_{20} hydroxy acids, e.g. *L. grandiflora* and *L. lasiocarpa* had haploid chromosome numbers 9 and 7 respectively whereas all the others in the group had n = 8. Very recently it has been suggested to move the latter species from the "auriculate-leaved" group (Barclay and Tallent, personal communication), which would make the fatty acid picture simpler. On the other hand, some species within the "auriculate-type" group previously reported to lack lesquerolic acid have been shown to contain 2 and 5 % of this acid. Fatty acid data for one species of the auriculate-type group *L. auriculata* were not known to Barclay *et al.* (1962), but on the basis of chromosome number and morphology, they suggested that it should contain densipolic acid. A report which was published 10 years later revealed that it contained only 2 % of densipolic acid but 32 % of a novel acid (called auricolic acid, see Fig. 2) which was shown to be 14-hydroxy-*cis*-11, *cis*-17-eicosadienoic acid (Kleiman *et al.*, 1972). It is interesting to note that auricolic acid is a homologue of densipolic acid whereas lesquerolic acid is a homologue of ricinoleic acid; both C_{20} acids are structurally "elongated" at the carboxyl end. The major fatty acids of many Cruciferae, *cis*-11-eicosenoic and *cis*-13-docosenoic acids are formed by elongation of *cis*-9-octadecenoic (oleic) acid (see Fig. 4).

It has been reported that auricolic acid is absent from at least four of the auriculate-type species but present (in minor amounts) in many of the other lesquerellas (Barclay and Tallent, personal communication). As more data are becoming available (Barclay, personal communication), it appears as though the presence of densipolic, auricolic and lesquerolic acids in *Lesquerella* species is of lesser phytochemical significance.

The studies of the *L. auriculata* seed oil also revealed the presence of large amounts of tetra-acid triglycerides (Kleiman *et al.,* 1972). These are formed by acylation of the hydroxyl group of the hydroxy acid which is esterified to glycerol (see Fig. 3). The structure formed by esterification of a hydroxy

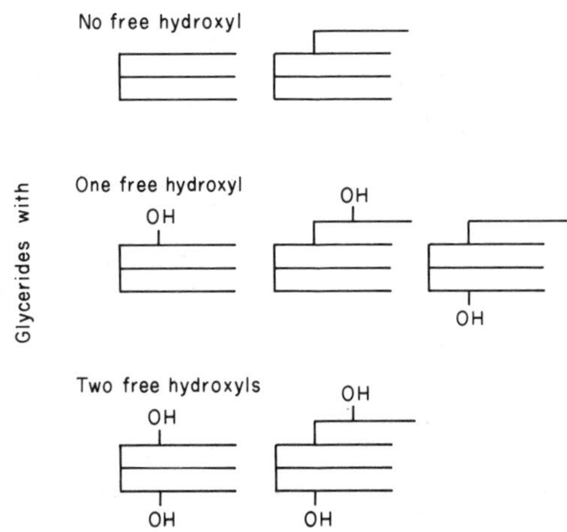

FIGURE 3. Structures of the estolides found in *Lesquerella*

group of one fatty acid with the carboxyl group of another long chain acid is called an "estolide".

Detailed structural studies demonstrated the presence in *L. auriculata* of both triglycerides (triacyl glycerols) and estolide glycerides (tetra-acid-triglycerides) each containing no, one or two free hydroxyl groups (Fig. 3). Similarly to what is known for other Cruciferae (Appelqvist and Dowdell and *loc. cit.*, 1968) and plants in general as well, the 2-position of the glycerol is esterified with the "common" unsaturated fatty acids, oleic, linoleic and linolenic acids, whereas the 1- and 3-positions contain the "unusual" fatty acids.

From these three sections above it is evident that at least three classes of "unusual" fatty acids besides those in the (n-7) and (n-9) series of monoenes such as eicosenoic and erucic acids (which hardly merit the name "unusual") occur in seed oils of the Cruciferae: epoxy-acids, monoacetylated dihydroxy acids and monohydroxy acids.

"Elongated" acids in various non-cultivated Cruciferae

As mentioned in the Introduction, eicosenoic and erucic acids are very common in the seed lipids of Cruciferae. Actually, the seed oils of ca 75 % of all the species of this family so far reported from modern GLC analyses contain erucic acid at levels from ca 1 % to ca 60 % (Mikolajczak *et al.*, 1961, Miller *et al.*, 1965, Goering *et al.*, 1965, Appelqvist, 1970a and 1971a, Thies, 1971).

Generally cruciferous seed oils are also rather rich in linolenic acid. Levels under 5 % are exceptional and no single species of this family seems to be completely devoid of linolenic acid in their seed oil (Mikolajczak *et al.*, 1961, Miller *et al.*, 1965, Appelqvist, 1970a and 1971a).

Usually 24:1 is the longest mono-ene listed in studies on cruciferous lipids and often the data presentation lists no fatty acid longer than 22:1. All the oils which contain erucic acid (22:1) also have variable amounts of eicosenoic acid (20:1). Many of the erucic acid-rich seed oils also contain nervonic acid (24:1), generally in very small quantities (up to 2 %). As has been pointed out previously, isothermal GLC analysis of seed oils usually is performed in such a manner that minute amounts of still longer homologues would never be detected (Appelqvist, 1968a). Since we considered it essential to know the number of elongated homologues present, heavily overloaded chromatograms were prepared. No peak for 26:1 could be seen on such chromatograms of fatty acid methyl esters from *Sinapis alba* seeds with 2 - 3 % of 24:1 (Appelqvist, 1968a). On the other hand Iverson (1966) reported 0.07 % 26:1 in such seeds.

Most papers on fatty acid patterns in the Cruciferae present no information on the position of the double bond in the fatty acid chain of 20:1, 22:1, and 24:1. In discussions of available data on inter- and intra-generic fatty acid variability it will be assumed that the 20:1 and 22:1 fatty acids are members of the (n-9) series, viz. *cis*-11-eicosenoic acid and *cis*-13-docosenoic (erucic) acid. This is warranted since it is known from detailed studies on rapeseed oil, that the major portion of the elongated mono-enes belong to the (n-9) series.

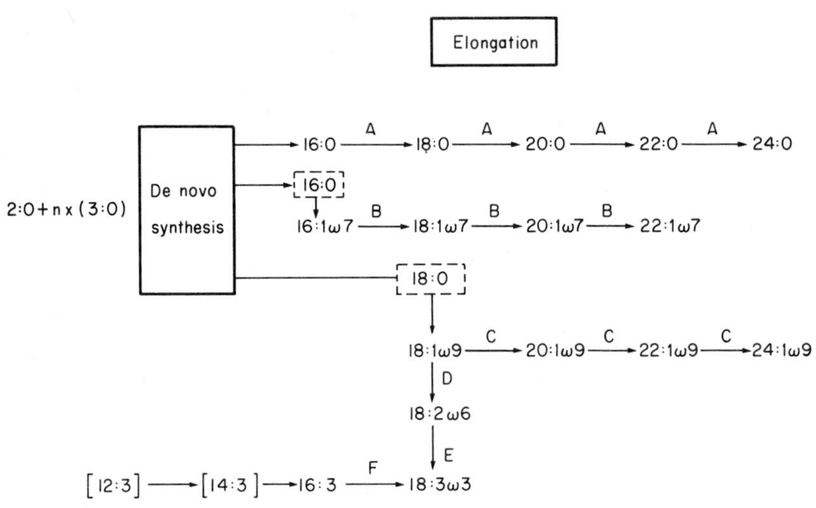

FIGURE 4. Fatty acids found in rapeseed lipids and their established or proposed metabolic interconnections.

However minor amounts of the (n-7) isomers of 18:1, 20:1 and 22:1 are also present (Kuemmel, 1964, Ackmann, 1966, Appelqvist, 1969).

Although most of the Crucifers have erucic acid (22:1) as their major "elongated" acid, there are examples of very high levels of eicosenoic acid (20:1) e.g. *Leavenworthia torulosa* with 53 % (Miller *et al.*, 1965), *Lobularia maritima* with 42 %, *Selenia grandis* with 58 % (Mikolajczak *et al.*, 1961) and *Teesdalia nudicaulis* with 56 % eicosenoic acid (Appelqvist, 1971a). Fatty acid patterns for the species discussed in this and a few following paragraphs appear in Table 1. The erucic acid content of some eicosenoic acid-rich species varies to a great extent. Whereas very little or no erucic acid is reported from the three species just mentioned, there are also examples of high levels of both the 20:1 and 22:1 acids, e.g. *Conringia*

Table 1

Fatty acid data for seeds of some species and genera of Cruciferae

Species		16:0 %	18:0 %	18:1 %	18:2 %	18:3 %	20:1 %	22:1 %	24:1 %	Other acids %	Ref.
Conringia orientalis 64-1027		2.2	0.3	6.7	24	2.2	23.6	29.2	5	6.6	c
C. orientalis		2	0.3	7	29	2	27	26	3		b
Hesperis matronalis		8	2	13	24	51	–	–	–	–	a
H. matronalis		6.5	2.4	13.8	21.9	54.5	–	–	–	–	c
Leavenworthia torulosa		2	0.6	20	12	7	53	–	–	5.3	b
Lepidium latifolium		5	2	15	34	36	4	–	–	1.4	b
Lobularia maritima		4	6	30	7	10	42	–	–	–	a
Lunaria annua		2	0.2	23	7	2	2	42	21	–	a
Matthiola fruticulosa (*M. tristis*)		5	2	12	14	65	0.4	–	–	–	b
Nasturtium officinale		9	2	34	23	0.5	11	18	–	–	a
Selenia grandis		2	1	28	4	2	58	3	–	–	a
Sinapis arvensis 1964-1414		3.3	1.1	39.2	20.8	16.8	11.7	5.7	ND[x)]	1.4	c
S. arvensis		4	1	10	13	17	16	35	1	–	b
Teesdalia nudicaulis		3.4	1.4	20.4	7.2	6.8	56.1	1.4	–	3.3	c
Thlaspi perfoliatum		4	0.8	14	20	5	7	29	19	0.2	b
Genus	**Number of species (samples)**										
Arabis	5 (9)	4-9	1-3	8-17	15-30	5-55	0-13	0-44	0-1		a,b,c
Alyssum	9 (9)	5-11	1-3	10-24	9-24	39-66	0	0	0		a,b
Crambe	6 (9)	0.3-4	0.3-0.8	17-25	9-25	4-11	2-21	27-59	0.1-1		a,b,c
Erysimum	7 (12)	3-7	1-2	5-13	13-27	14-39	5-9	17-46	0.6-3		a,b,c
Sisymbrium	10 (16)	4-14	0.4 -3	5-19	10-22	4-43	4-9	6-47	0-8		a,b,c

x) Not Determined; a) Mikolajczak *et al.*, 1961; b) Miller *et al.*, 1965; c) Appelqvist, 1971a.

orientalis with ca 25 % of each of eicosenoic and erucic acids (Miller *et al.*, 1965, Appelqvist, 1971a). Although no species in the Cruciferae seems to have very large amounts of nervonic acid (24:1), a few have more than 10 %. Thus a sample of *Lunaria annua* had 21 % in the seed (minus the seed coat)(Mikolajczak *et al.*, 1961) and one sample of *Thlaspi perfoliatum* had 19 % nervonic acid in the seed oil (Miller *et al.*, 1965). The nervonic acid-rich species also have large amounts of erucic acid but very small amounts of eicosenoic acid.

As mentioned previously, the seed lipids of the Cruciferae also contain various amounts of the "common" fatty acids, palmitic, stearic, oleic, linoleic and linolenic acids, and variability in levels of these acids will now be considered.

The palmitic acid content of most samples reported is rather low, typically 4 - 7 % and in a few species slightly above 10 %. The low palmitic acid content of rapeseed oil has been found to be a negative factor in nutritional studies (see e.g. Aaes-Jörgensen, 1972). The stearic acid content is typically a few per cent with 6 % being the highest figure reported.

Few natural crucifers reported so far have very high levels of oleic acid. High figures have been reported for *Nasturtium officinale* with 34 % (Mikolajczak *et al.*, 1962) and one out of several samples of *Sinapis arvensis* studied which had 39 % oleic acid (Appelqvist, 1971a). On the other hand very high levels of oleic acid are found in some "zero-erucic acid" genotypes of rapeseed (see Table 3 discussed on page 234). Ca 5 % oleic acid appears to be the lowest figure (see *Erysimum* and *Sisymbrium* in Table 1).

The linoleic acid content varies within wide ranges. Examples of low figures are the aforementioned *Selenia grandis* with 4 % and also *Lesquerella* species with 2-3 % linoleic acid (Barclay *et al.*, 1962, Mikolajczak *et al.*, 1962). High figures are exemplified by ca 27 % in *Erysimum* species, 34 % in *Lepidium latifolium*, up to 30 % in *Arabis* species and 29 % in *Conringia orientalis* (see Table 1).

Variation in linolenic acid percentages extends from less than 1 % in *Nasturtium officinale* to very high figures of 50 - 60 % for *Arabis* and *Alyssum* species, ca 50 % in *Hesperis matronalis* and 65 % in *Matthiola fruticulosa (M. tristis)* (see Table 1).

In this context it seems warranted to mention the intra-generic and intra-specific variability in erucic acid content in non-cultivated species. Considerable intra-generic variability in erucic acid content has been noted for *Arabis*, 0 - 44 %, for *Crambe*, 26 - 59 %, for *Erysimum*, 15 - 46 % and for *Sisymbrium*, 6 - 47 % (see Table 1). Previously in this survey, the intra-generic variability in fatty acid patterns in *Cardamine* has been discussed.

At the intra-specific level remarkable variability in erucic acid content was noted for *Sinapis arvensis* with a range in erucic acid content among 7 samples from 6 to 39 % (Appelqvist, 1971a).

Minor amounts of di- and tri-unsaturated fatty acids with 16, 20 and 22 carbon atoms are present in cruciferous seed lipids, as well as saturated fatty acids of chain lengths 14, 20, 22 and 24 (see Fig. 4). Whereas small amounts of 20:2, 20:3 and 22:2 are reported only from oils rich in erucic acid, the presence of 20:0, 22:0 and 24:0 is more widespread in seed oils.

Although the Cruciferae appears to be one of the more extensively studied plant families as regards seed fatty acid patterns, as yet figures for only a few hundred of the ca 3,000 or more species within the Cruciferae have been reported in the literature.

No attempt will be made in this survey to relate the data available for fatty acid composition to one or more of the several classification systems used for the Cruciferae. It should however be mentioned that Miller *et al.* (1965) grouped data from some publications according to the classification of Prantl. They then noted that the tribe Sinapeae contained the oils richest in erucic acid. However this tribe also had species lacking erucic acid. The species in the tribe Schizopetaleae, on the other hand, entirely lacked or had only low levels of erucic acid. With one exception, the tribe Hesperideae was represented by seeds with a maximum of 30 % erucic acid, many species however, lacked erucic acid.

"Elongated" acids in some cultivated Cruciferae

Quite a few cruciferous species are grown as oil seed crops. The seed oils from these species have, quite naturally, been

Table 2

Typical ranges of variation in content of common fatty acids in the oils of some cultivars or breeding lines of some cruciferous seeds

Species and type	Ranges in percentage content of					
	Palmitic	Oleic	Linoleic	Linolenic	Eicosenoic	Erucic acid
Brassica campestris						
Winter turnip rape	2-3	14-16	13-17	8-12	8-10	42-46
Summer turnip rape, classical cultivars	2-3	17-34	14-18	9-11	10-12	24-40
Summer turnip rape, low erucic acid lines[x)]	4-7	48-55	27-31	10-14	0-1	0
Sarson and Toria	2-3	9-16	11-16	6-9	3-8	46-61
Brassica juncea	2-4	7-22	12-24	10-15	6-14	18-49
Brassica napus						
Winter rape, classical cultivars	3-4	8-14	11-15	6-11	6-10	45-54
Winter rape, low erucic acid cultivars or lines[x)]	4-5	40-48	15-25	10-15	3-19	3-11
Summer rape, classical cultivars[xx)]	3-4	12-23	12-16	5-10	9-14	41-47
Summer rape, low erucic acid cultivars or lines[x)]	5	52-55	24-31	10-13	0-2	0-1
Brassica tournefortii	2-4	6-12	11-16	10-16	6-8	46-52
Sinapis alba	2-3	16-28	7-10	9-12	6-11	33-51

x) Results from only a few samples available. The range of variation in fatty acid compositions is expected to increase as new cultivars are being released.

xx) Except for the Polish cultivar Bronowski, which is not grown to any significant extent. This cultivar has ca. 10 % erucic acid. (Appelqvist, 1971b. Compilation)

subjected to extensive chemical studies. For details in this area the reader can consult some recent reviews (Appelqvist, 1971b and 1972a). Some key facts about the ruciferous oilseed crops are presented in this paper in conjunction with data on related "wild" species.

All natural populations and classical cultivars of the *Brassica* species of interest, viz. *B. campestris, B. juncea* and *B. napus*, contain considerable percentages of eicosenoic and erucic acids (Table 2). By single plant selection in some cultivars, it has been possible to isolate seeds of *B. campestris* and *B. napus* essentially free of erucic acid and with only small amounts of eicosenoic acid (Stefansson *et al.*, 1961, Downey, 1964 and Jönsson, 1973). This is of interest for the utilization of these species as oilseed crops, since erucic acid-rich oils are shown to cause adverse physiological effects when ingested in large amounts by experimental animals (see e.g. a review by Aaes-Jörgensen, 1972). Presently the commercial production of rapeseed oil (from *B. napus* and *B. campestris*) is gradually phasing over to so called LEAR-varieties (L E A R = Low Erucic Acid Rapeseed).

Due to mechanical admixture with high erucic acid rapeseed and outcrossing with high erucic acid plants (from voluntary seeds) and for other reasons, the commercial product often contains a few per cent of erucic acid (see Craig *et al.*, 1973), although the seed genotype often has less than 0.5 % erucic acid and thus qualifies for the name "zero-erucic acid rapeseed".

From Table 2 it is apparent that the range of variation in linoleic and linolenic acid levels of the classical cultivars of *B. campestris* and *B. napus* is very small. Further, it appears that the oleic/linoleic/linolenic ratios of the Brassicas are different from those noted for *Sinapis alba* (see discussion in Appelqvist, 1970a). More detailed fatty acid patterns for one classical genotype of *B. napus* (cv. Gulle) and three low or zero-erucic acid lines are presented in Table 3. It should be noticed that the zero-erucic acid lines have essentially unchanged percentages of 20:0 and 22:0, indicative of separate enzymes for synthesis of elongated saturated acids and elongated mono-enes (cf. Fig. 4).

Furthermore the linolenic acid content has changed very little whereas both oleic and linoleic acids percentages increase in different proportions in the zero-erucic acid lines. Efforts among plant breeders are now among other things, directed toward development of "zero-erucic acid" cultivars

Table 3

The fatty acid composition of a classical and some low erucic acid cultivars of *Brassica napus*

Sample	16:0 %	18:0 %	18:1 %	18:2 %	18:3 %	20:0 %	20:1 %	22:0 %	22:1 %
Gulle	3.8	1.0	15.3	15.6	11.4	0.6	12.6	tr	38.4
Oro	4.1	1.9	61.6	19.1	9.2	0.5	1.4	1.0	1.0
Line 314	3.9	1.9	65.1	14.3	10.0	0.6	2.2	0.5	1.2
Line 802	4.9	1.1	43.4	33.6	13.6	0.3	1.4	0.4	1.0

with highest possible linoleic acid percentages (for increased nutritive value) and lowest possible linolenic acid percentages (for maximum oxidative stability)(see Lööf and Appelqvist, 1972 for details). So far however, these efforts have met with only moderate success, highest linoleic acid percentages in single plants being ca 40 % and lowest linolenic being ca 4 % (see e.g. Röbbelen, 1972).

Brassica tournefortii, being a noxious weed with considerable productivity in Australia and therefore sometimes utilized as oilseed, displayed a rather small variability in erucic acid content among several collections analysed (Appelqvist, 1971a). This is probably related to the strong self-fertilizing behaviour of this species. Comparison of the single-seed variability in fatty acid patterns of another self-fertilizing *Brassica* species, viz. *B. oxyrrhina* with that of the strongly cross-fertilizing *B. campestris* revealed a statistically significant much larger variability in oleic and erucic acid percentages in the latter compared to the former (Appelqvist, 1969). That most of this variability is genetically determined appears to be very likely in view of the rapid success in development of zero-erucic acid lines of *Brassica campestris* by repeated selection in natural populations (Downey, 1964, Jönsson, 1973).

In this discussion of fatty acids in related Brassicas, it should also be mentioned that the erucic acid percentages of

Brassica oleracea and its non-domesticated ancestor *Brassica cretica* are rather high, often 40 - 50 % (Appelqvist, 1970a and 1971a). The fatty acid patterns of *B. juncea*, *B. carinata*, *B. nigra* and *B. oleracea* are generally rather similar to those of the classical cultivars of *B. campestris* and *B. napus* (Appelqvist, 1970). Also various cultivars of *Sinapis alba* are rather similar to the aforementioned Brassicas in fatty acid patterns (Appelqvist, 1968a and 1970).

Some taxonomic implications of the small differences noted between some of these species have however been made. The fatty acid data have thus supported the findings of Vaughan (1968) that *B. nigra* appears to be somewhat less related to *B. campestris* and *B. oleracea* than these latter two are related to each other (Appelqvist, 1970a). Furthermore the data support the independent generic status of *Sinapis alba* (in the US and Canada referred to as *Brassica hirta*). It has been remarked that the fatty acid pattern of *Sinapis arvensis* has some characteristics of the Brassicas and some of *Sinapis alba* (Appelqvist, 1971a).

It is well known that the fatty acids of polar and neutral lipids are not randomly distributed among the positions of the glycerol molecule (Litchfield, 1972 and Hitchcock and Nichols, 1971). Several investigations have shown that oleic, linoleic and linolenic acids are located at the 2-position of the triacyl glycerols of different Crucifers whereas the 1- and 3-positions are esterified with saturated and "elongated acids" (see Litchfield, 1972). More detailed studies on one sample of rapeseed oil (Brockerhoff and Yurkowski, 1966) revealed that the erucic acid is preferentially esterified at the 3-position (Table 4). Previously in this survey it has been

Table 4

Stereospecific analysis of the triacyl glycerols of a sample of rapeseed oil

Position	Fatty acid composition (mole %)								
	16:0	16:1	18:0	18:1	18:2	18:3	20:1	22:0	22:1
1	4.1	0.3	2.2	23.1	11.1	6.4	16.4	1.4	34.9
2	0.6	0.2	-	37.3	36.1	20.3	2.0	-	3.6
3	4.3	0.3	3.0	16.6	4.0	2.6	17.3	1.2	51.0

(From Brockerhoff and Yurkowski, 1966)

mentioned that the hydroxy acids of *Cardamine* were preferentially located at the 3-position and the hydroxy acids of *Lesquerella auriculata* at the 1- and 3-positions. It has been suggested that the unusual fatty acids of triacyl glycerols are in general preferentially esterified at the 3-position (Litchfield, 1972).

From a comparative point of view it might be interesting to note that erucic acid in *Limnanthes douglasii* (Limnanthaceae) is preferentially located at the 2-position in contrast to the situation with Crucifers where at the most a trace is found at the 2-position (Phillips *et al.*, 1971). In *Limnanthes douglasii* the outer positions are mainly occupied by acids with a double bond in the 5-position. It should be interesting to know whether this reflects a discrimination at the enzyme level of 5-*cis* acids as being still more "unusual" than the 11-*cis* and 13-*cis* acids.

In *Tropaeolum majus* (Tropaeolaceae) erucic acid is found at all positions since this species contains trierucyl glycerol (Litchfield, 1972).

As a consequence of the absence of erucic acid in the 2-position of Crucifers there is no trierucyl glycerol (trierucin) present in the Cruciferous oils (Appelqvist, 1972a). Efforts to increase the erucic acid content of Crucifers by plant breeding (aimed at increasing the value for non-food uses, see Ohlson, 1972) have been only partially successful (Appelqvist and Jönsson, 1970). No single plant with more than 67 moles % of "saturated + elongated acids" was found, reflecting the very low capacity or inability of Crucifers to incorporate erucic acid and related acids at the 2-position.

At this point in the text it appears appropriate to mention several weaknesses in the aforementioned classical link between erucic acid and the Cruciferae. First, there are many Crucifers which are totally devoid of erucic acid and second, erucic acid has been found in several plant families regarded as very distant from the Cruciferae. The monocotyledonous *Luzuriaga parviflora* (Philesiaceae) is reported to contain 15 % eicosenoic, 12 % erucic and 7 % nervonic acids (Moricé, 1970). Seeds of some cultivated Graminae (*Avena sativa, Hordeum vulgare, Triticum vulgare, Secale cereale* and *Zea mays)* also contain eicosenoic and erucic acids. The levels are small

(0.3 - 1 %) but the identities of the fatty acids have been established by GLC-mass spectrometry and other chemical means (Appelqvist, to be published). As well as in the Cruciferae, erucic acid occurs in at least two other dicotyledonous families, namely Limnanthaceae and Tropaeoleaceae. *Limnanthes douglasii* has ca 14 % erucic acid (Phillips *et al.*, 1971) and *Tropaeolum majus* ca 80 % erucic acid (Harlow *et al.*, 1966).

Thus, it should be noted that erucic acid occurs more widespread in the plant kingdom than hitherto assumed and that its level varies from zero to ca 60 % among Crucifers, many of which do contain this acid in their seed oils. The variation in erucic acid content can be very large at the intra-generic and intra-specific levels as well as among individual seeds in a heterozygous population of one species.

Anatomical parts of seeds

Fatty acids occur in seeds mainly as triacyl glycerols and only to a very small extent as non-esterified free acids. Whereas "total fatty acid patterns of entire seeds" is the most commonly available information for the lipids of seed materials, detailed studies on a few Cruciferous seeds have demonstrated that there are marked variations in fatty acid patterns among acyl lipid classes such as triacyl glycerols and various phospholipids. This is discussed in the next section. Furthermore, the mechanically easily separated anatomical parts of these seeds, viz. 1) the cotyledons, 2) the hypocotyl/radicle and 3) the seed coat with a thin layer of endosperm tissue, differ in fatty acid composition.

It has been demonstrated for *Brassica napus* (Appelqvist, 1969) and *Crambe abyssinica* (Earle *et al.*, 1965) that the erucic acid percentage in the cotyledons is considerably higher than that in other seed parts (Tables 5 and 6). From the data on *Brassica napus* presented in Table 5 many interesting differences can be noted. It is noteworthy for example that the two structures cotyledons and hypocotyl, both of embryonic origin, differ so much in total fatty acid distribution, mainly reflecting triacyl glycerols. The higher palmitic and linoleic but lower erucic acid levels in hypocotyls compared to cotyledons of both species reported might mirror an earlier deposition of hypocotyl triacyl glycerols, since the triacyl glycerols of the entire seeds during earlier

Table 5

Fatty acid composition of cotyledons, hypocotyl and seed coat of *Brassica napus* cv. Regina

Fatty acid	Fatty acid composition, %		
	Cotyledons	Hypocotyl	Seed coat
16:0	3.3	6.6	5.2
16:1	0.3	0.6	2.0
18:0	1.2	1.6	1.2
18:1	12.4	15.3	18.7
18:2	15.2	21.3	17.0
18:3	9.0	9.8	6.1
20:0	0.8	0.8	0.6
20:1	9.5	10.3	14.4
22:0	0.5	0.5	0.7
22:1	44.6	29.9	30.0
Isomer proportions (n-9)/(n-7)			
18:1	12/1	8/1	0.9/1
20:1	8/1	8/1	0.3/1
22:1	25/1	16/1	3.0

(Appelqvist, 1969)

stages of seed development are characterized by higher palmitic and linoleic but lower erucic acid percentages (McKillican, 1966).

More striking differences are however noted between the embryonic structures and the seed coat (+ a minute amount of endosperm) when the positional isomers of the mono-enes are considered. Whereas it had been demonstrated for rapeseed oil and other seed oils that small amounts of (n-7) mono-enes accompany the major isomers, viz. the (n-9) fatty acids (Kuemmel, 1964, Ackman, 1966) studies in our laboratory revealed that the total lipids of the seed coat of *Brassica napus*, cv. Regina II had about equal proportions of the (n-9) and (n-7) isomers of 18:1, viz. oleic and vaccenic acids (Appelqvist, 1969). The (n-7) isomers of 20:1 dominated 3 to 1 over the

Table 6

Fatty acid patterns in seed parts of *Crambe abyssinica*

Seed part	Fatty acid percentages											
	16:0	16:1	18:0	18:1	18:2	18:3	20:0	20:1	22:0	22:1	24:0	24:1
Pericarp	11.8	1.6	2.3	8.7	12.0	7.3	1.9	8.9	1.4	39.6	1.2	1.1
Seed coat	2.8	4.1	0.3	12.5	12.7	4.0	0.5	15.2	0.8	45.7	...	...
Hypocotyl	4.5	0.5	0.9	13.4	13.2	7.2	0.5	4.7	0.5	46.0	4.7	3.4
Cotyledons	1.5	0.3	0.5	15.1	6.7	6.1	0.2	2.0	0.7	59.1	2.4	4.5

(From Earle *et al.*, 1965)

Table 7

Percentage distribution among lipid classes of the total lipids of mature seeds of *Crambe abyssinica* and *Brassica napus*

Species	Hydro-carbons	Sterol esters	Triacyl glycerols	Free fatty acids	Free sterols	Mono- and di-acyl glycerols	Phospho- and glycolipids
Crambe abyssinica	0.2	1.3	94.9	0.2	1.1	1.2	1.1
Brassica napus cv. Golden	0.2	3.4	90.3	0.0	0.5	2.6	3.0

(From McKillican, 1966)

(n-9) isomers, whereas the opposite proportion was found for the 22:1 acids. Assuming 16:1 to be the parent fatty acid in the (n-7) series and 18:1 in the (n-9) series, it is apparent that the peak in elongation in both series occurs after two C_2-unit additions (see Figure 4). One should observe that the content of 16:1 is ca 10 times higher in the seed coat lipids than in the cotyledonary lipids of both rapeseed and *Crambe*. In this connection it is of interest to report that unpublished work in our laboratory has demonstrated the predominance of triacyl glycerols among the total lipids in all three anatomical parts of mature seeds of *Brassica napus*.

POLAR LIPID CLASSES AND THEIR FATTY ACIDS

Whereas the triacyl glycerols of oil rich seeds, deposited in the so called oil bodies of the embryo (see e.g. Rest and Vaughan, 1972), generally predominate among the lipid classes of mature oil seeds, there are also other acyl lipids present in such seeds, mainly phospho- and galactolipids, probably originating from the remains of chloroplasts and mitochondria (Table 7).

Yield data obtained in oilseed processing would indicate even larger proportions of triacyl glycerols among the total lipids than those indicated in Table 7.

So far no complete mapping of fatty acid distributions of all individual lipid classes of mature seeds of any Crucifer appears to be reported in the literature. From the results of McKillican (1966) it is obvious that the erucic acid content is highest in the triacyl glycerols.

However, the very slight reduction in erucic acid level of the other lipid classes of *Crambe* seeds appears to be contradictory to other observations on Crucifers. Generally, the levels of so called family-specific fatty acids in membraneous lipids, such as glyco- and phospholipids, tends to be very low (Hitchcock and Nichols, 1971 and Vijayalakshmi and Rao, 1972a). Data in our own laboratory from "slightly immature" seeds (Table 8) point to larger differences in erucic acid percentages among lipid classes than those shown by McKillican.

Table 8

The fatty acid composition of various lipid classes isolated from slightly immature seeds of *Brassica napus*

Genotype	Lipid class	Content of major fatty acids (per cent of total)						
		16:0	18:0	18:1	18:2	18:3	20:1	22:1
Gulle	Phospholipids and SQDG	21.7	1.1	23.1	38.0	9.4	1.1	2.6
	MGDG	12.7	8.9	14.5	13.7	14.0	6.0	18.9
	DGDG	12.8	0.7	27.1	40.1	11.7	1.8	2.0
	Neutral lipids, mainly triacyl glycerols	4.3	0.9	18.1	16.6	9.8	11.9	36.9
Zero-erucic line 802	Phospholipids and SQDG	18.3	0.6	22.3	47.9	7.4	-	-
	MGDG	25.4	8.7	42.2	11.2	3.0	2.1	-
	DGDG	19.6	6.2	21.9	28.5	13.1	-	-
	Neutral lipids, mainly triacyl glycerols	6.3	0.9	40.2	37.4	12.1	1.6	-

SQDG = sulphoquinovosyl diglyceride, MGDG = monogalactosyl diglyceride, DGDG = digalactosyl diglyceride.
(Appelqvist, 1972a)

The most detailed fatty acid data on "polar" lipids of rapeseed have been acquired on the commercial product rapeseed "lecithin", which is essentially all the polar lipids of crude rapeseed oil. Although the seeds from which these products were obtained were mixtures of Swedish crops, it appears appropriate to present them as well (Table 9).

Table 9

Fatty acid patterns in phospho- and galactolipids isolated from rapeseed "lecithin"

Compound	Fatty acid percentages							
	16:0	16:3	18:0	18:1	18:2	18:3	20:1	22:1
Phosphatidyl choline	12	-	1	30	40	9	1	5
Phosphatidyl ethanolamine	1	-	28	38	11	-	-	-
Phosphatidyl inositol	34	-	1	18	33	10	-	3
Monogalactosyl diglyceride	6	15	1	9	29	27	2	4
Digalactosyl diglyceride	5	6	1	6	37	39	1	0

(From Persmark, 1972 and Appelqvist, 1972b)

From the two sets of data (Table 8 and Table 9) it is easily seen that erucic acid is present in very small levels in phospholipids even when the triacyl glycerols in the same seeds are rich in erucic acid. Also the mono- and digalactosyl diglycerides are generally low in erucic acid. Marked differences in fatty acid patterns appear to exist between all the polar lipids.

The polar lipids generally have unsaturated acids at the 2-position. Data obtained with mustard lecithin might serve as an example (Vijayalakshmi and Rao, 1972b). From the data in Table 10 it is obvious that linoleic and linolenic acids are preferentially located at the 2-position and palmitic and stearic acids at the 1-position.

Table 10

Total and 2-position fatty acids in mustard "lecithin"

Fatty acid	Total acids	2-Position acids
Palmitic acid	14.2	3.3
Palmitoleic acid	-	tr
Stearic acid	1.3	-
Oleic acid	53.1	52.3
Linoleic acid	28.0	39.4
Linolenic acid	3.4	5.0

(From Vijayalakshmi and Rao, 1972b)

In conclusion to the two last sections it is appropriate to point to the fact that the fatty acid patterns vary with acyl lipid classes and tissue types. Although the major lipids of most Crucifers probably represent triacyl glycerols of embryonic tissues, the variability noted can give rise to atypical fatty acid patterns if the cotyledons of a seed sample taken for analysis are markedly underdeveloped. This aspect must be considered in phytochemical studies.

NON-GLYCERIDE LIPIDS

As mentioned previously, the triacyl glycerols predominate among the total lipids of mature seeds with few exceptions, none being a Crucifer (Hitchcock and Nichols, 1971). Minor components among seed lipids are both polar and non-polar in nature. The polar ones have been discussed on pages 240 - 242; the non-polar ones or non-glyceride lipids are to be treated in this section. This group of lipids in cruciferous seeds is composed of several classes of compounds, e.g. saturated hydrocarbons, carotenoids, sterols, sterol esters and tocopherols.

Hydrocarbons

A hydrocarbon fraction of a sample of rapeseed oil from undefined seed material has been found to contain 36 components:

n-hydrocarbons from C_{11} to C_{31}, iso- and/or anteiso-hydrocarbon from C_{11} to C_{17}, C_{19} to C_{21}. The major hydrocarbon was the C_{29} n-alkane (Capella *et al.*, 1963). It is interesting that the C_{29} hydrocarbon also dominates among the leaf hydrocarbons of *Brassica napus* (cf. p. 259).

Another sample of oil from rapeseed of undefined origin has been found to contain very little (less than 2 %) of β -carotene in the total carotenoid fraction (Box and Boekenoogen, 1967). Major components of this fraction were lutein, neo-lutein A and neo-lutein B.

Analysis of an oil sample, obtained from Canadian rapeseed, has shown that a major portion of the lutein is esterified (Froehling *et al.*, 1972). The fatty acid pattern of the lutein diesters was different from that of the triacyl glycerols of the same seeds (Table 11). Similar to the situation

Table 11

Fatty acid patterns of lutein diesters and triglycerides of rapeseed oil

Fatty acid	Fatty acid percentage in lutein diesters	triglycerides
14:0	3.4	0.1
16:0	9.0	3.1
16:1	0.5	0.2
18:0	1.1	1.0
18:1	21.6	32.1
18:2	48.8	22.1
18:3	2.1	9.4
20:0	0.4	-
20:1	3.8	10.8
22:1	9.3	20.6

(From Froehling *et al.*, 1972)

with the phospho- and galactolipids, the lutein diesters have less eicosenoic and erucic acids than the triacyl glycerols of the seed oil.

Sterols, 4-methylsterols and triterpenoids

Sterols, present in free form or as steryl esters, steryl glucosides or esterified steryl glucosides, predominate among the non-glyceride lipids. Generally, little is known about the proportions between the forms of sterols in tissue extracts, whereas considerable amounts of data are available on total sterols in cruciferous seeds, analysed after saponification of the seed oils. However, the different types of sterol derivatives in *Raphanus sativus* have been determined both in the cotyledons and the hypocotyl+radicle (Méance and Dupéron, 1973). Free sterols and steryl esters dominated in both tissue types, less than 1 % of the total sterols were found as steryl glucosides and esterified steryl glucosides. On a dry matter basis, 0.63 % free sterols and 0.37 % steryl esters were found in the hypocotyl+radicle fraction compared to 0.42 % and 0.08% of the two types in the cotyledons. Earlier it had been reported that β-sitosterol was the predominating sterol of the cotyledons (64 % of total sterols) as well as the hypocotyl+ radicle fraction of *Raphanus sativus*, cv. "National" Vilmorin. Minor sterols were, in order of decreasing amounts: campesterol, brassicasterol, stigmasterol, cholesterol and 24-methylene-cholesterol (Dupéron, 1967).

Unlike the situation for several of the minor lipid components, data on total sterol patterns are available for many seeds of well-defined status (Table 12). The paper by Knights and Berrie (1971) from which most of the data in Table 12 were taken, contains references to some earlier work on sterols in Cruciferous seeds or oils. From the data in Table 12 several interesting facts can be mentioned, e.g. (1) Campesterol and β-sitosterol are major components in most of the species and present in all samples studied. (2) Cholesterol is present in all the species, but the level varies from a trace to ca. 15 %. (3) The percentage of brassicasterol is very variable. Whereas the level in *Brassica* species is generally 10 - 20 %, there are also many Crucifers which entirely lack brassicasterol. One should however observe that Itoh *et al.* (1973a) from studies of 19 different vegetable oils reported that brassicasterol was present as a trace in all the oils but in large concentration in rapeseed oil only. (4) Stigmasterol and other sterols are present in variable amounts.

As a result of their studies of 41 species in 21 genera, Knights and Berrie (1971) grouped the species in 5 classes

Table 12

The percentage distribution of some common sterols in some Cruciferous seeds

Species	Individual sterols, % of total						Reference
	Chole-sterol	Campe-sterol	Brassica-sterol	β-Sito-sterol	Stigma-sterol	Other sterols	
Aethionema grandiflorum	10.9	6.9	1.9	78.7	1.6	-	c
A. pulchellum	3.8	6.5	tr	85.2	4.5	-	c
A. saxatile (as *A. creticum*)	8.8	8.2	tr	78.6	1.7	2.7	c
A. schistosum	4.0	6.0	-	89.0	1.0	-	c
Alyssum alpestre	8.7	3.8	-	66.6	10.4	10.5	c
A. argenteum	5.0	21.0	-	65.1	3.5	5.4	c
A. montanum A	6.0	6.5	-	72.0	7.7	7.8	c
A. montanum B	5.7	20.2	-	67.8	3.6	2.7	c
A. saxatile	1.9	22.5	-	73.1	tr	2.5	c
Arabis blepharophylla	1.0	15.7	-	81.1	-	2.2	c
A. caucasica (as *A. albida*)	1.3	22.7	-	76.0	-	-	c
Aubrietia deltoidea	3.0	17.5	-	76.9	2.6	-	c
Brassica campestris f. rapifera A. cv. Wallace	0.3	25.2	19.6	53.4	-	1.5	a
B. campestris f. rapifera B. cv. Golden Ball	2.7	22.4	13.4	61.5	-	-	a
B. campestris (Chinese Cabbage)	tr	34.4	17.8	47.8	-	-	c

B. napobrassica A	tr	38.2	19.1	42.7	-	-	c
B. napobrassica B	tr	34.8	8.2	57.0	-	-	c
B. napus cv. Matador	1.7	31.9	13.0	53.4	-	-	b
B. napus cv. Regina II	3.8	25.6	10.1	60.6	-	-	b
B. napus f. annua	tr	27.8	16.1	52.3	1.1	2.7	c
B. oleracea f. capitata (Primo)	tr	26.4	12.5	61.1	-	-	a
B. oleracea f. capitata	tr	26.4	12.5	61.1	-	-	c
B. oleracea f. cymosa	1.2	23.4	22.7	51.8	tr		
Cheiranthus cheiri A	15.3	17.9	-	38.3	-		c
C. cheiri B	15.0	19.5	-	51.4	-		c
C. cheiri C	15.3	15.7	-	54.3	-		c
C. cheiri (Blood Red)	15.1	19.5	-	51.5	-		a
Draba aizoon	12.3	25.1	4.4	58.0	-	-	c
Erysimum asperum	13.8	37.8	-	35.0	-		c
E. hieracifolium (as *E. marshallianum*)	8.8	28.1	-	53.1	-	10.0	c
E. linifolium	4.5	34.9	-	48.0	-		c
E. perofskianum	9.2	26.5	-	52.8	-	11.5	c
Eruca sativa	6.6	32.2	12.0	49.2	-	-	c
Heliophila longifolia	2.1	25.8	17.6	49.1	4.3	1.6	c
Hesperis matronalis	1.3	23.0	7.0	66.3	-	2.3	c
Hutchinsia alpina	12.5	38.9	6.0	42.6	-	-	c
Iberis gibraltarica	7.6	36.6	8.8	36.3	-	10.7	c
I. sempervirens	4.8	40.5	tr	51.6	-	3.1	c
I. umbellata A	1.2	32.3	20.0	45.2	-	1.3	c
I. umbellata B	tr	33.8	17.7	43.8			c

Table 12 continued

I. umbellata C	2.0	30.5	18.0	49.5	-		c
I. umbellata D	3.2	47.7	10.9	34.6	-	3.6	c
I. umbellata E	5.3	42.7	8.8	39.3	-		c
Ionopsidum acaule (as *Cochlearia acaulis*)	8.4	24.3	16.8	39.0	-	11.5	c
Lepidium sativum	5.8	11.2	-	52.8	4.2	26.0	c
L. virginicum	2.5	30.9	-	51.4	12.1	3.1	c
Lobularia maritima A (as *Alyssum maritimum*)	1.1	14.3	4.3	78.8	-	1.5	c
L. maritima B (as *A. maritimum*)	1.4	10.3	3.8	78.1	-	6.4	c
Lunaria annua (as *L. biennis*)	0.8	29.8	-	67.1	2.3	-	c
Malcolmia maritima	3.7	25.4	5.1	64.2	-	1.6	c
Matthiola bicornis	3.1	20.3	3.1	70.4	3.1	-	c
M. incana A	4.9	13.7	-	81.4	-	-	c
M. incana B	0.9	12.3	-	84.6	-	2.2	c
Petrocallis pyrenaica (as *Draba pyrenaica*)	5.5	29.1	12.9	52.5	-	-	c
Raphanus sativus A	2.5	30.1	15.1	52.3	-	-	c
R. sativus B	2.4	24.2	8.4	62.0	-	3.0	c
R. sativus C	1.5	25.7	8.6	59.8	-	4.4	c
R. sativus (French Breakfast)	2.3	24.2	8.5	62.0	-	3.0	a
Sinapis alba	3.2	34.6	5.2	43.8	-	13.2	a
S. arvensis	1.5	28.2	9.4	60.9	-	-	c

a) Ingram *et al.*, 1968 b) Capella and Losi, 1968 c) Knights and Berrie, 1971

and discussed the phytochemical significance of the results. For the present review, the data are rearranged so that the species follow in alphabetical order. Furthermore, some data from two other papers are included. It can be noted that Knights and Berrie (1971) located *Brassica napus* in a group different from that of all the other brassicas due to the presence of 1.1 % of stigmasterol in the total sterol fraction of the former compared to no stigmasterol in the other brassicas. This should be compared to the reported presence of a trace of stigmasterol in *B. napus* by Itoh *et al.* (1973a) and in *B. campestris* by Ingram *et al.* (1968). Therefore it appears as though, based on the stigmasterol criterion, *B. napus* could as well be grouped with the other brassicas.

The content and composition of 4-methylsterols of seed oils are less well known, since they occur in much smaller amounts than the sterols themselves and their physical properties are very similar to those of the sterols.

However Knights and Berrie (1971) reported measurable quantities of 4-methyl-Δ^7-cholesten-3-β-ol in three species: 5 - 14 % of the total sterols in *Cheiranthus cheiri*, 11.5 % in *Ionopsidum acaule* (as *Cochlearia acaulis*) and 1.7 % in *Erysimum linifolium*. Itoh *et al.* (1973a) found that a sample of rapeseed oil of Canadian origin contained in the unsaponifiables 3 % methylsterols, 6 % triterpene alcohols and 68 % sterols. Ten different compounds were recorded from the analysis of the 4-methylsterol fraction (Itoh *et al.*, 1973b). Three components were tentatively identified: obtusifoliol (29 %), gramisterol (22 %) and citrostadienol (7 %). One report mentions 31 % citrostadienol and two other major, unidentified compounds in the 4-methylsterol fraction of another sample of rapeseed oil (Sawicki and Mordret, 1970).

Detailed studies on the triterpene alcohol fraction of rapeseed oil have been reported from two laboratories (Jacini *et al.*, 1967, Itoh *et al.*, 1973b). The former group reported the presence of at least 13 components of which β-amyrin, cycloartenol and 24-methylcycloartanol were identified. The latter reported eight components; cycloartanol, cycloartenol and 24-methylenecycloartanol were tentatively identified. It appears that data on the variation in triterpene alcohol composition with species and genotype among Crucifers are as yet largely lacking. A review article in "Phytochemistry" as late as 1972 (covering the period 1963 - 1970) does not contain a single reference to triterpenes in Cruciferae (Kulshreshtka *et al.*, 1972).

The production of low- or zero-erucic acid oils of *Brassica campestris* and *B. napus* (see page 233) makes it of interest to search for suitable "tags" on *Brassica* oils regardless of fatty acid composition. So far unpublished work communicated to the author from other scientists and studies undertaken at our laboratory indicate similar sterol patterns in high-erucic and zero-erucic acid cultivars. In view of the great complexity of the triterpene alcohol fraction, it is likely that additional information relating to this question can be obtained from analysis of the triterpenes of many cultivars of the commercial *Brassica* groups.

Tocopherols

The tocopherols also deserve brief mention among the minor lipids of Cruciferous seeds. Total levels in *Brassica* and *Sinapis* are about 800 mg/kg oil. In Brassicas the α-tocopherol is the major and γ-tocopherol is the minor component (Slover, 1971 and Persmark, 1972 and *loc. cit.).* Variation between species and cultivars appears to be larger than that between duplicate samples (Persmark, 1972). It is noteworthy that the relative proportions of the different tocopherols in *Sinapis alba* is different from that in the Brassicas, namely $\alpha\ \gamma\ \delta$ = 10/86/4 in *S. alba* compared to ca. 35/36/- for four *Brassica* samples (Persmark, unpublished, cited by Appelqvist, 1972a).

The minor components discussed under the previous three headings are certainly not the only ones reported from studies on Cruciferous seed lipids. One could for example mention the occurrence of sinapic acid and methyl sinapate in rapeseed oil (Noda and Matsumoto, 1971) but these compounds are not generally considered as lipids.

The very fragmentary information presented under these three headings should, however, serve to indicate that there are many classes of lipids which are rather easily amenable to quantitative analysis and thus potentially valuable in further phytochemical studies.

LIPIDS OF PLANTS AND PLANT ORGANS

Whereas the amount of data available on lipids of Cruciferous seeds is considerable, the situation is very different when it comes to lipids of growing plants or plant parts. A recent monograph on plant lipid biochemistry emphasized that no plant's lipid components have been fully characterized (Hitchcock and Nichols, 1971) and to the knowledge of the author of this review there have been no such additions during recent years.

ACYL LIPIDS AND FATTY ACIDS IN ROOT, STEM, LEAF, SILIQUA AND DEVELOPING SEEDS OF BRASSICA NAPUS

Our laboratory has attempted to map the major classes of fatty acid-containing lipids and their fatty acid patterns in major organs or tissue types of a standard cultivar of *Brassica napus* (Appelqvist, 1970b) which is also used in our studies on the mode of control of lipid patterns in various tissues. From our data, presented in Tables 13, 14 and 15, the following points can be made. In all vegetative parts of the rapeseed

Table 13

Content of fatty acids in lipid fractions of different organs of *Brassica napus* (mg fatty acids/g.f.w.)

Organ	Phospholipids + SQDG	MGDG	DGDG	Neutral lipids
	Plants in stage of early blooming sampling date July 1.			
Leaf	0.54	0.83	0.65	a)
Stalk	0.27	0.09	0.21	0.10
Root	0.24	0.06	0.20	0.11
	Plants in a stage of late maturation[b)]			
Leaf	0.53	0.90	0.62	0.98
Stalk	0.10	0.14	0.12	0.32
Root	0.63	0.88	0.61	0.18
Siliqua	0.56	0.39	0.53	0.96
Seed	0.71	1.05	0.50	63.4

a) Figure missing b) Seed weight = 2.25 mg d.m., moisture content 60 % SQDG = sulphoquinovosyl diglyceride, MGDG = monogalactosyl diglyceride, DGDG = digalactosyl diglyceride.

Table 14

Fatty acid composition of lipids or lipid classes of leaves, stalks and roots from *Brassica napus* L. cv. Gulle. The plants were grown outdoors and were in a stage of early blooming; sampling date July 1

Lipid class (Major constituents)	16:0	16:3	18:0	18:1	18:2	18:3	Other acids
				Leaves			
PC + PI + PE	15.2	0.2	3.4	4.5	24.2	47.6	3.9
PG + SQDG	23.1	0.5	2.7	2.2	20.7	42.1	8.7[a]
DGDG	15.9	4.4	1.4	1.4	6.6	62.6	7.7
MGDG	1.9	32.2	-	0.7	3.0	61.8	0.4
Neutral lipids	43.7	4.4	2.2	3.6	8.8[b]	21.8	15.5[c]
				Stalks			
PC + PI + PE	29.0	-	3.6	6.3	16.5	44.6	-
PC + SQDG	23.8	0.6	2.9	5.6	12.3	54.8	-
DGDG	21.0	0.4	3.1	8.1	18.1	48.8	0.5
MGDG	10.0	17.6	2.6	3.1	3.1	62.6	-
Neutral lipids	26.0	1.1	3.3	6.8	13.3[b]	45.8	3.7
				Roots			
PC + PI + PE	25.0	-	2.3	13.3	15.7	41.3	2.4
PG + SQDG	25.0	-	2.5	11.8	13.4	44.0	3.3
DGDG	18.4	-	3.6	14.2	16.0	45.1	2.7
MGDG	27.1	1.8	3.9	14.9	7.7	37.7	6.9[d]
Neutral lipids	17.9	-	2.5	11.1	14.7[b]	49.5	4.3

Column heading for 16:0 to 18:3: Fatty acid composition, %

a) Mainly a fatty acid with the retention time of *trans*-3-hexadecenoic acid .

b) Including smaller amounts of a fatty acid with retention time slightly shorter than that of 18:2, probably a branched chain saturated fatty acid.

c) Mainly a fatty acid with carbon number 15.9 on BDS, probably a branched chain saturated fatty acid.

d) Including 1.7 % of each of 12.0 and 14:0, which is considerably more than in other lipid classes of roots.

SQDG, MGDG, DGDG - see Table 12 for explanation.

PC = phosphatidyl choline, PI = phosphatidyl inositol, PE = phosphatidyl ethanolamine, PG = phosphatidyl glycerol.

plant at the stages of flowering and late maturation, the phospholipids and galactolipids predominate among the total lipids. The fatty acid patterns of the phospholipids of the various tissues at the two stages of development studied vary relatively little, and are rather typical of phospholipids of vegetative tissue with palmitic, linoleic and linolenic acids as dominating fatty acids. The differences observed between various samples could be due to different proportions of the lipid classes grouped together or to real tissue differences in fatty acid patterns of any of the major phospholipid classes. Looking at the digalactosyl diglycerides one observes only minor differences in fatty acid composition among the various samples. On the other hand, there are major differences in fatty acid patterns for the monogalactosyl glycerides. Thus for the leaf tissue the content of palmitic acid is very low and that of hexadecatrienoic acid (16:3) is high. The reverse situation is apparent for root tissue and the stalks are somewhat intermediate. Other studies at our laboratory have revealed that the outer, green portion of the stalks has a monogalactosyl diglyceride fatty acid pattern similar to that of leaves, whereas the inner white tissue has one similar to that of the roots. Thus non-photosynthetic tissue also contains the chloroplast-typical monogalactosyl diglycerides but essentially lacks the chloroplast-unique fatty acid, 16:3.

The neutral lipid fraction is a very complex fraction and of interest for this discussion only when it comes to content of fatty acids longer than 18 carbon atoms. A comparison of leaf, root and stalk tissues at the flowering stage and late maturation reveals a slight trend towards relatively less of linolenic acid and relatively more of palmitic acid. However, at the stage of late maturation considerable amounts of arachidic acid (20:0) appears in those three tissue types. The siliques which are a major photosynthetic organ of the rapeseed plant at a late stage of seed development have one characteristic feature in all lipid classes namely the high content of stearic acid (cf Appelqvist, 1971c). Continuing studies in our laboratory are designed to reveal whether this high stearic acid content of the chloroplast-typical galactolipids reflects the presence of non-chloroplast located excessive amounts of galactolipids in siliquae or the chloroplasts of siliquas do contain such relatively high amounts of stearic acid. A comparison of the lipid patterns of the two major photosynthetic tissues of the plant, the leaves and the siliquae

Table 15

Fatty acid composition of lipids or lipid classes of leaves, stalks roots, pods, and seeds from *Brassica napus* L. cv. Gulle. The plants were grown outdoors and were in a stage of late maturation; sampling date August 14.

Lipid class (Major constituents)	Fatty acid composition, %										Other acids
	16:0	16:3	18:0	18:1	18:2	18:3	20:0	20:1	22:0	22:1	
Leaves											
PC + PI + PE	17.3	0.8	2.1	2.7	24.8	49.9	-	-	-	-	2.4
PG + SQDG	28.3	0.4	2.1	1.3	23.4	39.9	-	-	-	-	3.6[a)]
DGDG	16.1	2.5	2.3	1.0	9.5	60.9	3.4	-	-	-	4.3
MGDG	4.9	25.4	3.2	0.7	4.7	52.6	6.9	-	-	-	1.6
Neutral lipids	20.1	6.9	6.3	2.3	7.5[b)]	16.5	21.2	-	2.3	0.5	16.4[c)]
Stalks											
PC + PI + PE	25.1	0.3	2.5	5.4	26.2	38.1	0.4	-	-	-	2.0
PG + SQDG	29.9	0.4	2.1	4.4	25.8	36.7	0.2	-	-	-	0.5
DGDG	16.8	1.8	1.8	3.9	18.9	55.8	-	-	-	-	1.0
MGDG	14.3	7.8	2.8	4.1	17.5	50.9	1.4	-	-	-	1.2
Neutral lipids	17.9	2.5	7.1	3.1	13.5[b)]	28.4	19.7	-	-	-	7.8
Roots											
PC + PI + PE	19.8	0.2	3.0	17.5	17.0	38.5	1.0	-	-	-	3.0
PG + SQDG	26.4	0.5	1.8	12.3	17.1	38.6	0.2	-	-	-	3.1
DGDG	19.4	tr	1.6	10.0	14.0	52.1	-	-	-	-	2.9
MGDG	19.3	0.4	2.8	14.9	14.9	43.8	1.0	-	-	-	2.9
Neutral lipids	14.2	tr	1.9	10.1	16.3[b)]	48.5	3.2	-	-	-	5.8

					Siliquae						
PC + PI + PE	16.3	0.3	6.8	6.4	33.2	35.2	tr	-	-	-	1.8
PG + SQDG	23.6	0.4	6.9	3.2	29.5	32.1	tr	-	-	-	4.3
DGDG	16.7	1.6	4.8	2.3	19.0	52.2	-	-	-	-	3.4
MGDG	10.5	10.2	5.8	2.2	16.0	51.6	1.6	-	-	-	2.1
Neutral lipids	12.6	2.9	4.1	15.5	19.8	21.3	3.7	5.1	0.5	10.2	4.3
					Seeds						
PC + PI + PE	16.9	1.0	5.4	9.4	39.1	21.7	3.3	0.9	-	-	2.3
PG + SQDG	26.2	0.2	4.7	9.4	38.7	18.8	0.2	0.8	-	-	1.0
DGDG	16.0	0.8	3.0	12.6	28.9	35.9	-	1.0	-	-	1.8
MGDG	8.8	7.2	2.0	14.5	29.6	28.6	0.1	3.0	4.0	0.8	1.4
Neutral lipids	4.9	0.1	1.5	18.4	17.7	9.9	0.8	12.0	tr	34.3	0.4

a), b), c), SQDG, MGDG, DGDG, PC, PI, PE, PG
See Table 14 for explanation

in a late maturation stage makes apparent another major difference besides the high stearic acid content in the siliquae namely the rather high palmitic acid and low 16:3 acid content in the monogalactosyl diglycerides. Studies of the lipids in the outer, green portion of the siliquae and the inner, white portion revealed differences similar to those of the stalks, namely lower palmitic acid and higher 16:3 acid content of the green portion, but higher palmitic acid, lower 16:3 acid content in the white portion compared to the entire stalk. The fatty acid patterns of the phospholipids and the galactolipids of the immature seeds are characterized by rather low linolenic and rather high linoleic and oleic acid levels. They resembled slightly the phospho- and galactolipid composition of the roots and the siliquae The neutral lipid fraction of the seeds, which is the quantitatively dominant lipid fraction (see Table 13), has considerable amounts of long chain fatty acids and relatively little linolenic acid. This is similar to the pattern of the mature seeds. (Changes in seed composition from flowering to full maturity have been reported for *Brassica napus*, *Sinapis alba* and *Crambe abyssinica* but these results will be discussed in another review, Appelqvist, 1975.

Referring to the data presented in Table 15, consider the content of very long-chain fatty acids and their appearance in different lipid classes. Whereas the triacyl glycerols predominate in the neutral lipid fraction of the developing seeds, these lipids are only very minor in other tissues. Table 13 presents data for the total neutral lipid fractions; the triacyl glycerols were not quantitatively determined by us in this study but they often amount to less than 20 % of the neutral lipids. When a triacyl glycerol fraction was isolated we observed that the eicosenoic and erucic acids were almost exclusively located in that fraction, whereas the 20:0 and 22:0 acids were found predominantly in the wax fractions (see further, p 258). The eicosenoic and erucic acid peaks from the chromatogram were identified as 11-eicosenoic and 13-docosenoic acids respectively by several techniques including GLC-mass spectrometry. The interesting finding is that erucic acid is definitely present in leaf tissue in a plant bearing high erucic acid seed in their siliquae There is work currently continuing in our laboratory trying to reveal the mode of control of synthesis of seed-specific fatty acids in various tissues. Some data from such studies are presented in another review (Appelqvist, 1975) and briefly discussed on page 266 .

Lipids in Various Tissues of Different Cruciferae

Some miscellaneous reports on lipids in Cruciferous plant parts, such as the sterols of different organs of *Brassica napus* and *Raphanus sativus*, the wax coating on the leaves of cabbage (*Brassica oleracea* var. *capitata*) and the fatty acids in callus cultures of *B. campestris* and *B. napus* will be mentioned under this heading.

Sterols in seedlings and plant parts

Germinating *Raphanus sativus* seeds were found to increase in total sterol content both in the cotyledons and the hypocotyl-radicle fraction (Dupéron, 1968). Minor variations were observed as a result of whether the germination occurred in the light or in the dark, and with or without supply of nutrients. The two steryl derivatives which are essentially absent in the dry seeds, namely steryl glucosides and esterified steryl glucosides, appeared in substantial amounts at four days after the onset of germination of *R. sativus* seeds (Méance and Dupéron, 1973). Their levels on a per seedling basis generally rose to even higher levels at 8 and 16 days. The rise was especially marked for the steryl glucosides of the hypocotyl + radicle fraction of the seedling. Also the levels of free sterols increased on a per seedling basis, whereas that of the steryl esters varied without clear trends.

The roots of *R. sativus* plants were found to be richer in total sterols in the lipid fraction than the leaves (Eichenberger and Grob, 1970). Free and esterified sterols dominated the sterol fraction in both tissues, but the roots had substantial amounts of acylated steryl glucosides and both tissues had minor amounts of steryl glucosides. A detailed mapping of the sterols of *Brassica napus* at various stages of seedling development from the dry seed up to the fruiting stage has been reported by Ingram *et al.* (1968). It is of great interest to note that the percentage content of brassicasterol gradually diminished in the sterol fraction during seedling development and it was not detected at all under normal analytical conditions in the plant before flowering. In the flowering stem (including developing fruits) there was some brassicasterol, but in the leaves of these plants none could be detected. It is noteworthy that eicosenoic and erucic acids also disappear during germination and then reappear in the pods and developing seeds (cf. page 256). Ingram *et al.* (1968)

also studied the sterol patterns of dry seeds and young seedlings of five other Cruciferous species. All except *Cheiranthus cheiri* displayed decreasing levels of brassicasterol during germination. *C. cheiri* contained no brassicasterol but had a high percentage of cholesterol in the sterol fraction of the dry seeds and decreasing percentages during germination. In the other species the content of cholesterol generally increased during germination. This is of interest, since it has been reported that the "bound" sterols of chloroplasts generally are rich in cholesterol (Knights, 1971). The chloroplasts of *Sinapis alba*, besides being rich in cholesterol, had a high percentage of brassicasterol in the "bound" sterol fraction but a low percentage of β-sitosterol, compared to the predominance of this sterol in the "free", easily extracted fraction. A comprehensive review of the very interesting subject "Sterol metabolism in plants" has recently been published (Knights, 1973).

Wax of Brassica *and* Sinapis *leaves*

Whereas most of the lipids extracted from plant tissues are located inside the cells in the living plant, there is often a complex mixture of neutral lipids on the surface of leaves and stems. The surface lipids of *Brassica oleracea* have been studied by many groups. As shown in Table 16, which presents data on the surface lipids of cabbage leaves reported by Purdy and Truter (1963a,b,c), the paraffins are the predominant lipid class in the total wax fraction. The residual amounts are proportioned approximately equally among esters, primary alcohols, free acids, secondary alcohols and ketones. Great differences in chainlength of various components obviously exist. The C_{29} compounds predominate among the paraffins, secondary alcohols and ketones whereas even chainlength compounds from C_{12} to C_{28} comprise the primary alcohols and fatty acids in both their free form and esterified form. More recent studies have further elucidated the structures of some of the wax components of cabbage (Laseter *et al.*, 1968, Netting and Macey, 1971) and have compared the wax composition of "wild-type" cabbage with that of some glossy mutants (Macey and Barber, 1970).

From a phytochemical point of view it is of interest to note that Waldron *et al.* (1961) reported that leaves of "swede turnip" (probably *Brassica napus* var. *napobrassica*) and

Table 16

Composition of wax from cabbage leaves

Fraction	Per cent in total waxes	C_{12}	C_{14}	C_{16}	C_{18}	C_{20}	C_{22}	C_{23}	C_{24}	C_{25}	C_{26}	C_{27}	C_{28}	C_{29}	C_{30}	C_{31}
		Per cent of major constituents in each fraction														
Paraffins	36.0	-	-	-	-	-	-	-	-	-	-	1	1	93	1	3
Esters: alcohol moiety	12.6	14	14	-	-	-	14	-	8	-	52	-	14	-	-	-
Esters: acid moiety		14	28	-	28	-	8	-	8	-	-	-	-	-	-	-
Primary alcohols	8.7	6	-	-	24	6	12	-	6	-	36	-	6	-	-	-
Free acids	9.2	24	-	24	-	41.5	5.5	-	5.5	-	-	-	-	-	-	-
Secondary alcohols	11.1	-	-	-	-	-	-	-	-	-	-	-	-	100	-	-
Ketones	13.8	-	-	-	-	-	-	-	-	-	-	-	-	100	-	-
Ketols	0.9	-	-	-	-	-	-	-	-	-	-	-	-	-	-	-

(From Purdy and Truter, 1963c)

Brussel sprouts (*Brassica oleracea* var. *gemmifera*) had predominantly the C_{29} paraffin, whereas leaves of white mustard (*Sinapis alba)* had more of the C_{31} paraffin (52 %) than of the C_{29} (36 %) besides smaller amounts of paraffins of other chain-lengths. This adds to the many other compositional differences between *Sinapis alba* and the *Brassica* species. It is noteworthy that the seed paraffins of *Brassica napus* also have the C_{29} as the predominant component (Capella *et al.*, 1963).

Lipids in roots of Brassica campestris *var.* rapifera *and* B. napus *var.* napobrassica

The lipid composition of the roots of two cultivars of turnip (*Brassica campestris* var. *rapifera*) have been reported to be very similar (Lepage, 1967). The fatty acid patterns of some lipid classes are presented in Table 17. Similar to the figures reported for the roots of *B. napus* var. *oleifera* (see Tables 14 and 15) linolenic acid is a predominant fatty acid in all lipid classes. Notable is the high palmitic acid content of phosphatidyl inositol. It was specially reported that no erucic acid was detected. Among the carotenoids, lycopene dominated over γ-carotene and two other, minor components. In the sterol fraction, β-sitosterol was the major sterol (90 %) and campesterol the minor. There was no mention of any brassicasterol or cholesterol but stigmasterol was present as a trace. The sterol pattern of *B. campestris* roots obviously differs much from that in the seeds (see Table 12). The absence of brassicasterol in the roots of *B. campestris* adds further weight to the observations on *B. napus* (page 257) that brassicasterol might be a seed-specific sterol in these species. It should also be remarked that the carotenoid fraction of *B. campestris* roots differed very much from that in *B. napus* seeds (page 244).

The results from extensive analyses of the carotenoids of "partially sprouted" rutabagas (*Brassica napus* var. *napobrassica*) have been published by Joyce (1959). The isolation of six identified and 12 partially characterized components was reported, but no clear quantitative data were published.

*Phospholipids of florets of cauliflower (*Brassica oleracea *var.* botrytis).

As background information for biosynthetic studies, Abdel-kader and Mazliak (1970) presented data for lipid class

Table 17

The fatty acid composition of different lipid classes isolated from Laurentian Turnips (*Brassica campestris* var. *rapifera)*

Fatty acids	Neutral lipids %	Phosphatidyl choline %	Phosphatidyl ethanolamine %	Phosphatidyl inositol %	Digalactosyl diglyceride %	Monogalactosyl diglyceride %
16:0	10.9	10.2	12.6	33.6	21.2	12.1
16:1	1.2	1.0	0.7	0.7	1.8	1.1
18:0	1.2	0.8	0.9	0.8	1.2	0.9
18:1	8.8	10.7	11.3	4.0	7.7	9.6
18:2	17.0	19.6	24.9	14.6	13.5	20.4
18:3	60.9	57.7	49.7	47.1	54.7	55.8

(From Lepage, 1967)

distribution and fatty acid patterns of mitochondria and microsomes of cauliflowers (*Brassica oleracea* var. *botrytis*). From Table 18 it is apparent that phosphatidyl choline and phosphatidyl ethanolamine are the predominating polar lipids in both mitochondrial and microsomal fractions from this tissue. No striking differences in relative distribution of phospholipids

Table 18

Lipid class distribution and fatty acid patterns in mitochondria and microsomes of cauliflower florets

Lipid classes	Mitochondria	Microsomes
	Lipid class distribution, % of total	
Phosphatidyl inositol	11	13
" choline	43	31
" glycerol	3	9
" serine	1	4
" ethanolamine	32	31
" glycerol phosphate	7	5
Phosphatidic acid	2	7
	Fatty acid distribution, % of total	
Palmitic acid	18	24
Palmitoleic acid	2	-
Stearic acid	2	2
Oleic acid	10	10
Linoleic acid	12	13
Linolenic acid	45	51

(From Abdelkader and Mazliak, 1970)

were observed for the two preparations. Also the overall fatty acid composition of the two fractions was rather similar, linolenic acid being the major fatty acid followed by palmitic and linoleic acids.

At this point it might be appropriate to mention that the chloroplasts of all photosynthetic tissues so far analysed are very rich in galactolipids and also have considerable amounts of phospholipids (Hitchcock and Nichols, 1971). Although no quantitative data on lipid classes and fatty acids in chloroplast preparations of Crucifers seem to be reported, one can by analogy certainly assume that the chloroplast lipids of a Crucifer are very different from those of the mitochondria of the same tissue. We are presently working out methods for analysing fatty acids of isolated chloroplasts from various tissues of *Brassica napus* in our laboratory.

Lipids in pollens of three Crucifers

In a series of papers, the isolation and physiological effects of a mixture of "novel" fatty acid-containing compounds from pollen of *Brassica napus* have been reported (Mitchell *et al.*, 1970, Mandava and Mitchell, 1972 and *loc. cit.*). The compounds isolated were termed "brassins" and are claimed to have specific hormonal effects. The compounds with the physiological effect recorded were present also in seed tissue and in pollen from other species, but *B. napus* pollen was found to be a rich source. It has been reported that the "brassins" are glucose esters of fatty acids, structures which are novel to the plant kingdom (Mandava and Mitchell, 1972). However, other authors have criticised these findings and questioned both the elucidation of the chemical structure and the claim that the biological effects were novel (Milborrow and Pryce, 1973). The latter authors conclude that the physiological effects recorded are highly similar to those demonstrated by gibberellins. Thus the question on the nature of the "brassins" seems to remain open.

Analysis of the sterols of pollen from *Brassica nigra* and *Sisymbrium irio* demonstrated that 24-methylenecholesterol was the principal sterol in these species, similar to what is found in many other pollen samples (Standifer *et al.*, 1968). A total of six different sterols were found in both samples. These authors conclude, based on studies of a total of 15 species and older data in the literature, that no taxonomic relationships seem to exist between sterols in the pollen and the plant families investigated.

Lipids of tissue cultures of Brassica campestris *and* B. napus

Callus cultures grown from germinating seeds of *B. campestris* and *B. napus* had lipid class distribution patterns similar to those of stem and root tissues with galactolipids and phosphatidyl glycerol as major components (Staba *et al.*, 1971). The triacyl glycerols of the callus tissue had fatty acid patterns very different from those of seeds or seedlings with no erucic acid and over 50 % of linolenic acid being typical of the triacyl glycerols of callus (Table 19). The absence of erucic acid from the triacyl glycerols of callus grown from

Table 19

The fatty acid patterns of the triacyl glycerols from various tissues of *Brassica napus*

Fatty acids	Seeds %	Seedlings: Cotyledons %	Seedlings: Stems and roots %	Tissue culture %
below 16	0.2	1.6	3.8	1.0
16:0	4.1	2.8	16.5	16.1
16:1	4.2	0.4	4.1	1.0
18:0	1.0	0.8	6.4	3.7
18:1	20.9	19.2	17.7	14.5
18:2	16.7	14.8	17.3	6.7
18:3	14.2	12.6	8.0	53.8
20:0	0.4	0.9	tr	1.0
20:1	4.2	4.8	3.1	tr
22:0	-	-	tr	0.5
22:1	36.4	40.7	16.8	-
24:0	-	tr	tr	0.5
24:1	0.3	0.7	tr	0.6

(From Staba *et al.*, 1971)

germinating seeds can be expected, since it is known that the capacity to synthesize some "family-typical" fatty acids (e.g. ricinoleic acid in *Ricinus communis* and erucic acid in *Brassica napus*) does not occur in germinating but only in developing seeds.

ASPECTS ON THE CONTROL OF LIPID PATTERNS

The dominant theme of this review has been a straightforward mapping of the lipids reported to be present in various tissues. Some dynamic aspects will be discussed in a review on changes in developing seeds from any higher plant

(Appelqvist, 1975). However, in the present paper a brief account will be made on what is known about the control of the various lipid components.

Control expressed in Genetic Terminology

It has been demonstrated by several authors that the erucic acid content of seeds of *Brassica campestris* and *B. napus* is controlled by the genotype of the embryo (see Lööf and Appelqvist, 1972 for review and references to original work). The level of erucic acid is approximately intermediate between that of the parents and appears to be controlled by two "major genes" in the allotetraploid *B. napus* and one "major gene" in the diploid *B. campestris*. However, results from later crossing experiments have indicated that "minor genes" also contribute and that there are probably several alleles at one locus. The levels of oleic, linoleic and linolenic acids in the zero-erucic acid rapeseed are dependent both on the genotype of the embryo and that of the maternal plant (Thomas and Kondra, 1973 and *loc. cit.)*.

Control by Environmental Factors

It has been demonstrated that seeds obtained on *Brassica napus* plants, supplied with various amounts of nitrogen, potassium and phosphorus salts in a soil-free culture are affected to a rather small extent by the nutrient supply (Appelqvist, 1968b). The influence of temperature during seed development on the fatty acid patterns of the mature seeds of *B. napus* appears to vary with the genotype. Whereas Canvin (1965) in growth-chamber experiments with erucic acid-rich rapeseed noted progressively lower linolenic acid percentages with increasing temperature, studies on zero-erucic acid genotypes in our laboratory demonstrated an increasing level of linoleic acid and essentially constant linolenic acid percentage with increasing day temperature (Appelqvist, 1971c). A rather low night temperature was used in our experiments. Recent studies at our laboratory have demonstrated that two zero-erucic acid genotypes of *B. napus* respond differently to the same temperature treatment. One genotype obtained lower percentages of polyunsaturated fatty acids (essentially constant 18:2 acid and decreasing 18:3 acid) with increasing day temperature, whereas the other genotype had increased levels of polyunsaturated fatty acids (increasing 18:2 acid and constant

18:3 acid), regardless of whether a warm or a cool night was applied (Appelqvist, to be published). Also recent work by van Hal and van Baarsel (1974) has demonstrated that different genotypes of *B. napus* vary in their response as regards fatty acid patterns in growth-chamber experiments. For outdoor plantings of classical cultivars of *B. campestris*, *B. napus* and *Sinapis alba*, the traditional rule "A warmer climate yields a less unsaturated vegetable oil" appears to be verified (see Appelqvist, 1968c and *loc. cit.)*. However, the aforementioned data on zero-erucic acid rapeseed demonstrate that there are exceptions.

Control Expressed in Cell-physiological and Biochemical Terminology

In this review many figures have been presented which demonstrate tissue specificities in qualitative and quantitative composition of several lipid components. Almost nothing seems to be known, however, about the mechanisms by which these patterns are controlled. Two components, which show promise as candidates for elucidating such mechanisms are erucic acid and brassicasterol.

It has been stated in several texts (see e.g. Shorland, 1963, Hilditch and Williams, 1964) that erucic acid does not occur in the leaves of rapeseed plants although the seeds are rich in erucic acid, often 40 - 50 % of the total lipids. Studies in our laboratory have however revealed (as discussed on page 256) that leaves from plants of *Brassica napus* bearing erucic acid-rich immature seeds do contain small amounts of erucic acid (Appelqvist, 1970b). It has also often been claimed in the literature (without references to original work) that lipids are not translocated within a plant. The discovery that erucic acid is present in leaf tissue of erucic acid-rich genotypes bearing immature seeds but not in flowering plants probably has to be explained in one of two ways. Either 1) small amounts of erucic acid are translocated, as triacyl glycerols or in another form from which the acid is esterified almost exclusively into the triacyl glycerols of the recipient tissue or 2) the capacity to synthesize erucic acid is obtained by adult, maternal tissue as a result of a translocated factor (a hormone) which is being synthesized in the developing embryo. Experiments in our laboratory (e.g. grafting of silique-halves of immature zero-erucic acid genotypes on high-erucic acid plants and studies with ^{14}Clabelled acetate) have so far not yielded positive evidence for either of the two alternatives. Growth of callus tissue from immature cotyledons of erucic acid-synthesizing plants of *B. napus* is presently used at our laboratory as another tool in the attempts to shed some light on this interesting question. For details on this problem including literature references to the statements above and for information on what is known about biosynthesis of the "elongated" acids in various tissues, the reader is referred to another review (Appelqvist, 1975).

The occurrence of brassicasterol in rather high levels in mature *Brassica* seeds but not in the green plant until the onset of flowering and then not in the leaves but in the stalks plus the "as-yet-unopened" flowers is very interesting (cf. page 257). At a later stage in development, still no brassicasterol was detected in the leaves, although it was present in the "stalks plus the pods" fraction. Based on these data it has been suggested that brassicasterol might be implicated in the flowering process (Knights, 1973). It has also been suggested that sterols in plant tissue in general might be regulatory agents in the fertilization process, since there is often a great similarity in physiological control principles in the biosphere (Heftman, 1970). However, since brassicasterol is absent from (or present in very minute amounts in) other Cruciferae (see Table 12) it is also likely that this sterol is an "inert", secondary metabolite which is primarily synthesized in young, embryonic tissue (like erucic acid), leaving the proposed rôle in fertilization control to another, more generally occurring sterol or sterol derivative.

CONCLUDING REMARKS

Those data in the literature, which are the basis of this review have been acquired in laboratories with widely different programs. A major proportion of the data were accumulated as a basis for utilization of Brassicas and related species as oil seed crops, fodder crops or vegetables. Other data were a result of phytochemical studies or a "spin-off" from biochemical research, where the reaction was of prime interest and a Crucifer happened to be a handy substrate. Consequently, from a systematic point of view our knowledge as regards lipid patterns in the family Cruciferae is very imbalanced in favour of the genus *Brassica*. Hopefully, some of the discussions in this review will stimulate further research on the non-cultivated Cruciferae.

In the execution of such programs, there are a few matters for which the author of this review has special concern. One is the overestimation which still seems to occur of the exactness of information obtained by a single gas chromatographic separation. Further solid analytical data would for example be of great importance as a basis for statements whether erucic acid or brassicasterol are present in small amounts in a certain tissue. Besides running the risk of mistaking the methyl ester of behenic acid (22:0) for that of erucic acid (22:1), other volatile components of a crude lipid extract subjected to methanolysis could elute at the position of erucic acid. In case of doubts, other instrumental methods (such as mass spectrometry) should be utilized for proper identification. In this connection it may be appropriate to mention that erucic acid has been reported as a minor component also of the seed oils of sunflower (*Helianthus annuus*) and safflower (*Carthamus tinctorius*). Until such reports are supported by mass spectrometric data and/or other instrumental data, it is reasonable to assume that erucic acid is not present in carefully extracted oils from clean seeds of these species. As pointed out on page however, it is definitely present in several families outside the Cruciferae.

Another problem to be considered is the variation in fatty acid patterns with cultivar, anatomical part of seed and lipid class. Consequently, total fatty acid pattern of dry seeds can be a misleading figure in comparative studies if the seeds analysed were underdeveloped and therefore had subnormal amounts of cotyledonary triacyl glycerols and supernormal levels of cotyledonary polar lipids and seed coat lipids. Also a proper seed identification number for non-cultivated seeds or the cultivar used should be reported. For tissues other than dry, mature seed overall fatty acid data are of little value in view of the very large differences found in fatty acid patterns of various acyl lipids.

A third matter of concern is the frequent mislabelling of cruciferous specimens received from other laboratories or even botanical gardens. A few examples of such mislabelling revealed from fatty acid data are presented in an earlier paper (Appelqvist, 1970). The problems associated with checking the taxa by planting in close proximity different collects or cultivars of a species have been discussed earlier (Appelqvist, 1971a).

For the precautious investigator of cruciferous lipids, the statement of Carolus Linnaeus about the advantages of rapeseed cropping can be applied metaphorically: ". . . those who become interested in this crop have no reason to regret their toil, when they in this manner can derive rich remuneration from a well cultivated soil" (Linnaeus, 1751).

ACKNOWLEDGEMENTS

Financial support of the investigations in the author's own laboratory by the Swedish Extraction Association, the Swedish Oil Plant Growers' Association, the Swedish Council for Forestry and Agricultural Research, the Swedish Natural Science Research Council and the Bank of Sweden Tricentennial Fund, which also granted money for the participation in this symposium, is gratefully acknowledged.

REFERENCES

Aaes-Jørgensen, E. (1972). *In* "Rapeseed" (L-Å. Appelqvist and R. Ohlson, eds), pp. 301 - 353. Elsevier Publ. Co., Amsterdam.

Abdelkader, A. B. and Mazliak, P. (1970). *Eur.J.Biochem.* 15, 250.

Ackman, R. G. (1966). *J.Am.Oil Chem.Soc.* 43, 483.

Appelqvist, L-Å. (1968a). *Acta Agric.Scand.* 18, 3.

Appelqvist, L-Å. (1968b). *Physiol.Plant.* 21, 455.

Appelqvist, L-Å. (1968c). *Physiol.Plant.* 21, 615.

Appelqvist, L-Å. (1969). *Hereditas* 61, 9.

Appelqvist, L-Å. (1970a). *Fette Seifen Anstrichmittel* 72, 783.

Appelqvist, L-Å. (1970b). Abstr. no. 303, World Fat Congress, Chicago, *J.Am. Oil Chem.Soc.* 47, 7.

Appelqvist, L-Å. (1971a). *J.Am. Oil Chem.Soc.* 48, 740.

Appelqvist, L-Å. (1971b). *J.Am. Oil Chem.Soc.* 48, 851.

Appelqvist, L-Å. (1971c). *Physiol.Plant.* 25, 493.

Appelqvist, L-Å. (1972a). *In* "Rapeseed" (L-Å. Appelqvist and R. Ohlson, eds), pp. 123 - 173. Elsevier Publ.Co., Amsterdam.

Appelqvist, L-Å. (1972b). *J.Am. Oil Chem.Soc.* 49, 151.

Appelqvist, L-Å. (1975). *In* "Recent Advances in the Chemistry and Biochemistry of Plant Lipids" (T. Galliard and I. Mercer, eds), pp. 247 - 286. Academic Press, New York.

Appelqvist, L-Å. and Dowdell, R. D. (1968). *Arkiv för Kemi* 28, 539.

Appelqvist, L-Å. and Jönsson, R. (1970). *Z.für Pflanzenzüchtung* 64, 340.

Appelqvist, L-Å. and Ohlson, R. (1972). "Rapeseed". Elsevier Publ. Co., Amsterdam.

Barclay, A. S., Gentry, H. S. and Jones, Q. (1962). *Economic Botany* 16, 95.

Box, J. A. G. and Boekenoogen, H. A. (1967). *Fette Seifen Anstrichmittel* 69, 724.

Brockerhoof, D. and Yurkowski, M. (1966). *J.Lipid Res.* 7, 62.

Canvin, D. T. (1965). *Canad.J.Botany* 43, 63.

Capella, P. and Losi, G. (1968). *Ind.Agr.* 6, 277.

Capella, P., Fedeli, E., Cirimele, M. and Jacini, G. (1963). *Riv.Ital.Sostanze Grasse* 40, 603.

Craig, B. M., Mallard, T. M., Wight, R. E., Irvine, G. N. and Reynolds, J. R. (1973). *J.Am. Oil Chem.Soc.* 50, 395.

Downey, R. K. (1964). *Canad.J.Plant Sci.* 44, 295.

Dupéron, P. (1967). *C.R.Acad.Sc. Paris* 265, 409.

Dupéron, P. (1968). *C.R.Acad.Sc. Paris* 266, 1658.

Earle, F. R., Peters, J. E., Wolff, I. A. and White, G. A. (1965). *J.Am. Oil Chem.Soc.* 43, 330.

Eichenberger, W. and Grob, E. C. (1970). *FEBS Letters* 11, 177

Froehling, P. E., van den Bosch, G. and Boekenoogen, H. A. (1972). *Lipids* 7, 447.

Goering, K. J., Eslick, R. and Brelsford, D. L. (1965). *Economic Botany* 19, 251.

Gunstone, F. D. and Morris, L. J. (1959). *J.Chem.Soc.* 2127.

van Hal, J. and van Baarsel, J. (1974). Abstr. 4th International Rapeseed Conference, Giessen. *Fette Seifen Anstrichmittel* 76, 362.

Harlow, R. D., Litchfield, C. and Reiser, R. (1966). *Lipids* 1, 216.

Heftmann, E. (1971). *Lipids* 6, 128.

Hilditch, T. P. and Williams, P. N. (1964). "The Chemical Constitution of Natural Fats". 4th ed. Chapman & Hall, London.

Hitchcock, C. and Nichols, B. W. (1971). "Plant Lipid Biochemistry. Experimental Botany: An International Series of Monographs". Vol. 4. Academic Press, London.

Ingram, D. S., Knights, B. A., McEvoy, I. J. and MacKay, P. (1968). *Phytochemistry* 7, 1241.

Itoh, T., Tamura, T. and Matsumoto, T. (1973a). *J.Am. Oil Chem.Soc.* 50, 122.

Itoh, T., Tamura, T. and Matsumoto, T. (1973b). *J.Am. Oil Chem.Soc.* 50, 300.

Iverson, J. L. (1966). *J.Assoc.Offic.Anal. Chemists* 49, 332.

Jacini, G., Fedeli, E. and Lanzani, A. (1967). *J.Assoc.Offic. Anal.Chemists* 50, 84.

Joyce, A. E. (1959). *J.Sci.Fd Agric.* 6, 342.

Jönsson, R. (1973). Z. *Pflanzenzüchtung* 69, 1.

Kleiman, R., Spencer, G. F., Earle, F. R., Nieschlag, H. J. and Barclay, A. S. (1972). *Lipids* 7, 660.

Knights, B. A. (1971). *Lipids* 6, 215.

Knights, B. A. (1973). *Chemistry in Brit.* 9, 106.

Knights, B. A. and Berrie, A. M. M. (1971). *Phytochemistry* 10, 131.

Kuemmel, D. F. (1964). *J.Am. Oil Chem.Soc.* 41, 667.

Kulschreshtha, M. J., Kulschreshtha, D. K. and Rastogi, R. P. (1972). *Phytochemistry* 11, 2369.

Laseter, J. L., Weber, D. J. and Oró, J. (1968). *Phytochemistry* 7, 1005.

Lepage, M. (1967). *Lipids* 2, 244.

Linnaeus, C. "Skånska Resa" Stockholm (1751). p. 189 in Swedish, actual pages translated into English as pp. 5 - 6 in "Rapeseed" (L-Å. Appelqvist and R. Ohlson, eds), Elsevier Publ. Co., Amsterdam.

Litchfield, C. (1972). "Analysis of Triglycerides". Academic Press, New York.

Lööf, B. and Appelqvist, L-Å. (1972). *In* "Rapeseed" (L-Å. Appelqvist and R. Ohlson, eds), pp. 101 - 122. Elsevier Publ. Co., Amsterdam.

Macey, M. J. K. and Barber, H. N. (1970). *Phytochemistry* 9, 13.

Mandava, N. and Mitchell, J. W. (1972). *Chem. & Ind.* 930.

McKillican, M. E. (1966). *J.Am. Oil Chem.Soc.* 43, 461.

Méance, J. and Dupéron, R. (1973). *C.R.Acad.Sc. Paris* 277, 849.

Mikolajczak, K. L., Miwa, T. K., Earle, F. R., Wolff, I. A. and Jones, Q. (1961). *J.Am.Oil Chem.Soc.* 38, 678.

Mikolajczak, K. L., Earle, F. R. and Wolff, I. A. (1962). *J.Am. Oil Chem.Soc.* 42, 939.

Mikolajczak, K. L., Smith Jr, C. R. and Wolff, I. A. (1968). *Lipids* 3, 215.

Milborrow, B. V. and Pryce, R. J. (1973). *Nature* 243, 46.

Miller, R. W., Earle, F. R., Wolff, I. A. and Jones, Q. (1965). *J.Am.Oil Chem. Soc.* 42, 817.

Mitchell, J. W., Mandava, N., Worley, J. F., Plimmer, J. R. and Smith, M. V. (1970). *Nature* 225, 1065.

Moricé, P. P. (1970). *Phytochemistry* 9, 1829.

Netting, A. G. and Macey, M. J. K. (1971). *Phytochemistry* 10, 1917.

Noda, M. and Matsumoto, M. (1971). *Biochim.Biophys.Acta* 231, 131.

Ohlson, R. (1972). *In* "Rapeseed" (L-Å. Appelqvist and R. Ohlson, eds), pp. 274 - 287. Elsevier Publ. Co., Amsterdam.

Persmark, U. (1972). *In* "Rapeseed" (L-Å. Appelqvist and R. Ohlson, R., eds), pp. 174 - 197. Elsevier Publ. Co., Amsterdam.

Phillips, B. E., Smith Jr., C. R. and Tallent, W. H. (1971). *Lipids* 6, 93.

Purdy, S. J. and Truter, E. V. (1963a). *Proc. of the Royal Soc.B.* 158, 536.

Purdy, S. J. and Truter, E. V. (1963b). *Proc. of the Royal Soc.B.* 158, 544.

Purdy, S. J. and Truter, E. V. (1963c). *Proc. of the Royal Soc.B.* 158, 553.

Rest, J. A. and Vaughan, J. G. (1972). *Planta* 105, 245.

Röbbelen, G. (1972). *In* "The Way Ahead in Plant Breeding". (Plant Breeding Institute, Cambridge 1972), pp. 207 - 214. Proc. 6. Congr.Eucarpia, Cambridge, 1971).

Sawicki, J. and Mordret, F. (1970). *Rev.Franc. des Corps Gras* 17, 685.

Shorland, F. B. (1963). *In* "Chemical Plant Taxonomy". (T. Swain, ed.), pp. 253 - 303. Academic Press, London.

Slover, H. T. (1971). *Lipids* 6, 291.

Smith, C. R. Jr., Wilson, T. L., Miwa, T. K., Zobel, H., Lohmar, R. L. and Wolff, I. A. (1961). *J.org.Chem.* 26, 2903.

Staba, E. J., Shik Shin, B. and Mangold, H. K. (1971). *Chem. Phys.Lipids* 6, 291.

Standifer, L. N., Devys, M. and Barbier, M. (1968). *Phytochemistry* 7, 1361.

Stefansson, B. R., Hougen, F. W. and Downey, R. K. (1961). *Canad.J.Plant Sci.* 41, 218.

Stumpf, P. K. (1975). *In* "Recent Advances in the Chemistry and Biochemistry of Plant Lipids". (T. Galliard and T. Mercer, eds), pp. 93 - 113, Academic Press, New York.

Thies, W. (1971). *Fette Seifen Anstrichmittel* 73, 710.

Thomas, P. M. and Kondra, Z. P. (1973). *Canad.J.Plant Sci.* 53, 221.

Waldron, J. D., Gowers, D. S., Chibnall, A. C. and Piper, S. H. (1961). *Biochem.J.* 78, 435.

Vaughan, J. G. (1968). *In* "Chemotaxonomy and Serotaxonomy" (J. G. Hawkes, ed.), p. 103 - 110, Academic Press, London.

Vijayalakshmi, B. and Venkob Rao, S. (1972a). *Chem.Phys. Lipids* 9, 82.

Vijayalakshmi, B. and Venkob Rao, S. (1972b). *Fette Seifen Anstrichmittel* 74, 404.

Wolff, I. A. (1966). *Science* 154, 1140.

THE SEED PROTEIN CONTENTS OF SOME CRUCIFERAE

A. J. FINLAYSON

Prairie Regional Laboratory, National Research Council of Canada, Saskatoon, Saskatchewan, Canada.

INTRODUCTION

It has been realized during the last twenty years or so that there must be an increase in the production of protein throughout the world. Since seeds are the major source of proteins for animals and man, studies of seed proteins are necessary because their utilization depends partly on the quality and types of proteins produced in a particular crop. Consequently, to improve the protein quality of a crop, for either industrial or nutritional reasons, it is necessary to understand the chemistry of the seed proteins, how environment affects their synthesis and deposition, and to understand the relationship existing between the proteins and other seed constituents.

Many plants of the family Cruciferae such as *Crambe*, *Raphanus* and *Nasturtium* have a potentially great economic value, but at present those of greatest importance belong to the *Brassica* species. Subspecies of both *B. napus* L. (Argentine rape) and *B. campestris* L. (Summer turnip rape) are grown in Canada for the domestic vegetable oil market while the meal has some use as an animal feed (Downey, 1965) and for the preparation of a high protein "flour". Some *B. oleracea* cultivars are grown for the vegetable market and a small amount of mustard (*B. juncea)* is grown for food flavouring. *Crambe abyssinica* has been suggested as an industrial source of erucic acid. The seeds of the mature *Brassica* and *Crambe* cultivars contain about 22 - 24 % protein (N x 6.25) and the meal, after oil extraction, has a good potential as a protein supplement because of its nutritionally acceptable amino acid composition (Downey, 1965). The defatted meal may contain glucosinolate hydrolysis products which cause some toxicity problems when it is fed to animals; however, research by the Canada Department of Agriculture and the University of Manitoba has resulted in the development of cultivars with low glucosinolate contents (Kondra and Stefansson, 1970) thus alleviating the toxicity problem. Consequently, the removal of glucosinolates from rapeseed will provide a greater possibility of using *Brassica* seed proteins as food supplements. However, the effects of this extended plant breeding program on the seed protein composition has not yet been catalogued.

Research into the structures of many non-cereal seed constituents, which is necessary before crop improvement studies are initiated, is a development of the last twenty years. Enzymes and the reactions they catalyze in the leaves and stems have been carefully studied but research into reactions occurring in the developing and mature seed are not so well documented. There have been a number of reviews on seed proteins (Altschul, 1963; Inglett, 1972) and an examination of them shows there are many unsolved questions concerning both the developing and mature seed. For instance, genetic studies to improve seed proteins for functional properties and nutritive value have just started. In this review the author intends to describe the physical and chemical properties of the storage proteins in the seeds of some Cruciferae and to present what is known about their sub-cellular location and their deposition in the maturing plant.

The storage or reserve proteins in the seeds of the *Brassica* species as well as in a number of legumes constitute the major portion of the seed nitrogen (about 80 % in soybean and 75 % in rape). They apparently possess very little, if any, biological activity and are thought to provide a source of nitrogen and amino acids at germination. There are other proteins in the seed as well but the enzymes, haemaglutinins, and ribosomal proteins are present in small amounts relative to the storage protein. Since the storage proteins have, as yet, undiscovered biological activities they have been classified by physical and chemical means. Many of these seed proteins from botanically distantly related sources have similar properties; they are globulins using the Osborne classification

(Osborne, 1924). The globulins from a number of sources: phaseolin from *Phaseolus vulgaris* L., the 11s globulin from *Glycine max.* m Merr., arachin from *Arachis hypogea* L. are soluble in 0.5 - 1.0 M sodium chloride solution but have a lower solubility in water. They are aggregates of a number of polypeptide chains and have large molecular weight (1.5 x 10^5) but dissociate into the constituent polypeptides with a change in pH or a reduction in ionic strength of the solvent (Wolf, 1970). These globulins are usually rich in arginine and amides of the dicarboxylic amino acids. It appears that they are found mainly in the seeds of dicotyledons such as rape, cotton, peanut and the legumes although there is evidence to suggest they form only a small part of the reserve protein in monocotyledons (Graham *et al.*, 1962). There are other non-enzyme proteins in rapeseed which constitute about 20 % of the seed nitrogen. It appears that rape contains a greater variety of these polypeptides than either soybean or cottonseed. They are more basic than the globular proteins and readily extractable from the meal with water. Apparently, they are not associated with the globular proteins but nevertheless form part of the reserve protein of the seed. Although work on the structures of these low molecular weight proteins has only started, their amounts in the seed and their amino acid compositions appear to be highly cultivar and species variable.

The concept of a "protein body" or "aleurone grain" (Hartig, 1856; Altschul *et al.*, 1964) in which the reserve protein is stored in a seed has been discussed for many years. The advent of electron microscopy and density gradient centrifugation has simplified both the observation and isolation of protein bodies although isolating what is observed under the microscope is still a difficult problem. The protein body is thought to be limited by a membrane with other non-enzyme proteins, free amino acids, peptides and some enzymes outside of it; it has been suggested (Altschul *et al.*, 1964) that the globulin of the protein body be called "aleurin". The cottonseed protein body contains most of the seed protein, phospholipid, phytic acid and a large fraction of certain metals (Yatsu and Jacks, 1968). While the microscopic work with a number of oilseeds has shown them to have certain similarities in seed cellular structure, the cell structure and protein bodies of rape have received relatively little attention.

Table 1

Approximate Compositions of Seed of some Cruciferae

Plant	Lipid %	Protein (Nx6.25) %		Soluble carbo-hydrate %	Fibre %	Gluco-sinolates %	References
		Whole Seed	Meal				
B. campestris L. cv. Arlo	36-43	21-24	35-36		7-11	0.6-0.8[2]	Downey, 1965
B. napus L. cv. Target	40-47	21-24[1]	38-42	4.5[3]	7-11	0.6-1.0[2]	Downey, 1965
B. juncea L. Coss	38-41	24-25	38-42				Van Etten *et al.*, 1961
B. hirta Moench (*Sinapis alba* L.)		24-25	37-40				Van Etten *et al.*, 1961
Crambe abyssinica Hochst. ex R.E. Fries	36-38	32	45			9.0-10.0[2]	Van Etten *et al.*, 1961
Raphanus sativus L.	40-42	30-31					Miller *et al.*, 1962

1. 5% of seed N is nucleic acid.
2. Determined as isothiocyanates and 5-vinyloxazolidinethione.
3. 5.4% sucrose, 0.3% raffinose, 0.8% stachyose.

SEED CONTENTS OF SOME CRUCIFERAE

Some of the Cruciferae upon which detailed seed analyses have been made are listed in Table 1. Although amino acid analyses and glucosinolate contents have been reported for many Cruciferae, there has been little seed constituent analysis published except for those in Table 1. The seed contains about 40 % by weight lipid and from 23 - 25 % (N x 6.25) protein. The second figure is not an accurate measure of the amount of seed protein since 2 - 3 % of the seed nitrogen is free amino acids and low molecular weight peptides (Finlayson *et al.*, 1969) and an additional 5 % of the seed nitrogen is nucleic acid. The hull of *B. napus* L. cv Target is 1.5 % N and contains about 12 % of the total seed weight, thus, a more realistic figure for seed protein would be 20 - 22 %.

The meal amino acid analyses for five species of Cruciferae listed in Table 2 show a general similarity. Meal amino acid compositions of 41 Cruciferae have been reported by Miller *et al.* (1962) and all of them have large amounts of glutamic acid, proline, and glycine while the sulphur-containing amino acids and histidine are present in small amounts. The meals contain 3.0 - 7.0 mg methionine and from 19.0 - 23.0 mg lysine per gram. The corresponding figures for soybean are approximately 8.0 mg methionine and 32.0 mg lysine per gram of meal. Since soybean meal contains about 10 % more protein than the meal from a *B. napus* cultivar, it appears that some of the proteins from certain rapeseed cultivars have methionine and lysine contents equal or somewhat greater than that of soybean. Although an examination of the meal amino acid composition will not necessarily give an accurate estimate of the amino acid compositions of the proteins constituting the meal, a study of the amino acid compositions of the seed of 41 Cruciferae (Miller *et al.*, 1962) indicated that the sulphur-containing amino acids were the limiting ones nutritionally in all but six of the cruciferous seed meals. Furthermore, some of the seed proteins will contain greater amounts of methionine than others (Table 3), thus the possibility remains of breeding a rape cultivar with an increased methionine content.

Table 2

Amino Acid Compositions of Seed Meals (amino acid m moles/gm meal)(Based on 6.7% N)

Amino Acid	*B. campestris* cv. Arlo	*B. napus* cv. Target	*B. juncea* L. Coss	*Crambe abyssinica*	*Raphanus sativus*
Aspartic acid	0.22	0.18	0.33	0.21	0.20
Threonine	0.13	0.14	0.12	0.15	0.14
Serine	0.15	0.15	0.33	0.15	0.14
Glutamic acid	0.40	0.61	0.51	0.44	0.46
Proline	0.24	0.22	0.21	0.18	0.24
Glycine	0.24	0.28	0.24	0.27	0.23
Alanine	0.195	0.20	0.19	0.18	0.18
1/2-Cystine	0.02	0.02	--	0.02	0.06
Valine	0.17	0.16	0.14	0.16	0.16
Methionine	0.02	0.02	0.02	0.03	0.05
Leucine	0.19	0.20	0.19	0.18	0.20
Phenylalanine	0.07	0.09	0.06	0.08	0.09
Tyrosine	0.05	0.05	0.05	0.05	0.06
Ammonia	0.57	0.60	0.62	0.52	0.45
Lysine	0.16	0.13	0.14	0.13	0.14
Histidine	0.08	0.06	0.06	0.08	0.11
Arginine	0.11	0.11	0.15	0.13	0.17
Total N	3.81	3.96	3.94	3.75	3.96
% Recovery	79	82	82	78	82

Table 3

Amino Acid Compositions of the 12s Aleurins from five *Brassica* Species
(m moles/gm protein)(17.0 % N)

Amino Acid	*B. napus*	*B. campestris*	*B. nigra*	*B. juncea*	*B. hirta* (*Sinapis alba*)
Aspartic acid	0.70	0.78	0.88	0.67	0.60
Threonine	0.34	0.35	0.38	0.47	0.43
Serine	0.39	0.37	0.52	0.58	0.72
Glutamic acid	1.26	1.51	1.22	1.49	0.99
Proline	0.44	0.43	0.78	0.58	0.75
Glycine	0.68	0.77	0.01	9.81	0.91
Alanine	0.48	0.50	0.63	0.61	1.09
Valine	0.43	0.46	0.54	0.51	0.50
1/2-Cystine	0.04	0.15	trace	trace	trace
Methionine	0.11	0.09	trace	trace	trace
Isoleucine	0.33	0.33	0.43	0.41	0.44
Leucine	0.58	0.61	0.79	0.79	0.61
Phenylalanine	0.27	0.31	0.33	0.36	0.25
Tyrosine	0.16	0.15	0.16	0.19	0.20
Ammonia	1.13	1.62	2.06	1.55	1.60
Lysine	0.27	0.22	0.27	0.26	0.49
Histidine	0.12	0.12	0.15	0.10	0.15
Arginine	0.35	0.42	0.43	0.33	0.35
Tryptophan	0.05	0.05			

SEED RESERVE PROTEINS OF THE *BRASSICA* SPECIES

The data in Table 1 show that the defatted meal in some of the Cruciferae contains about 38 % protein (N x 6.25) of which approximately 65 % is soluble in 10 % sodium chloride solution or in 0.5 M sodium chloride - 0.01 M sodium borate buffer (pH 8.0). Neutral, 0.01 M sodium pyrophosphate solution dissolves about 45 % of the meal nitrogen, water dissolves about 20 - 25 % of it, and 60 - 70 % ethanol, a solvent for prolamines (Van Etten *et al.*, 1965), extracts about 5 % of the meal nitrogen of the *Brassica* species meals. Thus, the protein solubilities depend in part upon molecular size in this salting-in phenomenon. The smallest protein molecules dissolve at the lower salt concentrations, while the large ones (12s aggregate) dissolve at the higher salt concentrations. The solubility characteristics of the protein-containing extracts of the *Brassica* species is similar to those of cottonseed and soybean (Altschul *et al.*, 1966). Most of the protein nitrogen is solubilized in solutions of ionic strengths between 0.2 and 1.0 at pH values greater than 7.0. There is a solubility minimum between pH 4.0 and 6.5 where about 30 % of the nitrogen soluble at pH 8.0 remains in solution. The solubility vs pH plot for protein extracts from both *Crambe abyssinica* and *Raphanus sativus* (radish) are similar. The solubilities of soy meal extracts at pH 4.0 - 6.5 are much less, indicating that the soy contains more protein insoluble in this pH range. All the *Brassica* species tested contain very little alcohol-soluble nitrogen while some 20 - 30 % of the meal nitrogen from *Crambe abyssinica* is soluble in 70 % ethanol (Van Etten *et al.*, 1965). On the basis of classification by solubility, it appears that *Crambe* contains more prolamine-type proteins than the *Brassica* species.

Gel electrophoresis of the saline extracts from the *Brassica* seed meals separates a number of proteins (Fig. 1) into eight or ten distinct bands. The intense band near the top of the gel represents the seed globulin and is the major protein constituent in the seed. Those migrating further in the gel are present in much lesser amounts in the seed but are the more basic protein components. Although the gels show there are at least nine or ten protein components extractable from the meal, undoubtedly there are more since some are present in small amounts and are not detectable while several others may run as a single band.

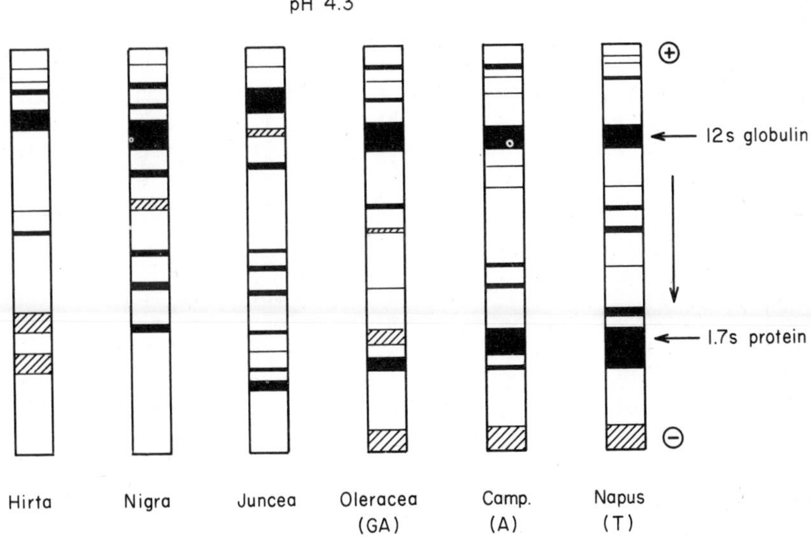

FIGURE 1. Reproductions of the disc gel electrophoresis separations of the 10 % sodium chloride extracts of the meal (from left to right): *B. hirta (Sinapis alba); B. nigra; B. juncea; B. oleracea; B. campestris; B. napus.*

Gel filtration of the saline extracts of the meals from the five *Brassica* species on Sephadex (Fig. 2) resolved the extract components into three ultra-violet absorbing peaks. The material in peak 1 which is eluted near the solvent front contains most of the extract nitrogen, the second peak contains most of the low molecular weight proteins and the contents of the third are mostly water soluble pigments and polyphenols (Bhatty *et al.*, 1968). Gel filtration of the material from peak 1 on G-200 separates the major protein component from small amounts of other protein and nucleic acids; its elution characteristics indicate its molecular weight is greater than 10^5. Gel electrophoresis of this protein fraction showed the presence of two protein bands, the major one which was subsequently shown to have a sedimentation coefficient of 12s and a minor one of sedimentation coefficient of 17s (Fig. 3a). Separation of these two proteins was achieved with great difficulty and the results, which are not conclusive, indicate that the 17s component may be a dimer of the 12s component. This conclusion is supported by the similar behaviour of the soybean globulin (Wolf, 1970). The major reserve protein (12s globulin) may also be isolated directly from saline meal extracts by preparative ultracentrifugation which yields a preparation free of low molecular weight material but containing small amounts of nucleic acids (MacKenzie and Blakley, 1972). The reserve proteins or "aleurins" from each of the five *Brassica* species had similar solubility properties and sedimentation coefficients between 11.0 and 12.0 (MacKenzie and Blakley, 1972). The concentration dependences of these aleurins were comparable in all five cases and the low magnitude (ds/dc=0.2) indicates that these proteins are essentially globular in shape. Furthermore, since their chromatographic and sedimentation characteristics are essentially the same, it is reasonable to assume that the aleurins from the five species have similar molecular weights. The properties of the seed proteins described above should be representative of those of the other members of the species.

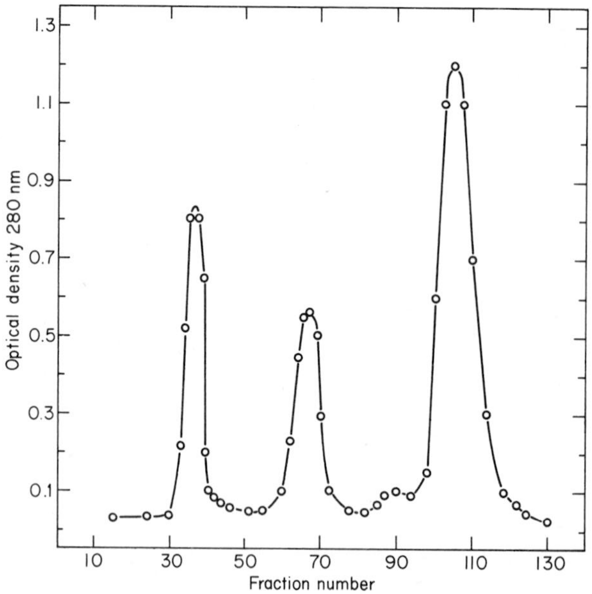

FIGURE 2. Elution curve for the chromatography on Sephadex G-100 of the 10 % sodium chloride - 0.01M sodium borate extract of rapeseed meal.

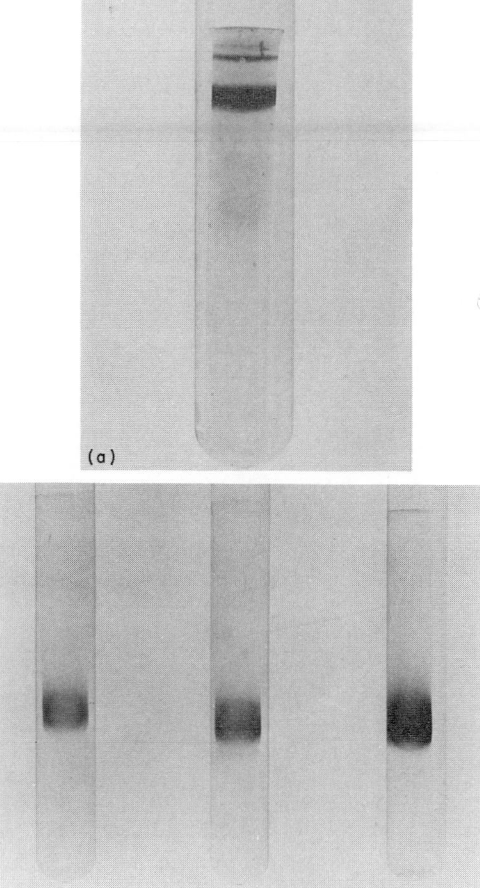

FIGURE 3. Photographs of the gel electrophoresis runs of the:

a) 12s aleurin, b) 1.7s protein.

Qualitative experiments have shown (Van Etten *et al.*, 1965) the minimum solubilities of aleurins occur between pH 4.0 and 6.5 with solubilities increasing as the extremes of the pH scale are approached. However, the sedimentation behaviour of the aleurin is different at low pH from that at pH 8.5 - 9.0. For instance, at pH 3.6 a solution of the aleurin contains two components: a minor one (S^{0}_{20} 1%, buffer 7s) and a major one (S^{0}_{20} 1%, buffer 3s) with only traces of the 12s component evident (Fig. 4a). In solutions of 6M urea, the major component of the aleurin solution has a sedimentation coefficient of 2.3s (Bhatty *et al.*, 1968)(Fig. 4b). A restoration of the original conditions (0.5M sodium chloride, 0.01M sodium borate; pH 8.8) did not yield material with the properties of the 12s aleurin (Goding *et al.*, 1970)(Fig. 4c). It appears, then, that the dissociation, 12s - 7s - 3s, produced by the pH reduction or urea treatment is irreversible. This dissociation is general for the aleurins of the five species although there will be probably slight differences in subunit behaviour. Furthermore, the dissociative character of the globulins, as affected by a pH change, is similar to that of the soybean aleurin which undergoes the dissociation: 11s - 7s $\overline{-}$ 4s with a reduction in pH or in urea solution. The sub-fractions of the aleurin after separation become water soluble and may be partly separated from one another by gel filtration of an urea solution of the protein (Goding *et al.*, 1970). There are four components recoverable although electrophoresis of these fractions indicates that aleurin is composed of at least seven polypeptides. Isoelectricfocusing separations of the aleurin from *B. juncea* showed it contained nine polypeptides, three of which are basic and six were neutral or acidic (MacKenzie, 1971). The addition of 2-mercaptoethanol to the original extraction or its presence in any of the above manipulations did not change the chromatographic of electrophoretic behaviour of the aleurin or its sub-fractions (Goding *et al.*, 1970). The results of the urea experiments indicate that hydrogen bonding is important in the structure of the 12s aggregate and those done with the reducing agent suggest the sulphydryl interactions do not play a large rôle in the isolation of the aleurin.

One of the polypeptide components of the 12s aleurin is a glycoprotein (Goding *et al.*, 1970) and contains about 20 % of the aleurin nitrogen. Hydrolysis of it yields 0.15 % galactosamine and about 1.5 % neutral sugar whose hexose (glucose)

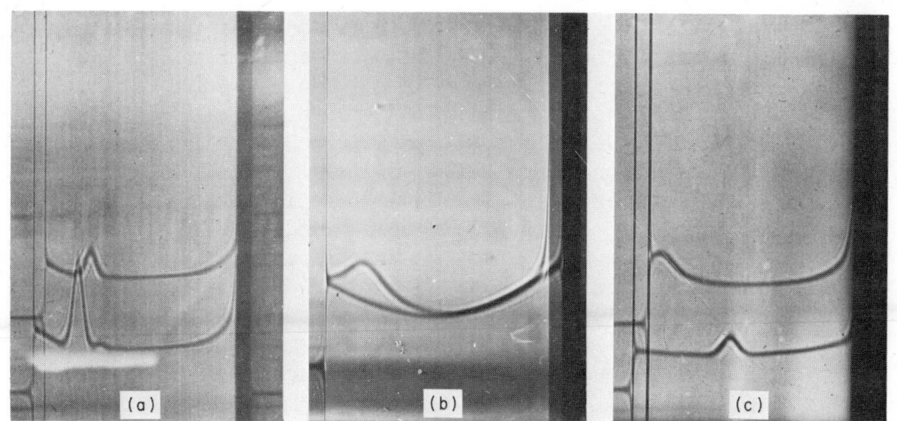

FIGURE 4. Photographs of schlieren patterns of the *Brassica napus* L. cv Target 12s aleurin.

a) 12s Aleurin preparation in 0.05M sodium borate, 0.5M sodium chloride solution.
b) 12s Aleurin in 6M urea solution (85 min at 60,000 rpm).
c) Lower, 12s aleurin (12 min at 60,000 rpm). Upper, reconstituted aleurin in 0.05M sodium borate, 0.5M sodium chloride.

to pentose (arabinose) ratio is about 1:8. Many of the aleurins and haemaglutinins isolated from seeds contain a glycoprotein component although most of them (Putzai, 1966; Koshiyama, 1971) have N-acetylglucosamine as their amino sugar instead of the galactosamine isomer.

There is substantial evidence (Inglett, 1972; von Hofsten, 1971) to show that the major seed storage proteins or globulins are located in a sub-cellular body called a "protein body" or "aleurone grain" which is present in the mature seed but disintegrates upon seed germination. Such a particle was originally suggested by Hartig (1856) who isolated proteinaceous particles from a number of oilseeds. Aleurone grains from a number of sources have been extensively analyzed and their synthesis in the developing seed is currently under investigation (Inglett, 1972). The soybean work has shown that the 11s aleurin (glycinin) is located exclusively in the protein body and not found in any other part of the seed. Recently, Altschul *et al.* (1964) suggested that proteins found in aleurone grains be called "aleurins' and consequently, many globulins isolated from legumes and oilseeds would be thus classified. Analyses of isolated protein bodies from peanut seeds (Dieckert, 1962) have shown them to contain 60 - 70 % of the total seed protein, large amounts of the cellular potassium and manganese, phospholipid and all the phytic acid found in the seed. Enzymes are also found in the protein bodies: 70 % of the acid phosphatase activity of cottonseed was found in the protein body (Yatsu and Jacks, 1968). Less work has been done with rapeseed but photographs (Figs. 5, 6) (von Hofsten, 1971) of ultrathin sections of the central region of a mature seed show large protein grains (A) which are surrounded by lipid (L). The whole system including the cell nucleus is enclosed by the cell wall (CW). Preliminary studies by MacKenzie (unpublished results) on the isolation of the

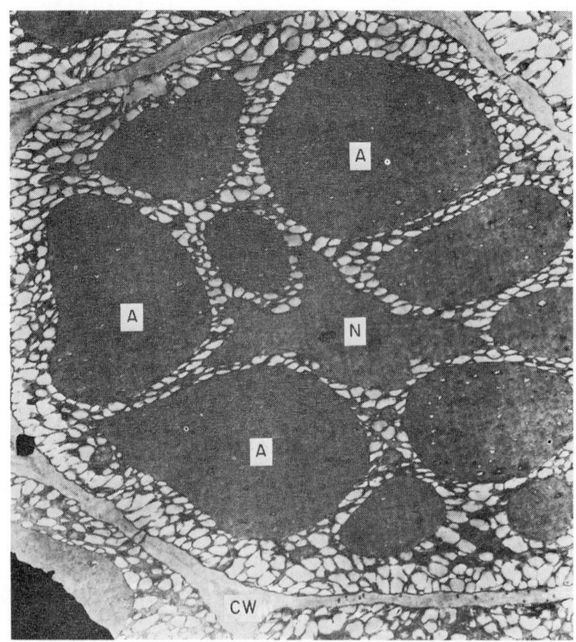

FIGURE 5. Electron micrograph of oilseed rape (*Brassica napus)* with cell wall (CW), nucleus (N), and protein rich aleurones (A).

rapeseed protein bodies by sucrose density gradient centrifugation have shown them to contain the 12s globulin and possibly its dimer, the aggregate with a sedimentation coefficient of 17s. The aleurin isolated by this method accounts for 50 % of the protein in the seed. Rapeseed contains other non-enzyme proteins; no evidence for these was found in the protein body preparations. Although more analyses are necessary, it appears that the 12s aleurin of rapeseed is the major storage protein of the seed and is found in a subcellular inclusion limited by some type of membrane.

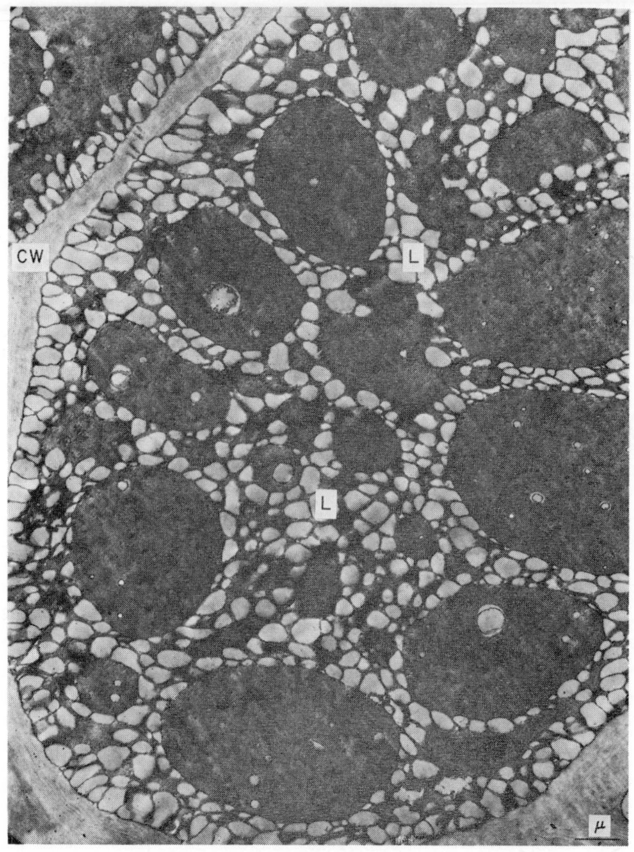

FIGURE 6. Electron micrograph of turnip rape *(Brassica campestris)*. L = lipid, CW = cell wall.

Disc gel electrophoresis of the saline extracts (Fig. 1) of *Brassica* seed meals shows there are a number of other proteins extractable besides the 12s aleurin. Some of these are eluted in the second peak (Fig. 2) from the Sephadex chromatography of the saline extract of the meal. One of these lower molecular weight proteins has been isolated from a number of cultivars of the five *Brassica* species. They are also readily water soluble and may be recovered from the meal by water extraction. Unlike the globulin these proteins are basic and hence easily isolated from protein mixtures through their strong adsorption on resins like carboxymethyl cellulose. Work with other cultivars indicates that there might be a series of basic proteins in rape whose properties are very closely related (Lonnerdahl and Janson, 1972). Nevertheless, a strongly basic protein ($S^{0}_{20,w}$ 1.7s) with a molecular weight of 13,500-800, accounting for 7 - 10 % of the seed nitrogen, may be isolated from the *B. napus* cultivar, Nugget (Table 4). This protein, which gives a single well defined band on acrylamide gel electrophoresis (Fig. 3b), appears to be monodisperse from a consideration of the molecular weight determinations (Bhatty *et al.*, 1968). The results published by Lonnerdahl and Janson (1972) indicated that some rapeseed and mustard cultivars may contain a series of basic proteins or polypeptides whose amino acid compositions have only slight differences. Although Bhatty *et al.* (1968) reported two basic proteins in the *B. napus* extracts, differences in isolation procedures used by the two groups of workers may account for the reported results. It is also possible that the observed differences in protein content of this fraction may be genetic since the parent stock of most of the present day cultivars are not well defined from an evolutionary standpoint. Both the *B. napus* cultivars, Nugget and Target, are well-established lines that are compatible; some other lines possibly have had heterozygous parents such as *B. campestris* cv Arlo which may account for the considerable variation in the seed protein amino acid composition (Goding *et al.*, 1972). However, the proteins isolated by both groups of workers have amino acid compositions different from the 12s aleurin: they have high cystine and methionine contents and 8 - 10 % arginine. Gel electrophoresis of the urea dissociated aleurin showed that it contained no polypeptides with electrophoretic properties similar to the 1.7s protein. Although the exact nature of this fraction is not yet clear, it is apparent that these basic proteins are not located in the protein body and hence are separate from the 12s aleurin. Presumably this protein and some of the others detected by gel electrophoresis (Fig. 1) are located in the cell cytoplasm. No biological function has been described for the 1.7s protein and it appears to be present in much greater amounts in the *Brassica* species than in certain leguminosae, if present there at all.

The proteins from the *Brassica* species have been more extensively studied than those from other Cruciferae and of the *Brassica*, the two rapeseed species have received the most attention. Fragmentary studies on protein solubilities have been made with other species such as *B. oleracea* var. *botrytis* (Ivanova and Tsonev, 1970). The results, while not relating well to work on *B. napus*, etc. show the *B. oleracea* cultivar contains globulins soluble in 0.3 - 0.5 M sodium chloride solution which may be fractioned into acidic, neutral and basic components. Less than 5 % of the seed protein from the *Brassica* species is soluble in 70 % ethanol, that is, by the Osborne classification they have a very low prolamine content. However, the *Crambe* species contains about 24 % of the seed nitrogen soluble in 70 % ethanol showing a major solubility difference in the proteins of the two species (Van Etten *et al.*, 1965). This solubility difference is not indicated by the amino acid compositions of the meals.

Many of the leguminosae contain trypsin inhibitors in the mature seed (Altschul *et al.*, 1966). It is not known if rape or any of the other *Brassica* species contain trypsin or other enzyme inhibitors, however, Ogawa *et al.* (1971) have isolated two protease inhibitors (R-1, arginine type inhibitor, R-III, lysine type) from the seeds of *Raphanus sativus*. The inhibitors form stable complexes with trypsin and the formation results in a total inhibition of proteolytic activity. The trypsin-inhibitor complex is stable at neutral pH but dissociates when the pH is lowered below 5.0 and is inactivated by heat in proportion to the heat inactivation of the enzyme. The inhibitors have relatively low molecular weights (8,000 and 12,000) and have amino acid compositions significantly different from the soybean trypsin inhibitors.

COMPARATIVE STUDIES OF *BRASSICA* SEED PROTEINS

Since proteins are the direct result of gene expression, analyses of their conformations and sequences have had increasing use in taxonomic studies. Boulter and Ramshaw (1972) have

Table 4

Amino Acid Compositions of the *Brassica* Species 1.7s Proteins
(m moles/gm protein)(17.0% N)

Amino Acid	*B. napus*	*B. juncea*	*B. hirta* (*Sinapis alba*)	*B. campestris*	*B. campestris* Arlo x Sarson F_1-12	F_1-16
Aspartic acid	0.18	0.18	0.95	0.20	0.21	0.21
Threonine	0.33	0.30	0.37	0.29	0.32	0.30
Serine	0.55	0.45	0.48	0.45	0.46	0.43
Glutamic acid	2.66	2.14	1.74	2.17	2.25	2.10
Proline	0.92	0.84	0.87	1.10	0.98	1.14
Glycine	0.56	0.62	1.13	0.57	0.61	0.56
Alanine	0.48	0.34	0.55	0.45	0.42	0.34
1/2-Cystine	0.16	trace	trace	0.13	0.50	0.54
Methionine	0.08	0.07	trace	0.06	0.08	0.07
Isoleucine	0.31	0.30	0.53	0.29	0.28	0.26
Leucine	0.67	0.56	0.89	0.57	0.58	0.55
Phenylalanine	0.16	0.21	0.37	0.22	0.21	0.21
Tyrosine	0.07	0.08	0.20	0.11	0.07	0.07
Ammonia	1.76	1.83	1.18	1.67	1.33	1.39
Lysine	0.64	0.50	0.33	0.62	0.63	0.65
Histidine	0.31	0.29	0.15	0.27	0.31	0.29
Arginine	0.40	0.50	0.50	0.35	0.23	0.36

sequenced a series of 14 cytochromes c from 11 families of plants including a *B. oleracea* cultivar. They found all but two of the cytochromes c to have 111 amino acids residues with 86 positions identical. The proteins had identical stretches of sequences for the haeme attachment sites and the 16 hydrophobic residues which point inward towards haeme in horse heart cytochrome c have identical counterparts in the plant proteins. The plant and animal cytochromes c have some differences; the animal protein is more basic than the plant protein and the latter contains two residues of trimethyllysine which does not appear in the animal protein. The limited variations of plant sequences for the monocotyledons, dicotyledons, and the gymnosperm agrees with the view that cytochrome c is a conservative molecule in evolutionary terms (Boulter and Ramshaw, 1972). Thus, it is safe to assume that the other *Brassica* species cytochromes c will be similar, if not identical, to the one described by Boulter and Ramshaw and, if species variations do occur, they will not be as numerous as those observed for storage proteins (Tables 3, 4). Vaughan and Denford (1968) have made comparative studies of seed proteins from a number of *Brassica* species using serological and gel electrophoresis techniques. They also wished to investigate the concept that *B. napus*, *B. juncea* and *B. carinata* were amphidiploids. The differences in serological reactions and relative mobilities of the albumins and globulins in acrylamide gels supported the morphological data for the separation of the plants into distinct species (Vaughan and Denford, 1968). Both methods of analysis indicated a closer relationship between certain species than with others; for instance, they found a closer relationship between proteins of *B. campestris* and *B. oleracea* than between either of these with *B. nigra*. A compositional analysis of the individual electrophoretic bands would make conclusions derived from electrophoretic data much better but there are considerable technical difficulties associated with obtaining amino acid analyses of bands from acrylamide gels. Vaughan and Waite (1967) also found that in the genus a *B. campestris* cultivar was the only taxon with 100 % of high frequency bands and that all its bands are found distributed throughout the remainder of the taxa. Vaughan concludes that this is support for the cytological work of Sikka (1940) and suggests that *B. campestris* (turnip) might be closest to the archetype of the taxa examined.

MacKenzie and Blakley (1972) compared the amino acid compositions of the 12s aleurins obtained from cultivars of five *Brassica* species. The amino acid analyses (Table 3) are generally similar although the *B. hirta (Sinapis alba)* aleurin has some obvious differences to the other four. Nevertheless, it is difficult to establish relatedness to the overall compositions by visual comparisons. Using Metzger's method of multivariant statistical analysis, MacKenzie was able to derive an assessment of the overall relatedness among the 12s aleurins of the five *Brassica* species. For instance, the amino acid compositions of the aleurins from *B. juncea* are more closely related to those of *B. campestris* and *B. nigra*, the two parents of *B. juncea*, than to the aleurin from *B. hirta (Sinapis alba)*. Applying the method to cultivar variations, he showed that differences in amino acid compositions of globulins isolated from cultivars within a species were small and thus the proteins should be similar. The smallest differences (about experimental error) and hence the closest similarities were found for proteins from seeds obtained from the one cultivar grown in different locations (MacKenzie and Blakley, 1972). The last finding would be expected since the primary structure of a protein should not be affected by environmental factors. Although conclusions could not be made about the amphidiploid nature of *B. juncea*, the results support those of Vaughan and agree with taxonomic data regarding the relationships within the five *Brassica* species.

There have been a large number of interspecific crosses made in the *Brassica* species designed to reduce both the seed glucosinolate and erucic acid contents. How these experiments have affected the seed protein compositions of the progeny is not clear but it is an area of research which needs investigation. Initial studies of this problem have produced difficulties: there is some dispute in the interpretation of the results of crossing experiments in cereals. For instance, Yong and Unrau (1964) claim that "new" protein has been synthesized in Triticale, a cross between *Secale cereale* and *Triticum durum*. The authors did not define the term "new", i.e. does the substitution of one amino acid for another which may change the physical properties of a protein slightly constitute the synthesis of a "new" protein? Other experiments with the synthesis of Triticale have confirmed that the proteins of the progeny are simply inherited from the parents (Chen and Bushuk, 1970), a conclusion also indicated by the work of Vaughan with *Brassica*. The electrophoretic studies of the seed proteins of *Brassica* showed that there were no specific proteins in *B. juncea* or a synthesized *B. napus*; all bands present in the *B. napus* electropherograms could be accounted for in its putative parents, *B. campestris* and *B. oleracea*. This work supports that of Chen and Bushuk (1970) which indicates that the protein composition of progeny is the sum of that of its parents. Another aspect of this problem has been shown by the analyses of the 1.7s proteins of the F_1 generation of a cross between two *B. campestris* cultivars, Arlo and Yellow Sarson (Goding *et al.*, 1970). The 1.7s proteins from the F_1 plants had the same electrophoretic properties as did those from the parents but had considerably different amino acid compositions particularly with regards to the cystine and methionine contents (Table 4). The Arlo plant was the maternal cultivar and is genetically heterogenous. While these results are not significant in terms of the amphidiploid problem in some *Brassica* species, it shows the difficulties which may arise if protein identification is based on one or two physical measurements. Thus, measurements of changes in protein structures to study genetic changes in plants will probably require investigations of the sequences of certain proteins since many of the proteins from the five *Brassica* species (in particular, the ones present in greatest amount in the seed) have similar physical properties. Some of the cultivars used in Canada for commercial purposes and plant breeding (*B. napus* L. cv Target and Bronowski) do not have a well-defined parentage and thus changes in the protein amino acid compositions may not be significant in evolutionary terms. However, it is important to study the genetic structures of both parents and crosses to support the plant breeding experiments designed to improve the commercial value of the crop and the functional properties of the seed proteins.

Considering overall amino acid compositions and sedimentation characteristics, the five 12s aleurins from the *Brassica* species are "similar" to that isolated from soybean. Since these proteins are not enzymes and their function presumably is to provide reserves of amino acids and nitrogen for the germinating seed, a certain degree of similarity is not surprsing even though they are from different plants. In most seeds, the most abundant protein amino acids are those which are readily converted into metabolic cycle intermediates (glutamic acid, proline, glycine). Thus, the similarities in the aleurins from different seeds may not be entirely accidental.

The 1.7s protein appears to be more characteristic of the *Brassica* species; soybean does not contain one similar to it in amounts that are present in rape or the mustards.

The effects of the environment on plant growth and development have been studied for many years. Because of the increasing use of seed proteins as food sources for both humans and animals, such research is necessary to support plant breeding experiments designed to improve the agronomic performance of the plant and the nutritional quality of the seed. The growth and subsequent maturing of a plant depends upon both its genetic background and environmental conditions of growth. For instance, shortages of soil nutrients affect the amounts of protein deposited in the seed and change the relative proportions of the seed constituents (Finlayson *et al.*, 1970). Rape grown on a sulphur-deficient soil has two to three times the amount of free amino acids in the mature seed than do plants grown under conditions of adequate soil nutrients (Finlayson *et al.*, 1970). Although the seed nitrogen content is not changed greatly, free methionine and cystine are not detectable under such circumstances and the amounts of some of the seed proteins are reduced. It appears that the methionine and cystine deficiency has an effect on protein synthesis and they have become the limiting amino acids in this case. Glucosinolate synthesis is also reduced by a sulphur deficiency in the soil and partial results have indicated that sulphur from glucosinolates is not used for cystine and methionine synthesis in cases of soil sulphur deficiencies. Thus, the results indicate that the synthesis of protein and glucosinolates proceed independently. Furthermore, they show that the free amino acid content of a seed is partly dependent on available nutrients and the recoveries of certain amounts of them is not characteristic of a particular species. The work quoted above and that of others (Margolis, 1960) shows that relative proportions of some seed constituents depend to a certain extent on external conditions. They also raise the question, "what are the normal amounts of the seed constituents" and how is the synthesis of these constituents controlled?

BIOSYNTHETIC STUDIES

The synthesis and deposition of the seed storage proteins, lipids and carbohydrates in rape occurs during the six to eight weeks between flowering and maturity. Nitrogen deposition in the seed is approximately linear during the first five or six weeks of development but the rate decreases as maturity approaches (Finlayson and Christ, 1971). Similarly, the amounts of trichloroacetic acid precipitatable nitrogen shows a linear increase during the first half of seed development but levels off in the second half of the seed growth period. Also, there is no evidence in the immature seed during the first five weeks of growth for the proteins whose physical and chemical characteristics are the same as those of the mature seed (Fig. 7). The electron photomicrograph of

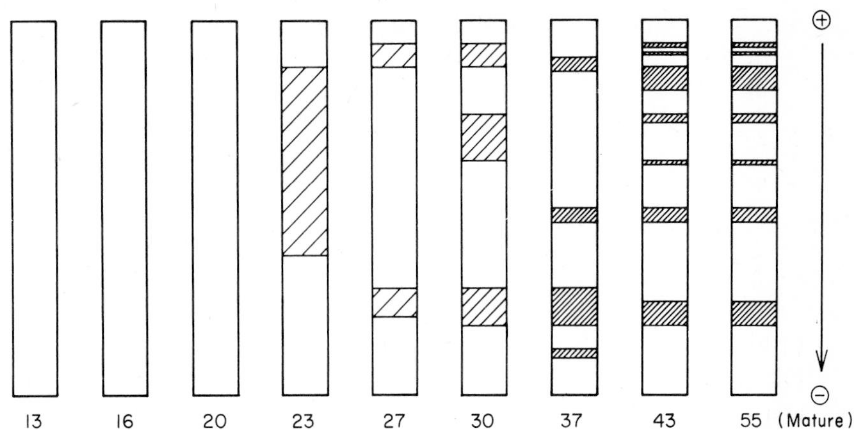

FIGURE 7. Disc gel electrophoresis reproductions of protein patterns obtained from an aliquot of an extract of maturing rapeseed. The numbers refer to days after flowering.

the immature seed shows a similar result (Fig. 8); the developing seed (10 days after pollination) contains starch and endoplasmic reticulum and there is no sign of aleurone grains or lipid droplets. The time of the maximum rate of nitrogen deposition does not correspond to the time of appearance of the reserve proteins and the completion of the synthesis of the 12s aleurin and 1.7s protein occurs during the last three weeks of seed development. There are protein staining bands present on the thirtieth and thirty-seventh days after flowering (Fig. 7) but how these are related to the polypeptides which eventually will form the 12s aleurin is, at present, not known.

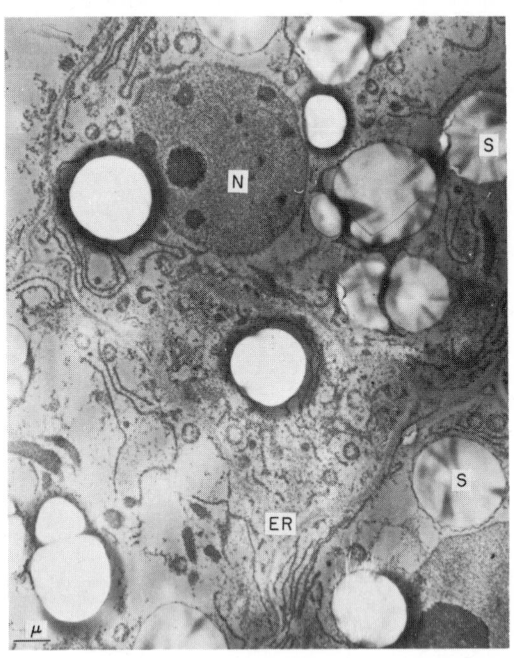

FIGURE 8. Electron micrograph of *Brassica campestris*, ten days after pollination. Endoplasmic reticulum (ER) and starch (S) occupy the cell. N = nucleus.

The synthesis of oilseed globulins (aleurins or vacuolar proteins (Dieckert and Dieckert, 1972)) has received much study in the past 8 to 10 years although speculation about their synthesis has been made for a much longer time. The currently accepted hypothesis is that the protein bodies of a seed develop in a vacuole while the polypeptides composing the aleurin are synthesized elsewhere in the developing seed (Dieckert and Dieckert, 1972). The available evidence indicates that the aleurin or the polypeptides composing it are synthesized on the polyribosomes of the rough endoplasmic reticulum and are passed to the lumen of the organelle. The incipient aleurin is transported to dictyosomes where it is organized into droplets. The membrane-bound protein droplets then migrate through the cytoplasm to the aleurone vacuoles where they pass through the vacuolar membranes by a process of membrane fusion. Some of the evidence that has been accumulated is that the rough endoplasmic reticulum contains polyribosomes on its surface; cells of the developing seeds of two species of plants studied (cotton, Shepherd's purse) contain vacuoles partly filled with protein whose staining properties are the same as those in the dictyosomal droplets and in the sacules of the rough endoplasmic reticulum. Although this evidence indicates that protein is deposited continuously throughout the seed growth, it appears (von Hofsten, 1971; Dieckert and Dieckert, 1972) that the aleurins are not synthesized and sequestered in aleurone vacuoles until a certain stage of growth is reached. This result agrees with the data that is available for rapeseed: there is no evidence for the appearance of the 12s aleurin or any other protein characteristic of the mature seed until five weeks after flowering. After this period, protein deposition appears to be rapid (Dieckert and Dieckert, 1972). This mechanism of aleurin synthesis derived from studies on cottonseed and Shepherd's purse embryo probably applies to rapeseed since it has been established that the aleurin (12s globulin) is located in a protein body and that the immature rapeseed is structurally similar to other oilseeds where the mechanism of aleurin deposition has been studied.

REFERENCES

Altschul, A. M. (1963). *In* "Proceedings of a Seed Protein Conference" (C.H. Fisher, ed.), U.S. Department of Agriculture, New Orleans, La.

Altschul, A. M., Neucere, N. J., Woodham, A. A. and Dechary, J. M. (1964). *Nature* 203, 501.

Altschul, A. M., Yatsu, L. Y., Ory, R. L. and Engleman, E. M. (1966). *In* "Annual Review of Plant Physiology" Vol. 17 (L. Machlis, ed.), Annual Reviews Inc., Palo Alto, Ca.

Bhatty, R. S., MacKenzie, S. L. and Finlayson, A. J. (1968). *Canad.J.Biochem.* 46, 1191.

Boulter, D. and Ramshaw, J. A. M. (1972). *Phytochemistry* 11, 553.

Chen, C. H. and Bushuk, W. (1970). *Canad. J. Plant Sci.* 50, 25.

Dieckert, J. W. (1962). *J. Fd Sci.* 27, 321.

Dieckert, J. W. and Dieckert, M. C. (1972). *In* "Symposium: Seed Proteins" (G.E. Inglett, ed.), The AVI Publishing Co. Inc., Westport, Conn.

Downey, R. K. (1965). *In* "Rapeseed Meal for Livestock and Poultry" (J.P. Bowland, ed.) Canada Department of Agriculture, Ottawa, Ontario.

Finlayson, A. J., Christ, C. M. and Bhatty, R. S. (1969). *Canad.J. Botany* 47, 679.

Finlayson, A. J., Christ, C. M. and Downey, R. K. (1970). *Canad.J.Plant Sci.* 50, 705.

Finlayson, A. J. and Christ, C. M. (1971). *Canad.J.Bot.* 49, 173

Goding, L. A., Bhatty, R. S. and Finlayson, A. J. (1970). *Canad.J.Biochem.* 48, 1096.

Goding, L. A., Downey, R. K. and Finlayson, A. J. (1972). *Canad.J.Plant Sci.* 52, 63.

Graham, J. S. D., Jennings, A. C., Morton, R. K., Palk, B. A., and Raison, J. K. (1962). *Nature* 196, 967.

Hartig, T. (1856). *Botan. Zeit.* 14, 257.

Inglett, G. E. (1972). *In* "Symposium: Seed Proteins" (G.E. Inglett, ed.), The AVI Publishing Co. Inc., Westport, Conn.

Ivanova, M. and Tsonev, D. (1970). *Chem. Abs.* 73, 11221f.

Kondra, Z. P. and Stefansson (1970). *Canad. J. Plant Sci.* 50, 643.

Koshiyama, I. (1971). *Agric. Biol. Chem.* 35, 385.

Lonnerdahl, B. and Janson, J. (1972). *Biochem. et Biophys. Acta* 278, 175.

MacKenzie, S. L. Unpublished results.

MacKenzie, S. L. (1971). A paper presented at the Annual Meeting of the American Association of Cereal Chemists, Dallas, Texas.

MacKenzie, S. L. and Blakley, J. A. (1972). *Canad. J. Botany* 50, 1825.

Margolis, D. (1960). *Contributions of the Boyce Thompson Inst.* 20, 425.

Miller, R. W., Van Etten, C. H., McGrew, C. and Jones, Q. (1962). *J.Afric.Fd Chem.* 10, 427.

Ogawa, T., Higash, T. and Hata, T. (1971). *Agric.Biol.Chem.* 35, 712.

Osborne, T. B. (1924). "The Vegetable Proteins" 2nd Edn., Longmans, Green and Co., New York.

Putzai, A. (1966). *Biochem.J.* 101, 379.

Sikka, S. M. (1940). *J.Genet.* 40, 441.

Van Etten, C. H., Miller, R. W., Wolff, I. A. and Jones, Q. (1961). *J.Agric.Fd Chem.* 9, 79.

Van Etten, C. H., Daxenbichler, M. E., Peters, J. E., Wolff, I. A. and Booth, A. N. (1965). *J.Agric.Fd Chem.* 13, 24.

Vaughan, J. G. and Waite, A. (1967). *J.Exp.Bot.* 18, 269.

Vaughan, J. G. and Denford, K. E. (1968). *J.Exp.Bot.* 19, 724.

von Hofsten, A. (1971). *In* "The Proceedings of the Internationa Conference on the Science, Technology and Marketing of Rapeseed and Rapeseed Products", p. 70, Rapeseed Assoc. of Canada Ottawa, Ontario.

Wolf, W. J. (1970). *J.Agric.Fd Chem.* 18, 969.

Yatsu, L. Y. and Jacks, T. J. (1968). *Arch.Biochem.Biophys.* 124, 466.

Yong, F. C. and Unrau, A. M. (1964). *Canad.J.Biochem.* 42, 1647

VOLATILE FLAVOUR COMPOUNDS OF THE CRUCIFERAE

A. J. MACLEOD

Department of Chemistry, Queen Elizabeth College, University of London, London, England

THE NATURE OF FLAVOUR

Flavour of food is a composite sensation, the two most important factors involved being the senses of taste (gustation) and of smell (olfaction). Of these by far the more important is the aroma contribution—in fact, there are only four primary taste sensations, although some authorities describe six. As a result, without the olfactory ability it would be possible to discriminate only the sweet, bitter, salt and sour sensations.

It should just be noted in passing, however, that others of the primary human senses do also play an apparent small part in flavour perception. Sight is a good example. It is well known that a consumer is likely to pronounce a lime-flavoured, although orange-coloured drink or sweet as having an orange flavour. Similarly, feel or texture is important and an ice cream or margarine without a smooth mouth-feel would be generally unacceptable. Even sound plays a rôle in flavour perception and appreciation, and many foods should provide a suitable sound when bitten into, e.g. the satisfying "crunch" of a stick of fresh celery.

Nevertheless, the most important factor in flavour by a very long way is olfaction. Food never has the same flavour, for example, when one has a cold and the olfactory reception centres in the nasal cavity are smothered. The important point about olfaction is that for any chemical compound to have any significant effect on flavour (the very limited number of taste sensations excluded) it must be volatile, hence to be able to reach the olfactory reception centres in the nasal cavity. In some cases it need not be very volatile, since with powerfully odorous substances only a few molecules are required to elicit a response. Some chlorinated anisoles, for example, which can cause musty taint in chicken meat, are extraordinarily potent and can be detected by the human nose at levels of one part in 10^{15} of water or lower (Land, 1973). Just to stress this point, in other words 0.001μg in one million litres of water would give a detectable aroma!

Two points which should be appreciated at this stage and which contribute greatly to the difficulties of flavour research are the following. First, the mechanism or mechanisms whereby molecules cause a particular aroma response are not understood. Why one molecule elicits one aroma response whilst a very similar molecule (even sometimes a stereoisomer) elicits a totally different response, and why two very different molecules can cause very much the same aroma response, are virtually inexplicable at the present level of knowledge. Admittedly theories do exist to explain the olfaction phenomenon at a molecular level, but none are entirely satisfactory to say the least. As a result, attempts to investigate food flavour must proceed without much understanding of the mechanism of perception. The second problem relates to the methodology of the accurate assessment of a subjective response. Regrettably there is no instrument to measure or describe flavours nor, for that matter is there even a language for odour, as there is for colour. Whilst we now refer to an object as red, rather than fire-coloured, we are still in the dark ages with regard to odour description.

Despite these difficulties it is obvious that ultimately in flavour research, whether one likes it or not, the various methods of objective study have to be linked with human assessment with all its frailties and inexactitudes and extreme problems of communication.

TECHNIQUES OF FLAVOUR ANALYSIS

It is intended to describe, very briefly indeed, the types of general methods of flavour analysis currently employed, emphasising the objective methods. The important point to remember is the restrictive interest in only volatile compounds. Analysis of the volatile components responsible for the flavour of a particular food comprises four distinct stages.

First, the *extraction* of the volatile flavour compounds from the food must be accomplished. This has to be carried out as delicately as possible to avoid abuse of the generally susceptible flavour molecules and hence risk of artefact formation. Even so, frequently various distillation methods are employed, separating the flavour components from the bulk of the food by virtue of their volatility. Alternatively various solvent extraction techniques are possible but these, of course, tend to extract involatile, interfering components as well. Since vegetables are nearly always cooked before being eaten, interest is in the cooked flavour and thus distillation methods are generally employed for extraction. Such methods need not be very carefully controlled since thermal degradation, if it occurs, is a necessity rather than a problem. After extraction of the aroma sample it must be checked subjectively (i.e. by the human nose) to ensure that it retains the correct aroma of the foodstuff. If it does not, then there is no point in further effort and an alternative extraction method should be employed.

The second stage of the analysis involves a *concentration* step. One of the main difficulties of flavour research is that the flavour components are usually liberated only in minute amounts (remember that the nose is remarkably sensitive) so that it is nearly always necessary to concentrate the aroma extract to provide the components at a concentration sufficient for objective methods of detection and analysis. Again, the resultant essence must be tested subjectively to ensure retention of the correct aroma. Techniques often employed for concentration include many forms of high vacuum/low temperature distillation, either to remove a volatile solvent from the extract or to "strip" the volatiles from a less volatile solvent.

Most flavour essences produced by these or similar techniques are complex mixtures and the third stage of the analysis is *separation* of the mixture into its various components. This is nearly always achieved nowadays by gas chromatography. This technique is ideally suited to this problem in being highly sensitive, highly efficient, and dealing specifically with volatile compounds. In many respects advances in flavour research have paralleled advances in the development of gas chromatography.

Having separated the mixture, the final stage is the *determination*, qualitatively, quantitatively and subjectively of the individual components. Quantitative assessments can be deduced from the gas chromatogram by peak area measurements, and limited qualitative information is possible from retention time or index measurements. However, the best way of qualitative analysis is by combined gas chromatography/mass spectrometry (GC/MS), whereby highly diagnostic mass spectra are obtained on-line of the components separated by gas chromatography. Generally, even concentrated flavour extracts are too dilute for the basically inefficient preparative gas chromatographic methods and on-line analytical methods are essential. Subjective assessments of components separated by gas chromatography are also achieved on-line, by splitting the effluent from the chromatographic column and whilst passing one portion as usual to the detector, sending the major fraction through an "odour port" (a heated glass line) to the outside of the chromatography oven for sniffing by the human nose and odour description.

Only a very few of the many techniques of flavour analysis have been mentioned, but some idea will have been gained of general procedures.

FLAVOUR COMPONENTS OF THE CRUCIFERAE

Having introduced the nature of flavour very briefly and described some of the experimental techniques and methodology involved in flavour analysis, again very briefly, it is now possible to consider the chemistry and nature of some of the volatile flavour components of some of the Cruciferae.

Glucosinolate Degradation Products

First it is intended to consider the compounds which are not only probably of most importance in Cruciferae flavour, but which are also those generating most interest—the volatile flavour products of the degradation of the glucosinolates. Understandably, much work has been carried out on this subject, but here is reported mainly our own work as being fairly representative and not overlapping with what is described elsewhere in this book.

It is well-known that on enzymic degradation, all glucosinolates produce corresponding isothiocyanates. Other important possible products of glucosinolate decomposition, formed depending upon the conditions, are thiocyanates and nitriles.

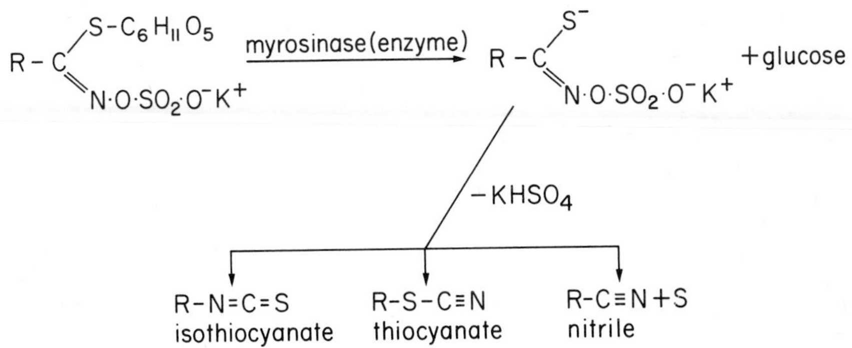

Isothiocyanates are of considerable flavour importance. Allyl isothiocyanate itself, (R=allyl, $CH_2=CH-CH_2-$) formed from sinigrin (potassium allylglucosinolate), is a pungent, lachrymatory, very bitter compound and it is quite potent, having a low flavour threshold value. Consequently, production of appreciable amounts of this in vegetables and other food plants imparts quite characteristic bite to the flavour, but equally important, loss below the natural level results in abnormally flat and dull products. Consider the following findings which illustrate the importance of this compound to *Brassica* flavour.

First, a simple example: it is generally agreed that the heart of the cabbage has a much stronger flavour than the outer leaves. Indeed at one time it was thought a good idea for patients suffering from anaemia to be fed the cabbage heart since, due to its slightly bitter flavour, it was thought to contain iron. As it happens it is now known that most of the iron content of the plant is in fact located in the outer leaves. In work on cooked cabbage, allyl isothiocyanate production was investigated from both heart alone and outer leaves alone and the results are shown in Table 1 (MacLeod and MacLeod, 1970c). The figures here, and throughout, refer to the percentage relative abundance of the components in the appropriate aroma extract, relative to the total organic volatiles collected. These results explain quite adequately the difference in flavour in this particular respect

Table 1

Comparison of some of the flavour volatiles of cooked cabbage

	Produced from inner leaves alone %	Produced from outer leaves alone %
allyl cyanide	3.5	1.0
allyl isothiocyanate	16.5	3.0
trans-hex-2-enal	0.05	8.5
cis-hex-3-en-1-ol	-	6.5

between the heart of the cabbage and the remainder, the far larger proportion of allyl isothiocyanate produced by the inner parts of the plant being almost totally responsible for the stronger and more bitter flavour of these leaves. Note that one of the other products of sinigrin degradation, allyl cyanide, shows similar behaviour to allyl isothiocyanate, as perhaps might be expected, although this would not greatly affect the flavour. Cabbage aroma components other than those shown in Table 1 did not vary greatly between the two appropriate aroma extracts.

Perhaps the most important point about isothiocyanate production from a glucosinolate is that it is enzymic. Therefore, any process, which, prior to consumption, destroys or inactivates the enzyme will cause decreased isothiocyanate production well below normal, if indeed any is obtained, and the result will be a product of less distinctive flavour. This, unfortunately, is usually the case when *Brassica* foodstuffs are commercially preserved. For cooked Brussels sprouts it was found that fresh sprouts normally gave allyl isothiocyanate to the extent of about 4% of the total organic volatiles collected, whereas frozen sprouts gave none or 0.1% at the most—see Table 2 (MacLeod and MacLeod, 1970a). The reason for this is that prior to freezing, the sprouts are blanched by plunging into boiling water. The purpose of this is indeed expressly to inactivate enzymes, but basically those which would be responsible for undesirable deterioration of

Table 2

Comparison of some of the flavour volatiles of fresh and frozen Brussels sprouts

	Fresh %	Frozen %
allyl cyanide	7.0	13.5
allyl isothiocyanate	4.0	0.1
trans-hex-2-enal	0.1	-
cis-hex-3-en-1-ol	1.5	-

the food even when frozen. Unfortunately, it is not possible, of course, to inactivate only the "undesirable" enzymes and leave intact the important flavour-producing ones. Therefore, no normal frozen vegetable food can ever completely simulate fresh flavour, since it must be lacking completely all flavour components produced enzymically. The consequent lack of allyl isothiocyanate in frozen Brussels sprouts is at least partly responsible for the flatter and less distinctive flavour of these compared with fresh sprouts.

Another interesting feature of glucosinolate degradation is also illustrated in Table 2 in that it can be seen that allyl cyanide is not only produced by frozen Brussels sprouts but it is produced in almost double its relative abundance in fresh sprouts. This does not improve the flavour of the frozen vegetable, but it is more important in that it shows that in sprouts at least sinigrin can degrade non-enzymically to form the nitrile—a mode of degradation of sinigrin which has occasionally been disputed.

Although cabbage is not preserved by freezing it is possible to obtain, mainly on the non-retail market, samples of de-hydrated cabbage. These too will have been blanched to inactivate enzymes before the dehydration procedure. Inves-tigating allyl isothiocyanate production in fresh and dehydrated samples, on average about 6.5% relative abundance of allyl isothiocyanate was found for fresh cabbage, but for all four dehydrated samples examined the value never rose above a minimal 0.1%—see Table 3 (MacLeod and MacLeod, 1970b). In confirmation it can be reported that subjectively by tasting the dehydrated cabbage samples had very poor flavour indeed.

Table 3

Comparison of some of the flavour volatiles of fresh and dehydrated cabbage

	Fresh %	Dehydrated %
allyl cyanide	3.0	23.5 - 48-5
allyl isothiocyanate	6.5	0.1
trans-hex-2-enal	1.5	-
cis-hex-3-en-1-ol	4.5	-

Again, apart from the lack of isothiocyanate this may have been due in part to the extraordinary increases in the allyl cyanide percentages observed for the four dehydrated samples. Normally about 3% relative abundance for fresh cabbage, the value increased to a minimum of 23.5% and a maximum of 48.5% over the four samples, thus confirming the previous finding that in such *Brassica* vegetables sinigrin is capable of degrading very readily non-enzymically to give allyl cyanide.

It is obvious,therefore, that the destruction of enzymes and consequent loss of important flavour components is a serious drawback of preserved vegetable foods. With this in mind many workers have accepted the enzyme loss and tackled the problem by considering restoration of the natural flavour to the preserved food by adding enzyme preparations at a stage just prior to consumption or cooking. The enzyme is best obtained from that particular food, although enzymes from closely (and some not so closely) related foodstuffs have been used. Bailey *et al.* (1961) treated dehydrated cabbage with a cabbage myrosinase enzyme preparation during reconstitution and obtained a vegetable with normal isothiocyanate content and good flavour. Schwimmer (1963) used enzymes for the same purpose from non-cabbage sources and although none was as satisfactory as cabbage myrosinase itself, all were better than simple water rehydration alone. As perhaps would be expected, mustard myrosinase gave a cabbage product with an excessively pungent flavour and onion enzyme gave an onion tinged flavour. Unfortunately, this work was carried out using taste-panel assessment only—a practice as superficial in flavour research as using objective methods only—and hence there is no valid information concerning the differing nature of the produced flavour components under these interesting circumstances. Nevertheless, from this sort of approach it can be suggested that eventually a preserved food might be supplied commercially with its own packet of "enzymes" to be added to the food during reconstitution, hence providing a product similar in flavour to the fresh. This statement would be more true if it were not for the depressing fact that we are rapidly breeding a race of youngsters who have been brought up on the modern insipid frozen vegetable foods and who now reject, say, fresh Brussels sprouts as being "nasty and bitter".

Apart from isothiocyanate and nitrile production varying with any processing of the plant, the proportions produced also vary depending upon the horticultural history of the plant. A whole series of experiments were carried out on a range of cultivars of cabbage grown under different conditions. Some of the results obtained, again with reference specifically to allyl isothiocyanate and allyl cyanide, are worth mentioning briefly. To begin with, it was noticeable that all but one of the cultivars studied gave much the same results in all instances. One, however, was consistently exceptional, namely Ennes Cross. The reason for this seemingly unique behaviour of this cultivar could be interesting but no further work can yet be reported.

In one series of experiments seeds were sown at weekly intervals and resultant plants harvested and analysed at weekly intervals. In this way cabbages of the same age could be examined for any seasonal variations—incidentally, all the cultivars studied were summer cabbages. Apart from Ennes Cross, all cultivars showed the same interesting trend, summarised in Table 4. Note that intermediate figures for the many results between early season and late season have been omitted for the sake of clarity, but the variations were roughly linear with time. Early and late season here were separated by two months. Except for Ennes Cross, which is therefore shown separately in the Table, all cultivars (e.g. Elsoms New Hybrid, Summer Monarch) gave very much the same

Table 4

Comparison of production of some flavour volatiles of cabbage during a season

	Early season %	Late season %
allyl cyanide (Ennes Cross)	11.0	50.0
allyl isothiocyanate (Ennes Cross)	23.5	0.05
allyl cyanide (other cultivars)	6.0	3.5
allyl isothiocyanate (other cultivars)	13.0	0.1

results, within experimental error, in all instances in this series and therefore common values are quoted for all. It can be seen that in all the cultivars examined high concentrations of allyl isothiocyanate were obtained with early season plants, but very much lower concentrations were obtained from late season plants. The same trend, although to a much lesser extent, was observed for the nitrile, except in the case of Ennes Cross when it increased markedly throughout the season. Subjective assessments confirmed the considerably superior flavour of all the early season cabbages. This was particularly noticeable with Ennes Cross, since it was about the only occasion when it did possess reasonable flavour, and late season Ennes Cross cabbages had virtually no detectable characteristic flavour.

Studies were also carried out on crop spacing and its effect on the composition of the flavour volatiles, since the tendency is, of course, to closer spacings and hence higher yield per acre. It was found that in general the closer together the plants were grown the greater were the relative abundances of the glucosinolate degradation products, particularly the isothiocyanate (Table 5). Again, a number of intermediate values have been omitted for the sake of clarity. In this instance the anomalous figures for Ennes Cross are not shown.

Table 5

Comparison of production of some flavour volatiles from cabbages grown at different crop spacings

	Wide spacing (3ft apart) %	Close spacing (1ft apart) %
allyl cyanide	2.5	5.5
allyl isothiocyanate	1.0	19.0
trans-hex-2-enal	1.5	3.5
cis-hex-3-en-1-ol	1.5	3.0

This same trend was confirmed for Brussels sprouts as well (Table 6). This is such an interesting differentiation shown by both of the two plants investigated that it is worth theorising briefly on the possible reason for this.

Table 6

Comparison of production of some flavour volatiles from Brussels sprouts grown at different crop spacings

	Wide spacing (3ft apart) %	Close spacing (1ft apart) %
allyl cyanide	2.5	4.0
allyl isothiocyanate	0.5	10.0
trans-hex-2-enal	0.1	1.5
cis-hex-3-en-1-ol	0.1	1.0

Freeman and Mossadeghi (1972) have shown that allyl isothiocyanate production in cabbage correlates well with sulphur nutrition, so the fact that the closely grown cabbages and sprouts produced "excess" isothiocyanate implies that sufficient sulphate was available and that the lesser amount of nutrients available to a closely grown plant is probably not an important factor in this instance. A possible explanation is the following. It is well known that certain metabolic pathways flourish more in a plant when it is grown under so-called "hard" conditions such as when plants are grown very close together. In particular, amino acid biosynthesis is much increased, and since glucosinolates are themselves produced in the plant from amino acids this may explain this observation. Thus, "hard" conditions ⟶ more amino acid ⟶ more glucosinolate ⟶ more isothiocyanate.

In flavour terms the type of work just described is quite valuable. Sensory tests confirmed the stronger, better flavour of closely grown cabbages (as well as early season ones, as described earlier), so that in effect it is possible, in a rather limited sense admittedly, to grow cabbages (and possibly sprouts also) ranging from strong to weak flavour as required, depending upon the cultivar selected and the horticultural conditions employed.

It is now intended to consider some important glucosinolates of members of the Cruciferae other than those of the genus *Brassica*. Recently the volatile flavour components of cress have been investigated and the results with regard to garden cress (*Lepidium sativum*) are interesting. It has been known for some time that garden cress gives benzyl cyanide (phenylacetonitrile) as a major volatile product (Hofmann, 1874b) and Gmelin and Virtanen (1959) obtained the corresponding isothiocyanate and thiocyanate from the seeds. The appropriate glucosinolate precursor, where $C_6H_5CH_2$- is the side-chain, is potassium benzylglucosinolate (glucotropaeolin).

Virtanen and Saarivirta (1962) have conducted a detailed study of the formation of benzyl isothiocyanate, thiocyanate and nitrile in the moistened seed powder of *Lepidium* and come to the conclusion that all are formed enzymically, although it is suggested that the thiocyanate is produced from the isothiocyanate by means of an isomerase, with reduced temperatures favouring this process. The proposed scheme is shown below. Incidentally, in this instance a nitrile is produced enzymically, whereas in cabbage it will be remembered that it was seen that allyl cyanide could be produced non-enzymically.

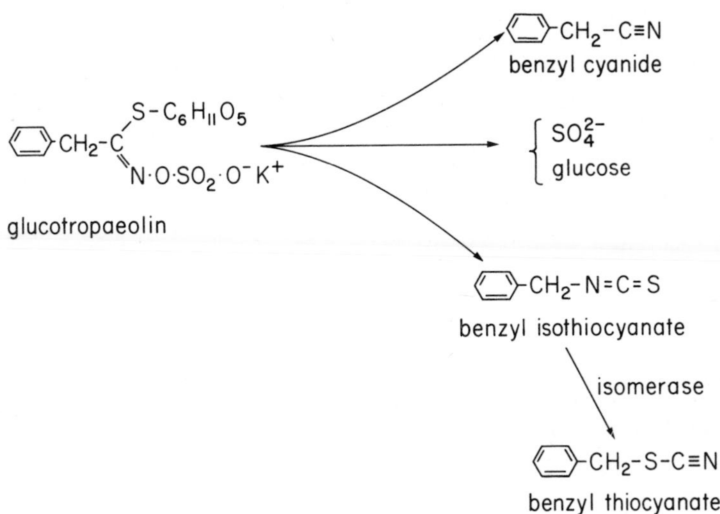

Virtanen (1965) reported that the thiocyanate could not be obtained from the green leaves of *Lepidium sativum* and we have confirmed this. It may be that the isomerase is absent from the leaves, but why this should be the case is obscure. Furthermore, recent work has cast doubt on the existence of this isomerase and it is suggested that in *Lepidium* seeds benzyl thiocyanate and nitrile are the main enzymic products with isothiocyanate only produced when formation of the main products is inhibited (Saarivirta, 1973). This may be the case, although much work is needed to evaluate fully this system, but even so there is no certainty that anything like the same mechanism would necessarily apply in the fresh green leaves as in the seeds particularly since no thiocyanate is obtained from the leaves.

Our work on the volatile flavour components of the green leaves of garden cress confirmed the production of benzyl isothiocyanate and cyanide, and also the lack of any thiocyanate. However, far more nitrile was found to be produced than isothiocyanate and also it was observed that these two are not the only glucosinolate degradation components. In fact, of the nine major aroma components observed (a remarkably simple system in flavour terms), eight are four sets of nitrile/isothiocyanate pairs. In order of elution from a PEG 20M gas chromatography column, the identified volatiles of garden cress are given in Table 7, together with their percentage relative abundances in the flavour extract.

Table 7

Volatile flavour components of *Lepidium sativum*

	%
$CH_2 = CH - CH_2 - CH_2 - CN$	7
$CH_2 = CH - CH_2 - CH_2 - CH_2 - CN$	10
$CH_2 = CH - CH_2 - CH_2 - NCS$	5
$CH_2 = CH - CH_2 - CH_2 - CH_2 - NCS$	8
$C_6H_5 - CH_2 - CN$	51
$C_6H_5 - CH_2 - CH_2 - CN$	6
$C_6H_5 - CH_2 - NCS$	5
$C_6H_5 - CH_2 - CH_2 - NCS$	3

The benzyl derivatives are the major pair (56% total), followed by the 4-pentenyl (18%), the 3-butenyl (12%) and the 2-phenyl ethyl (9%) derivatives. An interesting feature of all four pairs is the predominance of the nitrile.

The presence of the 2-phenylethyl derivatives is interesting since these are reputed to be the chief aroma components of water cress (*Nasturtium officinale*) (Hofmann, 1874a; Gadamer, 1899). The green leaves of this plant have also been examined in detail and it has been confirmed that these derivatives are the two major volatile components of the aroma extract, with the nitrile again predominating and to a considerable extent providing ~(95%)of the total organic volatiles.

One of the most intriguing aspects of the volatile components of garden cress leaves is that all the major components are glucosinolate degradation products. Only 5% of the organic volatiles remains unassigned as such products. Also, the very neat and tidy pair relationship of nitrile and isothiocyanate is remarkable and can be considered a tribute to the good order of the plant. Usually, of course, a whole range of volatile flavour components of all sorts of different types and origins is obtained from a foodstuff. The flavour of garden cress leaves is thus basically simply due to a blend of these isothiocyanates (the nitriles contribute little to the flavour).

It must be appreciated that in the preceding discussion of glucosinolates and their relevance to flavour it has not been possible to give the complete picture, and certain glucosinolates, degradation products and plants have been emphasised. The problem of the various mechanisms of the production of nitrile has only been touched upon and much interesting work could be reported, although in truth the relevance to flavour is limited. The importance of the thiocyanates and their mode of production have been almost totally ignored and again much work has been conducted on the formation of the thiocyanates from glucosinolates and on isothiocyanate/thiocyanate isomerisations under various circumstances. The thiocyanates do have importance in flavour, generally bestowing a more garlic aroma; in addition, they may cleave to thiols to give a foetid character.

Cis-Hex-3-en-1-ol and *Trans*-Hex-2-enal

The types of compounds just described in the first section are by no means the only volatile flavour components produced by the Cruciferae. There are very many other compounds of importance which have been located in flavour extracts. It is not possible to deal with all of these in the space available so again a fairly detailed description will be given of a restricted aspect taken from our own work. It is important to understand that in many respects the glucosinolates are one of the successes of flavour chemistry in that the flavour compounds are important, widespread, of distinctive flavour, and the mechanism of their formation is quite well understood. In addition, there is the interest of the chemotaxonomy of the glucosinolates. Too often in flavour research a list of volatile components is compiled with little concern for the importance of the compounds in flavour or of their biogenesis. Nowadays there is a little more interest in the biogenesis of flavour components since it is at last being realised that there cannot be a full understanding of any system without this knowledge. Furthermore, in applied terms, it is much more sensible to consider the addition to a substrate (processed or synthetic food) of the appropriate precursor of the flavour volatile rather than the volatile itself, which may well suffer problems of stability, toxicity, etc. In addition, it is obvious that generally a "natural" food additive is more acceptable than a synthetic one.

The mode of formation of many flavour components can only be guessed at and there is little detailed knowledge as there is for the glucosinolates. Recently, however, a number of workers have been investigating the biogenesis of *cis*-hex-3-en-1-ol and *trans*-hex-2-enal, and we have been studying the compounds in detail in the Cruciferae. The point about the two compounds is that they are extremely common constituents of the aroma volatiles of green leaves. They are so common as to be popularly known as "leaf alcohol" and "leaf aldehyde" and the alcohol has an aroma which is highly reminiscent of freshly mown grass—it is a classic "green" aroma. Incidentally, natural occurrence crosses to the animal kingdom and the aldehyde is the main active component of the defensive secretion of the cockroach—indeed nearly 100% pure aldehyde is produced and it is highly toxic to cockroaches, and to other insects as well. The interest in the biogenesis of these two compounds is thus obvious and although findings and results for cabbage are described here, similar conclusions have been reached with regard to other foods, e.g. tomatoes (Kazeniac and Hall, 1970).

First, it is necessary to summarise the early findings with respect to cabbage which provoked initial interest in the biogenesis of the two compounds. Table 1 shows a truly remarkable clear-cut differentiation between their production from inner and outer leaves of cabbage. Table 2, for Brussels sprouts, implies an enzymic mode of formation in that they are absent from the frozen vegetables; Table 3 for cabbage shows this better and supports the enzymic biogenesis theory. Bearing in mind the toxicity of the compounds to insects, and the fact that they also exhibit bacteriostatic action, then their presence in the outer parts of the plant only and their probable enzymic production when the plant tissue is ruptured (for example by an invading insect pest), is supremely logical. The biogenesis is a very rapid process; in confirmation, squeeze and rub some grass between the fingers and the aroma, consisting in part of these compounds, is generated almost immediately.

Tables 5 and 6 show that, as with the glucosinolates, the precursors of these compounds also thrive in a "hard" horticultural environment.

Concerning the mechanism of the biogenesis of the two compounds, it was recognized that the products are similar in structure to the products of autoxidation of lipids, and furthermore it is well-known that important odour and flavour compounds are derived from lipid degradation (e.g. Forss, 1972; Schultz *et al.*, 1962), often lipid oxidation. A simple experiment confirmed that cabbage aroma extracts produced in an inert, nitrogen atmosphere gave far less *cis*-hex-3-en-1-ol and *trans*-hex-2-enal than under normal circumstances (i.e. extract prepared in air). This, with the earlier evidence, suggested an enzymic oxidation and probably of a lipid. Further experiments implicated linolenic acid as the lipid material, in that cabbage extracts prepared in the presence of excess added linolenic acid produced far more (twice as much) of the two products than under normal circumstances with no added linolenic acid. Other fatty acids, e.g. linoleic, did not behave in the same manner. The enzyme responsible for the oxidation of lipids is lipoxygenase, the first products being hydroperoxides, essentially the same as those produced during the first stages of autoxidation although usually in different relative proportions depending upon the conditions (Galliard, 1973). The lipoxygenase catalysed oxidation of linolenic acid which is relevant in this instance is as shown below, the product of interest being 13-hydroperoxyoctadeca-9,

$$CH_3-CH_2-CH\overset{c}{=}CH-CH_2-CH\overset{c}{=}CH-CH_2-CH\overset{c}{=}CH-(CH_2)_7COOH$$

linolenic acid

↓ lipoxygenase

$$CH_3-CH_2-CH\overset{c}{=}CH-CH_2-\underset{\displaystyle O-OH}{\underset{|}{CH}}-CH\overset{t}{=}CH-CH\overset{c}{=}CH-(CH_2=_7COOH$$

linolenate hydroperoxide

11, 15-trienoic acid. Other hydroperoxide products are possible. Geometric configurations of the double bonds are shown by letters c (*cis*) or t (*trans*) above the bonds. To determine whether or not this reaction was in fact the first stage in the formation of *cis*-hex-3-en-1-ol and *trans*-hex-2-enal, the 13-hydroperoxyoctadeca-9, 11, 15-trienoic acid (linolenate hydroperoxide) was prepared in the laboratory from linolenic acid and lipoxygenase. Cabbage extracts prepared in the presence of this hydroperoxide were then examined and found to produce much increased amounts of *cis*-hex-3-en-1-ol and *trans*-hex-2-enal over a blank experiment with no added hydroperoxide, thus implicating the hydroperoxide in the reaction pathway and substantiating the first stage of the biogenesis as shown above.

To discover which of the two reactants was responsible for the formation of the products in the outer leaves of cabbage only (see Table 1), both linolenic acid and lipoxygenase were estimated in inner leaves alone and outer leaves alone. Surprisingly, approximately equal amounts of both were produced by the two parts of the plant.

The main problem, however, remained as how the hydroperoxide degraded to give the two required products. Various approaches were attempted including heat, different pH, metal ions, ultraviolet radiation, etc., most borrowed from knowledge of autoxidation mechanisms, but with no significant success. Some influences functioned to some extent in giving the required products, but never in sufficient amounts to explain the quantities produced by the cabbage. Eventually, the possibility was examined of inactivated haemoprotein enzyme catalysts being functional at this stage (Eriksson *et al.*, 1970). The theory is that when haemoprotein enzymes such as peroxidase or catalase are inactivated by heat, acid or other treatment, the molecule uncoils exposing the haeme moiety which is active in this instance. If this is true then it would appear that a compound such as haematin should be even more active in being the isolated haeme fragment with no protein interference present. Table 8 shows the effect of addition of various relevant agents to synthetic linolenate hydroperoxide. After allowing the reaction mixture to stand for one hour a major product was observed on submitting the mixture to gas chromatography—this was shown to be *cis*-hex-3-enal. The Table shows the relative amounts of this product formed under the influence of the different reagents and the efficiency of the inactivated haemoprotein enzyme catalyst is obvious, with acid-denaturation being the best method. As suspected, haematin gave the most product.

Table 8

Effect of various degrading agents on linolenate hydroperoxide (LH)

	relative amount of product (*cis*-hex-3-enal)
linolenate hydroperoxide (LH)—blank	408
LH + peroxidase	490
LH + heat-denatured peroxidase	593
LH + acid-denatured peroxidase	738
LH + haematin	812

The second stage of the proposed pathway is thus as shown below—the production of the *cis*-hex-3-enal from the linolenate hydroperoxide is presumably by simple fission at the hydroperoxide grouping.

$$CH_3\text{-}CH_2\text{-}CH\overset{c}{=}CH\text{-}CH_2\text{-}CH\text{-}CH\overset{t}{=}CH\text{-}CH\overset{c}{=}CH\text{-}(CH_2)_7COOH$$
$$\quad\quad O\text{-}OH$$

$$\downarrow \text{ inactivated haemoprotein enzyme catalyst}$$

$$CH_3\text{-}CH_2\text{-}CH\overset{c}{=}CH\text{-}CH_2\text{-}CH{=}O \quad \textit{cis}\text{-hex-3-enal}$$

A possible answer to the production of *cis*-hex-3-en-1-ol and *trans*-hex-2-enal by the outer leaves of cabbage alone is given by the fact that on estimating the iron content of cabbage, it was observed that at least four times as much iron is found in the outer leaves as in the inner leaves. The method of analysis determined total iron and did not distinguish between inorganic and organic iron; the obvious assessment of haemoprotein enzyme distribution in cabbage has yet to be carried out.

At this stage *cis*-hex-3-enal has not been proved as intermediate in the production of *cis*-hex-3-en-1-ol and *trans*-hex-2-enal since it has only been shown to be produced from the linolenate hydroperoxide *in vitro*. However, Table 9 does show the supporting evidence for the hypothesis, in that cabbage extract prepared in the presence of excess added *cis*-hex-3-enal gave more *cis*-hex-3-en-1-ol and a vastly increased amount of *trans*-hex-2-enal over the amounts produced by cabbage alone.

Table 9

Effect on reaction products of addition of excess *cis*-hex-3-enal to cabbage extract

	relative amount of product		
	trans-hex-2-enal	*cis*-hex-3-enal	*cis*-hex-3-en-1-ol
cabbage alone - blank	144	112	972
cabbage plus *cis*-hex-3-enal	2960	533	1070

The final stage of the proposed biogenetic reaction pathway is shown below. Having arrived at the *cis*-hex-3-enal intermediate the formation of the *cis*-hex-3-en-1-ol would not be expected to be too difficult and it was confirmed by *in vitro* experiments that one of the normal biological reduction mechanisms could be operative, namely alcohol dehydrogenase in the presence of reduced NAD. The other product, *trans*-hex-2-enal was formed *in vitro* very readily from the *cis*-hex-3-enal, the double bond migrating to achieve the more stable conjugated structure with the carbonyl group, and the molecule at the same time resorting to the conformationally more acceptable *trans* state to accommodate the chain and the bulky carbonyl group as far apart, and hence as stable, as possible. This isomerisation seemed to be provoked by all sorts of influences, including heat, ultraviolet radiation, etc., and it was not possible to pinpoint for sure one particular reagent as chiefly responsible in cabbage.

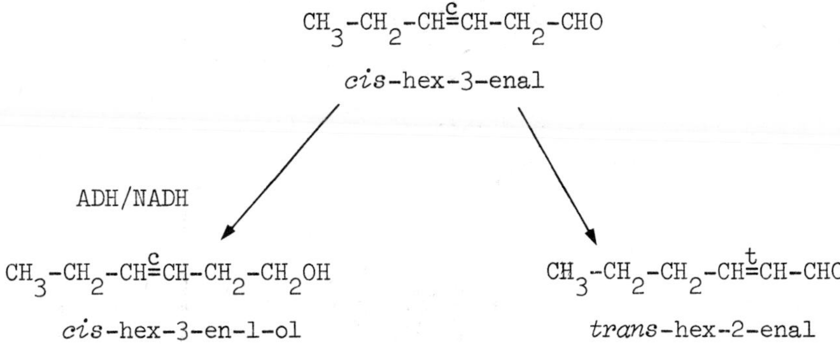

The fact that the pathway branches at *cis*-hex-3-enal rather than either *cis*-hex-3-en-1-ol or *trans*-hex-2-enal being formed from the other was indicated by preparing a cabbage extract in the presence of both *cis*-hex-3-en-1-ol alone and *trans*-hex-2-enal alone and comparing the products obtained with those of a blank cabbage extract with no additions. In neither case was there any difference between the blank and the extract with the added compound, suggesting that both products are separate ends of the biogenetic pathway. Table 10 shows the results for the addition of *trans*-hex-2-enal, as illustration. Similar results were obtained with added *cis*-hex-3-en-1-ol.

Table 10

Effect on reaction products of addition of excess *trans*-hex-2-enal to cabbage extract

	relative amount of product		
	trans-hex-2-enal	*cis*-hex-3-enal	*cis*-hex-3-en-1-ol
cabbage alone - blank	144	112	972
cabbage plus *trans*-hex-2-enal	632	111	970

Thus a possible pathway for the production of *cis*-hex-3-en-1-ol and *trans*-hex-2-enal in cabbage has been determined and it is shown in its entirety below. This type of pathway would appear to apply in other green plants as well.

$$CH_3 - CH_2 - CH \overset{c}{=} CH - CH_2 - CH \overset{c}{=} CH - CH_2 - CH \overset{c}{=} CH - (CH_2)7\ COOH$$

$$\downarrow$$

$$CH_3 - CH_2 - CH \overset{c}{=} CH - CH_2 - \underset{O - OH}{\underset{|}{CH}} - CH \overset{t}{=} CH - CH \overset{c}{=} CH - (CH_2)7\ COOH$$

$$\downarrow$$

$$CH_3 - CH_2 - CH \overset{c}{=} CH - CH_2 - CHO$$

$$\swarrow \qquad \searrow$$

$$CH_3\text{-}CH_2\text{-}CH\overset{c}{=}CH\text{-}CH_2\text{-}CH_2\ OH \qquad CH_3\text{-}CH_2\text{-}CH_2\text{-}CH\overset{t}{=}CH\text{-}CHO$$

The above, and the glucosinolate story, are prime examples of the way in which flavour chemistry must now progress. More and more of these pathways must be determined and evaluated to enable a fuller understanding to be achieved of the chemistry of flavour.

ACKNOWLEDGEMENTS

The unpublished work described in this paper was carried out in our laboratories by Mrs. R. Islam, Mr. J. W. Letcher, Dr. M. L. Nussbaum and Dr. H. E. Pikk.

REFERENCES

Bailey, S. D., Bazinet, M. L., Driscoll, J. L. and McCarthy, A. I. (1961). *J.Fd.Sci.* 26, 163 - 170.

Eriksson, C. E., Olsson, P. A. Svensson, S. G. (1970). *Lipids* 5, 365 - 366.

Forss, D. A. (1972). *In* "Progress in the Chemistry of Fats and other Lipids" (R. T. Holman, ed.), Vol. XIII (Part 4, pp. 181 - 258. Pergamon Press, Oxford.

Freeman, G. G. and Mossadeghi, N. (1972). *J.Sci.Fd Agric* 23, 387 - 402.

Gadamer, J. (1899). *Ber.dt.chem.Ges.* 32, 2335 - 2341.

Galliard, T. (1973). *Proc.Inst.Fd Sci.Technol.* 6, 188 - 190.

Gmelin, R. and Virtanen, A. I. (1959). *Acta Chem.Scand.* 13, 1474 - 1475.

Hofmann, A. W. (1874a). *Ber.dt.chem.Ges.* 7, 520 - 523.

Hofmann, A. W. (1874b). *Ber.dt.chem.Ges.* 7, 1293 - 1294.

Kazeniac, S. J. and Hall, R. M. (1970). *J.Fd Sci* 35, 519 - 530.

Land, D. G. (1973). *Proc.4th.Europ.Poult.Conf., London.* 447 - 452.

MacLeod, A. J. and MacLeod, G. (1970a). *J.Fd Sci* 35, 734 - 738.

MacLeod, A. J. and MacLeod, G. (1970b). *J.Fd Sci* 35, 739 - 743.

MacLeod, A. J. and MacLeod, G. (1970c). *J.Fd Sci* 35, 744 - 750.

Saarivirta, M. (1973). *Planta Med.* 24, 112 - 119.

Schultz, H. W., Day, E. A. and Sinnhuber, R. O., eds. (1962). "Lipids and their Oxidation". AVI, Westport, Conn.

Schwimmer, S. (1963). *J. Fd Sci.* 28, 460 - 466.

Virtanen, A. I. (1965). *Phytochem.* 4, 207 - 228.

Virtanen, A. I. and Saarivirta, M. (1962). *Suomen Kem.B.* 35, 248 - 249.

THE BIOLOGY AND CHEMISTRY OF THE CRUCIFERAE - GENERAL CONCLUSIONS

V. H. HEYWOOD

Department of Botany, Plant Science Laboratories, University of Reading, England

The biology and chemistry of any large angiosperm family such as the Cruciferae embraces so many diverse disciplines, approaches and even philosophies, as this symposium has clearly illustrated, that I shall limit this summary to attempting to single out what progress has been made in particular areas, seek to find parallels with the situation obtaining in other families, single out major problems and suggest fruitful topics and priorities for future research.

This symposium forms part of a series which was initiated by a similar review of the biology and chemistry of the Umbelliferae (Heywood, 1971) and it is only natural that a comparison should be made between our state of knowledge of the two families.

Large, natural families, such as the Cruciferae, Umbelliferae, Compositae and Leguminosae, pose similar problems. By and large, members of them are easily recognisable as belonging to the family through their common possession of a syndrome of conspicuous characters or character-complexes, usually referring to inflorescence, flower and fruit. At the same time these characters serve to separate off the family from any others. However, these same characters impose upon the family as a whole an apparent uniformity which makes recognition of tribes and genera a more difficult task than normal. It is a common characteristic of such natural families that many of the tribes and genera are regarded as largely artificial, based on trivial characters selected on an unscientific basis. Hedge, in his valuable review of the classification of the Old World species, suggests that probably only the tribes Brassiceae and Lepideae are largely natural, which is a distressing judgement in view of the almost heroic efforts of O. E. Schulz in preparing a major new classification of the family after a life-time's study, based on a much wider range of characters than that used by his predecessors. Despite the later revisions and modifications to Schulz's system, notably by Janchen, we have today no better general system available, despite its recognised weaknesses. A similar situation is found in the Umbelliferae and other large, natural families, where, for practical purposes, we are obliged to use a largely unsatisfactory tribal classification because some subdivision of the family is needed, due to its very size, for convenient handling and reference, and the task of preparing a satisfactory alternative is too daunting to envisage. Provided the situation is recognised by the users of these classifications no great harm is done but it does limit severely their value as a basis for evolutionary, phylogenetic and phytogeographical interpretations.

Not all parts of the system are artificial, as has been noted, but the basic uniformity in floral structure (there are, of course, exceptions as Hedge and Rollins point out) forces us to focus on smaller-scale features for tribal and generic recognition than we would perhaps prefer, and this in turn leads the uninformed observer to distrust the classification even more. We are dealing with the common phenomenon in classification of scale-effects—the less easily visible the character, the less we understand it and, therefore, the less we trust it.

When we look in detail at the flowers and fruits of the Cruciferae, we find that there are in fact many usable characters—Hedge suggests about twenty—but they are not easy to use or appreciate in many cases because of their small-scale, as just mentioned, and the difficulty in observing them accurately or rapidly. It is not surprising that the recent renewed interest in tribal and generic classification has coincided with the development of techniques which permit the easy observation and assessment of micro-characters. Notable has been the scanning electron microscope, which has transformed the study of indumentum, seed, fruit and pollen surfaces, etc. Of course, these features have been looked at previously—indeed much of O. E. Schulz's remarkable achievement rests on the fact that he used features such as nectaries, trichomes, embryos, etc. But anyone who has attempted to analyse detailed trichome and nectary structure with the light microscope only knows how tedious, time-consuming, and often incomplete or at least ambiguous such attempts often are.

The scanning electron microscope has made possible the detailed study of the most bewildering diversity shown by the trichomes in the family, as Rollins and Banerjee's paper beautifully demonstrates. The diversity can be broken down into a series of characters referring to general form, branching, density, webbing, tuberculation, etc. but is best conveyed by scanning electron migrographs accompanied by a brief commentary rather than in inaccurate word-pictures requiring a complex terminology. Not to use such an approach is to handicap taxonomy unnecessarily. Of course, some trichome features are regularly used in the family, employing only a hand lens or dissecting microscope, but these are limited in scope: simple, branched, stellate, squamate, etc. tend to be the categories used. It is to be hoped that the much richer information of the type that Rollins and Banerjee describe within *Lesquerella* can be obtained for a much wider sample of the family covering a range of genera in each tribe. This would be of great value in any attempt to prepare a new tribal classification.

A source of characters that has been surprisingly neglected is the nectary-gland, which shows a remarkable diversity in some tribes. We tend to pay lip service to the use of nectary-gland characters, just as the stylopodium has received scant attention in the Umbelliferae, and we seldom scrutinise them closely, tending to accept what Prantl, Schulz or other authors say. A scanning electron microscope study would almost certainly provide the needed stimulus for a broadly-based consideration of these characters, which would not only be of value in classificatory studies but provide data of considerable biological importance.

A further area where much remains to be done is that of pollen studies. Rollins presented preliminary studies at this symposium (not, however, published in this volume) which gave us a foretaste of the wealth of information to be obtained from the pollen grains. A full study would require (a) light microscope studies (b) scanning electron microscope studies of the exine surface and sectioning of the exine or ultrasonic fracturing so as to study its 3-dimensional features, and (c) transmission electron microscope studies of development and fine structure, along the lines of the research on the palynology of the Umbelliferae published by Cerceau-Larrival (1971) and her school.

Yet another source of valuable information is illustrated by Gómez-Campo and Tortosa's studies on seedling characters (1974). Again, the parallel with similar work on the Umbelliferae is worth noting. Seedling features have been reported frequently in the past in view of their importance in the recognition of seedlings in breeding programmes and identification of weeds, but these studies had a very restricted purpose and only limited conclusions were sought and obtained.

Research on the anatomy and structure of Cruciferous seeds has again been coloured by the large number of species of economic importance as Vaughan and his collaborators point out in their review of seed studies in the family. As they further note, the seed has also been extensively used as a source of compounds in chemosystematic studies and there is enormous potential in extending these studies in conjunction with breeding programmes and investigations into the origin and evolution of crop species and their wild relatives. Few scanning electron microscope studies on the surface features of the testa have yet been made and there is clearly a case to be made for the survey of such characters throughout the family, especially in genera and species of economic value.

The contribution of biochemical studies to our understanding of the Cruciferae has been substantial but restricted largely to the study of compounds and processes of agronomic or economic importance, such as the mustard oils and their precursors, the glucosinolates, and the enzymes (myrosinases) involved in their production; lipids; and seed and leaf proteins. This is not perhaps surprising if one considers that the Cruciferae is one of the major crop plant families and, while not nutritionally and economically as important as the cereals and legumes, contains a remarkably wide range of species used for oil seed crops, vegetables, and animal feed. In addition, again showing a parallel with the Umbelliferae, it contains many minor crop species used as condiments, spices, salads. In view of these uses of cultivated Crucifers it is not surprising that much of the chemical research is devoted to study and analysis of the volatile flavour compounds found in the family. MacLeod's paper illustrates clearly how essential this research is in breeding, selection, cultivation and processing. The belief that brussel sprouts taste better after a touch of frost receives confirmation from the discovery that hard conditions lead to a greater amino acid production which leads to more glucosinolates which in turn give rise to greater production of isothiocyanates and consequently more flavour!

Finlayson's paper on the seed proteins of certain crop Crucifers such as *Brassica* points to the great potential value of this family as a source of useful protein both for animals and man. Not only do some *Brassica* and *Crambe* cultivars contain a high percentage of protein (22 - 24 %) but the meal after oil extraction is potentially a good protein supplement because of its nutritionally acceptable amino acid balance. As Finlayson points out, it seems that some of the proteins from certain rapeseed cultivars are equal in methionine and lysine contents or even greater than that of soybean.

More important from an economic viewpoint are the seed oils and their fatty acid composition. As Crisp points out, oil crops such as oil seed rape and similar crops are likely to increase considerably in importance in view of the shortage, uncertainties, and high costs of supplies of mineral and animal oils. This is especially true of temperate regions to which Cruciferous oil crops are well adapted.

Appelqvist's review of lipids in the Cruciferae highlights the restricted approach to the phytochemistry of the family from a systematic point of view. The amount of what one might call speculative phytochemical research in the family is very limited—it is not a favourite hunting ground for the biochemical systematist—and most of the data that have been accumulated stem from those studies on the utilization of *Brassicas* and related seeds as oil crops or "as a "spinoff" from biochemical research where the reaction was of prime interest and a Crucifer happened to be a handy tool". The consequent imbalance in favour of the genus *Brassica* as regards our knowledge of lipid patterns is equally true of other classes of compound. Yet as the papers by Appelqvist, Björkmann and Kjaer reveal, there is a vast, if unequal, body of data available for the biologist seeking information on relationships, chemical characters for use in classification, evolutionary trends, and so on, to sieve through and interpret. These data range from the distribution of erucic acid—in the plant kingdom—more widespread than previously believed, occurring in such taxonomically distant families (from the Cruciferae) as the Philesiaceae, Gramineae, Limnanthaceae and Tropaeolaceae, and no doubt it will be found to be a constituent of further families, to the effects of seasonal and developmental conditions on the occurrence and concentration of compounds as well as variation between tissues, organs, cultivars and species.

Kjaer's elegant studies on the structure and biosynthesis of the glucosinolates prompts one to ask whether it might not be possible to arrange some of his data into evolutionary levels and sequences on chemical grounds (not as is customary by the usual circularity of working out their chemical evolutionary status from their taxonomic position). It is frequently stated, not without justification,that the emphasis in descriptive phytochemistry should move from classification of compounds and their distribution to comparative studies of biosynthesis and the distribution of processes, refined by comparative enzyme studies. I feel, however, we are still awaiting a lead from phytochemists and biochemists in these matters, since it is not realistic to expect the present generation of taxonomists to make full use of the available data. More co-operation and discussion is needed if the information is to be effectively used since, with rare exceptions, the chemist disclaims a sufficiently wide knowledge of the biological and taxonomic problems involved (to say nothing of nomenclature and synonymy) and the biologist/taxonomist disclaims a deep enough understanding of the chemistry.

As it is the taxonomists grasp at threads such as the fact that methyl side chains are not found in unbranched alkyl glucosinolates in the Cruciferae while they are apparently universal in the members of the Capparaceae studied; or the frequency distribution of erucic acid in the different tribes of the Cruciferae mentioned by Appelqvist. While, no doubt, future generations of chemists and taxonomists will have bridged this communication and comprehension gap, largely through changes in their training, it is idle to expect the majority of present day workers to be able to make full use of the available taxonomic and chemical data. A conscious effort is needed to sort, predigest and simplify the information so as to make it readily accessible and comprehensible. Taxonomists have made greater progress here than have the chemists and phytochemists. Many of these problems are discussed in two recent papers (Heywood, 1973, 1974).

The chemical parallelism (or convergence) shown by the Cruciferae and Capparaceae is of great interest and should help us in our elucidation of the relative evolutionary status and relationships of these two families. Again this brings to mind the situation vis à vis the Umbelliferae and the Araliaceae. In both cases the chemical evidence seems to support the view that is obtained from other lines of evidence that the Cruciferae—Capparaceae and Umbelliferae—Araliaceae have evolved in parallel from common stocks and have attained different stages of evolution in each family.

I shall not comment in detail on the problems highlighted by several authors in the volume, especially the phytochemists, in trying to interpret diverse nomenclatures and taxonomy for the same entities, nor the difficulties found by misidentification of seed obtained from Botanic Garden Seedlists. Progress is being made in both these areas but there is no alternative to full mutual consultation between chemists and taxonomists. What is, perhaps, more disturbing is the fact that very different generic treatments are accepted on the different sides of the Atlantic. In general it can be said that in questions of generic classification and status we in Europe are one cycle ahead of our North American counterparts. This is a reflection of the different ways in which taxonomy has developed in the two areas in the last few decades but presents a somewhat shocking picture to the non-taxonomist. It should be noted that this problem is by no means confined to the Cruciferae but occurs in other families such as the Caryophyllaceae, Umbelliferae, etc.

The problems of generic classification are touched upon by Hedge and I shall return to this at the end of this commentary. Harberd, on the other hand, is concerned with the lack of intercourse between plant breeders and taxonomists, often translated into a lack of sympathy with each other's approach to similar materials—wild and cultivated plants. Harberd's use of cytodemes in his cytogenetic studies is understandable in view of his particular interest in the Brassiceae as an agricultural geneticist. While one sympathises with his comment that he is glad he is not a taxonomist, I feel that he has perhaps extended the concept of the cytodeme to an extent that limits its usefulness in relation to taxonomy. I get the impression that he gets the answers he wants (in terms of groups) by making his own rules with a very limited set of defining criteria. The use of cytodemes is a means of circumventing taxonomic problems and I should like to see a more detailed analysis of the relationship between his cytodemes and more or less acceptable taxonomic species. Unless this is attempted the auxiliary terminology of cytodemes will become an end in itself and no rapprochement will be possible. This may sound a harsh criticism but it is levelled at both sides—the plant breeders and the taxonomists. Certainly I feel somewhat confused and unhappy with his groupings and with his reference to being left with a residue of "species" within a single cytodeme which reached a certain level of evolution and then diverged. Perhaps we are back to the time-honoured question of what do you, as a plant breeder, mean by a species? Do you accept the taxonomists' species or do you wish to redefine them yourselves by a selected range of cytogenetic criteria and still retain the name species for your new group? Some clear thinking is needed here if we are not to lapse into sterile debates on semantics.

Harberd's review of chromosome and cytogenetic studies is valuable and thought provoking. It is, I feel, a sad commentary on the very way we prosecute our subject that no-one has attempted to update Manton's classic study on the cytology of the Cruciferae. Much of what Manton proposed some forty years ago is valid today in general outline but the amount of data has of course increased enormously and is only accessible in a very summary form in the various chromosome handbooks. Here then is a very worthwhile task that would provide results of value to cytologists, taxonomists, plant breeders, evolutionists and other biologists. Likewise the amount of cytogenetic information available in the Brassiceae is enormous and Harberd's own researches have been a major contribution. Added to this is the related chemical studies of Vaughan and his group, and it would be extremely profitable if a review, possibly even a book, summarising and interpreting all this information could be produced. We seem so intent on adding to already large bodies of information that we tend to overlook the need to add to our understanding by bringing data and ideas together. Rollins has given us a lead in this connexion by publishing his recent book synthesizing his work on *Lesquerella*. How much more needed is a similar compendium for the *Brassicas!* At the same time, more attention needs to be given to questions of classification of the species, subspecies and cultivars concerned—it is difficult at times to interpret the nomenclature used in many papers (even in this volume!) due to lack of an agreed system of classification and nomenclature.

Returning to cytotaxonomic studies, a particular example is Manton's classic studies on the distribution and origin of the diploid and tetraploid races in the *Biscutella laevigata* complex. This was necessarily incomplete when written in 1934 and 1937 due to a lack of data from certain critical areas such as France, the Iberian Peninsula, Italy, etc., but since then many additional counts have been made but no overall synthesis has yet been attempted, nor a correlation with modern views on the taxonomy of the complex, and so we still refer to generalizations made some 30 - 40 years ago.

I shall only mention in passing the problem of commercial breeding work in the Cruciferae which Crisp has so fully covered in his paper. The extraordinarily diverse ways in which different parts (stems, leaves, apical buds, inflorescence, etc.) of species such as *Brassica oleracea* have been exploited as crop plants is a remarkable lesson to us all aside from providing good course material for classes on economic botany. Why the British should be the world's greatest consumers of brussel sprouts is a sociological problem about which a Ph.D. thesis may one day be written. The breeding of mini-cauliflowers seems to be an example evoked by parallel psychosocial evolution! The techniques of Crucifer crop breeding contrast starkly with the position in the Umbelliferae due to their very different floral structure, biology and breeding systems. A light hearted comment may be made on the fact that much of the economic return comes from selling mustard most of which is left on the plate and from parsley which likewise is seldom consumed when provided as a garnish! Colour is important in both cases and their role in both cases is as much psychological and decorative as nutritive.

Lawrence's excellent work on variation in *Arabidopsis* is the kind that might well be applied to crop studies. Finally in the area of breeding, I would echo Crisp's comments on the value of conservation work on wild species and primitive cultivars. The Cruciferae seed bank being established by Gómez-Campo is a model of what can be done efficiently and effectively with little manpower and a great deal of personal initiative and enthusiasm. The need to extend breeding programmes by taking into account wild relatives is again dependent to some degree on there being a workable classification available so that likely sources of genetic material can be readily identified.

I shall conclude this review by returning to the question of tribes and genera. Hedge's statistics indicate a ratio of about 8 species to a genus on average. There is usually, however, a pattern of one or two (or a few) large genera in each tribe plus a number of small ones, often mono- or ditypic. This seems to be a common feature of large families (again cf. the Umbelliferae) and may be as much a reflection of the taxonomic process as of the inherent biological correctness of the situation. Certainly some of the small genera are of uncertain affinity as in the examples cited by Hedge of *Physocardum* and *Fabrisinapis* so that there may be some justification for this pattern and it would do little service to taxonomy if very disparate elements were brought together for the sake of uniformity of generic size.

Tribes should ideally be constructed by putting together similar genera—from below upwards, not as is commonly the case by subdivision of the family from above together with accretion since the last classification was prepared. It would be possible in some parts of the family to try this synthetic approach and again the *Brassica* group would be an excellent choice given the amount of available information. It should be relatively easy to complete a character survey using a wide range of disciplines and see if the Brassicae does in fact hold together.

The Cruciferae illustrate excellently many of the problems and ills facing taxonomy as well as the remarkable advances made in the past few decades. I do not think we should be depressed by the enormous tasks still facing us but be stimulated by the challenges they pose and encouraged by the fact that the results will be of direct use in furthering the exploitation of a family of such actual and potential economic value.

REFERENCES

Cerceau-Larrival, M.-T. (1971). *In* (V.H. Heywood, ed.), "The Biology and Chemistry of the Umbelliferae", pp. 109 - 155. Academic Press, London.

Gómez-Campo, C. and Tortosa, Maria E. (1974). *Bot.J.Linn. Soc.* 69(2), 105 - 124.

Heywood, V. H. (ed.) (1971). "The Biology and Chemistry of the Umbelliferae". *Suppl.*1, *Bot.J.Linn.Soc.* 64. Academic Press, London.

Heywood, V. H. (1973). *Chimie pure et Appliquée.* 34, 355 - 375.

Heywood, V. H. (1973). *In* "Nobel 25, Chemistry in botanical classification". 41 - 54.

SUBJECT INDEX

S

T

U

V

SPECIES INDEX